Preservation and Protest

Preservation and Protest

Theological Foundations for an Eco-Eschatological Ethics

Ryan Patrick McLaughlin

Fortress Press
Minneapolis

PRESERVATION AND PROTEST

Theological Foundations for an Eco-Eschatological Ethics

Cover design: Alisha Lofgren

Library of Congress Cataloging-in-Publication Data

Print ISBN: 978-1-4514-8040-5

eBook ISBN: 978-1-4514-8948-4

The paper used in this publication meets the minimum requirements of
American National Standard for Information Sciences — Permanence of Paper
for Printed Library Materials, ANSI Z329.48-1984.

Manufactured in the U.S.A.

This book was produced using PressBooks.com, and PDF rendering was done by
PrinceXML.

Contents

Conclusion

List of Tables and Illustrations

Tables

Illustrations

Acknowledgements

This book would not have been possible without the help of others. I wish to offer special thanks to those who have read drafts of the work and provided important feedback. First and foremost in this category is Daniel Scheid, who directed the project in its earliest form as a dissertation at Duquesne University. James Bailey and Anna Floerke Scheid, both readers on my committee, were also extremely helpful in improving the work. Indeed, I am grateful to all the faculty of Duquesne's Theology Department for their support and guidance. I would also like to express my appreciation to Duquesne University, in particular the McAnutly College and Graduate School of Liberal Arts, for providing financial support in the form of the McAnutly Dissertation Fellowship Award.

More personally, I would like to thank my wife, Melissa, who not only provided valuable editorial feedback of the manuscript but also supported me, encouraged me, and put up with me during the often arduous path to its completion. Support has also been abundant from my family, not only in this work but also in the entirety of my educational pursuits. I am also grateful to my friends and colleagues, conversations with many of whom remain immeasurably helpful in my thought process. Brenda Colijn, a dear friend and mentor, warrants special mention here. I would also like to thank Jonathan

Paul Pepper and Ryan Mimidis for thoughtful conversations and feedback that helped hone my position.

Special thanks go to Cambridge University Press for permission to include in this book a version of an article previously published in *Horizons*.

Finally, I would like to thank Fortress Press for publishing this work.

Preface

This book is the result of a number of years of personal experience and research. It draws on research from previous works, including sermons, student projects, comprehensive exams, published articles, and my most recent book, *Christian Theology and the Status of Animals*. It furthermore develops out of my doctoral dissertation—though, while similar in content, it is different in its format.

Introduction

"That's how it's supposed to be." Those were the marveling words of Calvin DeWitt, a scientifically astute evangelical, in response to a description of how every year at a wetland preserve in Ohio, half of a pond would dry up quickly, leaving whatever fish happened to be on that side stranded in insufficient puddles. The birds would swoop down to the flopping feast, gathering the easy prey. Life and death; predator and prey; pleasure and suffering. For DeWitt, these are the necessary and beautiful antitheses of nature.

It was DeWitt's position that impressed upon me that not all scholars who reject—as both DeWitt and I do—the notion that everything exists for the well-being of humans shares my dismay for the suffering in the natural world. I am a vegetarian because I want to witness against this suffering—to protest it in some small fashion. However, it is possible to be "pro-creation" in a non-anthropocentric manner while at once awe-struck over predation.

The stark difference between DeWitt's passing comment and my own response to the thought of the fish stranded to die facilitated the beginning of a long academic journey which culminates in the present work. I have two primary aims. First, I want to delineate a novel taxonomy of four paradigms of nonhuman theological ethics by examining the intersection of tensions within value terms ("anthropocentrism" and "cosmocentrism") and teleological terms ("conservation" and "transfiguration"). Second, out of the four paradigms that take shape at this intersection, I hope to develop constructively a paradigm of "cosmocentric transfiguration" that maintains that the entire cosmos—including all instantiations of life therein—shares in the eschatological hope of a harmonious participation in God's triune life that entails the end of suffering, predation, and death. This paradigm yields an ethics based upon a tension between preservation (i.e., the letting-be and protection of nature, which requires embracing suffering, predation, and death) and protest (i.e., the personal witness against suffering, predation, and death through non-violent living).

Project Outline

The work is divided into three parts, each comprised of multiple chapters. Part I (chapters 1–6) delineates my taxonomy of nonhuman theological ethics. Part II engages the theologies of Jürgen Moltmann and Andrew Linzey in order to provide parameters for the ethics I ultimately seek to construct. Finally, I begin the effort of systematizing my nonhuman theological ethics in part III.

Chapter 1 situates my own taxonomy by exploring others in the field. Chapter 2 engages the theological loci of cosmology, anthropology, and eschatology. These loci highlight and explicate the tensions between value terms (anthropocentrism and cosmocentrism) and teleological terms (conservation and transfiguration) within which the paradigms of my taxonomy take shape (chapter 3).

Chapters 4–6 examine three of these paradigms. The first is anthropocentric conservation (chapter 4), which is skillfully represented in the work of Thomas Aquinas. According to this paradigm, humans possess an essentially unique dignity that makes them the central subjects of divine concern. Corporeal nonhumans are a gift from God—a good and ordered network of resources—for the well-being of the entire human community, including future generations.

The second paradigm is cosmocentric conservation (chapter 5). It is powerfully represented in the writings of the Passionist priest, Thomas Berry. This paradigm maintains that humans are members of a larger cosmic community and therefore not the absolute center of divine concern. It furthermore de-emphasizes the need for eschatological redemption by claiming that the current order of the nonhuman world, including its continuing evolutionary emergence, is fully good.

The third paradigm is anthropocentric transfiguration (chapter 6), which is most evident in the writings of certain Eastern Orthodox writers, including the Romanian priest Dumitru Staniloae. In this view, the telos of the entire creation is transfiguration, which, in light of the fall, entails eschatological redemption. However, the role of the nonhuman creation in the eschaton is to be the eternal sacrament for the divine-human drama.

In chapters 7–13, I engage Moltmann and Linzey in order to highlight the broad parameters of cosmocentric transfiguration. I devote four chapters (7, 8, 10, and 11) to the theology of Moltmann and Linzey, two chapters each. Chapters 9 (Moltmann) and 12 (Linzey) examine the ethics deriving out of these theological foundations. In chapter 13, I offer a comparative analysis of Moltmann and Linzey, suggesting how I think each is helpful in his own way for constructing a theological ethics of cosmocentric transfiguration.

Chapters 14–16 are dedicated to a nascent systematic construction of cosmocentric transfiguration, burgeoning out of my engagement with both Moltmann and Linzey and in dialogue with the many positive aspects of the other paradigms. In chapter 14, I offer a theological framework for cosmocentric transfiguration. In this endeavor, I attempt to take seriously insights from the natural sciences, particularly Darwinian evolution, and theology, particularly cosmic eschatology. I apologetically defend this paradigm against potential critiques in chapter 15. Finally, chapter 16 considers the ethics that emerges from this paradigm with regard to individual sentient life, individual non-sentient life, and holistic systems of life. At these intersecting considerations, cosmocentric transfiguration bears two essential facets: preservation and protest. Regarding preservation, humans bear responsibility both to allow wild nature its own space to be and to engage nature, both domesticated and wild, in a sustainable manner. Regarding protest, humans bear the calling to witness proleptically to the maximally inclusive eschatological hope of the cosmos. Such a witness entails increasing practices of peace and diminishing practices that elicit harm for both the earth and its human and nonhuman inhabitants.

Rationale for Engaging Particular Theologians

I have already noted which theologians I will engage for each paradigm. My choice has mainly to do with my previous research. As I explored the work of those like Aquinas, Moltmann, and Linzey, I began to note what I perceived to be the most important differences among them. The discovery of Aquinas's value for conservation helped me to distinguish between approaches commensurable with Aquinas and those that emphasize the transfigurative dimension of Christian thought. Aquinas also taught me that practical anthropocentrism (within a theocentric framework) is not incompatible with a strong environmental ethics of conservation.

While examining the work of creation spiritualists and other cosmocentric thinkers, including DeWitt, I felt unsettled by their ecological ethics that sought only to preserve the integrity of the natural order. I could not marvel at the predatory nature of the cosmos. Indeed, such a view seemed to me to overlook the central import of eschatology for Christian theology. It was in these encounters that I came to the personal conclusion that a shift to cosmocentrism was not theologically sufficient to explain my ethics. As I read the work of Thomas Berry, I saw a clear expression of the issues that had only partially formed in my mind up to that point.

At first, I intended only three paradigms of nonhuman theological ethics. I expected to include all Orthodox writers in a large category of transfiguration that stood in tension with conservationist paradigms. However, when I began to read the work of Maximus the Confessor, Dumitru Staniloae, and John Meyendorff, I realized that transfiguration and anthropocentrism were not mutually exclusive terms. It was then that I included a fourth paradigm.

Finally, my first interactions with both Moltmann and Linzey occurred early in my explorations into animal theology and ethics. I found both of them important expressions of my own leanings. Yet, it was only when I was able to juxtapose them to the aforementioned thinkers that I understood the potential significance of their contributions.

This brief rationale reveals that my proposed paradigms arise out of inductive searches into individual theologians. After having moved from individual examples to the general paradigms, I think it best to return to the thinkers who most influenced this generalization. Such a return enables me to take the reader on a similar journey that I experienced. Such is the justification for the authors I engage.

Other Methodological Considerations

Before continuing, I should like to address a few methodological issues. I begin with a consideration of terminology. Next, I offer a word of caution concerning the endeavor of categorization. Then, I acknowledge the inevitability of interpretation for finite creatures. Finally, I present a caveat regarding my constructive work in comparison with the other paradigms.

Animal-Talk

In Andrew Linzey's view, terminology for nonhuman animals (e.g., brutes, pests, beasts, etc.) has perpetuated abuse. Even the term "animal" "is itself a term of abuse" because it "hides the reality of what it purports to describe, namely, a range of differentiated beings of startling variety and complexity."[1] Linzey sees one of the challenges of the animal theology/rights movement as the advancement of terms that do not perpetuate oversimplification or denigration to nonhuman creatures. Similarly, Northcott suggests that both deep ecology and process theology run the risk of "a homogenising view of the natural world" that "undermines the legitimate difference and otherness of the different orders of matter and life in the cosmos."[2] Such a danger has also been highlighted by the continental philosopher Jacques Derrida.[3]

It is thus important to address the language I will use concerning animals in this project.[4] In his recent book, *On Animals*, David

1. Andrew Linzey, *Why Animal Suffering Matters: Philosophy, Theology, and Practical Ethics* (New York, NY: Oxford University Press, 2009), 44–45.
2. Michael Northcott, *The Environment and Christian Ethics* (New York, NY: Cambridge University Press, 1996), 150.
3. David Clough, *On Animals* (New York, NY: Bloomsbury, 2014), xv–xvi; Jacques Derrida, "The Animal That Therefore I Am," printed in *The Animal That Therefore I Am*, ed. Marie-Louise Mallet, trans. David Wills (New York: Fordham University Press, 2008), 29–35, 47–48.

Clough astutely notes, "We treat 'human' and 'non-human' as parallel categories, instead of recognizing that 'human' names one species of animal and 'non-human' names about 1,250,000 species."[5] I prefer terms such as "nonhuman creation" and "nonhuman animal," though at times I simply use "creation" or "animal." While I acknowledge that these terms run the risk of downplaying the differences among nonhumans, I use them mainly to highlight the traditional separation between the two categories of corporeal creation: human and nonhuman. The use of "nonhuman" is meant mainly to express the reality that human beings are part of creation, and more specifically of the animal kingdom. I am not aiming at the homogenization of the nonhuman creation. As evidence, I will at times consider more specifically the role of sentience, consciousness, and life, as differentiating elements among nonhumans. Most often, however, I use more generalized terms in order to participate in traditional conversations. The reader should be aware of my intention with these uses.

The Dangers (and Promises) of Proposing a Taxonomy

Categories always risk (and perhaps inevitably end in) oversimplification. They furthermore hazard inadequacies and inaccuracies. I want here to highlight my awareness of these dangers. What I offer in this project is *my interpretation* of particular theologians and *my categorization* of those interpretations into a taxonomy of paradigms. Whether or not the individual theologians (or those who have spent many years studying their work) would

---

4. For an enlightening discussion on this topic, see Robert Wennberg, *God, Humans, and Animals: An Invitation to Enlarge Our Moral Universe* (Grand Rapids, MI: William B. Eerdmans Publishing Company, 2003), 23–26.
5. Clough, *On Animals*, 74.

agree with my categorization is open to debate. For this reason, I offer this project not as the "final word" but as a contribution—the opening for a clearer dialogue concerning nonhuman theological ethics. I do not harbor the hubris of thinking I have perfectly and without remainder defined all possibilities in my taxonomy.

These issues notwithstanding, taxonomies such as the one I am proposing offer promise to the field. Even if other scholars disagree with my classification, the act of classifying itself opens the door for further dialogue regarding the criteria used to structure the taxonomy. Furthermore, it allows other thinkers in the field to examine their own positions vis-à-vis the new taxonomy. In this sense, a well-structured taxonomy aids in the clarification of the field.

You Can't Spell "Interpretation" without an "I"

To be human is to be finite. To be finite is to be located—here instead of there, now instead of then. To be located is to see the world from a particular perspective, one different from others differently located. As already noted, all that I offer in this text is my perspective of the research I have done. While I hope readers will find this perspective justified, I also recognize that my interpretation is influenced by my epistemic location.

I am a white male living in the United States of America. I grew up in suburbs. I have never lived or worked on a farm. My primary field is theology and ethics. My knowledge of the intricacies of biology, theoretical physics, and cosmology are limited. I have hunted before, many years ago. I fell asleep in the woods with a loaded gun (the safety was on) and decided it was not a good practice for me. For most of my life, I ate meat and used various animal products. For eight years, I have been a strict vegetarian. For two years, I have been a vegan—though, admittedly less strictly so. These factors, among more too numerous to list, inform my understanding and interpretation of the world. Because all of these influences affect my work, I strive to be humble in my approach. It is my hope that this humility is detected by readers.

The Superiority of Cosmocentric Transfiguration?

Lastly, in light of what I have just stated, I want to acknowledge clearly my bias. I find the paradigm of cosmocentric transfiguration to be the most satisfying of those presented here. However, that does not mean that I find the other paradigms to be objectively wrong or inadequate. While I make a case that cosmocentric transfiguration offers a vision that accounts for both theological doctrines and scientific evidence, I do not maintain that it is in any sense the only—or even the obvious—choice for Christian ethics. I leave that judgment to the reader.

A New Taxonomy of Nonhuman Theological Ethics

Part I Introduction

To best establish the theological foundations of an eco-eschatological nonhuman ethics, it is pertinent to frame this ethics within the wider field. Such is the aim of part I. I begin by critically examining current options of the table for mapping nonhuman theological ethics. From this examination, I offer a new taxonomy to categorize the field better than existing taxonomies do. I achieve this aim by exploring the theological loci I detect to be central concerning the moral status of nonhumans. Out of the tensions that arise from these loci, four paradigms of nonhuman theological ethics take shape. While my central focus is only one of those paradigms (cosmocentric transfiguration), I consider the three other paradigms in order to highlight the uniqueness of the fourth. In an effort to avoid simplistic overgeneralizations and abstractions, I focus on a particular thinker or group of thinkers for each paradigm. Collectively, these chapters culminate in solidifying the four paradigms of nonhuman theological ethics.

Current Taxonomies of Nonhuman Theological Ethics

Does the world really need another classification of environmental ethics? Or am I simply so desperate to find a niche and write a book that I will stoop to reinventing the wheel? Desperation notwithstanding, the past seven years of research has convinced me that a new taxonomy will greatly benefit the current field. My aim in this chapter and the next is to delineate and supplement existing classifications, combine their strengths, and ameliorate their weaknesses. To achieve this goal, I must first critically engage the writings of those who have mapped the field, suggest why I think a novel approach is warranted, and provide the foundations that facilitate this approach.

Classifications of Eco-Theological Ethics

Susan J. Armstrong and Richard G. Botzler explore four categories of ecological thought based primarily on the criteria of value and moral consideration.[1] The first category, represented first and foremost by René Descartes, is anthropocentrism, which intimates the chief or sole relegation of intrinsic value to humans. The second category, advocated by Tom Regan, is individualism, which entails the rejection of the relegation of ethical import to species, ecosystems, or the cosmos at large. The third category, including both Aldo Leopold's land ethic and Arne Naess's deep ecology, is ecocentrism, which places both the earth and the land into the category of intrinsic value. The fourth category is ecofeminism, which entails the political dismantling of hierarchical claims in favor of an egalitarian view of the cosmos.

William French offers a similar value-based distinction in his categorization of contemporary Catholic thought.[2] French highlights two basic categories: subject-centered and creation-centered approaches to ecological ethics. Subject-centered approaches emphasize the significance of both human subjects (including the capacities of their being) and human history.[3] French places Pierre Teilhard de Chardin in this category for his optimistic evaluation of human progress within the evolutionary emergence of the universe.[4] He also includes the writings of Vatican II, stating, "The council follows the generally anthropocentric scale of the natural law

---

1. The following is taken from Susan J. Armstrong and Richard G. Botzler, *Environmental Ethics: Divergence and Convergence*, third edition (New York, NY: McGraw Hill, 2003), 271–463.
2. See William C. French, "Subject-centered and Creation-centered Paradigms in Recent Catholic Thought," *The Journal of Religion*, 70, 1 (January 1990): 48–72.
3. Ibid., 48–49.
4. Ibid., 53–54. While French acknowledges that Chardin is "a creation-centered thinker," he maintains that he is the "dean of Catholic subject-centered theology because of his insistence that humanity is called to further the 'personalization' of the planet by 'building the earth.'" Ibid., 53.

tradition."[5] Finally, he includes both the political theologian Johannes Baptist Metz and Pope John Paul II on account of their interest in transforming the world for human benefit.[6]

While there are variations within this category (French distinguishes between Chardin's "sovereignty-within" model and the "sovereignty-over" model of the other voices), French draws out some basic commonalities. Both models bear (1) A processive, eschatological focus; (2) a *homo faber* anthropology; (3) a wide-ranging endorsement of technology, industry, and science; and (4) a buoyant optimism regarding our possibilities for progress.[7] Although he recognizes the value of an affirmation of individual human subjects, French ultimately criticizes the subject-centered approach for its "triumphalist endorsement of technology, economic development, and historical transformation."[8]

Creation-centered theologies "do not dispense with emphasizing subjectivity and history; rather, they highlight their interrelation with embodiment and creation."[9] Under this category, French includes the creation spirituality of Thomas Berry, the feminism of Rosemary Radford Ruether, and the liberation theology evident in the Filipino bishops' "Pastoral Letter on Ecology."[10] Again, French detects two sub-categories: the stewardship model of the Filipino bishops and the "ecological egalitarian" models of Berry and Ruether.[11]

Not all classifications center on value. In response to the emphasis on anthropocentrism in the wake of Lynn White's critique of Christianity, Willis Jenkins maps the field of environmental thought according to soteriological concepts of grace.[12] In doing so, he seeks

5. Ibid., 54.
6. Ibid., 55–57.
7. Ibid., 58.
8. Ibid., 61.
9. Ibid., 50.
10. Ibid., 62–68.
11. Ibid., 69. French opts for the stewardship model.

to avoid the common use of anthropocentrism as the sole litmus test for viable environmental contributions. Jenkins employs the notions of sanctification, redemption, and deification to classify eco-theological thought. Drawing on the taxonomical work of the sociologist Laurel Kearns, he traces these soteriological terms to three strategies for environmental ethics. These three strategies are ecojustice, stewardship, and creation spirituality, each of which loosely corresponds to ecclesial traditions.[13]

Sanctification corresponds to the strategy of ecojustice, most typically practiced by Roman Catholicism. Although, Jenkins lists among the advocates of this view the Lutherans Larry Rasmussen and Jürgen Moltmann and the Episcopalian Michael Northcott.[14] This strategy predicates human duty to the environment on account of its being God's creation.[15] Redemption corresponds to the strategy of stewardship, most typically emphasized in Protestant circles.[16] Jenkins cites thinkers like Calvin DeWitt, Wendell Berry, and John Douglas Hall as advocates of this strategy. He also engages Anabaptist thought.[17] He spends most of his time in later chapters focusing on the work of Karl Barth.[18] Whereas ecojustice emphasizes creation's integrity, advocates of stewardship emphasize God's command to humanity to care for the earth. Humanity is responsible for the earth before God. Deification corresponds to the strategy of creation spiritualism, most typically embodied in Eastern Orthodox theologians like Maximus the Confessor, Patriarch Ignatius IV of Antioch, John Zizioulas, and the sophiologists.[19] Jenkins also locates

---

12. For Jenkins's engagement of White, see Willis Jenkins, *Ecologies of Grace: Environmental Ethics and Christian Theology* (New York, NY: Oxford University Press, 2008), 11–12.

13. Ibid., 18–19.

14. See ibid., 66–75.

15. Ibid., 64–66.

16. See ibid., 78–80.

17. Ibid., chapter 4.

18. Ibid., chapters 8 and 9.

this strategy in the work of creation spiritualists like Matthew Fox, Thomas Berry, and Pierre Teilhard de Chardin.[20] Creation spiritualism locates environmental concern in both the communion within the cosmos and between the cosmos and God.

Regarding the classification of eco-theological thought, Michael Northcott establishes three fluid terms: humanocentric, theocentric, and ecocentric.[21] He describes the terms as fluid because ethicists and theologians shift back and forth between them.[22] For Northcott, these terms are not about value but rather framework. A humanocentric framework is one that approaches ecological issues with an emphasis on human issues and needs. Northcott includes thinkers with diverse content in this category, such as Eastern Orthodox theologians, Rosemary Radford Ruether, and Pope John Paul II.[23] A theocentric framework considers environmental concerns vis-à-vis God's relation to the cosmos, emphasizing the import of creation for God and the ethical ramification of this import. Northcott lists both Jürgen Moltmann and Andrew Linzey in this category.[24] An ecocentric framework develops around the cosmos itself, emphasizing the nonhuman creation in its own right. This category includes process theologians and creation spiritualists.[25]

Another important classification of eco-theological thought is offered by Celia Deane-Drummond.[26] Her taxonomy is couched within a geographical framework in which she explores and evaluates voices from the North, South, East, and West. Deane-Drummond

19. See ibid., 108–111.
20. See ibid., 93–108.
21. See Michael Northcott, *The Environment and Christian Ethics* (New York, NY: Cambridge University Press, 1996), chapter 4.
22. Ibid., 124.
23. Ibid., 125–141.
24. See Ibid., 141–147.
25. Ibid., 147–161. I am uncertain why Northcott labels McFague as eco-centric. By his criteria, it seems she could more easily be classified as theocentric.
26. Celia Deane-Drummond, *Eco-Theology* (Winona, MN: Anselm Academic, 2008).

explores three forms of ecological ethics from the Northern hemisphere (which includes "most notably the United States").[27] These forms include Aldo Leopold's land ethic; Arne Naess's deep ecology; and the creation spirituality of Teilhard de Chardin, Matthew Fox, and Thomas Berry.[28] With regard to voices from the South, Deane-Drummond admittedly only scratches the surface. Her two basic explorations engage liberation theologians and indigenous thought. In her examination of contributions from Eastern thought, Deane-Drummond basically delineates approaches of Eastern Orthodox eco-theology. She includes the liturgical emphasis of Elizabeth Theokritoff, John Zizioulas's vision of humans as the priests of creation, the revelatory value of the cosmos as expressed in the work of Kallistos Ware, the sophiology of Sergii Bulgakov, and the monastic and ascetic tradition of Saint Symeon.[29] Deane-Drummond limits her initial engagement with Western thinkers to socio-political writers.[30] She very briefly explores Northcott's natural law critique of modernity, Murray Bookchin's social ecology that critiques capitalistic hierarchies in both human and nonhuman realms in favor of "eco-anarchy," and Peter Scott's theological (and more specifically, trinitarian) appropriation of Bookchin's work.[31]

Classifications of Animal Ethics

In his work, *God, Animals, and Humans*, Robert Wennberg limits the focus of his thesis:

> This is a book on animal advocacy. It is not a book on ecology nor is it an attempt to construct an environmental ethic, for animal advocacy and

27. Ibid., 32.
28. Ibid., 32–42.
29. Ibid., 57–66.
30. Ibid., 69.
31. Ibid., 69–74.

environmentalism are not the same thing. Indeed, according to some, they are not only not the same thing, but they are seriously at odds with each other, so much so that ultimately one will have to choose between the agenda of the animal advocate and that of the environmentalist.[32]

Wennberg is not alone in noting this difference within the larger field of nonhuman ethics,[33] a difference exacerbated because "the environmentalist has a higher standing in the community, both inside and outside the church, than does the animal advocate, who is often viewed with suspicion."[34] Wennberg offers three reasons for this suspicion. First, animal advocacy is linked in the minds of many to violence. Second, "animal advocacy is viewed as anti-scientific." And third, animal advocacy is always anti-anthropocentric.[35] For Wennberg, the main difference between an environmentalist and an animal advocate pertains to the unit of primary moral concern—more specifically, whether the individual animal has any moral claims.[36]

Under the category "animal advocate," Wennberg notes two general divisions, and subdivisions within each. The general division is between direct or indirect moral concern.[37] The latter category includes Immanuel Kant's emphasis on personhood, Aquinas's moral hierarchy, and social contract theory.[38] The former category includes Regan's animal rights approach, Singer's utilitarianism, Linzey's theos-rights, Hall's vision of stewardship, and various virtue theory approaches.[39]

32. Robert Wennberg, *God, Humans, and Animals: An Invitation to Enlarge Our Moral Universe* (Grand Rapids, MI: William B. Eerdmans Publishing Company, 2003), 29.
33. See, for instance, Lisa H. Sideris, *Environmental Ethics, Ecological Theology, and Natural Selection* (New York, NY: Columbia University Press, 2003), 13; Stephen Webb, "Ecology vs. The Peaceable Kingdom: Toward a Better Theology of Nature," *Soundings* 79/1–2 (Spring/Summer 1996): 239–52.
34. Wennberg, *God, Animals, and Humans*, 30.
35. Ibid., 30–32.
36. See ibid., 32–36. Also, Sideris, *Environmental Ethics*, 21.
37. Regan also makes this general distinction. See Regan, *The Case for Animal Rights*, chapters 5 and 6.
38. Wennberg, *God, Humans, and Animals*, 119–37.

In the *Encyclopedia of Animal Rights and Animal Welfare*, Tom Regan notes the difference between animal welfare (welfarism) and the animal rights movement. "Animal welfare holds that humans do nothing wrong when they use nonhuman animals . . . if the overall benefits of engaging in these activities outweigh the harms these animals endure."[40] Animal rights, on the other hand, maintain that "human utilization of nonhuman animals . . . is wrong in principle and should be abolished in practice."[41]

In his work, *The Moral Menagerie*, Marc R. Fellenz traces extensionist animal ethics by categorizing their development within the framework of traditional Western ethical categories. He thus devises a taxonomy of animal ethics by delineating utilitarian, deontological, virtue, and contractual approaches.[42] Utilitarian approaches include the work of Jeremy Bentham and Peter Singer.[43] Fellenz explores the work of Tom Regan—because he seeks to establish animal *rights*—as a deontological approach.[44] As an example of a virtue approach to animal ethics, Fellenz considers Bernard Rollin's retrieval of Aristotle and Lawrence Becker's systematic virtue ethics for animals.[45] Fellenz's engagement with contractualism focuses on developments of Johns Rawls's veil of ignorance and the meaning it might have for animal ethics.[46]

39. Ibid., 137–79.
40. Tom Regan, "Animal Rights," *Encyclopedia of Animal Rights and Animal Welfare*, ed. Marc Bekoff and Carron A. Meaney (Westport, CT: Greenwood, 1998), 42.
41. Ibid. For further differentiation among welfarism, see the subsequent entries in the encyclopedia by David Sztybel and Gary L. Francione.
42. Marc R. Fellenz, *The Moral Menagerie: Philosophy and Animal Rights* (Chicago, IL: University of Illinois Press, 2007), 57–117.
43. Ibid., 57–67.
44. Ibid., 82–87.
45. Ibid., 92–102.
46. Ibid., 108–116

Warrant for a New Taxonomy

Between general classifications of environmental and animal theological ethics, there exists a great host of alternatives regarding human engagement with the nonhuman creation. While contemporary authors have offered various means of categorizing these alternatives, there remains a level of confusion regarding central tensions in the field. For example, while Jenkins emphasizes soteriology in his erudite classification and French emphasizes the question of intrinsic value, neither approach engages both dimensions of soteriological telos and intrinsic value. French makes an unwarranted leap in equating subject-centered paradigms with transformation and creation-centered paradigms with preservation.[47] Jenkins's work is problematic inasmuch as it critiques the transformational view of ecojustice and stewardship but ignores the nearly ubiquitous view in Orthodox theology that creation is fallen and in need of eschatological redemption.[48] It is this misstep that leads Jenkins to list Orthodox theology with the creation spiritualism of Matthew Fox and Thomas Berry, both of whom deny cosmic fallenness. Northcott's approach is helpful in terms of framework, but is somewhat misleading in terms of content (e.g., the common categorization of Ruether and John Paul II as humanocentric). Deane-Drummond's survey of the field is also helpful, but does not really offer a taxonomy in terms of comparative ethics. The contrast between ecological ethics and animal ethics with regard to the emphasis of individuals or species/ecosystems makes classification all the more difficult.

I believe there is a need for a taxonomy that attends to the problems of the above classifications. Such a taxonomy is possible if one

47. See French, "Subject-centered and Creation-centered Paradigms," 58–59.
48. On Jenkins's critique of ecojustice and stewardship, see Jenkins, *Ecologies of Grace*, 70–74, 89.

addresses the central tensions evident in various theologies of the nonhuman creation and the ethics that these theologies ground. In my view, these tensions exist at the level of cosmology (i.e., the status and purpose of the nonhuman creation), anthropology (i.e., the status and purpose of human beings), and eschatology (i.e., the extent of God's redemptive aim for the created order). Collectively, these three theological facets address issues of both salvation and value. They include (and surpass) the somewhat narrow (though still valuable) approaches of French and Jenkins. They provide a framework that classifies the content of nonhuman ethics, which both Northcott and Deane-Drummond avoid. They furthermore help bridge the gap between ecological ethics and animal ethics within a broader theological framework.

Conclusion

This short chapter provides a sketch of current classifications of nonhuman theological ethics. Each of these classifications has strengths and weaknesses. The weaknesses tend toward odd groupings (such as creation spirituality and Orthodox theology) that contain theologians and ethicists that have much uncommon ground. They also tend to oversimplify nuances by focusing only on value, teleology, or method. To circumvent these weaknesses, I offer three theological loci, cosmology, anthropology, and eschatology, as a superior classificatory framework. Such is the subject the next chapter.

2

Three Theological Loci for a New Taxonomy

If you gather a group of theologians into a room and ask "Is death good?", "Does creation require redemption?", or "Do human beings have dominion over the nonhuman creation?", you are bound to receive a wide variety of answers—some of which sound the same but mean completely different things! What is at the root of these differences? In this chapter, I explore in detail the three theological categories I propose for a new taxomony of nonhuman theological ethics. I intend this exploration to draw out fundamental tensions I detect in disparate positions within the field.

The Loci in Broader Perspective

In his effort to develop an environmental theology that is at once faithful to Christian history and pertinent to the contemporary environmental context, Stephen Bouma-Prediger explores the theological and philosophical loci of anthropology, ontology, and theology proper.[1] To facilitate this exploration, he examines the theologies of Rosemary Radford Ruether, Joseph Sittler, and Jürgen Moltmann. Based on his work, Bouma-Prediger proposes a three-fold theological vision. First, anthropology must reflect a non-dualistic worldview, especially with regard to nature and history.[2] Second, ontology must be conceived relationally and theocentrically for both the human and nonhuman creation.[3] Third, theology proper must take the form of a social doctrine of the Trinity that rejects both androcentric and anthropocentric hierarchies and recovers divine immanence.[4]

There are similarities between the present work and Bouma-Prediger's. The most important of these is the use of three theological categories to frame the discussion. We both engage anthropology. His exploration of ontology is not dissimilar from my use of cosmology—especially with regard to an emphasis on relationality and various value-centric possibilities. His third category is theology proper. While the doctrine of God does not constitute a specific category of exploration in his project, it is nonetheless a ubiquitous theme. Indeed, my categories of cosmology, anthropology, and eschatology should be understood as *theological* categories (i.e., categories within a larger framework that implies a theology proper).

As noted in chapter 1, Willis Jenkins avoids classifying environmental thought according to centric value systems and instead employs a soteriological categorization. Soteriology is not one of the three theological dimensions of this project. However, like theology proper it is present, in this case at the intersection of

1. See Steven Bouma–Prediger, *The Greening of Theology: The Ecological Models of Rosemary Radford Ruether, Joseph Sittler, and Jürgen Moltmann* (Atlanta: Scholars Press, 1995).
2. Ibid., 266–74.
3. Ibid., 274–83.
4. Ibid., 284–301.

cosmology, anthropology, and eschatology. Theological cosmology expresses fundamentally what the created order was and is in relation to both God and itself. Theological anthropology expresses fundamentally what humanity was and is within the framework of theological cosmology. Eschatology expresses fundamentally what the cosmos (including humans) is becoming and will, in a final sense, be in relation to both God and itself.

The theological dimensions of cosmology, anthropology, and eschatology thus embrace the entire temporal and spatial scope of the Trinity's history with the cosmos and therefore include both theology proper and soteriology. They furthermore account for the relationality of the cosmos both spatially (each part of the cosmos in relation to others and the whole and each part and the whole in relation to God) and temporally (the relation among protological claims about the cosmos, the present condition of the cosmos, and the future God desires for the cosmos). Lastly, these theological dimensions are dominant driving forces (even when they are excluded from a theological framework) of environmental ethics. It is for these reasons that I adopt these three loci.

Cosmology

Traditionally, the term "creation" refers to all that is not God. Yet, in most explorations of cosmology, anthropology is relegated to a separate category (or at least an essentially distinct sub-category). I am here honoring that distinction for the sake of clarity. However, inasmuch as cosmology is the doctrine of the Creator's creation, it is also the doctrine of human beings. There can be no sharp partition here.[5] *Anthropology can only be the doctrine of human beings in, with, and as the Creator's creation*—that is, a dimension of cosmology.

The Christian doctrine of creation is always influenced by historical contexts. Early Christian cosmologies reflect both a milieu of blended Jewish and Greek thought and challenges raised by groups like the Gnostics and Manicheans.[6] In this context, Christians address questions concerning the goodness of creation, the fallenness/ distortion of the cosmos, the purpose of the created order, and the relationship between God and the world. Questions concerning these facets of cosmology continue to be central in modern Christian thought. However, contemporary theologians are influenced by new contexts, most particularly the findings of science and the earth's present ecological disposition.[7] Here, I aim to delineate and explicate the broad dimensions of cosmology pertinent to the purpose of this project. These dimensions are the goodness of creation and the order of the cosmos in tension with the doctrine of the fall and the hope for redemption.[8]

The Goodness of Creation

A strong affirmation of the goodness of the cosmos has rarely, if ever, been absent in Christian history. The biblical claim of creation's

5. See Elizabeth Theokritoff, *Living in God's Creation: Orthodox Perspectives on Ecology* (Crestwood, NY: St Vladimir's Seminary Press, 2009), 25–26; Anne M. Clifford, "Creation," in *Systematic Theology: Roman Catholic Perspectives*, ed. Francis Schüssler Fiorenza and John P. Galvin (Minneapolis, MN: Fortress Press, 2011), 202.
6. See ibid., 214–23.
7. For considerations, see The Worldwatch Institute, *Vital Signs 2012: The Trends That Are Shaping Our Future* (Washington DC: Worldwatch Institute, 2012); Michael Northcott, *The Environment and Christian Ethics* (New York: Cambridge University Press, 1996), 1–32; Celia Deane-Drummond, *Eco-Theology* (Winona, MN: Anselm Academic, 2008), 1–31.
8. Another dimension of cosmology that will arise is nature of the ontological relationship between God and the cosmos. For considerations, see Stanley J. Grenz and Roger E. Olson, *20th Century Theology: God and the World in a Transitional Age* (Downers Grove, IL: Intervarsity, 1992).

goodness is firmly imbedded in the first creation narrative.[9] In the second century, Irenaeus of Lyons defended creation's goodness against the criticisms of Gnosticism, which viewed matter as a degradation of spirit.[10] In the fifth century, Augustine maintained the goodness of the entire created order against his once fellow Manicheans, who believed that the physical creation represented a fundamental barrier to the spiritual (i.e., incorporeal) telos of humanity.[11] In the thirteenth century, Thomas Aquinas preserved the notion of cosmic goodness, arguing that the creation's hierarchical order evinces God's fundamental concern for human beings.[12] These three examples are among many in the Christian narrative.[13] Each maintains that the creation is good inasmuch as it is the work of a good Creator.[14] The physical world is not the mistake of some lesser or evil deity.[15] It is rather the mode of existence in which humanity comes to communion with God. In modern contexts of ecological concern, an affirmation of the goodness of creation is strongly emphasized in ecclesial statements of Roman Catholicism, Orthodoxy, and Protestantism.[16]

The dominant theological claim in Christian history concerning creation's goodness signifies that Christianity is not necessarily an

---

9. E.g., Genesis 1:4, 10, 12, 18, 21, 25, and 31.

10. See Irenaeus of Lyons, *Irenaeus: Against Heresies*, Ante-Nicene Fathers, ed. A. Roberts and J. Donaldson (Grand Rapids, MI: Eerdmans, 1996), book 1; Matthew Craig Steenberg, *Irenaeus on Creation: The Cosmic Christ and the Saga of Redemntion* (Boston: Brill, 2008), 1–15, 21–38.

11. On Augustine's position, see Jame Schaefer, *Theological Foundations for Environmental Ethics: Reconstructing Patristic & Medieval Concepts* (Washington, DC: Georgetown University Press, 2009), 18–27.

12. See Chapter 4.

13. See Schaefer, *Theological Foundations*, 17–42.

14. See, for instance, Augustine, *The Enchiridion: On Faith, Hope and Love*, trans. J. F. Shaw, ed. Henry Paolucci (Chicago, IL: Regnery Gateway, 1961), 10:10–11.

15. See Steenberg, *Irenaeus on Creation*, 22–38.

16. See, for instance, Pope John Paul II and Patriarch Bartholomew I, *Common Declaration on Environmental Ethics*. 2002. Available online at http://www.vatican.va/holy_father/john_paul_ii; "An Evangelical Declaration on the Care of Creation," printed in *The Care of Creation: Focusing Our Concern and Action*, ed. R. J. Berry (Downers Grove, IL: Intervarsity, 2000), 18–22.

unfriendly voice with regard to environmental issues. While certain strands may indeed be indictable for the development of an anthropocentric and utilitarian view of nature, there are alternative strands. At the same time, the claim that creation is good highlights one of the main tensions in nonhuman theology regarding nature. Namely, are all aspects of creation—including the gratuity of suffering and predation—good? Or is there something *not good* about the cosmos?

The Fallenness/Incompleteness of Creation

Nearly as common as affirmations of creation's goodness in Christian history is the recognition that the created order is in some manner fallen. Irenaeus maintains the historicity of Eden and the cosmic effects of Adam and Eve's sin.[17] Theophilus of Antioch argues that predation among nonhuman animals evinces that they followed humanity into sin.[18] Ephrem the Syrian writes that the relationship between humans and the nonhuman world—and within the nonhuman world itself—was greatly harmed by sin.[19] These thinkers, among others, maintain that the nonhuman creation, while remaining in some sense good, is at once distorted.[20]

Yet, the creation's fallenness is by no means unambiguously affirmed in Christian history. One of Western Christianity's most dominant voices, Thomas Aquinas, maintains that the nonhuman creation is not fallen.[21] Predation among animals is part of the divine

17. See Irenaeus, *Against Heresies*, 5.33.4.
18. Theophilus of Antioch, *Letter to Autolycus*, Ante-Nicene Christian Library, ed. Alexander Roberts and James Donaldson (Edinburgh: T & T Clark, 1880), II.16–17 (83–84).
19. Ephrem, *Commentary on Genesis*, St. Ephrem the Syrian: Selected Prose Works, ed. Kathleen McVey, trans. Edward G. Mathews and Joseph P Amar (Washingon DC: The Catholic University of America Press, 1994), 2.9.3 and 6.9.3.
20. For further biblical, historical, and contemporary considerations, see David Clough, *On Animals* (New York: Bloomsbury, 2014), 119–21.

order of the nonhuman cosmos. (Though, Aquinas does maintain that animal aggression toward humans is a result of human sin.[22]) Thus, while the goodness of the cosmos was rarely challenged in Christian thought, the notion of cosmic fallenness is less consistent.[23]

This inconsistency is further complicated today by the dismantling of the viability of an historical Eden.[24] The natural sciences leave little room for the claim that there was an historical period in which predation, death, and violence did not exist.[25] Biologically, human sin cannot be the cause of a cosmic fall that introduces predation and death into existence.[26] Furthermore, without facets of evolutionary emergence such as the violent destruction of stars, the competition and predation among species, and ultimately the ubiquity of death, there could not be the complexity and diversity of life that exists.[27] As John Polkinghorne notes, it was only because of the destruction of the dinosaurs that "little furry mammals, who are our ancestors, were given their evolutionary opportunity."[28] Based on such claims, Neil Ormerod maintains that evolutionary suffering is not synonymous with evil but rather "has an intrinsic relationship to finitude."[29] Others, such as David Clough, note a theological issue: "If non-human predation and suffering are judged to be intrinsically evil, it

---

21. See Thomas Aquinas, *Summa Theologica*, trans. Fathers of the English Dominican Province (Benziger Brothers, 1947), 1.96.1.

22. Ibid., 1.72.6.

23. Holmes Rolston III notes this point. See "Does Nature Need to be Redeemed?" *Zygon* 29 (1994): 208.

24. See Patricia Williams, *Doing without Adam and Eve: Sociobiology and Original Sin* (Minneapolis, MN: Fortress Press, 2001).

25. See Christopher Southgate, *The Groaning of Creation: God, Evolution, and the Problem of Evil* (Louisville, KY: Westminster John Knox Press, 2008), 5, 28–29; Arthur Peacocke, *Theology for a Scientific Age: Being and Becoming—Natural, Divine and Human* (Minneapolis, MN: Fortress Press, 1993), 222–23.

26. Southgate, *The Groaning of Creation*, 28.

27. See ibid., 29.

28. John Polkinghorne, *The God of Hope and the End of the World* (New Haven, CT: Yale University Press, 2002), 6.

29. Neil Ormerod, *Creation, Grace, and Redemption* (Maryknoll, NY: Orbis Books, 2007), 14.

seems that creation was fallen long before human beings had any opportunity to respond positively or negatively to God."[30]

The question of cosmic fallenness stands alongside the issue of the nature of the protological state of creation. Origen's vision of creation and the fall takes the form of a Platonic distortion of static perfection.[31] Irenaeus's vision is starkly different, suggesting rather that the creation was made in a state of dynamism that required growth. Adam and Eve were created as children whom God intended would grow into adulthood.[32] Thus, for Irenaeus, the fall is more a straying from the path to the proper telos of the cosmos than a loss of perfection.[33]

Irenaeus's cosmology has been taken up, whether purposefully or not, by modern thinkers who want to emphasize the dynamism and relational nature of the cosmos, a vision more consummate with science than that of Origen.[34] David Fergusson maintains that both Scripture and science witness to the dynamism of the cosmos. In both accounts, "the good creation is not one which is already perfect. It is fit for its purpose and displays the constant love of God for creatures. . . . Yet its destiny awaits it in the future."[35] Theologically, Vladimir Lossky states, "The primitive beatitude was not a state of deification, but a condition of order, a perfection of the creature

30. Clough, *On Animals*, 122.

31. See Colin E. Gunton, "Between Allegory and Myth: The Legacy of the Spiritualising of Genesis," in *The Doctrine of Creation: Essays in Dogmatics, History and Philosophy*, ed. Colin E. Gunton (New York: T&T Clark International, 2004),53–58.

32. See Irenaeus of Lyons, *Irenaeus' Demonstration of the Apostolic Preaching: A Theological Commentary and Translation*, ed. Iain M. Mackenzie, trans. J. Armitage Robinson (Burlington: Ashgate, 2002), 12, 14.

33. On this point, see Ryan Patrick McLaughlin, *Christianity and the Status of Animals* (New York: Palgrave Macmillan, 2014), chapter 4.

34. See John Polkinghorne, "The Demise of Democritus," in *The Trinity and an Entangled World: Relationality in Physical Science and Theology*, ed. John Polkinghorne (Grand Rapids, MI: William B. Eerdmans Publishing Company, 2010), 15–31; Peacocke, *Theology for a Scientific Age*, 41–70.

35. David Fergusson, "Creation," in *The Oxford Handbook of Systematic Theology*, ed. John Webster, Kathryn Tanner, and Iain Torrance (New York: Oxford University Press, 2007), 76.

which was ordained and tending towards its end."[36] It is in this sense that Wolfhart Pannenberg offers his eschatological remark concerning creation's goodness:

> The verdict of "very good" does not apply simply to the world of creation in its state at any given time. It is true, rather, of the whole course of history in which God is present with his creatures in incursions of love that will finally lead it through the hazards and sufferings of finitude to participation in his glory.[37]

Irenaeus's cosmological dynamism notwithstanding, many appropriations of his work carve his protology and eschatology away. The main reason is that Irenaeus's protology does not square with biological evolution. However, evolution presents its own problems, both biblically and theologically. In the words of Michael Northcott, "The vision of nature's original goodness and harmony in the first chapters of Genesis contrasts with other Ancient Near Eastern myths of origin, and it contrasts significantly with modern scientific accounts of human society and the non-human world."[38] What is at stake in this tension is the very character of God. To express this point, I turn to the first creation narrative (Gen. 1:1–2:3).

Conventional wisdom in biblical scholarship suggests that this narrative draws on a milieu of myths from the Ancient Near East.[39] One such myth is the *Enuma Elish*.[40] This cosmogony is of import because it belongs to the Babylonians by whom Israel was taken into exile in the sixth century B.C.E.. The narrative has the gods at

---

36. Vladimir Lossky, *The Mystical Theology of the Eastern Church* (Crestwood, NY: St. Vladimir's, 1976), 99.

37. Wolfhart Pannenberg, *Systematic Theology*, trans. Geoffrey W. Bromiley (Grand Rapids, MI: William B. Eerdmans Publishing Company, 1991), 3:645.

38. Northcott, *The Environment and Christian Ethics*, 174.

39. See John J. Collins, *Introduction to the Hebrew Bible* (Minneapolis, MN: Fortress Press, 2004), 25–45.

40. For a translation, see Ellen van Wolde, *Stories of the Beginning: Genesis 1–11 and Other Creation Stories* (Ridgefield, CT: Morehouse Publishing, 1995), 189–194.

war with each other prior to the creation of humanity. In a final battle, Marduk, in order to achieve a divine kingship among his peers, defeats his rival/mother, Tiamat. He splits her body and uses it to create the world. With the cosmos in place, Marduk creates human beings as slaves so that they might facilitate divine ease.[41]

Marduk's creative act stands in sharp juxtaposition to Elohim's. Ellen van Wolde points out that the Genesis account does not present human beings as slaves of the gods, but rather as a royal representation of God on earth.[42] Similarly, J. Richard Middleton skillfully argues that, contra the *Enuma Elish*, Genesis 1 does not fit the category of *chaoskampf* (that is, creation through a struggle with chaos). Indeed, whereas Marduk must contend with the dragons of Tiamat, Elohim sets the sea dragons (Hebrew *tannînîm*) free to be "part of God's peaceable kingdom."[43] Marduk creates by overcoming others with power; Elohim creates by empowering others to be free.[44] Marduk creates slaves; Elohim shares his image and likeness. Marduk engages in war; Elohim creates harmony devoid of even natural predation.[45]

The process and realization of Marduk's creation reflects Marduk's character. The same is true for Elohim. This juxtaposition is theological in the most proper sense, for it addresses the very nature of the divine. Consider this juxtaposition alongside a Darwinian worldview evident in table 2.1:

---

41. See ibid., 193.
42. Ibid., 28.
43. J. Richard Middleton, *The Liberating Image: The Imago Dei in Genesis 1* (Grand Rapids, MI: Brazos, 2005), 264. Contrarily, See Rosemary Radford Ruether, *Gaia and God: An Ecofeminist Theology of Earth Healing* (New York: HarperCollins, 1992), 19–22.
44. See Middleton, *The Liberating Image*, chapter 6; also Clifford, "Creation," 204–205.
45. On the non–predatory nature of the original creation in Genesis 1, see McLaughlin, *Christianity and the Status of Animals*, chapter 5.

Table 2.1 – Creation and Divine Character			
	Deity	Creative Action	Cosmic Identity
Narrative/ Myth "A" (Gen. 1:1–2:3)	Elohim	Creates through peaceful and cooperative divine fiat	A world of empowered creatures absent of predation
Narrative/ Myth "B" (*Enuma Elish*)	Marduk	Creates out of a divine war for existence	An enslaved and competitive world for divine benefit
Narrative/ Theory "C" (Darwinian Evolution)	???	???	A world in which "loss and death on an unthinkable scale are built into the way things are"[46]

The theologians of Israel differentiate Elohim ("God A") from Marduk ("God B") by juxtaposing both the process of creation and nature of the world they create ("World A" versus "World B"). "God A" (Elohim), through peaceful means ("Act A"), creates a world that reflects "God A": a peaceful world ("World A"). "God B" (Marduk), through chaotic struggle, murder, and death ("Act B"), creates a world that reflects "God B": a world of struggle and slavery ("World B").

If (1) there has never been a "World A," but only a "World C" and (2) "World C" reflects more elements of "World B" than "World A," then how can one affirm the *theological* vision of Genesis 1? Is Elohim revealed by science to be none other than Marduk? After all, Darwinian evolution is much more commensurable with Marduk than Elohim.[47] Here is the crux of the theological matter: One is all but forced by scientific evidence to reject the historicity of "World

---

46. Denis Edwards, "Every Sparrow that Falls to the Ground: The Cost of Evolution and the Christ-Event," *Ecotheology* 11/1 (2006): 104; also Lisa Sideris, *Environmental Ethics, Ecological Theology, and Natural Selection* (New York: Columbia University Press, 2003), 19.
47. See Northcott, *The Environment and Christian Ethics*, 74–75.

A"[48]; however, it is unclear how such a rejection does not at the same time necessitate the *theological* rejection of "God A."[49] As David Hull writes, "The God of Galapagos is careless, wasteful, indifferent, and almost diabolical."[50] Or, in the worlds of James Rachels: "Countless animals have suffered terribly in the millions of years that preceded the emergence of man, and the traditional theistic rejoinders do not even come close to justifying *that* evil."[51]

Clough, in light of an affirmation of evolution and a survey of biblical texts that intimate God's intention for creation is cosmic peace absent of predation, recognizes this same tension:

> One response to this difficulty is to deny the doctrine of the fall altogether and instead affirm that the world was always intended by God to contain the predation and suffering we see about us. This provokes the obvious question of how to reconcile the goodness of God with such a world, particularly given the strength of biblical witness concerning God's desire for peace between creatures.[52]

Clough offers an insightful place to begin in reference to the fall, writing, "the primary evidence for the fall is that Christ came to effect reconciliation between all things and God."[53] The nature of Jesus' work reveals something is not right about the world. Indeed, one might suggest that the death of God (speaking in terms of Christ on the cross) evinces the severity of predation in the cosmos—not even God can survive it! That God succumbs to it reveals the fallenness of the world. That God overcomes it reveals that this fallenness requires redemption. Clough claims that his position renders the fall an historical event in that the cross, as the clear expression of creatures

---

48. Rolston, "Does Nature Need Redeemed?" 205.
49. The force of this point is captured well by Southgate, *The Groaning of Creation*, 1–10.
50. David L. Hull, "God of the Galapagos," *Nature* 352 (August 1992): 486.
51. James Rachel, *Created from Animals: The Moral Implications of Darwinism* (New York: Oxford University Press, 1990), 105.
52. Clough, *On Animals*, 122.
53. Ibid.

turning on God, occurs within history. It is not, however, history "in the sense that a single fateful decision is a temporal cause of all the sin that follows."[54]

While Clough's position provides a good place to begin with the doctrine of the fall (i.e., the Christ-event as opposed to Genesis 3), he does no heavy lifting in delineating the etiology of evil. Ultimately, he appeals to a vague notion of will: "The only account we can give in a theological context to the existence of evil is creaturely rebellion against God's graciousness in creation."[55] Clough couples this appeal with an acknowledgement of ignorance—that we cannot know "how God's goodness, power and love relate to the darkest parts of creation" until we "see as the angels do."[56] There is thus no attempt at the resolution of "God A" and "World C." There is rather an acknowledgement of both and an appeal to ignorance and mystery.

Thus, in Clough's position the tension remains because there is no account of how God's goodness is amenable with the history of evolutionary emergence. Clough is happy to avoid addressing this tension because he sees it, ultimately, as a theodicy. And, as he rightly critiques about many theodicies, they attempt to exonerate God by somehow justifying the suffering of victims. "The danger that theodicy may become a rationale for oppression is acute in the context of the suffering of non-human animals."[57] Clough is here critical of Christopher Southgate's "only way" argument (that evolution is the only way God could bring about the goodness of the present world, including its biodiversity), writing, "This theodicy risks rationalizing the suffering of non-human animals, making it an acceptable cost as part of an overall divine plan, rather than seeing

54. Ibid., 126.
55. Ibid.
56. Ibid.
57. Ibid., 148.

in it a motivation for practical action, together with lament and protest."[58]

It is important to take heed to Clough's warning about exonerating God and justifying the suffering of victims. I have no such aim here. The exoneration of God is God's business—business that in my view still requires much to be done. For my part, addressing the tension that arises between God's goodness and the predatory nature of our universe is an attempt to respond to those who embrace the mechanisms of evolution as good by exploring possible scenarios in which God does not ordain them. In this sense, addressing the tension becomes a way not of exonerating God but rather of *refusing* to justify the suffering of victims by appealing to some divine plan. Indeed, Clough suggests that such suffering calls for "lament and protest," a point in which my work will fully concur.

So, how can this theological tension between God's goodness and evolution be relieved? There are three prominent options: (1) Reinterpret the doctrine of the fall in a manner that takes scientific evidence seriously and thereby maintains in some sense the identity of both "World A" and "God A"; (2) Interpret the doctrine of God in such a way as to lessen divine culpability for "World C"; and (3) Interpret the Hebrew worldview of Genesis 1 so that "World C" and "God A" are not incompatible.[59]

A combination of the first and second options is evident in the approaches of Moltmann and Linzey. The second option is significant and utilized to varying degrees by a host of theologians,

---

58. Ibid.
59. For instance, Northcott, *The Environment and Christian Ethics*, 179. See also Robert Wennberg's discussion of deep ecology in *God, Humans, and Animals: An Invitation to Enlarge Our Moral Universe* (Grand Rapids, MI: William B. Eerdmans Publishing Company, 2003), 43–49.

especially those influenced by open and relational theologies.[60] Here, however, it is the third route I wish to explore.

Creation spiritualists, for instance Matthew Fox and Thomas Berry, maintain that the mechanisms that facilitate the emerging of the universe are not only not fallen, but good. Fox's "Eucharistic Law of the Universe" maintains that the great law of existence consists of evolutionary transformation through sacrifice—more specifically, by "eating and being eaten." He thus contends, "We too will be food one day for other generations of living things. So we might as well begin today by letting go of hoarding and entering the chain of beings as food for one another."[61] Wendell Berry offers a similar view.[62] Thomas Berry, whom I will engage in much greater detail in chapter 5, maintains that the violent episodes of evolutionary emergence are "cosmological moments of grace."[63]

Certain ecofeminists, such as Rosemary Radford Ruether, argue that death ought to be embraced as part of the beautiful cycle of life rather than an enemy resulting from some cosmic fall. One living thing dies while another receives life. Thus, when an individual dies, his or her "existence ceases as individuated ego/organism and dissolves back into the cosmic matrix of matter/energy, from which new centers of the individuation arise."[64] As such, death is an "essential component" of cosmic existence and is therefore "a friend of the life process."[65]

60. See David Ray Griffin, *God, Power, and Evil* (Louisville: Westminster John Knox, 2004); John Sanders, *The God Who Risks: A Theology of Providence* (Downers Grove, IL: Intervarsity, 1998).

61. Matthew Fox, *Creation Spirituality: Liberating Gifts for the Peoples of the Earth* (San Francisco: HarperCollins, 1991), 51.

62. Wendell Berry, *The Gift of Good Land: Further Essays Cultural and Agricultural* (San Francisco: North Point, 1981), 281.

63. Thomas Berry, "Wisdom of the Cross," in *The Christian Future and the Fate of the Earth*, ed. Mary Evelyn Tucker and John Grim (Maryknoll, NY: Orbis Books, 2009), 89.

64. Rosemary Radford Ruether, *Sexism and God-Talk: Toward A Feminist Theology* (Boston: Beacon, 1983), 257.

65. Ruether, *Gaia and God*, 53.

Many of these approaches fail to take seriously the chaotic struggle of nature, a criticism leveled by Lisa Sideris against Ruether, Sallie McFague, and Northcott, all of whom overemphasize the cooperative aspects of nature while downplaying the competitive aspects.[66] Sideris argues that such ecotheologians ignore that the "harmonious" balances within nature "are maintained at great cost to *individual* animal lives." Indeed, "the ecological community…does not aim toward the good of each individual within that community, as (ideally) human communities do."[67]

Taking his lead from Sideris, Jenkins writes,

> It is not just the religious right voicing skepticism of the natural sciences. Whenever a theological ethicist privileges interdependence, balance, and cooperation in nature over evolution, predation, or death, she appears to let theological criteria determine her view of the natural world, in the face of credible scientific reports.[68]

In doing so, "a number of environmental theologians rewrite descriptions of the natural world even as they call Christians to respect creation on its own principles."[69]

Sideris and Jenkins highlight theological attempts to remedy the disparity between "God A" and "World C" by re-envisioning the latter in a manner that it is less offensive to the former. However, as Sideris astutely notes, "Something must be given up: either the traditional understanding of God must be altered or the processes of evolution must be reinterpreted along less Darwinian lines."[70] Thus, an "ecological" emphasis at the expense of the reality of suffering,

66. See Sideris, *Environmental Ethics*, 45–90.
67. Ibid., 81.
68. Willis Jenkins, *Ecologies of Grace: Environmental Ethics and Christian Theology* (New York: Oxford University Press, 2008), 70–71.
69. Ibid.
70. Sideris, *Environmental Ethics*, 279, n. 19.

predation, and death, does not hold the scientific high ground—even though its advocates often make such a claim.

Regardless of the solution, the import of the cosmological tension surrounding the notion of the fall for nonhuman theology can hardly be overstated. At its heart is the question of what we understand as "tragic."[71] Phrased differently, the question is whether or not the world as we experience it, and most notably the darker dimensions of evolution, is the way God desires it to be. If so, how does one make sense of God's eternal goodness? Of Christ's victory over death? If not, how are these mechanisms of evolution set into motion, if not by God?

Anthropology

Are humans essentially unique creatures in the cosmos? If so, does that uniqueness constitute the exclusion of other creatures from direct moral concern, as anthropocentric worldviews tend to maintain? Such questions constitute central issues in environmental and animal theologies vis-à-vis anthropology.

To answer these questions, it is prudent to consider the doctrine of the *imago Dei*. This phrase actually receives very little attention in the Hebrew Scriptures.[72] Nonetheless, theologians have devoted a great deal of ink to it. This interest has resulted in multiple interpretations.[73] Authors such as Middleton identify three major categories for these interpretations: substantive, relational, and functional.[74]

---

71. Wennberg, *God, Humans, and Animals*, 48.
72. The only explicit appearances of "image" (*selem*) in the context of "image of God" are Genesis 1:26, 28; 9:6 (in deuterocanonical works, Wis 2:23 and Sir 17:3).
73. See David Cairns, *The Image of God in Man*, revised edition (London: Collins, 1973).

The substantive interpretation is the most common, historically. Stanley Grenz provides a good overview of its rise and perpetuation, including its Hellenistic roots.[75] Advocates of this interpretation view the *imago* as ingrained in human nature, which bears an essential commonality with the divine.[76] Frequently, rationality and freewill constitute this commonality.[77] These characteristics not only express an ontological similarity between humanity and God, but also a discontinuity between humanity and the rest of creation. As Augustine writes, "God . . . made man in His own image. For He created for him a soul endowed with reason and intelligence so that he might excel all the creatures of the earth, air, and sea, which were not so gifted."[78]

The substantive interpretation evokes Douglas John Hall's criticism: "It can readily appear—if one follows the history of the interpretation of this symbol closely—that the whole enterprise of defining the *imago Dei* in our Christian conventions centers on the apparent need to show that human beings are different from all other creatures."[79] Hall delineates two negative effects of this view. First, that the boundaries created by the *imago* necessarily denote a difference between greater and lesser creatures in which "'different' almost invariably implies 'higher,' 'nobler,' 'loftier,' 'better.'"[80]

74. See Middleton, *The Liberating Image*; Douglas John Hall in *Imaging God: Dominion as Stewardship* (Grand Rapids, MI: William B. Eerdmans Publishing Company, 1986); Millard J. Erickson, *Christian Theology*, second edition (Grand Rapids, MI: Baker Books, 1998), 520–29.

75. Stanley J. Grenz, *The Social God and the Relational Self: A Trinitarian Theology of the Imago Dei* (Louisville, KY: Westminster John Knox, 2001), 143–73.

76. Hall, *Imaging God*, 89.

77. For historical considerations, see Grenz, *Social God*, 142–61.

78. Augustine, *City of God*, Basic Writings of Saint Augustine, ed. Whitney J. Oates (New York: Random House, 1948), 12:24.

79. Hall, *Imaging God*, 90.

80. Ibid. In response to such emphases, Clough argues that, in the face of the claim that the cosmic Christ incarnate as creature is *the* image of God, the *imago* must be democratized into the entire created order. Humans image God *in via* a particular mode (or better, through a particular vocation). See Clough, *On Animals*, 101–2.

Second—and related to the first danger—ascribing greater worth to humanity on account of nonmaterial qualities seems to serve as a polemic against physicality.[81]

In the relational interpretation, favored in contemporary theology, the *imago* denotes humanity's relational capacity. Humans, as *imago Dei*, have the ability to relate to each other and to God. Hall links this view to Luther and Calvin, both of whom view the *imago* not as intrinsic to humanity but rather as a reality derived from a proper rapport with God.[82] Without this rapport, the *imago* is not realized.[83] In this sense, the image constitutes a calling to reciprocate the divine openness to the creation.

Karl Barth promulgates this view when he claims that, as the image of God, humanity is fundamentally relational, evident in the "male and female" of Genesis 1. This relationality reflects the relationality in the Trinity, the "I and the Thou of God Himself."[84] Emil Brunner makes comparable claims in his systematic theology.[85] Hence, similar to the early Reformers, for Barth and Brunner humans cannot lose the image as it is not a human possession. However, humans can fail to inhabit or fully realize it.[86]

Modern biblical scholars tend to favor the functional interpretation of the *imago*, as exegetical factors of Genesis 1 substantiate it.[87] In this reading, the *imago* places humans in a relationship to the nonhuman creation. Specifically, God calls all humans to a position of both royal

---

81. Hall, *Imaging God*, 90.
82. The Reformers did not differentiate between "image" and "likeness."
83. See Hall, *Imaging God*, 98–108.
84. Karl Barth, *Church Dogmatics*, ed. G. W. Bromiley and T. F. Torrance (Edinburgh: T&T Clark, 1958), III/1:191–98.
85. Emil Brunner, *Church Dogmatics* (Cambridge, UK: James Clark and Company, 1952), 2:55–61.
86. See Barth, *Dogmatics*, III/1:200.
87. For instance, one finds a functional interpretation of the *imago Dei* in Middleton, *The Liberating Image*; Hall, *Dominion As Stewardship*; Towner, "Clones of God"; Terrance Fretheim, *God and World in the Old Testament: A Relational Theology of Creation* (Nashville: Abingdon, 2005), 48–53; Walter Brueggemann, *Genesis* (Atlanta: John Knox, 1982), 32.

dignity and responsibility as co-regents in the created order. Humans represent the presence of God in the created order. In Middleton's words, "The *imago Dei* designates the royal office or calling of human beings as God's representatives and agents in the world, granted authorized power to share in God's rule or administration of the earth's resources and creatures."[88]

Even more concise is Ellen van Wolde's statement: "The human being is created to make God present in his creation."[89]

These three interpretations highlight the dominant voices in the field.[90] With regard to nonhuman theology, each presents unique opportunities and problems. The substantive interpretation, as already noted, emphasizes the essential and incorporeal uniqueness of humans, which in turn tends toward the exclusion of *all* nonhuman life from anything akin to direct moral concern.[91] This position is furthermore problematic when juxtaposed with evolutionary biology. For instance, in *Humani Generis*, Pope Pius XII maintains that the human soul cannot be the result of evolutionary development.[92] Such a concession would weaken essential human uniqueness, a result that some scholars embrace.[93]

The relational interpretation in theory renders the ontological difference between humans and nonhumans less important. The anxiety of separating "us" from "them" diminishes—though, it seems that ontological aspects such as rationality and freewill are essential for responding to the relational calling constituted by the image. At any rate, this view often neglects to explore the significance of

88. Middleton, *The Liberating Image*, 27.
89. Wolde, *Stories of the Beginning*, 28.
90. Though, it should be noted that these interpretations can take christological/eschatological orientations. See Grenz, *The Social God and the Relational Self*.
91. See Fergusson, "Creation," 84.
92. Clifford, "Creation," 233. This point is later reiterated by John Paul II. Ibid., 234.
93. See Hoggard Creegan, "Being an Animal and Being Made in the Image of God," *Colloqium* 39/2 (November 2007): 185–203.

the *imago* for nonhumans, focusing rather on the relationship among humans and between humans and God.[94]

Positively, the functional interpretation directly places human beings in relation to the nonhuman creation. It is quite anthropocentric with regard to humanity's role—though, not necessarily with regard to value.[95] Also, like its relational counterpart, the functional interpretation relies on essential human qualities necessary for humanity's representative role in creation. Following Genesis 1, scholars have tended to define this role in terms of "dominion." While this term bears negative historical baggage, modern advocates of the functional interpretation, including those who understand dominion in terms of stewardship and those, like myself, who view humanity's role as sacramentally rendering present in history the eschatological peaceable kingdom, tend to dismantle the notion that the nonhuman creation exists for humanity.[96] Indeed, some maintain the opposite: humans exist, at least in part, for the sake of cosmic well-being.

Collectively, these three interpretative strands highlight two fundamental anthropological questions. First, what constitutes the human being (substance)? Second, what meaning does this constitution bear for human activity in the cosmos (function/relation) vis-à-vis the human disposition before the divine (relation)? These questions highlight the contributions theological anthropology will make to my exploratory framework.

---

94. For example, see Barth, *Dogmatics*, III/1:194–96. For exceptions, see Bradley C. Hanson, *Introduction to Christian Theology* (Minneapolis, MN: Fortress Press, 1997), 84–85; Shirley C. Guthrie, *Christian Doctrine*, revised edition (Louisville, KY: John Knox, 1994), 196–210.

95. See, for instance, Hall, *Dominion as Stewardship*.

96. On stewardship, see Ibid. On eschatological perspectives, see Andrew Linzey, *Animal Theology* (Chicago: University of Illinois Press, 1994), 72.

Eschatology

Eschatology has perhaps received more attention than any other doctrine in the twentieth century. This vigorous exploration is due largely to the work of Johannes Weiss and Albert Schweitzer, both of whom highlighted the significance of eschatology for Jesus's life and ministry.[97] While the claims of both scholars have been widely contested with regard to their christological implications, my interest consists in other eschatological issues that have arisen in their wake—namely, the scope of the community for which eschatological redemption bears significance, the interplay between eschatology and history, and the extent of both the continuality and discontinuity of the present creation and the new creation.

The Scope of the Eschatological Community

The question of what parts of the cosmos will persist in the eschaton yields a wide variety of answers in Christian history. These answers can be expressed through expanding circles of inclusion.[98] The first circle is the inclusion of the individual human soul/spirit. Modern theologians tend to decry an exclusively spiritualized eschatology by emphasizing the importance of the resurrection of the flesh over and against the Platonic immortality of the soul.[99] The future of humanity is an embodied one, not simply a spiritual one.[100] Thus, the second

---

97. See Hans Schwarz, *Eschatology* (Grand Rapids, MI: William B. Eerdmans Publishing Company, 2000), 107–115; Benedict T. Viviano, "Eschatology and the Quest for the Historical Jesus," in *The Orthodox Handbook of Eschatology*, ed. Jerry L. Walls (New York: Oxford University Press, 2008), 73–90.

98. This imagery is my own.

99. See, for instance, Oscar Cullman's classic work: *The Resurrection of the Dead or the Immortality of the Soul?: The Witness of the New Testament* (Eugene, OR: Wipf & Stock Publishers, 2010). For a survey and critical consideration of this trend, see Joseph Ratzinger, *Eschatology: Death and Eternal Life*, second edition, trans. Michael Waldstein (Washington DC: The Catholic University of America Press, 1988), 104–61; also, Pannenberg, *Systematic Theology*, 3:570–73.

circle of inclusion is the individual human body—the flesh—which includes the elements and chemicals necessary for such matter.[101]

The third circle of inclusion is exemplified in Joseph Ratzinger's *Eschatology*, in which he emphasizes the communal dimension of eschatology. He rejects, for instance, the possibility of an individual's instant experience of the resurrection of the dead through an appeal to eternity as diachronic time because such a position downplays the communal significance of history's unfolding.[102] While Ratzinger thus moves beyond individualistic eschatologies to include the human community, he is less developed in his cosmic eschatology.[103] This limited focus is evident in his description of the "task of contemporary eschatology," which is "to marry perspectives, so that person and community, present and future, are seen in their unity."[104]

The cosmic dimension of eschatology, which constitutes the fourth inclusive circle, is the beginning of the most important dividing marks with regard to the present work. It is strongly present in Eastern theology.[105] Contemporary Eastern Orthodox theologians tend to maintain consistently that the entire cosmos will in some manner participate in eschatological redemption through transfiguration.[106] Contrarily, in the West theological giants such as Augustine and Aquinas reserve eschatological redemption for

100. See John Polkinghorne, *Scientists as Theologians: A Comparison of the Writings of Ian Barbour, Arthur Peacocke and John Polkinghorne* (London: SPCK, 1996), chapter 3.
101. See Thomas Aquinas, *Summa Contra Gentiles*, ed. Joseph Kenny (New York: Hanover House, 1955–57), IV.97.5; Ratzinger, *Eschatology*, 168–94.
102. Ratzinger, *Eschatology*, 251–55. See also Pannenberg, *Systematic Theology*, 3: 546–47.
103. For a criticism of Ratzinger, see Jürgen Moltmann, "Horizons of Hope," *The Christian Century*, May 20 (2009): 31–33.
104. Ratzinger, *Eschatology*, 12.
105. See McLaughlin, *Christian Theology and the Status of Animals*, chapters 4 and 7; chapter 6 of the present work.
106. See Andrew Louth, "Eastern Orthodox Eschatology," in *The Orthodox Handbook of Eschatology*, ed. Jerry L. Walls (New York: Oxford University Press, 2008,) 237–238.

humans (and inanimate elements).[107] In modern times, some Western theologians advocate a more cosmic eschatology.[108]

The problem with the cosmic eschatologies of the East and West is that they are vague with regard to the nature of the nonhuman creation's participation in the eschaton. They are unclear if the eschatological community includes simply cosmic matter and energy, or an earth-like environment, or plants, or nonhuman animals. Furthermore, they remain unclear—regarding plants and animals especially—if there is a bodily resurrection of those individual entities that existed during history (whether some or all) or a generic eschatological representation of each species.

The persistent vagueness of cosmic eschatologies points to a fifth circle of inclusion in which all individual creatures that existed in history will participate in the eschatological resurrection. Moltmann's eschatology exemplifies such a view.[109] Indeed, his is perhaps the most inclusive eschatology in the field—although, Clough highlights (and echoes) the extreme inclusivity of John Hildrop's eschatology in which "every individual creature will have a place in immortality."[110] Clough's research also reveals that, historically, a great deal of discussions (and reticence) concerning the presence of animals in the eschaton has focused on whether or not they have immortal souls as opposed to whether or not they shall experience a resurrection of the flesh.[111]

---

107. See Augustine, *Miscellany of Eighty-Three Questions*, The Works of Saint Augustine, ed. Raymond Canning, trans. Boniface Ramsey (New York City Press, New York: 2008), XXX. On Aquinas, see Chapter 4.
108. See Andrew Linzey and Tom Regan, eds., *Animals and Christianity: A Book of Readings* (Eugene, OR: Wipf and Stock, 1990), 81–109.
109. Jürgen Moltmann, *The Coming of God: Christian Eschatology*, trans. Margaret Kohl (Minneapolis, MN: Fortress Press, 1996), 69–70.
110. Clough, *On Animals*, 142.
111. See ibid., 137–144.

Eschatology and History

A cosmic eschatology bears significance for eco-theological ethics only to the extent that eschatology bears meaning for how humans live within the unfolding of history. This point raises the question, What is the relationship between the present and the eschatological future?[112] In contemporary theology, I detect five general approaches: existentially-oriented, future-oriented, present-oriented, hope-oriented, and politically-oriented.[113]

Ratzinger suggests that Karl Barth's transcendental eschatology paves the way for the existentially-oriented approach inasmuch as it renders eschatology fully transcendent to time and immanent to existence, facilitating the crisis of encounter between humanity and God.[114] This emphasis on encounter is taken up by Rudolph Bultmann, in whom "eschatology is stripped of any temporal component" and defined essentially as "an act of self-abandonment."[115]

In juxtaposition to existential approaches that emphasize encounter at the expense of temporality stands future-oriented approaches, which place temporality at the heart of eschatology.[116] An example is Oscar Cullman's "salvation history" approach to eschatology in which time is divided into the pre-Christ-event, the already/not yet of the Christ-event, and the future hope to come—the "not yet".[117] In this schema, "Faith means entering into solidarity with salvation history, taking up its 'already' and, on that basis, working towards the 'not yet.'"[118]

---

112. Ratzinger, *Eschatology*, 4.
113. I am here combining into my own categories insights from Ratzinger, Schwarz, and Moltmann.
114. Ratzinger, *Eschatology*, 47–48.
115. Ibid., 48–49. On Bultmann, see Schwarz, *Eschatology*, 120–27.
116. Ratzinger, *Eschatology*, 51.
117. See Ratzinger, *Eschatology*, 53–55; Schwarz, *Eschatology*, 136–37.

Present-oriented eschatologies bear a semblance to existential ones in their application of eschatology to the here and now. The difference is between "here" and the "now." Whereas existential eschatologies emphasize personal encounter (the "here"), present eschatologies emphasize the presence of the future in history (the "now"). There is overlap here with both Cullman's futurist approach and theologies of hope. However, C. H. Dodd's "realized eschatology" warrants a separate category. For Dodd, the Christ-event accomplished the work of rendering God's kingdom present on earth.[119] Thus, the Church's celebration is less a looking forward and more a looking back.[120] For "in Jesus the eternal entered decisively into history," forcing the "hour of decision."[121] Hans Schwarz classifies Dodd's approach as transcendentalist because history has already witnessed the coming of the kingdom. Therefore, the future hope is not at all future, but beyond history altogether.[122]

In Moltmann's view, whereas Barth transported eschatology into eternity, rendering it wholly other than time and history, future-oriented approaches mistakenly subsume eschatology into time.[123] Thus Moltmann, along with Wolfhart Pannenberg, advocates a different approach—one oriented around hope. Moltmann's earlier work, especially *Theology of Hope*, has been greatly influential in the rise of political theology.[124] Yet there is a distinct difference between both Moltmann and Pannenberg and strictly political theologies that transport eschatology into time in an effort to construct utopian societies.[125] There is also a difference between Moltmann's

---

118. Ratzinger, *Eschatology*, 54.
119. Schwarz, *Eschatology*, 130. On the difference between Dodd and Barth here, see Karl Barth, *Church Dogmatics*, trans. G. W. Bromiley (Edinburgh: T&T Clark, 1962), IV/3/2:903–905.
120. Ratzinger, *Eschatology*, 55–56.
121. Schwarz, *Eschatology*, 130.
122. Ibid., 132.
123. Moltmann, *The Coming of God*, 10–12.
124. Ratzinger, *Eschatology*, 58.

THREE THEOLOGICAL LOCI FOR A NEW TAXONOMY

eschatology and the future-oriented eschatology of Cullman;[126] for Moltmann differentiates between the phenomenological future (the irreversible time of history) and the eschatological future, which "is God's coming and his arrival."[127] Thus, for Moltmann, God's coming is the presence of the eschatological future, which is the source of phenomenological time, within history. This coming transforms time (and history) itself. Thus, the eschaton is both transcendent and immanent—it is present in history while at the same time being history's horizon. Christologically, this vision is different from Pannenberg, who maintains that God's coming in Christ is the prolepsis of the still future kingdom.[128]

Finally, there are the politically-oriented eschatologies of liberation theology.[129] These forms are influenced by the work of Johann Baptist Metz.[130] Many of them furthermore bear some affinity with existential approaches in that they tend to demythologize eschatology, rendering it more a call to work toward social utopias that are possible within the flow of history.[131] Said differently, eschatology is often deprived of its transcendence.[132] It becomes a fully historical, political, and ethical endeavor. This tendency is also evident in certain feminist approaches to eschatology, most notably that of Ruether.[133]

---

125. See Moltmann, *The Coming of God*, 195; Pannenberg, *Systematic Theology*, 3:585–86.
126. See ibid., 12–13.
127. Ibid., 22.
128. Schwarz, *Eschatology*, 145. However, on the practical overlap between Moltmann and Pannenberg, see Pannenberg, *Sysmatic Theology*, 3:552.
129. For an overview, see Schwarz, *Eschatology*, 152–66.
130. See ibid., 152–53.
131. See Ratzinger, *Eschatology*, 57–59. In my view, Ratzinger wrongly classifies Moltmann here.
132. See Schwarz's engagement with Gustavo Gutierrez in *Eschatology*, 159–60.
133. See, for instance, her mixture of agnosticism (about the future) and existentialism regarding personal eschatology in *Sexism and God Talk*, 257–58.

Eschatology and Ethics

Intimately connected to the question concerning the relationship between history and eschatology—and equally important for this project—is the relationship between eschatology and ethics.[134] To what extent does eschatology inform morality within the unfolding of history? It is just at this point that Ratzinger is critical of political theologies; for "the realization of God's Kingdom is not itself a political process."[135] Even more harshly, to make eschatological hope an achievable goal within history entails "the emasculation of Christian hope."[136] For Ratzinger, the kingdom of God bears meaning for politics, but not by way of eschatology. Thus he maintains that "the setting asunder of eschatology and politics is one of the fundamental tasks of Christian theology."[137] To the extent that eschatology ought not to become a political program in which the full realization of eschatological hope is transported into history and realized through human effort, I concur with Ratzinger's position. However, if he intends to claim that eschatology has no bearing on moral theology, his stance is much less tenable.

On the other hand, a complete relegation of eschatology into ethics and politics—which is what Ratzinger seems to fear—is also problematic. In the words of Barth, the undeniable "not yet" of history is the shattering of "the great Constantinian illusion."[138] For Barth, Christians are called to hope for the future kingdom in the midst of inevitable conflict.[139] This vision leans toward the approaches of Moltmann and Pannenberg. Schwarz summarizes Pannenberg's eschatological ethics well: "Since we are able to

134. See Moltmann, *The Coming of God*, 129–202.
135. Ratzinger, *Eschatology*, 58.
136. Ibid., 59.
137. Ibid.
138. Barth, *Church Dogmatics*, IV/3/2:918.
139. Ibid., 917–19.

participate proleptically in the promised future, we are encouraged to anticipate this future proleptically."[140]

Continuity and Discontinuity between the Present and the New Creation

Also connected to the question of the relationship between history and eschatology is the issue concerning the level of continuity (and discontinuity) between the present creation and the new creation. This issue is further complicated, however, by the introduction of an inbreaking eschatological future in which the radically new accosts history—for example the resurrection of Jesus *within history*. The question, then, is two-fold. First, to what extent will the new creation be continuous with the present creation? Second, to what extent does the Christ-event, including the ongoing work of the Spirit, enable the new to break into history? These questions will be of great significance in my discussion of Moltmann and Linzey and in my constructive work in chapter four.

At stake in these questions are both the object and nature of eschatological salvation. Is the present cosmos the object of salvation? Phrased differently, will the "new creation" be numerically identical—and thus continuous—with the present creation? Or, will the "new creation" replace the present one? If there is numerical identity between the present creation and the new creation, will the new creation be genuinely new—and thus discontinuous—or a mere evolutionary development of the present creation?[141]

---

140. Schwarz, *Eschatology*, 145. This position is commensurate with Schwarz's own constructive proposal. See ibid., chapter 7.

141. On these questions, see Polkinghorne, *God of Hope*, 14–26; John Polkinghorne, *Science and the Trinity: The Christian Encounter with Reality* (New Haven, CT: Yale University Press, 2004), 143–69.

In Sum

I have explored the following dimensions of eschatology:

1. The scope of the community of eschatological redemption;
2. The nature of the relationship between eschatology and history;
3. The nature of the relationship between eschatology and ethics;
4. The degree of continuity and discontinuity between the present and new creation.

Collectively, these dimensions reveal much about one's eco-theology.[142] Non-cosmic eschatologies tend to render the nonhuman creation less important—or important only insofar as it contributes to human well-being. Yet a cosmic eschatology that includes even the resurrection of individual creatures holds meaning for moral practice in history only if eschatology is not purely transcendent. Furthermore, existentially and politically oriented eschatologies tend to work toward only that which is achievable in the natural evolution of history. They are thus open to the restructuring of human communities, but they cannot logically bear the strain of the transfiguration of nature itself. If, however, an eschatology contains a cosmic scope (thus including nature), a transcendent dimension (thus offering hope for future beyond what the natural unfolding of history can provide), and a manner in which the "future" is somehow present within history (thus rendering the hope for the kingdom impactful for human practice within history), then it becomes cosmically significant *to history* without being completely subsumed *in history*. It

142. See Paul Santmire, *The Travail of Nature: The Ambiguous Ecological Promise of Christian Theology* (Minneapolis, MN: Fortress Press, 1985), 216–18.

is just such a vision that both Moltmann and Linzey offer.

Conclusion

I maintain that the theological loci of cosmology, anthropology, and eschatology provide a promising framework within which to develop a new taxonomy of eco-theological ethics that more thoroughly maps the field with regard to content than those I explored in chapter 1. They do so because they highlight central tensions that are often unaccounted for in other systems of classification. I now turn to these tensions in order to establish the parameters of my proposed taxonomy.

3

A New Taxonomy

In the previous chapter I explored three fundamental loci for nonhuman theological ethics: cosmology, anthropology, and eschatology. At the intersection of these loci, two fundamental tensions arise. The first burgeons out of the interplay between the historical telos of the nonhuman creation and that of the human creation. By "historical telos," I intimate the purpose of a thing or groups of things within the unfolding of the present creation. The term stands in juxtaposition to an "eternal" or "ultimate" telos, which denotes the eschatological destiny of a thing or group of things. Why do humans and nonhumans exist in history? To what end? Does the nonhuman find its meaning and value only in the human? Or, does it have, each part or creature, some value and relation with God in and of itself? Has God endowed the nonhuman cosmos with any meaning or value apart from its being in relation to humanity? I use two value terms, "anthropocentrism" and "cosmocentrism," to represent this tension.

The second tension derives from the divine intent for the created order (both human and nonhuman), the eternal telos of the nonhuman creation, and the manner in which these factors shape how humanity ought to engage the nonhuman world. Is the nonhuman world the way God desires it to be? Or, is it in some sense fallen or incomplete? What is the ultimate end God desires for the nonhuman world? Does it have a place in eternity or is it exhausted in the temporal realm? If it has a place, how much of the nonhuman creation will that place accommodate? Individuals? Species? Simple building blocks of matter? Time? For this tension I use the teleological terms "conservation" and "transfiguration."

Anthropocentrism versus Cosmocentrism

Willis Jenkins rightly notes that the most common form of classifying environmental theologies is whether or not they are anthropocentric. He is furthermore correct, in my view, that this label should not be the only one employed in mapping the field or adjudicating the potential contributions of voices within that field. However, I maintain that anthropocentrism is an important categorical marker in that it highlights significant divergences in eco-theological theory and practice. It is for want of his use of this categorical marker that Jenkins's taxonomy of grace faces its own challenges.[1] Namely, he categorizes voices together that bear striking differences. Indeed, he himself notes that there are wide (and not inconsequential) variations within ecojustice regarding natural evil.[2] Furthermore, the stark distinction between Moltmann and Aquinas ought to elicit curiosity at their common categorization. The reason I continue to distinguish

---

1. To be fair, Jenkins never claims that his map of the field is absolute or exhaustive.
2. See Willis Jenkins, *Ecologies of Grace: Environmental Ethics and Christian Theology* (New York: Oxford University Press, 2008), 70–71.

between anthropocentric and non-anthropocentric forms of nonhuman theological ethics is because I believe the question of intrinsic value, while not the only pertinent distinction in this field, remains key in establishing categories within it.

Defining the Terms

There are multiple ways to use terms like "anthropocentric" and "cosmocentric."[3] For instance, Northcott uses the term "humanocentric" to denote a conversational framework and a methodology of engaging ecological issues. Ruether approaches ecological issues within the framework of a sociological and theological critique of patriarchy. Because she starts with this critique of *human* thought, Northcott labels her humanocentric.[4] Pope John Paul II approaches ecological issues from a concern for universal human dignity—also a human-based category. It is this commonality that leads Northcott to place Ruether and the Pope in the same category. Similarly, Northcott categorizes Moltmann as theocentric because his "doctrine of creation is derived primarily from a new reading of the doctrine of God as Trinity."[5] Thus, Northcott uses centric terms to describe method as opposed to value.

Another use—which tends to have theological connotations—of anthropocentrism is concerned with functional roles. For instance, anthropocentrism can mean that humans bear a central role in the preservation and/or development of the cosmos, whether as stewards or co-creators.[6] Some of the thinkers that are cosmocentric with regard to *value* are anthropocentric with regard the *functional role* of

3. On "anthropocentrism," see David Clough, *On Animals* (New York: Bloomsbury, 2014), XV–XX.
4. Michael Northcott, *The Environment and Christian Ethics* (New York: Cambridge University Press, 1996), 137.
5. Ibid., 350, n. 53.

humanity.[7] This distinction is essential in later chapters of the present work.

Yet another form of centric terms is offered by Lisa Sideris. She writes that "The distinction between an ethic derived from nature and one extended to nature becomes blurred in the writings of some ecotheologians."[8] This statement highlights the crux of Sideris's understanding of various centric terms. For her, such terms are defined by their frame of reference for the establishment of value. In conjunction with James Gustafson, she states that "anthropocentrism constitutes a refusal to accept and respect a natural ordering that is neither of our own making nor completely under our control."[9] An anthropocentric ethic is thus one in which humans apply their subjective values and hopes to nature. For instance, Ruether is anthropocentric "insofar as her ecological ethic is filtered through the experiences and claims of women as an oppressed group." [10] Indeed, Sideris defines any failure to affirm the goodness of the natural order, any reading of the natural order in an anthropomorphic sense, and any hope for an eschatological transfiguration of nature as anthropocentric.[11] An *eco*centric ethic, which Sideris favors, is one in which humans allow nature to reveal its own set of principles and formulate from this revelation an ethic that respects those principles.[12] In Sideris's view, a *theo*centric ethics (by which she seems to mean the particular theocentric ethics of Gustafson) is one in which humans permit the order God has established in nature to reveal the

---

6. See John Meyendorff, *Christ in Eastern Christian Thought* (Washington, DC: Corpus Books, 1969), 105; Kallistos Ware, *The Orthodox Way*, Revised Edition (Crestwood, NY: St. Vladimir's Seminary Press, 1995), 49–50; Clough, *On Animals*, XIX.

7. As I will show, such is the view of Moltmann and Linzey.

8. Lisa Sideris, *Environmental Ethics, Ecological Theology, and Natural Selection* (New York: Columbia University Press, 2003), 46.

9. Ibid., 201.

10. Ibid., 85.

11. Sideris includes Ruether, McFague, Northcott, Moltmann, and Charles Birch in this camp.

12. Sideris, *Environmental Ethics*, 175.

framework for human engagement with nature. Such a perspective "fosters a sense of dependence, awe, and gratitude . . . for powers that sustain human life and life as a whole."[13] It thus does not denigrate the natural order, which is divinely established. Nor does it seek a better world: "However unappealing the perspective may be at times, a theocentric construal does not force God and nature into roles that better suit our own preferences for harmony and justice."[14]

These exceptions notwithstanding, most thinkers use terms like anthropocentrism, biocentrism, androcentrism, and cosmocentrism to refer to the question of teleology and value. In the words of Susan Armstrong and Richard Botzler, "*Anthropocentrism* is the philosophical perspective that ethical principles apply to humans only and that human needs and interests are of the highest, and even exclusive, value and importance." [15] In line with this definition, Paul Taylor distinguishes between two kinds of environmental ethics: anthropocentric and biocentric.[16] He maintains that an anthropocentric approach "holds that our moral duties with respect to the natural world are all ultimately derived from the duties we owe to one another as human beings."[17] Such a view makes ecological conservation a moral issue because of both the present and future human community. Contrarily, a biocentric approach maintains that

> our duties toward nature do not stem from the duties we owe to humans
> . . . the natural world is not there simply as an object to be exploited
> by us, nor are its living creatures to be regarded as nothing more
> than resources for our use and consumption. On the contrary, wild
> communities of life are understood to be deserving of our moral concern

13. Ibid., 201.
14. Ibid., 214.
15. Susan J. Armstrong and Richard G. Botzler, *Environmental Ethics: Divergence and Convergence,* third edition (New York: McGraw Hill, 2003), 271.
16. Paul Taylor, *Respect for Nature: A Theory of Environmental Ethics* (Princeton, NJ: Princeton University Press, 1986), 10–11.
17. Ibid., 11.

and consideration because they have a kind of value that belongs to them inherently.[18]

Thus, centric terms differentiate between direct and indirect moral concern for the nonhuman cosmos—between viewing nonhumans primarily as creatures of value in their own right and nonhumans viewing them primarily or exclusively as resources, the telos of which is realized in the facilitation of human well-being.

In this project, I have Taylor's value-based understanding of these terms in mind. I specifically use cosmocentrism as opposed to biocentrism in order to maximize moral inclusiveness—that is, not only life (*bio*) but non-living matter and the cosmos itself. However, by the term cosmocentrism I do not intend that *only* the cosmos as a whole has value or even that it has primary value. I thus seek to avoid the critique labeled against "nonanthropocentric ethics" noted by Sam Mickey:

> While anthropocentric ethics foster exploitative and manipulative attitudes toward the environment, nonanthropocentric ethics like eco- and bio-centrism threaten to become misanthropic and socially irresponsible as they marginalize problems faced by disenfranchised economic classes and ethnicities.[19]

By cosmocentrism I mean that both the cosmos as a whole and *all* of its individual components (including ecosystems, species, and individual creatures, both human and nonhuman) have *intrinsic* value. It thus entails the moral recognition of the nonhuman creation for its own sake. Contrarily, by anthropocentrism I intimate that humans bear intrinsic value and the value of the nonhuman creation is derivative of both the historical and ultimate import of humanity.

18. Ibid., 12–13.
19. Sam Mickey, "Contributions to Anthropocosmic Environmental Ethics." *Worldviews* 11 (2007), 227.

Why Not Theocentrism?

Referring positively to Joseph Sittler's ethics, Stephen Bouma-Prediger maintains,

> only such a theocentrism in which God is affirmed as the source of being and existence of ultimate meaning and value is able both to preserve human uniqueness and affirm the interdependence of creation and thereby avoid both an anthropocentrism that fails to acknowledge the commonality of humans with other creatures and a cosmocentrism that refuses to admit human distinctiveness.[20]

Bouma-Prediger is not alone in this sentiment. The notion that theocentrism is categorically superior to both anthropocentrism and cosmo/bio/ecocentrism is common. Defenders of Aquinas's contribution to nonhuman ethics argue his theocentrism trumps charges that he is anthropocentric.[21] The Orthodox theologian Radu Bordeianu critiques Thomas Berry for being cosmocentric as opposed to theocentric.[22] Other theologians, such as Moltmann and Linzey, define themselves as theocentric rather than cosmocentric or biocentric.[23]

Yet, it is unclear why theocentrism should be categorized with anthropocentrism or cosmocentrism. If theocentrism entails that this world belongs to God and not humans and that God is its source of value and meaning—which seems most often to be the case—then the term does little to stymie the *practical anthropocentrism* of many theologians in history. In fact, theocentrism sanctions such praxis. If

---

20. Stephen Bouma–Prediger, *The Greening of Theology: The ecological Models of Rosemary Radford Ruether, Joseph Sittler, and Jürgen Moltmann* (Atlanta: Scholars, 1995), 278.

21. Mark Wynn, "Thomas Aquinas: Reading the Idea of Dominion in the Light of the Doctrine of Creation" in *Ecological Hermeneutics: Biblical, Historical and Theological Perspectives*, ed. David G. Horrell, Cherryl Hunt, Christopher Southgate and Francesca Stavrakopoulou, (New York: T & T Clark, 2010), 156–162.

22. See Radu Bordeianu, "Maximus and Ecology: The Relevance of Maximus the Confessor's Theology of Creation for the Present Ecological Crisis," *Downside Review* 127/447 (2009): 115.

23. See Chapters 7–12 of the present work.

God is indeed the source of value and meaning for creation, and God orders the creation such that the nonhuman exists for the human, then theocentrism has in fact grounded anthropocentrism within the cosmos. As David Clough writes, such a vision "provides a divine mandate for humans to satisfy their needs and desires through the use of all other creatures in the confidence that this was the relationship God intended."[24]

Thus, with regard to the issue of intrinsic value, theocentrism is not one option among other centric terms. Theocentrism deals with *the foundation*—or lack thereof—for the value and meaning of creatures. It is thus the framework within which centric terms receive justification. Michael Hauskeller makes just this point:

> Both anthropocentrism and biocentrism (in a strong sense) require some sort of theocentric background. One cannot really believe that humans are at the centre of the universe (that is, that we matter or our existence has intrinsic value while nothing else does) if one does not believe (however vaguely) that we have been put there by some higher, cosmic authority. Similarly, one cannot really believe that all living beings matter and deserve moral consideration if one does not believe (again, however vaguely) that there is something in the universe that gives weight to those beings and to what is being done to them. Thus theocentrism is actually not a third position in addition to anthropocentrism and biocentrism but a background presupposition of intelligibility for both of them.[25]

Thomas Aquinas's anthropocentric hierarchy of creation is couched within a theocentrism as is Thomas Berry's biocentrism. The question, then, is not: Should theology be theocentric, cosmocentric, or anthropocentric? The question is: does theocentrism ground an anthropocentric or cosmocentric worldview?

---

24. Clough, *On Animals*, 4.
25. Michael Hauskeller, *Biotechnology and the Integrity of Life: Taking Public Fears Seriously* (Burlington, VT: Ashgate, 2007), 88–89.

This point is not lost on James Gustafson. He develops his theocentric ethics in an effort to overthrow the grip of anthropocentrism on Western thought—a grip in which "culturally, religiously, theologically, and ethically, man, the human species, has become the measure of all things; all things have been put in the service of man."[26] Gustafson aims to develop alternative strands that seek the welfare of the whole creation, not simply humanity. He draws on religious roots to achieve this end, stating, "God, rather than man, ought to be the measure of all things."[27] Such is the meaning of "theocentrism" for Gustafson. Note, however, the theocentrism is not mutually exclusive with value-centric terms. As Gustafson acknowledges, theocentrism can *ground an anthropocentric worldview* if "the good of human beings coincides with the ultimate divine purpose"; that is, if "what God wills is what is good for man."[28] I thus think Sideris is in error when she suggests a direct equivalence between theocentric ethics and Gustafson's delineation of this ethics (and then suggests that a theocentric ethics overlaps, apparently merely by being theocentric, with ecocentric ethics).[29] Theocentrism is not a value-centric term; rather, it grounds such terms. For Gustafson, it grounds a non-anthropocentric ethics; for others, it does the opposite.

At any rate, with the term "cosmocentrism" I intimate that all created things, living and not, have value in themselves *because* God intends them to have such value. My view is similar to that of Clough, who suggests that best path moving forward is jettisoning any teleological anthropocentrism (i.e., the proper end of all things

26. James Gustafson, *Ethics from a Theocentric Perspective* (Chicago: University of Chicago Press, 1981), 1:82.
27. Ibid.
28. Ibid., 1:91.
29. See Sideris, *Environmental Ethics*, chapter 6.

is the well-being of humans) and combing theocentrism with the notion that "God's purpose in creating is to do good to creatures."[30]

Conservation versus Transfiguration

The juxtaposition of conservation and transfiguration may appear odd at first. Conservation is a very common term in both secular and theological ethics. Transfiguration is not. Whereas my use of anthropocentrism and cosmocentrism pertains fundamentally to the question of value—and more specifically intrinsic value—my use of conservation and transfiguration pertains to the question of the telos of the nonhuman creation and the significance of this telos for human morality.

By conservation, I mean the notion that the proper human interaction with the nonhuman creation is both sustaining and preserving what exists, including the elements of evolutionary emergence. I am in this sense conflating *conservation* and *preservation*, the sustainable use *and* letting-be of the cosmos. In this view, the natural cycles of the cosmos, including those like predation, are typically envisioned as good—theologically speaking, unfallen with regard at least to the nonhuman cosmos—and therefore not in need of redemption. Humans bear the role of living within these cycles in such a manner as to permit the continued facilitation of nature's integrity. Here nature denotes something akin to Taylor's definition of the "the natural world": "the entire set of natural ecosystems on our planet, along with the populations of animals and plants that make up the biotic communities of those ecosystems."[31] Humans must limit their actions so that their presence does not disrupt the natural cycles

30. Clough, *On Animals*, 22.
31. Taylor, *Respect for Nature*, 3.

of the cosmos. Perpetuation of nature, not eschatological redemption, is the mantra of conservation.

In his delineation of Orthodox environmental theology, Andrew Louth draws out the meaning of transfiguration for the cosmos. "To speak of the transfiguration as the goal and purpose of creation is to suggest a genuine transformation, but not a transformation *into something else*, rather it is a transformation that reveals the true reality of what is transfigured."[32] In Christ's transfiguration, he "is revealed as he really is."[33] So also, "to see the cosmos as transfigured is to see it as it really is."[34] In line with this view, by transfiguration I intimate the notion that proper human interaction with the nonhuman creation is defined not by what is, but rather but what will be, eschatologically. In this view, parts of nature's cycle, including evolutionary dimensions such as predation, suffering, and death, are often viewed as fallen (or evidence of creation's incompleteness) and in need of redemption. Humans bear the role of being counter-natural with regard to such dimensions, if only by means of witness against the evolutionary process from within it. Humans ought not to live according to the "rule of nature," but rather in a manner that witnesses to creation's eschatological destiny. Proleptic protest, not mere preservation, is the mantra of transfiguration.

Four Paradigms of Eco-Theological Ethics

The terms conservation and transfiguration address *how* humans ought to engage the nonhuman creation. The terms

32. Andrew Louth, "Between Creation and Transfiguration: The Environment in the Eastern Orthodox Tradition," *Ecological Hermeneutics: Biblical, Historical and Theological Perspectives*, ed. David G. Horrell, Cherryl Hunt, Christopher Southgate, and Francesca Stavrakopoulou (New York: T & T Clark, 2010), 216.
33. Ibid.
34. Ibid., 217.

anthropocentrism and cosmocentrism address *why* humans ought to do so. The tensions between these two sets of terms provide a framework to establish four paradigms of eco-theological ethics. This framework is evident in illustration 3.1, a Cartesian coordinate diagram in which the X-axis represents the tension between conservation and transfiguration and the Y-axis represents the tension between anthropocentrism and cosmocentrism.

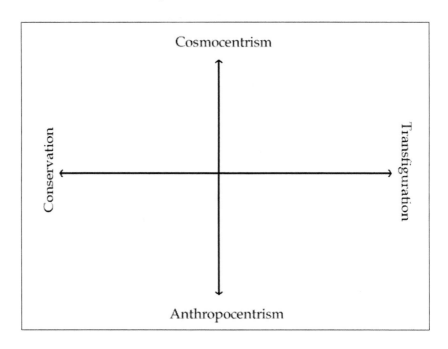

Illustration 3.1:
Tensions in Nonhuman Theological Ethics

With this coordinate plane, a position can be charted according to where it falls with regard to these to tensions. If, for instance, a thinker advocates a conservationist viewpoint as opposed to one of transfiguration (and thus falls in the [-X] dimension) while at the same time advocating a cosmocentric worldview as opposed to an anthropocentric one (and thus falls in the [Y] dimension), that thinker would then occupy the quarter of the coordinate plane that represents one of the paradigms, *cosmocentric conservation*. There are thus four possibilities, evident in illustration 3.2:

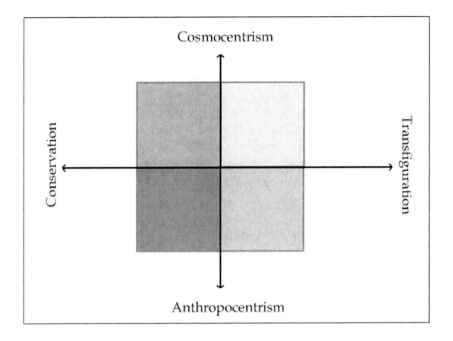

Illustration 3.2:
The Four Paradigms

For the sake of clarity, I label each paradigm according to its location on the plane. Thus, the (-X, -Y) coordinates are anthropocentric conservationism, a view which I establish through an engagement with the work of Saint Thomas Aquinas. The (-X, Y) coordinates are cosmocentric conservationism. To present this view, I examine the work of the Passionist priest, Thomas Berry. The (X, -Y) coordinates are anthropocentric transfiguration, a view which is best represented in the work of Orthodox theologians like Dumitru

Staniloae and John Meyendorff. Lastly, the (X, Y) coordinates are cosmocentric transfiguration. I construct this ethics through dialogue with Moltmann and Linzey.

The Primary Unit of Moral Consideration

Daniel Cowdin writes that the question of whether or not the nonhuman world bears moral worth

> has been explored along a spectrum ranging from individual organisms as exclusively considerable, on the one side, to species, ecosystems, and natural processes as exclusively considerable, on the other. Animal welfare as well as broader reverence for life approaches fall on the individualistic side of the spectrum, while a land ethic approach falls on the systematic side.[35]

Sideris notes the centrality of this issue: "Perhaps the most important question is whether individuals—as opposed to a collective entity such as species, populations, or biotic communities—are or ought to be the unit of moral consideration in environmental ethics."[36] In making ethical decisions, should moral priority rest with a particular individual life or the larger system that makes possible the existence of all individual lives? More basically still, what is the primary (note, not *exclusive*) unit of moral consideration? Individuals? Species? Ecosystems? The cosmos as a whole? Should the primary question of moral justification be whether or not an action violates the life of a single living organism? Or, should the primary question be whether or not an action interferes with either natural processes or endangered ecosystems?

35. Daniel Cowdin, "The Moral Status of Otherkind in Christian Ethics," in *Christianity and Ecology: Seeking the Well-Being of Earth and Humans*, ed. Dieter T. Hessel and Rosemary Radford Ruether (Cambridge, MA: Harvard University Press, 2000), 268.
36. Sideris, *Environmental Ethics*, 21.

These questions lead to one of the fundamental distinctions between many environmental ethicists and animals rights activists. Marc Fellenz notes this distinction:

> Whereas ecocentric criterion requires deep ecologists to place a prima facie higher value on the lives and interests of members of endangered species, animal advocates, while not insensitive to the issues of species extinction, generally have been hesitant to follow suit for fear of violating principles of moral quality.[37]

Northcott concurs, noting that the tension concerning the primary unit of moral concern establishes a divide between rights advocates, who tend to "privilege competition over co-operation, individuals over collectivities and moral claims over moral relationships and responsibilities," and other forms of ecological ethics.[38] Thus, whereas Aldo Leopold emphasizes the group or the system, animal rights activists like Tom Regan emphasize the individual "subject of a life" as the basic unit of moral concern.[39]

There is thus a divide between animal advocates and deep ecologists—and most eco-theologians in general.[40] Cowdin favors the systematic side over the individual side.[41] He is critical of animal rights thinkers like Linzey who emphasize the moral standing of individual creatures. For Cowdin, "exclusive moral concern for individual animals becomes incoherent at the level of land management."[42] Clough, on the other hand, argues that the individual animal must have a moral claim. "The place of animals needs securing against the rush to the totality of living things or

---

37. Fellenz, *The Moral Menagerie*, 163.
38. Northcott, *The Environment and Christian Ethics*, 102.
39. See Tom Regan, *The Case for Animals Rights*, second edition (Berkley, CA: University of California Press, 2004), 243–50.
40. See Clough, *On Animals*, xx–xxi.
41. Cowdin, "The Moral Status of Otherkind in Christian Ethics," 268.
42. Ibid., 271.

creatures . . . recognizing the particularly of what it means to be animal means resisting shifting directly from an anthropocentric perspective to one that values creatures only insofar as they are part of ecosystems."[43]

The import of this distinction for the formulation of ethical principles can hardly be overstated.[44] For instance, Deane-Drummond writes that Aldo Leopold's ethic "began to challenge the focus on the individuals' needs. . . . His focus on the ecological whole showed an underlying philosophical holism, so that hunting and other activities were still permitted as long as the ecology was not disturbed."[45] While Leopold's land ethic emphasizes the import of considering a violation of "the integrity, stability and beauty of the biotic community" as morally illicit,[46] there is no inherent wrong in taking the life of an individual in that community. Thus, Wennberg notes that the "environmentalist is fundamentally concerned with the preservation of animal *species* and with the *role* of animals in delicately functioning ecosystems, whereas the fundamental concern of the animal advocate is with the *individual* animal and its welfare."[47]

Sideris likewise recognizes this division. She also critiques environmental theologians for not recognizing its severity with regard to practical application:

> Ecotheologians tend to speak in broad terms of liberating and healing "life" in general or "nature" as a whole, whereas Singer and Regan typically focus on animals only, and often their concern is directed toward the plight of animals in very particular circumstances. Ecotheologians express much greater interest in, and concern for, the well-being of a large, ecological "community" of organisms or as a "web

43. Clough, *On Animals*, 44.
44. See Wennberg, *God, Humans, and Animals*, 32–57.
45. Deane-Drummond, *Eco–Theology*, 33.
46. Aldo Leopold, *A Sand County Almanac—and Sketches Here and There* (New York: Oxford University Press, 1987), 224.
47. Wennberg, *God, Humans, and Animals*, 32–33.

of life" (although they fail to understand why this focus is inconsistent with an ethic of liberation or care for each individual "subject" within that community).[48]

She further criticizes that ignoring this division leads eco-theologians to the inconsistent position of emphasizing holistic ethics while they "continue to concern themselves with issues of animal suffering, sentience, and liberation."[49] Sideris later writes, "Many ecotheologians view ecosystems as subordinate to the needs of the individual members (human and nonhuman) of the community."[50] It seems to me that the crux of her critique is that environmental theologians often write as if there were no conflict between the interests of individuals and the interest of the whole. That said, most eco-theologians still write in a manner that emphasizes the whole, even if this emphasis is ultimately inconsistent. Furthermore, they tend to promote a conservationist ethics, which favors the whole over the individual. As Sideris herself notes, both Ruether and McFague shy away from vegetarianism, which seems a logical outcome of their radically egalitarian claims.[51]

It ought to be noted that there is not an "either/or" with regard to the question of value. One can value intrinsically individuals, species, ecosystems, the land, and natural processes.[52] The issue is not one of intrinsic value or moral standing, but of the *primary unit of value*—the "locus of rights or value."[53] Here is the central point: one cannot hold both the individual creature and the species/ecosystem/cosmos to be the *primary* unit of moral value and concern, since the good of individuals and the good of the whole are often at odds

48. Sideris, *Environmental Ethics*, 132.
49. Ibid., 135.
50. Ibid., 227.
51. Ibid., 78.
52. Wennberg, *God, Humans, and Animals*, 35–36.
53. Ibid., 35.

with one another.[54] Given the nature of creaturely existence, the eco-theological "interpretation of interdependence fails to recognize that the good of the parts and the good of the whole cannot be harmonized."[55]

With this divide in the field, should there not be another dimension added to my coordinate plane? It would contain a Z-axis—evident in illustration 3.3—representing the tension between the general (e.g., species, ecosystems, etc.) and the particular (e.g., individual nonhuman plants and animals).

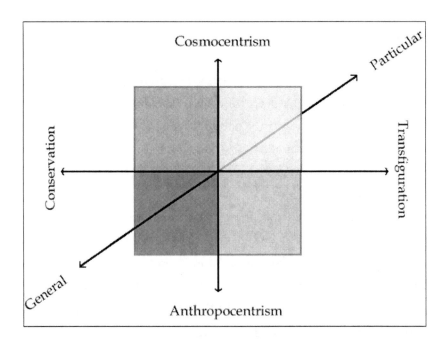

Illustration 3.3:
Primary Moral Concern

54. Ibid., 36; Gustafson, *Ethics from a Theocentric Perspective*, 2:239–43; Sideris, *Environmental Ethics*, 221.
55. Sideris, *Environmental Ethics*, 265.

It seems that this three-dimensional plane should elicit eight, as opposed to four, paradigms of nonhuman theological ethics. The reason I do not find it necessary to present this project within such a framework is that my research has yielded certain tendencies among the already existing paradigms with regard to the issue of the primary unit of value and moral standing. I emphasize here the nonhuman creation because, with regard to humans, anthropocentric paradigms tend to emphasize the individual. It is only with regard to nonhumans that the general overshadows the particular in ethical matters. Wennberg touches on this point when he juxtaposes deep ecology, sentientism, and traditional (anthropocentric) moral frameworks. For the latter, "ethical individualism applies to humans and ethical holism applies to animals." For sentientism, "ethical individualism applies to both humans and animals." For deep ecology, "ethical holism applies to both humans and animals."[56]

Regarding the nonhuman creation, anthropocentric worldviews tend to emphasize the general. When the central concern is the well-being of human individuals, it is not all that important whether an individual cow lives or dies. However, the cow as a species ought to be protected because it provides sustenance for the present human community (and will continue to do so for future generations). Likewise, a beautiful creature that is endangered will be protected so that future generations can appreciate the beauty of that species.

In a similar manner, conservationist worldviews emphasize the general. The mechanisms of evolutionary emergence, after all, do not evince much concern for individual creatures, which die all the time—and often in horrific deaths. Even so, the system as a whole trudges forward in all its complexity and diversity. Hence, the conservationist tends to accept the loss of the nonhuman individual

56. Wennberg, *God, Humans, and Animals*, 44–45.

for the sake of species, the ecosystem, or the cosmos as a whole. This position reflects the evolutionary process itself, as Daniel Deffenbaugh notes, "From an evolutionary perspective, the isolated organism is merely a token, a representative, which plays a small part in the propagation of a living historical form: the species. This is the real unity of evolution and therefore the more significant reality which demands human respect."[57]

Theologically speaking, only the combination of cosmocentrism and transfiguration tends to emphasize the particular, positing individual creatures as the basic unit of moral concern.[58] This point will become further evident in later chapters. For now, it suffices to note that the introduction of the tension between the general and particular (the Z-axis) does not necessarily change the four paradigms, as each paradigm tends strongly toward one direction of that axis (as displayed in illustration 1.4). For this reason, I will maintain the four paradigms while noting each paradigm's tendency concerning the primary unit of moral concern.

---

57. Daniel G. Deffenbaugh, "Toward Thinking Like a Mountain: The Evolution of an Ecological Conscience," *Soundings* 78/2 (Summer 1995), 255.
58. For example, see Clough, *On Animals*, 44.

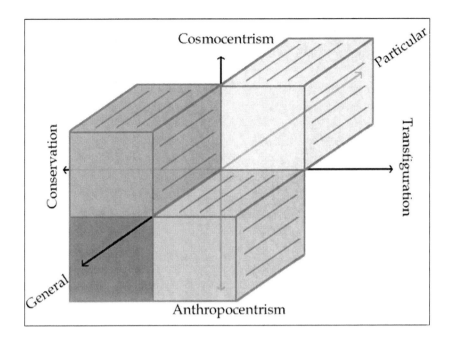

Illustration 3.4:
Paradigmatic Tendencies for Primary Moral Concern

Conclusion

The theological loci of cosmology, anthropology, and eschatology reveal central tensions between poles of value and poles of teleology. Regarding value, the issue is whether only humans alone bear intrinsic worth or if such worth is extended to other parts of the created order, including individual nonhuman animals and holistic systems of life. Regarding teleology, the issue is whether the nonhuman world is fine as it is or whether it requires some eschatological redemption, which entails, in some sense, the inclusion of nonhumans in eternity. Another tension exists between an emphasis on individual creatures and an emphasis on holistic systems of life. This tension resolves itself, at least in general tendencies, depending on how one resolves the other tensions.

4

Anthropocentric Conservation

Generally speaking, anthropocentric conservation is informed by three core principles.[1] First, the nonhuman creation exists, in history, for the sake of humanity. Second, the nonhuman creation exists, in history, for the entire human community, both present and future. Third, the eschatological telos of sharing in God's own life is reserved for rational (i.e., human and angelic) creatures and the elements/ matter necessary to facilitate this telos.

The role of the human creature is to use properly the gift of the cosmos. Proper use entails taking account of both the telos of that cosmos (in history, as an ordered source of sustenance and divine revelation for the entire human community) and the human creature (historically, a life of virtue in community before God, and ultimately, a sharing in God's own eternal life). Thus the role of the nonhuman creation is that of a good and ordered network of

---

1. Versions of this chapter have appeared elsewhere: Ryan Patrick McLaughlin, "Thomas Aquinas's Eco-Theological Ethics of Anthropocentric Conservation." *Horizons* 39, 1 (2012): 69–97; *Christianity and the Status of Animals* (New York: Palgrave Macmillan, 2014), chapter 1.

resources or gifts that exist for the well-being of all humans on their journey toward their essentially unique and ultimate telos.

The various foundations of this view have numerous representatives in the Christian tradition.[2] However, it is perhaps Thomas Aquinas who gives this theological ethics its clearest expressions. Thus, in this chapter I will delineate the paradigm through an exploration of Aquinas's work.

Aquinas's monumental genius commands respect. His appropriation of Aristotelian philosophy; his deep engagement with major Christian thinkers like Augustine, Dionysius, and Peter Lombard; his mastery of Christian scripture; and his interactions with medieval Jewish (e.g., Maimonides) and Muslim (e.g., Avicenna) philosophers provides a coherent framework of faith and practice from his historical context.[3]

Given Thomas's lasting and significant impact on Christian thought, his work has elicited a large corpus of secondary literature, even with regard to focused issues like nonhuman ethics. Hence, establishing Aquinas as a concrete example of anthropocentric conservation requires first situating his theological framework within this corpus. This move will allow us to dialogue with the secondary literature as we engage Aquinas's writings.

---

2. See, for instance, Gary Steiner, *Anthropocentrism and Its Discontents: The Moral Status of Animals in the History of Western Philosophy* (Pittsburgh, PA: University of Pittsburgh Press, 2005), 116–123; Morwenna Ludlow, "Power and Dominion: Patristic Interpretations of Genesis 1," in *Ecological Hermeneutics: Biblical, Historical and Theological Perspectives*, eds. David G. Horrell, Cherryl Hunt, Christopher Southgate and Francesca Stavrakopoulou (New York: T & T Clark, 2010), 140–153.

3. See Servais-Théodore Pinckaers, "The Source of Ethics of St. Thomas Aquinas," in *The Ethics of Aquinas*, ed. Stephen J. Pope (Washington, DC: Georgetown University Press, 2002), 17–28.

The Controversy over Aquinas's Environmental Contributions

When it comes to Aquinas's potential contribution for widening concern for ecological issues, scholars provide a diverse interpretative spectrum. Many of these interpretations follow Lynn White's 1967 essay in which he posits the accusation, "Christianity is the most anthropocentric religion the world has seen."[4] In the wake of White's contribution, "anthropocentrism" has become an inherently pejorative term. This climate framed one of the central debates concerning Aquinas: Is his theological framework anthropocentric?

Many within the animal rights movement accuse Aquinas of contributing to an anthropocentric and abusive attitude toward nonhuman animals. Peter Singer, in his seminal *Animal Liberation*, claims that Aquinas excludes nonhuman animals from the realm of morality with the one exception in which harming them may result in harm to humanity. Says Singer: "No argument could reveal the essence of speciesism more clearly."[5] In *The Encyclopedia of Animal Rights and Animal Welfare*, Joyce Salisbury argues that, for Aquinas, "here on earth there [is] no need to preserve animals that [are] seen as 'useless.'"[6] In Richard Ryder's estimation, Aquinas's thought has provided the justification for "several centuries of outstanding cruelty" toward animals.[7] In his book arguing for a widened scope of moral concern from within Christianity, Robert Wennberg claims that Aquinas adheres to a moral theory "that has no place for animals."[8]

4. Lynn White, "The Historical Roots of Our Ecological Crisis," reprinted in *This Sacred Earth: Religion, Nature, Environment*, ed. Roger S. Gottlieb(New York: Routledge), 189.
5. Peter Singer, *Animal Liberation: A New Ethics for Our Treatment of Animals* (New York: Avon Books, 1975), 203–204.
6. Joyce E. Salisbury, "Attitudes toward Animals: Changing Attitudes throughout History," in *Encyclopedia of Animal Rights and Animal Welfare*, ed. Marc Bekoff and Carron A. Meaney(Westport, CT: Greenwood, 1998), 78.
7. Richard D. Ryder, *Animal Revolution: Changing Attitudes towards Speciesism* (Cambridge, MA: Basil Blackwell, 1989), 43.

Andrew Linzey, perhaps the leading voice in the field of animal theology, is also rather critical of Aquinas. In his earlier *Christianity and the Rights of Animals*, Linzey cites Aquinas in conjunction with the "deeply anthropocentric" nature of contemporary Christianity.[9] In *Animal Theology*, he summarizes Aquinas as follows: "Considered *in themselves* animals have no reason and no rights, and humans no responsibility to them."[10] In Linzey's view, Aquinas's speciesist viewpoint "has left a bitter legacy in Christian theology."[11]

Other theologians have also critiqued Aquinas. Paul Santmire balances negative and positive views of Christianity's potential contribution to ecological sensitivity by exploring both harmful and promising voices in Christian history.[12] He labels Aquinas's theological framework as an "intramundane anthropocentrism" in which "nature is seen more as an object for human use, which satisfies biological needs and serves spiritual knowledge, than as a subject in its own right."[13]

Voices from other perspectives also depict Aquinas negatively with regard to animals and the environment. David Kinsley, in his cross-cultural exploration regarding the convergence of the intersection of nature and spirituality, places Aquinas in the chapter entitled "Christianity as Ecologically Harmful."[14] Kinsley critiques Aquinas's hierarchical view of the world, in which the natures of nonhuman animals "are defined in terms of their subservience to human beings."[15] (Given this critique, it is not overly clear how Kinsley

8. Robert N. Wennberg, *God, Humans, and Animals: An Invitation to Enlarge Our Moral Universe* (Grand Rapids, MI: William B. Eerdmans Publishing Company, 2003), 121.
9. Andrew Linzey, *Christianity and the Rights of Animals* (New York: Crossroad, 1987), 22.
10. Andrew Linzey, *Animal Theology* (Chicago: University of Illinois Press, 1995), 15.
11. Ibid., 19, also 64–65.
12. Paul Santmire, *The Travail of Nature: The Ambiguous Ecological Promise of Christian Theology* (Minneapolis, MN: Fortress Press, 1985).
13. Ibid., 91–92.
14. See David Kinsley, *Ecology and Religion: Ecological Spirituality in Cross-Cultural Perspective* (Upper Saddle River, NJ: Prentice Hall, 1995), 103–107.

so effortlessly classifies Augustine as a positive ecological voice in Christianity).[16] J. Claude Evans claims that Aquinas represents the "classic statements of anthropocentrism."[17] Similarly, Gary Steiner, in his work tracing the dominance of anthropocentrism in Western philosophy, categorizes Aquinas as "the apex of medieval anthropocentrism."[18] His legacy is an essential distinction between humans and nonhuman animals that establishes an ethics of dominion in which humans have no direct duties to animals.[19]

These critiques of Aquinas tend towards the claim that he contributes to a milieu of ecological degradation by advocating an anthropocentrism that renders the nonhuman world a resource for human benefit. In response to such accusations, defenders of Aquinas have sought to highlight his cosmological theocentrism. This response challenges simplistic charges of anthropocentrism in Aquinas's theological framework.

In the introduction to *Creaturely Theology*, Celia Deane-Drummond and David Clough critique Linzey's edited volume *Animals on the Agenda* because, in their view, its historical investigations are structured only "to set up certain theologians as instigators and culprits of a negative attitude toward animals."[20] This critique is no doubt aimed in part at Dorothy Yamamoto's essay on Aquinas.[21] As a remedy to such allegedly biased interpretations of Thomas, Deane-Drummond and Clough point to John Berkman's

---

15. Ibid., 109–110.
16. Ibid., 118–120.
17. J. Claude Evans, *With Respect for Nature: Living as Part of the Natural World* (Albany, NY: State University of New York Press, 2005), viii.
18. Steiner, *Anthropocentrism and Its Discontents*, 126.
19. Ibid., 130–131.
20. See Celia Deane-Drummond and David Clough, "Introduction," in *Creaturely Theology: On God, Humans and Other Animals*, eds. Celia Deane-Drummond and David Clough (London: SCM Press, 2009), 6–7; Dorothy Yamamoto, "Aquinas and Animals: Patrolling the Boundary?" in *Animals on the Agenda: Questions about Animal Ethics for Theology and Ethics*, ed. Andrew Linzey and Dorothy Yamamoto(Chicago: University of Illinois Press, 1998), 80–89.
21. See Yamamoto, "Aquinas and Animals," 80–89.

essay in their text as a "critical, but far more sensitive, reading of Aquinas."[22] Berkman acknowledges Aquinas's justification of human utility of the nonhuman creation in the temporal order. However, he quickly qualifies this acknowledgement with an affirmation of Aquinas's theocentrism. Berkman ultimately argues that, for Aquinas, "God's plan in creation . . . is by no means anthropocentric."[23]

In Anne Clifford's view, "a major part of Aquinas's legacy to the Roman Catholic tradition is his sacramental view of material creation."[24] In light of this view, Clifford argues that critiques of Aquinas's anthropocentrism are viable only when passages from his writings are "read in total isolation from other passages in which he affirms the inherent goodness of all creatures as unique manifestations of the Trinity and if his theology is interpreted ahistorically."[25]

Deane-Drummond claims that Aquinas's affirmation that "creation is an expression of God's wisdom" suggests that God's wisdom is still at work in the ongoing processes of the created order.[26] She acknowledges that his understanding of the cosmos requires adjustment in light of evolutionary biology.[27] Even so, Deane-Drummond defends Aquinas against "simplistic" views that criticize his damaging influence on eco-theological thought by acknowledging the interplay between grace and nature in his theology.[28]

---

22. Deane-Drummond and Clough, "Introduction," 7.
23. John Berkman, "Towards a Thomistic Theology of Animality," in *Creaturely Theology: On God, Humans and Other Animals*, ed. Celia Deane-Drummond and David Clough(London: SCM Press, 2009), 24.
24. Anne Clifford, "Foundations for a Catholic Ecological Theology of God," in *"And God Saw That It Was Good": Catholic Theology and the Environment*, ed. Drew Christiansen and Walter Grazer(Washington, DC: United States Catholic Conference, 1996), 38.
25. Clifford, "Foundations," 40. Clifford's critique is specifically aimed at Santmire. Seeibid., 46, n. 44.
26. Celia Deane-Drummond, *Eco-Theology* (Winona, MN: Anselm Academic, 2008), 159.
27. Ibid.
28. See ibid., 103–104, 213–214, n. 23.

Jame Schaefer acknowledges and concedes accusations of anthropocentrism in Aquinas's theology.[29] However, she also criticizes such accusations, claiming that they "have not been explored sufficiently from several perspectives," the dominant of which is contextual differences between modern readers and ancient writers. Schaefer continues: "Nor do these criticisms take into consideration the constraints that patristic and medieval theologians imposed on human use of Earth's constituents and their teachings about the faithful's responsibility to their neighbors and to God for how they regard and use other creatures."[30]

William French is also a qualified defender of Aquinas.[31] He concedes that Aquinas's instrumental view of animals in conjunction with his refusal to extend to them direct moral concern "helped establish a tradition of misnaming which has plagued Catholic moral theology until only very recently."[32] Even so, French laments simplistic critiques of Aquinas that miss his cosmological theocentrism. He sees in Aquinas's theological framework an interconnected cosmos in which each part contributes to the good of the whole, which has God as its final telos.[33]

In a collection of essays deriving from a research project at the University of Exeter, Mark Wynn begins by examining both critical (e.g. Linzey) and sympathetic (e.g. Deane-Drummond) readings of Aquinas.[34] Wynn contextualizes Aquinas's anthropocentrism within

---

29. Jame Schaefer, *Theological Foundations for Environmental Ethics: Reconstructing Patristic & Medieval Concepts* (Washington, DC: Georgetown University Press, 2009), 8–9.
30. Ibid., 9.
31. See William French, "Catholicism and the Common Good," in *An Ecology of the Spirit*, ed. Michael Barnes, (Lanham, MD: University Press of America Press, 1993), 182–83, 191; French, "Beast Machines and the Technocratic Reduction of Life," in *Good News for Animals? Christian Approaches to Animal Well-Being*, ed. Charles Pinches and Jay B. McDaniel (New York: Orbis Books, 1993), 24–43.
32. French, "Beast-Machines," 37.
33. Ibid., 37–38.
34. Mark Wynn, "Thomas Aquinas: Reading the Idea of Dominion in the Light of the Doctrine of Creation" in *Ecological Hermeneutics: Biblical, Historical and Theological Perspectives*, ed. David G.

his cosmological theocentrism.[35] Creatures, in their variety of being, reflect God's subsistent existence (i.e., that God *is* being itself). This reflection constitutes the good of the cosmos as a holistic system, of which all things are integrally a part and nothing is without meaning. Hence, the individual parts of the created order have a good telos that, in Wynn's estimation, "cannot simply consist in their service to human beings."[36] Rather, Wynn claims, "The fulfilment of the nature of 'lesser' creatures, and even of non-animate creatures, can count as a good, even when this results in a human being suffering some deprivation of good."[37]

Willis Jenkins also laments overly simplistic critiques of Aquinas. From the perspective of soteriology—as opposed to cosmology—Jenkins offers Aquinas as an influential foundation for ecojustice, a view which he claims is dominant in the Roman Catholic tradition and draws on the notion of sanctifying grace.[38] Ultimately, Jenkins seeks to

> demonstrate that [Aquinas] escapes facile categorization by cosmological centrisms. Instead he harmonizes (or resists the use of) anthropocentrism, theocentrism, and ecocentrism, precisely because he sees that God chooses to move creation to Godself by inviting humans into a friendship shaped by their intimacy with all creation.[39]

In Jenkins's view, "those who think that Thomas's anthropocentrism offers only problems for environmental theology miss the way he sets humans within a cosmos of creatures bearing their own integrity."[40]

Horrell, Cherryl Hunt, Christopher Southgate and Francesca Stavrakopoulou (New York: T & T Clark, 2010), 154–167.

35. Ibid., 156–162.
36. Ibid., 157.
37. Ibid., 162.
38. Willis Jenkins, *Ecologies of Grace: Environmental Ethics and Christian Theology* (New York: Oxford University Press, 2008), 16–17.
39. Ibid., 150.
40. Ibid., 118.

Within this integrity, all creatures bear a "common dignity" inasmuch as they seek the good together as a whole.[41] For humans, unique in the created order, desire for God includes knowing the world and using it properly, primarily in the contemplative sense.[42] Thus humanity acquires, through grace, an "ecological literacy."[43] Such literacy requires a genuine engagement with the created order—which Jenkins defines as charity. Thus, for Jenkins, charity qualifies Aquinas's anthropocentrism with a theocentrism in that virtuous humans will view creation as an invitation to divine friendship.[44]

In my view, almost all of the interpretations of Aquinas's nonhuman theological ethics bear some dimension of truth. At the same time, most of them also contain a certain lack of clarity.[45] Aquinas's critics tend to miss his sacramental understanding of the nonhuman world and the impact this understanding has for human behavior. Aquinas's defenders often too easily sidestep his anthropocentric tendencies and sanctify his work with an appeal to either context or theocentrism.

In what follows, I engage Thomas's writings, particularly his *summas*, to provide an example for the theological foundations for anthropocentric conservation. When necessary, I defend where my interpretation clashes with voices in the secondary literature. Ultimately, I aim to be more critical than defenders like Wynn and Jenkins, but (hopefully) more nuanced and cautious than critics like Singer and Linzey.

41. Ibid., 123.
42. Ibid., 125–127.
43. Ibid., 127.
44. Ibid., 142.
45. For a stark exception, see Francisco J. Benzoni, *Ecological Ethics and the Human Soul: Aquinas, Whitehead, and the Metaphysics of Value* (Notre Dame, IN: University of Notre Dame Press, 2007), parts I and II.

Theological Foundations for Aquinas's Anthropocentrism

For Aquinas, the multiplicity of formal distinctions in the created order is an aspect of the goodness of the cosmos.[46] However, "formal distinction always requires inequality" (*ST*, 1.47.2). Thus Aquinas affirms a hierarchical order within the cosmos. Within this hierarchy, Aquinas posits three classifications of soul: vegetative, sensitive, and rational.[47] Connected to these souls are the attributes of nutrition, sentience, and reason, respectively.[48] The human soul possesses the qualities of both the vegetative and sensitive souls; but it augments and excels them on account of rationality.[49] The human contains all dimensions of the soul because she is both corporeal and incorporeal, a microcosmic being that "is in a manner composed of all things" (*ST*, 1.91.1; also 1.96.2). Furthermore, for Aquinas, "what belongs to the inferior nature pre-exists more perfectly in the superior" (1.76.5). Thus, it is by rationality that humans exceed other creatures in perfection. It is this unique rational dimension of the human creature that constitutes the *imago Dei*. Whereas all creatures—and even humans in their bodiliness—bear a likeness to God in that they reveal a trace of God's design,[50] for nonhuman animals this trace is the limit of their likeness to God. In humans, only the rational component—the mind—bears the likeness of God as image.[51]

---

46. Thomas Aquinas, *Summa Theologica* (hereafter *ST*), trans. Fathers of the English Dominican Province (Benziger Brothers, 1947), 1.5.3 (Subsequentquotes will appear in the text in parentheses).
47. See *ST*, 1.78.1; Judith Barad, *Aquinas on the Nature and Treatment of Animals* (San Francisco: International Scholars Publication, 1995), 29–30.
48. Aquinas ascribes three types of power to the vegetative soul: nutritive, augmentative, and generative. See *ST*, 1.79.2.
49. On the difference of animal capacities in both animals and humans see *ST*, 1.78.4; 1.79.6; 1.81.3.
50. *ST*, 1.45.7.
51. *ST*, 1.93.6.

Aquinas's delineation of the hierarchical order of creation translates into a hierarchy of teloi. Concerning the link, Francisco Benzoni states, "It is only in light of Thomas' teleology that the moral import of his ontology becomes clear."[52] The human has a two-fold telos.[53] The first pertains to historical matters. The second is the ultimate telos of humanity, which Aquinas defines as "happiness" (*ST*, 1|2.1.8).[54] For Aquinas, "God alone constitutes man's happiness" (*ST*, 1|2.2.8). Thus, God is the ultimate telos of the human creature. Moreover, God is the end of every individual human creature in a manner unique to humanity's nature. For the rational creature, happiness is a shared life with God in which the rational soul contemplates the divine.[55] Says Aquinas, "Final and perfect happiness can consist in nothing else than the vision of the Divine Essence" (ST, 1|2.3.8). Aquinas goes on to link happiness to "union with God." In short, for Aquinas, the ultimate telos appropriate for humans is the Beatific Vision.

Regarding the historical telos of humanity, Aquinas posits that an imperfect happiness is possible in history. This happiness "depends, in a way, on the body" (*ST*, 1|2.4.5). Furthermore, "For imperfect happiness, such as can be had in this life, external goods are necessary, not as belonging to the essence of happiness, but by serving as instruments to happiness, which consists in an operation of virtue" (*ST*, 1|2.4.7). Because ultimate happiness is the Beatific Vision, happiness in history is always imperfect for Aquinas.[56] Based on his understanding of imperfect happiness, Aquinas maintains that the historical ends of humans (1) include care for the body (a dependence

---

52. Benzoni, *Ecological Ethics and the Human Soul*, 41.

53. *ST*, 1|2.62.1.

54. *ST*, 1|2.1.8.

55. On the communal dimension of happiness, see Bonnie Kent, "Habits and Virtues (Ia IIae, qq. 49–70)," in *The Ethics of Aquinas*, ed. Stephen J. Pope(Washington, DC: Georgetown University Press, 2002), 126.

56. See Thomas Aquinas, *Summa Contra Gentiles* (hereafter *SCG*), ed. Joseph Kenny (New York: Hanover House, 1955–57), III.48.

that stems from humanity's possession of nutritive and sentient souls)[57] and (2) are directed toward their ultimate end.[58] This understanding evinces the centrality of teleology in Aquinas's understanding of virtue.[59] For a human to live virtuously in history is for her to live toward her proper telos, whether historical or ultimate. Like Aristotle, Aquinas understands the cardinal virtues as directed toward temporal ends.[60] Aquinas differs from Aristotle in claiming that the perfection of the cardinal virtues occurs when, with and by the theological virtues, they are redirected to humanity's ultimate telos.[61] This point will bear significance when we consider whether or not humanity's ultimate telos is shared with nonhuman animals.

What of the telos of the nonhuman world? For Aquinas, all life is teleological.[62] The telos of a creature is its good.[63] And God is the ultimate good for the entire creation.[64] Therefore, the entire creation has God as its end. In this teleological sense, there is a commonality between humans and nonhumans.[65] However, God is not the telos of a flower in the same way that God is the telos of a human being.[66] The foundation of this difference is predicated upon the formal distinctions within nature.[67] Thus, "Reasonable creatures . . . have in some special and higher manner God as their end, since

---

57. See *ST*, 1.79.2.
58. See *ST*, 1|2.1.6.
59. Stephen J. Pope, "Overview of the Ethics of Thomas Aquinas," in *The Ethics of Aquinas*, ed. Stephen J. Pope (Washington, DC: Georgetown University Press, 2002), 32. Also, Alasdair MacIntyre, *After Virtue: A Study in Moral Theory*, third edition (Notre Dame, IN: University of Notre Dame Press, 2007), 53, 185.
60. *SCG*, III.34–35.
61. See Kent, "Habits and Virtues," 118; David Hollenbach, *The Common Good and Christian Ethics* (New York: Cambridge University Press, 2002), 123.
62. *ST*, 1.2; *SCG*, III.2. See also Pope, "Overview of the Ethics of Thomas Aquinas," 32.
63. *ST*, 1.5.1.
64. *SCG*, III.17.
65. See *SCG*, III.18–19; also *ST*, 1.4.3; 1|2.1.8.
66. See *ST*, 1|2.1.8; *SCG*, III.18.
67. See *ST*, 1.91.3; *SCG*, III.22. See also Schaefer, *Theological Foundations*, 22–24.

they can attain to Him by their own operations, by knowing and loving Him."[68]

The nonhuman creation glorifies God by acting according to the multiplicity of the variegated natures that compose it as a whole.[69] Says Aquinas,

> For He brought things into being in order that His goodness might be communicated to creatures, and be represented by them; and because His goodness could not be adequately represented by one creature alone, He produced many and diverse creatures, that what was wanting to one in the representation of the divine goodness might be supplied by another. For goodness, which in God is simple and uniform, in creatures is manifold and divided and hence the whole universe together participates the divine goodness more perfectly, and represents it better than any single creature whatever. (*ST*, 1.47.1)

For Aquinas, then, God is the ultimate good of the entire creation because God provides creatures with variegated natures predisposing them toward the appropriate teloi for which they live. In living thus, the created order, in the multiplicity of its formal distinctions, reveals the goodness of God.[70] Thus all life is derived from and directed toward God. But the manner in which God is the end of nonhumans is predicated upon their natures.

Of the three classes of souls Aquinas delineates (vegetative, sensitive, and rational), he applies greater goodness to the creatures with the capacities entailed by the higher souls.[71] These creatures are more perfect than those below them; and for Aquinas, "the imperfect are for the use of the perfect" (*ST*, 1.96.1). Because of their lower disposition in the hierarchy of the created order, non-rational animals are "naturally under slavery" (*SCG*, III.112). By "slavery" Thomas

---

68. *ST*, 1.65.2; also, 1|2.1.8.
69. *ST*, 1.47.2; 1.65.2.
70. See Benzoni, *Ecological Ethics and the Human Soul*, 42–43.
71. *SCG*, III.20.3.

denotes that nonhuman animals are, by nature, at the disposal of humanity's pursuit of the good. This pursuit must, of course, be informed by the virtues. At any rate, Aquinas follows Aristotle in claiming that humans can hunt nonhuman animals as a "natural right" *qua* humans.[72]

It is here that many defenders of Aquinas's theocentrism too easily rescue him on account of his affirmation that the entire nonhuman creation has God as its end. This claim is only true inasmuch as the nonhuman creation has God as its end *for the sake of humanity*.[73] (Benzoni qualifies this claim by noting a tension in Aquinas's thought between the good of the cosmos as a whole and the good of human beings.)[74] Thus, I take issue with Berkman's claim: "For Aquinas, God's plan in creation, while hierarchical, is by no means anthropocentric."[75] Says Aquinas, "The intellectual nature is the only one that is required in the universe, for its own sake, while all others are for its sake" (*SCG*, III.112.3). Based on passages such as this one—even contextually considered—I also find Schaefer's position that Aquinas's sacramental view of the cosmos imbues it with intrinsic value untenable.[76] Without humanity, the created order would have value *for no one*.[77] In this sense, the value of nonhuman animals in particular is fully predicated on their value *for*, in this case for humanity.[78] The point to be made is that Aquinas's position suggests that the nonhuman creation is *for God, through humanity*. In this sense, Aquinas's cosmological theocentrism actually reinforces his ethical

72. See *ST*, 1.96.1. Aquinas also grounds this view in scripture. See *ST*, 1.91.4.
73. See Santmire, *Travail of Nature*, 91; Kinsley, *Religion and Ecology*, 109.
74. Benzoni, *Ecological Ethics and the Human Soul*, 49–58.
75. Berkman, "Towards a Thomistic Theology of Animality," 24.
76. See Jame Schaefer, "Valuing Earth Intrinsically and Instrumentally: A Theological Framework for Environmental Ethics," *Theological Studies* 66 (2005): 783–814.
77. See *SCG*, III.112.3; *ST*, 2I2.64.1.
78. See Benzoni, *Ecological Ethics and the Human Soul*, 44.

anthropocentrism. The justification of humanity's use of nonhuman animals is solidified by the providential ordering of the cosmos.[79]

There is a still a question as to *how* nonhumans exist for God through humanity. There are two primary manners. First, Aquinas follows Aristotle in claiming using nonhuman animals for human benefit—even as food—constitutes a good.[80] Thus, the nonhuman creation provides bodily sustenance (e.g., food and clothing) for humanity.[81] Second, the nonhuman creation provides a sacramental revelation of God's goodness.[82] Thus Aquinas's redactor in the Supplement to the Third—which is derived from Aquinas's commentary on Peter Lombard's *Sentences*—appropriately represents him:

> We believe all corporeal things to have been made for man's sake, wherefore all things are stated to be subject to him. Now they serve man in two ways, first, as sustenance to his bodily life, secondly, as helping him to know God, inasmuch as man sees the invisible things of God by the things that are made. (*ST*, S3.91.1)

Ironically, here one of the very points that defenders of Aquinas use to exonerate him from accusations of anthropocentrism backfires.[83] It is true that the entire created order, in its multiplicity, reveals the glory of God better than one life form could.[84] Yet for Aquinas this revelation can only have meaning to those with the capacity to appropriate it through contemplation (i.e., rational creatures).[85] Thus even this revelatory showing forth is always a showing forth *for humanity*.

---

79. Ibid., 47–48; Andrew Linzey, *Why Animal Suffering Matters: Philosophy, Theology, and Practical Ethics* (New York: Oxford University Press, 2009), 14.

80. *ST*, 2I2.64.1.

81. *ST*, 1.96.1; *SCG*, III.112.

82. *ST*, 1.47.1.

83. See Benzoni, *Ecological Ethics and the Human Soul*, 56.

84. E.g., Wynn, "Thomas Aquinas," 158–162.

85. *ST*, S3.91.1.

Theological Foundations for Aquinas's Conservationism

I have delineated what I take to be the anthropocentric dimension of Aquinas's theological framework. His cosmological theocentrism does maintain that the entire cosmos has God as its end. However, this foundation only solidifies Aquinas's anthropocentrism in history. By divine ordering, the non-rational creatures of the cosmos fulfill this telos in their service to humanity.

Aquinas's conservational dimension is evident in two manners. First, the nonhuman creation, apart from the elements, is wholly relegated to history and is good *as it is*.[86] Second, the good cosmos belongs to the *entire* human community.

Two fundamental notions inform the first point. First, Aquinas does not view predation as a facet of fallenness.[87] Not only is predation not a sign of the fall, it is part of the good order of the cosmos inasmuch as humans may kill other creatures if such killing is done in a manner conducive to the telos proper to human nature.[88] For this reason, I am unconvinced by Jenkins's argument that Aquinas balances the goodness of creation with the ambiguity of death and suffering by the principle of double effect. That is, God wills the goodness of creatures (e.g., the ferocity of a lion) with the indirect "evil" effect that the lion then devours the gazelle.[89] Jenkins makes an even stranger claim when he writes that humanity, in innocence, would not have used animals for food. He provides no reference to Aquinas on this point.[90] In my view, Jenkins is misguided on both accounts. After all, "There is no sin in using a thing for the purpose for which it is" (*ST* 2|2.64.1). There is no need for the

---

86. See Susanne M. DeCrane, *Aquinas, Feminism, and the Common Good* (Washington, DC: Georgetown University Press, 2004), 44–45.
87. *ST*, 1.65.1.
88. *SCG*, III.112; *ST*, 1.91.6.
89. Jenkins, *Ecologies of Grace*, 137, 144–145.
90. See ibid., 135.

principle of double effect vis-à-vis predation because Aquinas does not consider predation evil. Indeed, he repudiates such a claim:

> In the opinion of some, those animals which now are fierce and kill others, would, in that state, have been tame, not only in regard to man, but also in regard to other animals. But this is quite unreasonable. For the nature of animals was not changed by man's sin, as if those whose nature now it is to devour the flesh of others, would then have lived on herbs, as the lion and falcon." (*ST*, I, Q 96 A 1, Ad 2)

Thus, there is also no reason why this facet of a properly ordered and good cosmos would not have existed from the beginning.

At any rate, because predation among nonhuman animals (whether from other animals or humans) is good, there is no need for an eschatological redemption for creatures in this cycle. This needlessness for eschatological redemption is further solidified by the second notion. Aquinas's redactor claims that, apart from the elements, the nonhuman creation lacks an eschatological telos.[91] The temporal function of nonhumans (i.e., sustenance and revelation for humanity) will cease to be necessary in eternity.[92] The redactor writes, "[I]f the end cease, those things which are directed to the end should cease. Now animals and plants were made for the upkeep of human life…Therefore when man's animal life ceases, animals and plants should cease" (*ST*, S3.91.5).[93]

While this point is made most forcibly by Aquinas's redactor in the Supplement, it accurately represents Aquinas.[94] He follows Augustine in claiming that "man's last end is happiness…but 'happiness is not possible for animals bereft of reason'… Therefore other things do

---

91. *ST*, S3.91.1. See also *ST*, 1.65.1.
92. *ST*, S3.91.1.
93. See also, *SCG*, IV.97.5.
94. On humanity's animal life ceasing, see Aquinas, *SCG*, IV.83–86. Also, see Benzoni's enlightening engagement with Aquinas's *On the Power of God*. Benzoni, *Ecological Ethics and the Human Soul*, 54–57.

not concur in man's last end" (ST, 1|2.1.8). Aquinas is explicit that happiness, in the ultimate sense, is an end suited only for humans.[95]

In short, for nonhumans, the temporal realm is the extent of their existence. Thus Aquinas writes that "death comes to both [humans and nonhumans] alike as to the body, but not as to the soul."[96] The death of a nonhuman body is the annihilation of its sensitive soul, which in Aquinas's view are necessarily and wholly dependent on their physicality.[97] Hence, referencing the incorruptibility that humanity (and the inanimate creation in service to humanity) will attain in the eschaton, Aquinas states, "But the other animals, the plants, and the mixed bodies, those entirely corruptible both wholly and in part, will not remain at all in that state of incorruption" (SCG, IV.97.5). Thus, Aquinas excludes the nonhuman creation—apart from the elements—from the eschatological community. He furthermore maintains that dimensions of the nonhuman order such as death and suffering are not evil, but rather part of its goodness.

Regarding the second point, for Aquinas the nonhuman creation exists for all humanity. This point is most evident in his affirmation of the common good.[98] For Aquinas, part of the good for humanity is that which is required for human bodily sustenance. Yet Aquinas claims that society cannot function unless, as individuals seeking this good, it is also established for the entire community.[99] Thus, in his admonition to the king of Cyprus, Aquinas writes that it is a requirement of the king to "see that there is a sufficient supply of

95. ST, 1|2.1.8. See also Carlo Leget, "Eschatology," in The Theology of Thomas Aquinas, ed. Rik Van Nieuwenhove and Joseph Wawrykow (Notre Dame, IN: Notre Dame University Press, 2005), 370.
96. ST, 1.75.6; also, SCG, II.79.
97. ST, 1.75.6; also SCG, II.82.
98. For a good summary of Aquinas's understanding of the common good, see DeCrane, The Common Good, 42–84.
99. Aquinas, On Kingship, trans. Gerald B. Phelan, revised edition (Toronto: Pontifical Institute of Medieval Studies, 1949), 1.1.8.

the necessities required to live well."[100] Susanne DeCrane notes these requirements include "physical goods necessary to maintain life."[101] Furthermore, Aquinas claims that "each one is entrusted with the stewardship of his own things, so that out of them he may come to the aid of those who are in need" (*ST*, 2|2.66.7).[102] The point is that the created order, which constitutes a good for the entire human community, must be conserved so that all members of that community can make use of it.

An Eco-Theological Ethics of Anthropocentric Conservation

Aquinas's theological framework elicits four fundamental concerns with regard to the nonhuman creation. Each of these concerns derives from concern for the welfare of the human being and human society *in via* through this temporal world toward an eschatological telos. As such, all moral concern for the nonhuman creation is indirect.

First, because in its multiplicity the nonhuman creation reveals God's goodness, if humans abuse a part of the created order to the point of eradication, we diminish the revelation of God's goodness.[103] For Aquinas, no creature is without purpose, for all creatures participate in revealing God's goodness more fully.[104] Because this revelation is for humanity, harming creation to the point of eradication *is* the same as harming humanity.[105] Thus, one can rightly claim that utilization with disregard for conservation is morally

---

100. Ibid., 2.4.118.
101. DeCrane, *The Common Good*, 64.
102. Aquinas goes on to say that it is licit for someone to take the possessions of another out of dire need. *ST*, 2|2.66.7. See also DeCrane, *The Common Good*, 77–79.
103. Clifford, "Foundations," 39; Jenkins, *Ecologies of Grace*, 125–131.
104. I make this point contra Salisbury, "Attitudes toward Animals," 78.
105. Many critics of Aquinas miss this point. See Steiner, *Anthropocentrism and Its Discontents*, 131; Wennberg, *God, Humans, and Animals*, 121.

reprehensible for Aquinas.[106] Indeed, Aquinas holds that God charges the human creature (as rational) with maintenance of the created order.[107]

Second, Aquinas is concerned about human property. Because nonhuman animals "are ordered to man's use in the natural course of things, according to divine providence" (SCG, III.112), Aquinas maintains that "he that kills another's ox, sins, not through killing the ox, but through injuring another man in his property" (ST, 2I2.64.1). Here again, harming part of the nonhuman creation is tantamount to harming humans.

Third, and regarding specifically nonhuman animals, Aquinas expresses concern that humans causing them gratuitous harm might lead to the desensitization of the one causing the harm. This desensitization, in turn, could lead to violence toward other humans.[108] In other words, causing harm to sensitive creatures that have no basis for direct moral concern could lead to causing harm to sensitive creatures that do have such a basis.

Fourth, human use of the nonhuman creation must adhere to the propriety of virtue. In particular, humans must not engage in immoderate use of resources that are meant first and foremost to direct them to their proper telos, both temporal and ultimate. Jame Schaefer makes this point well, noting how Aquinas taught that

> humans should use God's creation in proper ways for the purposes they fulfill in the scheme of creation. Plants exist for animals to eat, animals exist for other animals, and all exist for humans to eat or use in other ways to bring up children, support a family, and meet other bodily needs. . . . However, an individual who possesses or desires to possess immoderate amounts of material goods sins against another with the sin

---

106. ST, 2I2.141.3; SCG, III.129. Also, Shaefer, "Valuing Earth Intrinsically and Instrumentally," 792.

107. SCG, III.78; ST, 1.64.4; Porter, The Recovery of Virtue, 61, 178.

108. SCG, III.112.13.

of avarice, because on individual cannot have an abundance of external riches without other individuals lacking them.[109]

This point fundamentally concerns the just distribution of nonhuman resources for the entire human community.[110] This anthropocentric emphasis on ecological social justice remains an important part of modern magisterial documents.[111]

Before leaving this section, it is worth noting that Benzoni makes a strong case against Aquinas's viability as a source for conservationism. He writes that, according to Aquinas, it is God's providence that sustains species as opposed to humanity's moral actions. Thus, deriving from Aquinas an ethics that relegates the role of species preservation to humans appears a bit specious.[112] Benzoni's point is well-made. However, for my purposes it is not important whether or not *all* preservation be the responsibility of humans. It is enough to note that Aquinas's position dictates that conservation is a byproduct of living properly within the ordered world.

Anthropocentric Conservation
and Individual Nonhuman Animals

I have already adumbrated much of what can be said about the place of individual nonhuman animals within the eco-theological paradigm of anthropocentric conservation. The nature of nonhuman animals renders them resources meant to meet the needs of human creatures, both contemplative and bodily, as they journey toward

109. Schaefer, *Theological Foundations for Environmental Ethics*, 199.
110. See Benzoni, *Ecological Ethics and the Human Soul*, 63–73
111. See Michael Northcott, *The Environment and Christian Ethics* (New York: Cambridge University Press, 1996), 135–36; Ryan Patrick McLaughlin, *Christianity and the Status of Animals: The Dominant Tradition and Its Alternatives* (New York: Palgrave Macmillan, forthcoming), chapter 2.
112. Benzoni, *Ecological Ethics and the Human Soul*, 53–54.

God. It is true that the term "resources" is anachronistic; yet, it adequately describes Aquinas's view in my opinion. Nonhuman resources, lacking the dignity of human nature, have no grounds for direct moral concern. Thus Aquinas echoes Aristotle: "There is no sin in using a thing for the purpose for which it is. . . . Wherefore it is not unlawful if man use plants for the good of animals, and animals for the good of man, as the Philosopher states" (ST 2|2.64.1). More than "not unlawful," on account of God's providential ordering of the cosmos, this use of plants and animals is good. Indeed, for Aquinas humans cannot sin against nonhuman animals.[113]

Aquinas's view of the nature of nonhuman animals also excludes them from the eschatological community. This exclusion bears ethical consequences, a point consistent with Aquinas's teleological understanding of virtue. Thus, Aquinas claims that the extension of charity to nonhuman animals is improper because "charity is based on the fellowship of everlasting happiness, to which the irrational creature cannot attain" (ST, 2|2.25.3). Aquinas delineates two further reasons why one should not (or cannot) extend charity to nonhuman animals. First, "friendship is towards one to whom we wish good things, while, properly speaking, we cannot wish good things to an irrational creature." Second, "all friendship is based on some fellowship in life. . . . [and] irrational creatures can have no fellowship in human life which is regulated by reason."[114] Therefore, arguments that Aquinas's view demands charitable engagement for the nonhuman creation for its own sake lack validity.[115]

In part, then, Aquinas does not consider nonhuman animals as subjects of direct moral concern because their nature precludes them from the purview of God's redemptive scope. Individual nonhuman

113. See ibid., 62–63.
114. *ST*, II–II, Q 25 A 3.
115. For instance, Jenkins, *Ecologies of Grace*, 140–141.

animals exist in history for the sake of the well-being of the entire human community. Their suffering and death, deriving from the natural order that includes human use, is part of the goodness of the cosmos. While a species as a whole would be protected as a revelatory expression of the divine, use of individual animals is subject only to concerns of property and desensitization. As Benzoni rightly notes, for Aquinas,

> It is the species of creatures that are primarily needed for the universe to be perfect because this perfection consists in the order of diverse "grades of goodness" (that is, species) to one another. Corruptible individuals are important only in the secondary sense that they are necessary for the sake of preserving their species in existence. Corruptible individuals are for the sake of their species.[116]

As such, the suffering of the individual nonhuman creature needs to be embraced, not redeemed.

Humans, on the other hand, are proper subjects of direct moral concern on account of their rational nature, which is directed toward their ultimate telos.[117] Thus, Aquinas states that rational creatures "stand out above other creatures, both in natural perfection and in the dignity of their end" (*SCG*, III.111). Furthermore,

> [T]here should be a union in affection among those for whom there is one common end. Now, men share in common the one ultimate end which is happiness, to which they are divinely ordered. So, men should be united with each other by a mutual love. (*SCG*, III.117.2)[118]

---

116. Benzoni, *Ecological Ethics and the Human Soul*, 52.
117. *SCG*, III.117.2; also 117.3.
118. See also Hollenbach, *The Common Good*, 149.

Anthropocentric Conservation in Summation

An eco-theological ethics of anthropocentric conservation establishes a sharp distinction between the human community and nonhuman resources. The human community is made of up of essentially unique creatures that constitute the central aim of divine concern. Only humans have a particular eternal telos that is communion with God. The nonhuman creation is a good and ordered network of resources that enable all humans to move toward their eschatological end by aiding them with regard to bodily sustenance as food and clothing and with regard to contemplative matters as a means of divine self-disclosure. In short, the nonhuman world, including individual animals, exists for the well-being of humanity. This function, predicated upon its nature, exhausts its temporal telos and renders an eternal telos moot.

Within this paradigm, humans must use the nonhuman creation properly. Proper use entails a concern for one's own end (i.e., using in a manner consistent with virtue) and the end of one's fellow humans (i.e., permitting them access to the goods of creation so that they might also use them properly). There is no sin or evil in killing an individual animal as long as these requirements are met. Such killing is in fact part of the good order of the cosmos. It helps perpetuate the divinely established system in which all nonhuman animals, along with the rest of the created order, exist for well-being of self and neighbor.

5

Cosmocentric Conservation

Willis Jenkins notes that, in the wake of Lynn White's critique of Christianity, most eco-theological thinkers have accepted that one of the most fundamental aspects of retrieving Christianity's environmental potentials entails exploring whether or not it is bound to a human-centered worldview.[1] Subsidiary to this exploration are questions regarding the role of science in the construction of nonhuman ethics. On the one hand, a complete relinquishment of truth to the realm of science often engenders a demystification of the nonhuman cosmos. This demystification provides the groundwork for an anthropocentric worldview in which nonhumans do not attain to the status of direct moral concern.[2] On the other hand, a staunch rejection of science enables a blind affirmation of the essential uniqueness of the human creature by overlooking the stark

1. Willis Jenkins, *Ecologies of Grace: Environmental Ethics and Christian Theology* (New York: Oxford University Press, 2008), 11–12.
2. Such a result is evident in a Cartesian framework. See William French, "Beast Machines and the Technocratic Reduction of Life," in *Good News for Animals? Christian Approaches to Animal Well-Being*, ed. Charles Pinches and Jay B. McDaniel (New York: Orbis Books, 1993), 24–43.

similarities between humans and our closest genetic ancestors. The disregard for this evidence also grounds an anthropocentric worldview.

In response to the aforementioned new task, theologians, ethicists, and biblical scholars have turned to various authoritative historical sources to recover strands of Christian thought that resist accusations of anthropocentrism. In many cases, only a critical retrieval of these sources renders them relevant today. Attempts of critical retrieval have, in certain cases, led to the paradigm of nonhuman ethics that I label cosmocentric conservation. In this view, the insights of science inform the manner in which theological claims apply to the relationship between humanity and the nonhuman cosmos. In particular, new understandings of the interconnectedness of the created order, including common origins and historical struggles through the evolutionary process; the interdependency of life within particular ecosystems and the effect the loss of one creature can have on the larger created order; and the shocking similarity on the genetic level between humans and nonhuman animals, have led to a dethroning of humanity with regard to an essentially unique dignity. Humans are no longer transcendent, above the creation, and unique in the possession of intrinsic value. Rather, they are creatures within the cosmic community, which includes all living creatures and the earth itself.

Thomas Berry's Ethics of Cosmocentric Conservation

The basic parameters of cosmocentric conservation have numerous representatives across denominational lines. Many of these representations have been developed through the work of Teilhard de Chardin and, to varying degrees, Thomas Berry. The ex-Catholic priest and creation spiritualist Matthew Fox provides an example.[3] In

Protestant thought, cosmocentric conservation is evident in the work of Calvin DeWitt.[4] In Liberation theology, Leonardo Boff's work reflects this paradigm.[5] In feminist thought, the work of Rosemary Radford Ruether and Dorothy McDougall are examples.[6]

These fine representatives notwithstanding, one of the most artful representatives is the late Roman Catholic Passionist priest and self-proclaimed "geologian," Thomas Berry. While Berry is Roman Catholic, he is adamant that his tradition has certain shortcomings that must be redressed.[7] Peter Ellard identifies the "radical nature of Berry's view" by referring to it as "dark green."[8]

Berry's amendments to the shortcomings of his tradition develop under the influences of various world religions, most notably indigenous religions of the Americas, Asia, and India.[9] Berry has also been influenced by scholars of history, most notably Giambattista Vico and Christopher Dawson.[10] Regarding Christianity, Berry provides an example of a critical appropriation of the work of

---

3. Matthew Fox, *Creation Spirituality: Liberating Gifts for the Peoples of the Earth* (San Francisco: HarperCollins, 1991).

4. Calvin DeWitt, *Earthwise: A Guide to Hopeful Creation Care*, third edition (Grand Rapids, MI: Faith Alive Christian Resources, 2011).

5. Leonardo Boff, *Ecology and Liberation: A New Paradigm*, trans. John Cumming (Maryknoll, NY: Orbis Books, 1995).

6. See Rosemary Radford Ruether, *Gaia and God: An Ecofeminist Theology of Earth Healing* (New York: HarperCollins Publishers, 1992). On McDougall, see *The Cosmos as the Primary Sacrament: The Horizon for an Ecological Sacramental Theology* (New York: Peter Lang, 2003).

7. Peter Ellard, "Thomas Berry as the Groundwork for a Dark Green Catholic Theology," in *Confronting the Climate Crisis: Catholic Theological Perspectives*, ed. Jame Schaefer (Milwaukee, WI: Marquette University Press, 2011), 313–314.

8. Ibid., 301.

9. For biographical considerations, see Mary Evelyn Tucker, "Thomas Berry: A Brief Biography," *Religion and Intellectual Life*, 5/4 (Summer 1988): 107–114. See also Thomas Berry, "The Universe as Cosmic Liturgy" (2000), in *The Christian Future and the Fate of the Earth* (hereafter *CFFE*), ed. Mary Evelyn Tucker and John Grim (Maryknoll, NY: Orbis Books, 2009), 96–102; Mary Evelyn Tucker and John Grim's introduction in *CFFE*, xiii–xxvii. See also Tucker's foreword in Thomas Berry, *The Sacred Universe: Faith, Spirituality, and Religion in the Twenty-First Century* (hereafter *TSU*), ed. Mary Evelyn Tucker (New York: Columbia University Press, 2009), ix–xiii.

10. Tucker, "Thomas Berry," 109–111.

Thomas Aquinas. He appreciates passages in Aquinas's corpus that emphasize the importance of the cosmos as a whole.[11] However, he clearly rejects the notion of anthropocentrism he detects in Thomas's theological framework. Oddly, Berry is here more critical of Augustine than Aquinas.[12]

Berry's later ecological works are most strongly influenced by the Jesuit Pierre Teilhard de Chardin, who provides a scientific cosmology to frame Berry's understanding of history. Mary Evelyn Tucker identifies five major emphases that Berry derives from de Chardin:

> (1) his comprehensive view of evolution as both a psychic and a physical process; (2) his discussion of the human as the consciousness of the universe; (3) his shifting of theological concerns from redemption to creation; (4) his desire to activate human energies for building the earth; (5) his emphasis on the important role of science in understanding the universe.[13]

Michael Northcott, who considers de Chardin to be humanocentric on account of his emphasis on human uniqueness and praise of technological advancement, writes that Berry "takes the Teilhardian approach in a much more ecocentric direction."[14]

The Cosmocentrism of the "New Story of the Universe"

"It's all a question of story," writes Berry.[15] Our precarious ecological context has arisen from a story developed "within a culture that emerged from a biblical-Christian matrix."[16] In Berry's estimation,

---

11. Berry, "Christian Cosmology," 31.
12. See Berry, "Wisdom of the Cross," 85–87; "The Universe as Cosmic Liturgy," 105–107.
13. Tucker, "Thomas Berry," 113.
14. Michael Northcott, *The Environment and Christian Ethics* (New York: Cambridge University Press, 1996), 347, n. 7.
15. Thomas Berry, *The Dream of the Earth* (San Francisco: Sierra Club Books, 1990), 123.
16. Berry, "The Christian Future and the Fate of the Earth" (1989), in *CFFE*, 35.

the Western version of this story is particularly harmful, with chapters including the work of René Descartes, Francis Bacon, the colonialism of early America, and the Industrial Revolution.[17] Thus Berry affirms, to some degree, White's critique of Western Christian thought.[18]

For Berry, such thought too often evinces anthropocentric tendencies that denigrate the nonhuman world. The Christian story as developed within the West has negated intimacy with the world. Berry claims this negation occurred in three phases. The first stage was "the meeting of early Christian spirituality with Greek humanism to form the basis of a strong anthropocentrism." Second, the Black Plague gave rise to an escapism from a condemned world in need of redemption. Finally, the triumph of industrialism rendered the world merely "a collection of objects."[19]

Berry insists that, in the midst of ecological degradation, Christian theology requires a new shape for its cosmology, one formed within the parameters of the "New Story of the universe."[20] This New Story does not obliterate the foundations of the old stories—the religious myths of creation. However, it enhances and develops these myths by being attentive to the "voices of the natural world" often silenced in Christian theology.[21] That is, the story is developed within the parameters of the discoveries of science, which for Berry constitute a primary form of revelation.[22]

Even so, the story does not succumb to the scientific tendency of reducing the world to an exhaustively calculable object.[23] Berry is adamant that a scientific approach that demystifies the world is as dangerous as a faith perspective that ignores the mysterious "voice

17. Berry, "The Sacred Universe" (1998, 2001), in *TSU*, 153–161.
18. Berry, *The Dream of the Earth*, 80.
19. Berry, "Christianity and Ecology," in *CFFE*, 60–63; *The Dream of the Earth*, 125–128.
20. On this reshaping, see McDougall, *The Cosmos as Primary Sacrament*, 22.
21. Berry, "The Christian Future," in *CFFE*, 38.
22. Ellard, "Dark Green Catholic Theology," 303.
23. Berry, *The Dream of the Earth*, 130–131; "Christianity and Ecology," in *CFFE*, 62–65.

of the world."[24] Thus Berry seeks to move beyond Deep Ecology.[25] Says Ellard, "Nothing short of great spiritual traditions—or current traditions greatly transformed—are in order in response to the current terror."[26] Indeed, Ellard writes that theologians "need to mythologize scientific findings."[27] In Berry's view, the confident claims of both science and religion regarding their calculations of the nonhuman world and the resulting conceptualization of that world as "thing" ground our ecological crisis. "We no longer have a world of inherent value, no world of wonder, no untouched, unspoiled, unused world. We think we have understood everything. But we have not. We have *used* everything."[28]

Thus Berry draws on religion and science. Dorothy McDougall summarizes his view well: "Berry seeks to integrate postmodern scientific insights into a functional cosmology which can guide human aspirations and action *within* the governing principles of the universe."[29] Berry's balanced combination of religious myth, science, and a nature mysticism elicits a worldview in which the "integral universe . . . constitutes the sacred community par excellence."[30]

For Berry, integrating Christian thought into the New Story is "the Great Work to which Christianity is called in these times."[31] This New Story is a unifying story. In a literary sense, it is the metanarrative from which all other narratives—religious, political, and economic—derive.[32] Hence Berry frames his theological explorations within this narrative framework.[33]

---

24. See Berry, *The Dream of the Earth*, 130–131; "Christianity and Ecology," in *CFFE*, 62–65; "Wisdom of the Cross," in *CFFE*, 82–83. See also Berry's enlightening discussion on personhood and language in "The Universe as Divine Manifestation," in *TSU*, 145.
25. Berry, *The Dream of the Earth*, 2.
26. Ellard, "Dark Green Catholic Theology," 302.
27. Ibid., 305.
28. Berry, "The World of Wonder" (2001), in *TSU*, 171.
29. McDougall, *The Cosmos as Primary Sacrament*, 2.
30. Berry, "Christian Cosmology," in *CFFE*, 34.
31. Berry, "The Role of the Church," in *CFFE*, 53.

Berry describes the New Story as the tale of "a sequence of irreversible transformations" spanning around fourteen billion years.[34] The plot gives special attention to human beings, "that being in whom the universe in its evolutionary dimension became conscious of itself."[35] Yet the narrative is never dominated by these late arrivals.[36] In fact, "the Earth has a privileged role" because it is the space with which the entire interconnected biotic community develops.[37] (I write "with which" to denote that the earth is more than the setting for biotic development.) Furthermore, whatever unique qualities exist in the human species derive from the common history of living beings in the world.[38] As Ellard states, "We do not live *on* earth. We *are* earth as it has expressed itself in a unique way, an amazing way—self reflective and aware."[39]

For Berry, this derivative nature of the human being not only acknowledges the inescapable earth-ness of humans, but also the spiritual-ness of the entire cosmos.[40] This claim bears two important corollaries. First, it contradicts any scientific reductionism that treats the nonhuman cosmos as nothing more than the amalgam of its physical components. In other words, there is a mysteriousness to the cosmos—an excess that empiricism cannot calculate.

Second, it disrupts the dualistic dichotomy between humans as physical/spiritual and nonhumans as merely physical. In the words of

---

32. See Berry, "The Christian Future," in *CFFE*, 41; *The Dream of the Earth*, 136. See also Ellard, "Dark Green Catholic Theology," 304.
33. For more details of this narrative, see Brian Swimme and Thomas Berry, *The Universe Story: From the Primordial Flashing Forth to the Ecozoic Era—A Celebration of the Unfolding of the Cosmos* (New York: HarperCollins, 1994).
34. Berry, "Christian Cosmology," in *CFFE*, 29.
35. Berry, *The Dream of the Earth*, 128. See also "The Christian Future," *CFFE*, 42–43.
36. Berry, *The Dream of the Earth*, 14.
37. Berry, "Christian Cosmology," in *CFFE*, 29–30.
38. Berry, "The Role of the Church," in *CFFE*, 48.
39. Ellard, "Dark Green Catholic Theology," 308–309.
40. Berry, "Christian Cosmology," *CFFE*, 29; "Christianity and Ecology," in *CFFE*, 65.

Ellard, "All material interactions before humans arrived had a psychic component, a mind component, a soul component in them. . . . This psyche/mind/spirit/soul aspect of all material things remains in all things."[41] Thus the uniqueness of humanity is always uniqueness within the evolutionary emergence of the cosmos. The New Story is not anthropocentric, but rather radically cosmocentric. It draws all life into a community. More than that, it unveils a cosmic family; for human beings are "cousins to every other living being."[42] One could perhaps even point to a greater intimacy in which "everything *in* the universes *is* the universe."[43] That is, all that exists in the cosmos is irrevocably united both materially and spirituality. One senses here an Eastern influence on Berry.[44] Though, Berry does not reject selfhood. Rather, he subsumes it into the "Great Self" or "greater self" in which it is united with all things.[45] As Ellard writes, "More than the fact that we are cousins to everything else, we are everything else. Everything else is part of our 'Great Self' identity."[46]

Based on such claims, Berry has been accused of advocating pantheism.[47] Ellard defends him against such accusations, arguing that Berry's view is not pantheistic but theophanic. That is, humans encounter the divine not *as* the creation, but *in* the creation. This sacramental emphasis suggests a divine element beyond the cosmos.[48]

41. Ellard, "Dark Green Catholic Theology," 306.
42. Berry, "Wisdom of the Cross," in *CFFE*, 84; *The Dream of the Earth*, 1.
43. Ellard, "Dark Green Catholic Theology," 304.
44. For Berry's engagement with Eastern thought, see Thomas Berry, *The Great Work: Our Way into the Future* (New York: Bell Tower, 1999), 70–93.
45. Berry, *The Great Work*, 70; Berry, "Prologue: Loneliness and Presence," in *A Communion of Subjects: Animals in Religion, Science, and Ethics*, ed. Paul Waldau and Kimberly Patton (New York: Columbia University Press, 2006), 5.
46. Ellard, "Dark Green Catholic Theology," 309.
47. See Richard Bauckham, *Bible and Ecology: Rediscovering the Community of Creation* (Waco, TX: Baylor University Press, 2010), 82–83; Loren Wilkinson, "The Making of the *Declaration*," in *The Care of Creation: Focusing Concern and Action*, ed. R. J. Berry (Downers Grove, IL: Intervarsity, 2000), 55.
48. See Ellard, "Dark Green Catholic Theology," 305.

Though, Ellard does acknowledge that Berry does go to great lengths to downplay transcendence.[49] He furthermore states that "the divine, in a Berrian system, will be largely devoid of . . . theistic underpinnings."[50] Thus, the accusations are not fully without warrant.

Conservation of a Cosmos without Need of Redemption

I have demonstrated Berry's cosmocentrism. The cosmos constitutes a community in which all share in the materiality and spirituality of one another. The hierarchy of Aquinas is fully dismantled in Berry's view. To establish the conservational dimension of Berry's eco-theological ethics, I must address his views concerning eschatological redemption.

Ellard claims that Berry's critique of Christianity is sharpest with regard to the notions of transcendence and redemption.[51] Here my emphasis is redemption. For Berry, the New Story of the universe is the necessary framework for all Christian claims, including redemption. Within this framework, redemption is neither rescue from cosmic evolutionary processes nor the mechanisms that enable them. Rather, redemption, if there is such a thing in Berry's view, is the realization of these processes, even in their "awesome violence."[52] The violent occurrences in the natural world are not consequences of a cosmic fall or sin, but rather "cosmological moments of grace."[53] They correspond to Christ's sacrifice on the cross, for they are a "primary necessity in activating the more advanced modes of being."[54] Thus, the violence of the evolutionary process is a

49. Ibid., 313–14.
50. Ibid., 311.
51. Ibid., 314.
52. Berry, *The Dream of the Earth*, 89. See also McDougall, *The Cosmos as Primary Sacrament*, 121.
53. Berry, "Wisdom of the Cross," in *CFFE*, 89.

manifestation of the wisdom of the cross whereby sacrifice enables life.[55] For Berry, "every living being is sacrificed for other living beings."[56] In line with this incarnational understanding of violence, Ellard highlights the revelatory function of violence in the cosmos:

> Violence is one of the ways that the universe creates and it is part of the context. This means, of course, that, just like the universe, the divine is both wonderful and violent. The divine is life-giving and life-taking. The divine is made manifest through destruction, through cancer, and through plague. We need to take comfort in this.[57]

Ellard's point is that, for Berry, violence and goodness are not opposed. Thus he also writes, "There is little talk of intrinsic evil within a Berrian system. In a real sense, there is no room for it." That which occurs in nature (i.e., natural evil) is part of the order of nature, which is good and therefore in need of neither transcendent escape nor eschatological redemption. There is, however, a need for the repentance of humans for their violation of nature's balanced cycles. Thus, Berry maintains a strong sense of moral evil alongside his apparent dismissal of natural evil.

For Berry, therefore, death is part of the necessary, good, and divinely ordained mode of progress in the unfolding creation. As he writes, "The divine creates a phenomenal world with the power to develop greater complexity through emergent processes."[58] There is no "fall" of the nonhuman universe.[59] For this reason, humanity should not lament the violence of nature. For cosmic peace, which entails the sustaining of the balanced order within the creative

54. Berry, "Christian Cosmology," in *CFFE*, 33.
55. Berry, "Wisdom of the Cross," in *CFFE*, 88–91.
56. Thomas Berry, *Befriending the Earth: A Theology of Reconciliation between Humans and the Earth* (Mystic, CT: Twenty-Third Publications, 1991), 68.
57. Ellard, "Dark Green Catholic Theology," 312.
58. Berry, "Christianity and Ecology," in *CFFE*, 64–65.
59. See Berry's discussion on redemption in *The Dream of the Earth*, 124–126.

emergence of the universe, requires it.[60] Far from lamentation, Berry calls for liturgical outlets that enable "celebration of the evolutionary transformation moments."[61] Doing so would remedy one of Berry's critiques of Western religions: that they "have been so occupied with redemptive healing of a flawed world that they tend to ignore creation as it is experienced in our times."[62] Furthermore, such liturgical acts would incorporate our religious story into the story of the universe; for "the universe, by definition, is a single gorgeous celebratory event."[63]

On account of the goodness of the ordered cosmos, Berry seeks to surmount the notion that Christianity necessitates "redemption from a flawed world."[64] It is here that he demonstrates the conservational dimension of his cosmocentrism. Nonhumans are not excluded from the community of eschatological redemption, as was the case in Aquinas's theological framework. Nor are they included, as will be the case in Orthodox theology. For Berry, there is no community of eschatological redemption, nor is there need for one.[65] A chief human mistake, grounded though it is in Christian thought, is that human beings seek to overcome the order of nature.[66] But the laws of this order, established by God, require human assent, not correction. "The universe is the primary law-giver."[67] The ecological crisis does not need "a human answer to the earth problem, but an earth answer

60. Berry, *The Dream of the Earth*, 216–220.
61. Berry, "The Universe as Cosmic Liturgy," in *CFFE*, 111.
62. Berry, *The Dream of the Earth*, 25.
63. Ibid., 5.
64. Berry, "The Christian Future," in *CFFE*, 39.
65. Consider David Toolan's comparison of Moltmann and Berry with regard to the value of biblical promise and eschatological hope. Toolan, *At Home in the Cosmos* (Maryknoll, NY: Orbis Books, 2003), 150 n. 22.
66. Berry, "The Role of the Church," in *CFFE*, 47.
67. Ibid., 51.

to the earth problem."[68] Humanity, like all species, must fit into the mysterious whole.[69]

Many theologians critique Berry—along with others of the so-called creation spirituality category such as Matthew Fox—for overlooking the suffering in creation. Sallie McFague acknowledges the power of Berry's vision. Yet she levels the following critique:

> What Berry and other creation spirituality writers lack is a sense of the awful oppression that is part and parcel of the awesome mystery and splendor. The universe has not been for species, and certainly not for most individuals within species, a "gorgeous celebratory event." It has been a story of struggle, loss, and often early death.[70]

McFague's critique is common. Celia Deane-Drummond approvingly notes that "many would see that [Berry's] vision is overly idealistic, ignoring some of the more unsavoury, destructive aspects of evolutionary and cosmic history."[71] In line with this critique is another: the place of eschatology in Berry's framework. In McFague's estimation, the beauty of creation spirituality ought to be its eschatological promise. That is, it should represent the world as it ought to be, a community of intimacy.[72] Yet John Haught critiques the absence of such an eschatological promise in Berry's thought.[73]

In my estimation, McFague and others miss Berry's point. Berry is well aware of the violence in the created order:

> The universe, earth, life, and consciousness are all violent processes. The basic terms in cosmology, geology, biology, and anthropology all carry a heavy charge of tension and violence. Neither the universe as a whole nor any part of the universe is especially peaceful.[74]

68. Berry, *The Dream of the Earth*, 35.
69. Ibid., 208.
70. Sallie McFague, *The Body of God: An Ecological Theology* (Minneapolis, MN: Fortress Press, 1993), 71.
71. Deane-Drummond, *Eco-Theology*, 42.
72. McFague, *The Body of God*, 72.
73. See John Haught, *The Promise of Nature* (Mahwah, NJ: Paulist, 1993), 104–105.

Thus Berry clearly recognizes that "there is a violent as well as a benign aspect of nature."[75] The significant point to be made is that, for Berry and others like him, "the 'cosmic-earth' process . . . and the process of ultimate human transformation are one in the same."[76] That is, the evolutionary emergence of the cosmos is neither superseded by eschatological redemption from outside of history nor a burgeoning millennialism from within it. Rather, any notion of redemption is subsumed into the New Story. If anything, the cosmos itself is the harbinger of redemption through the very mechanisms of death and suffering that many theologians seek to redress by an appeal to eschatology.[77] For Berry, "the supremely beautiful is the integrity and harmony of the total cosmic order."[78] As this order not only includes but currently *requires* violence, death, predation, suffering, and evolutionary waste, these dimensions of the cosmos constitute part of its beauty and goodness. The human fault is the rejection of this beauty and goodness in pursuit of some future hope that leaves this natural order behind. In short, humans erred when we convinced ourselves that "we deserved a better world."[79]

A Nonhuman Ethics of Cosmocentric Conservation

I have established that Berry's vision of the world rejects both anthropocentrism and the need for an eschatological redemption of the cosmos. Concerning the latter, the cosmos is not a fallen

---

74. Berry, *The Dream of the Earth*, 216.

75. Ibid., 6.

76. Kusumita Pedersen, "Inclusion and Exclusion: Reflections on Moral Community and Salvation," in *Earth Habitat: Eco-Injustice and the Church's Response*, ed. Dieter Hessel and Larry Rasmussen (Minneapolis, MN: Fortress Press, 2001), 50.

77. See Berry's discussion on hope in *The Dream of the Earth*, 221–223. See also Deane-Drummond, *Eco-Theology*, 42.

78. Berry, *The Dream of the Earth*, 129.

79. Ibid., 205.

realm of ugliness; rather, it is a beautiful emergence of celebration. Concerning the former, the cosmos is not divided between ensouled, spiritual, thinking beings and "things." Based on these foundations—and with regard to this project—Berry's eco-theological ethics has one fundamental core with three practical corollaries. The core is the recognition of an egalitarian cosmic community of intrinsic value. The practical corollaries are the dismantling of human dominion, the vision of humanity's "living-with" the cosmos, and finally the extension of rights to the nonhuman creation in conjunction with the limiting of human rights.

Regarding the dismantling of dominion, Berry's notion of the cosmic community rescinds the unique and transcendent identity of humanity as above nature.[80] As McDougall notes, for Berry, "the universe is the primary sacred reality—the *imago Dei*."[81] Thus, Berry posits a democratization of the *imago*. This democratization grounds the dismissal of a functional anthropocentrism (i.e., human dominion):

> Apart from the primary intention of the scriptures, the practice of Westerns Christians has been to consider that every earthly reality is subject to the free disposition of humans insofar as we are able to assert . . . dominion. We do not feel responsible precisely to the world about us since the natural world has no inherent rights; we are responsible only to the creator and to ourselves, not to abuse anything. . . . Only in this detached situation could we have felt so free to intrude upon the forces of the natural world even when we had not the slightest idea of the long-range consequences of what we were doing.[82]

Berry's dismantling of human dominion even challenges the model of stewardship. For Berry, this model is "too extrinsic a mode of relating"; for "it strengthens our sense of human dominance" and

---

80. Berry, "Christian Cosmology," in *CFFE*, 30; *The Dream of the Earth*, 125–128.
81. McDougall, *The Cosmos as Primary Sacrament*, 65.
82. Berry, "The Christian Future," in *CFFE*, 40.

"does not recognize that nature has a prior stewardship over us as surely as we have a stewardship over nature."[83] Thus, in Berry's view, the role of the nonhuman world is one of mutuality with humans; for "humans and the universe were made for each other."[84] The human expresses the conscious appreciation and celebration of the universe. The universe, on the other hand, constitutes the primordial sacrament.[85] It is the "primary revelation of the divine."[86] In this mutuality, "human beings find their fulfillment in the universe even as the universe finds its fulfillment in the human."[87] There is thus a sacramental reciprocity between the human and the nonhuman. The celebration of the cosmos finds unique expression in humanity. Human fulfillment, in turn,. depends upon the "Book of Nature," which is an essential counterpart to other forms of divine revelation.[88] In other words, Berry's egalitarian value system is coupled with a functional egalitarianism in which humans express cosmic consciousness while at once being intrinsically and indissolubly dependent upon the cosmos. As such, there can be no claim of any form of functional anthropocentrism, even stewardship.

If dominion/stewardship is not the appropriate model of human interaction with the cosmos, what is? The model that Berry suggests is that of an "Ecozoic era, a period when humans [are] present to the planet in a mutually enhancing manner."[89] Humanity's role, apart from appreciation and celebration, is preservation, a humble living with and within the order of the cosmos, a letting be of the natural world.[90] The nonhuman world is not a network of resources for

83. Ibid., 41. For a similar position, see McDougall, *The Cosmos as the Primary Sacrament*, chapter 2.
84. Berry, "Loneliness and Presence," 6.
85. Berry, "Christian Cosmology," in *CFFE*, 31–32.
86. Ibid., 31.
87. Berry, "The Sacred Universe," in *TSU*, 166.
88. Berry, "The Christian Future," in *CFFE*, 38–39, 42; "The Universe as Divine Manifestation," *TSU*, 146.
89. Berry, "The Role of the Church," in *CFFE*, 47.

human consumption, but rather a vast mystery, a good and ordered community of intrinsic value with a spirit-imbued history that long predates humans. Even so, humanity's reverential "letting be" does not negate utility. Rather, it qualifies it with a harmonious "living with" the nonhuman world in which harmony suggests struggling for human survival without unhinging the community that enables that struggle.[91] Berry calls for balance between a gracious "letting be" of the cosmos and a reverential "living with" it, as it is in its beautiful evolutionary emergence. The following sentiment constitutes the heart of cosmocentric conservation:

> To learn how to live graciously together would make us worthy of this unique, beautiful, blue planet that evolved in its present splendor over some billions of years, a planet that we should give over to our children with the assurance that this great community of the living will lavish upon them the care that it has bestowed so abundantly upon ourselves.[92]

Note the multiple and interconnected dimensions of this ethics. Humans are not simply responsible for the cosmos; they are responsible *as the cosmos*. They do not simply protect the nonhuman creation; they *need the nonhuman creation*. Human celebration is not an act toward the cosmos. It is rather a participation in the cosmos—a "living-with." Thus preservation cannot simply be an "us" (i.e., humans) protecting "it" or even "them" (i.e., nonhumans). Berry is adamant that "nothing is simply an object to be used."[93] Preservation is rather an act within the sacred community itself. In short, Berry replaces dominion, which is an extrinsic model of the human/ nonhuman rapport, with a model of reverential "living-with," which emphasizes human immanence in the place of transcendence. In

90. Ibid., 48; Berry, "Wisdom of the Cross," in *CFFE*, 93–94.
91. Berry, "Reinventing the Human at the Species Level," in *CFFE*, 119.
92. Berry, *The Dream of the Earth*, 12.
93. Berry, "The Role of the Church," in *CFFE*, 55.

Mary Evelyn Tucker's terms, Berry calls for "a shift from an anthropocentric sense of domination to an anthropocosmic sense of communion with all life forms."[94]

An anthropocosmic worldview is similar, with regard to value, to my use of cosmocentrism. The term denotes, beyond the issue of value, a strong sense of mutuality between humanity (*anthropos*) and the world (*cosmos*).[95] However, the question of mutuality is, in my view, less important than the issue of intrinsic value. A strongly anthropocentric worldview can have a symbiotic understanding of humans and the cosmos. It can even maintain a strong sense of human immanence in the created order. Thus the notion of mutuality does not necessitate the dismantling of a centric value system. Nor does an extensive value system require equal mutuality (e.g., consider the relationship between a parent and a child). At any rate, a cosmocentric view, at least as I am using it, denotes mutuality in the sense that humans are not "other than" the cosmos. They are part of the cosmos. It furthermore denotes that this cosmos, along with its various components—including humans—bears intrinsic value. Thus, I find Berry to be amenable with the classification of cosmocentric. Regardless, the aim of reverential living-with all life constitutes the Great Work of humanity—an opening and embracing of cosmic mutuality. Says Berry, "The Great Work now . . . is to carry out the transition from a period of human devastation of the Earth to a period when humans would be present to the planet in a mutually beneficial manner."[96]

---

94. Mary Evelyn Tucker, "A Communion of Subjects and a Multiplicity of Intelligences," in *A Communion of Subjects: Animals in Religion, Science, and Ethics*, ed. Paul Waldau and Kimberly Patton (New York: Columbia University Press, 2006), 646.

95. See Sam Mickey, "Contributions to Anthropocosmic Environmental Ethics," *Worldviews* 11 (2007): 226–47.

96. Berry, *The Great Work*, 3.

Once the essential transcendence of humanity is dismantled, Berry is able to extend the notion of rights to the entire cosmos. When there is no longer the division between "I" and "it," then the notion that the "nonhuman nature is merely a 'good' to be distributed evenly" among humans vanishes.[97] Rather, "the basic referent in terms of reality and of value is the universe in its full expression in space and time."[98] Herein lies the "primary law of the universe."[99] Value belongs to the entire cosmic family in its irrevocable interconnectedness.[100]

Thus Berry staunchly rejects an anthropocentrism in which one measures value only with reference to humanity.[101] On the contrary, he advocates a biocentrism, a term related to my notion of cosmocentrism, in which the value of the nonhuman world is as intrinsic as the value of humanity.[102] All other anthropocentric approaches ground the industrial triumph of utility over communion.[103] Berry's biocentrism entails the rejection of the position that rights apply only to humanity.[104] In fact, the rights of nonhumans require "limited rights" for humanity.[105] While this use of the language of rights does not denote equal rights, it does denote rights for all: "Each being has rights according to its mode of being. Trees have tree rights, birds have bird rights."[106]

---

97. McDougall, *The Cosmos as Primary Sacrament*, 70.
98. Berry, "Christian Cosmology," in *CFFE*, 31.
99. Berry, *The Dream of the Earth*, 202.
100. Berry, "The Role of the Church," in *CFFE*, 48–49, 53; "Christianity and Ecology," *CFFE*, 60; "The Sacred Universe," in *TSU*, 152.
101. Berry, "Christian Cosmology," in *CFFE*, 31.
102. Berry, *The Dream of the Earth*, 21; "The Christian Future," in *CFFE*, 44.
103. Berry, "Christianity and Ecology," in *CFFE*, 63.
104. Berry, "The Universe as Cosmic Liturgy," in *CFFE*, 118–119.
105. Berry, "The Role of the Church," in *CFFE*, 50.
106. Berry, "Wisdom of the Cross," in *CFFE*, 91.

Cosmocentric Conservation
and Individual Nonhuman Animals

Within the paradigm of cosmocentric conservation, the human species is part of an evolutionary process that depends on predation, suffering, and death. In this cycle, "each individual life form has its own historical appearance, a moment when it must assert its identity, fulfill its role, and then give way to other individuals in the processes of the phenomenal world."[107] These dimensions of existence are not the result of sin or the fall, but rather cosmic grace in the unfolding of the universe. Thus they are not in need of redemption.

Because predation and death are part of the good order of nature, it seems that the killing of individual nonhuman animals for survival is not only acceptable, but, pending the context, good. However, a human-induced extinction of a species, even for great human benefit, is not.[108] As Berry notes, extinction is "not like the killing of individual lifeforms that can be renewed through normal processes of reproduction."[109] An evolutionary extinction of species is, of course, another matter. Such is part of the awesome violence of evolutionary emergence.

It is crucial to note that, for Berry, nonhuman animals are part of the cosmic family and thus kin to humans. The reverence due their dignity is profound. In Berry's words, "Every being has its own interior, its self, its mystery, its numinous aspect. To deprive any being of this sacred quality is to disrupt the larger order of the universe. Reverence will be total or it will not be at all."[110] Furthermore, Berry claims that animals "belong in our conscious human world in a special manner."[111] The treatment of animals

---

107. Berry, "Loneliness and Presence," 6.
108. Berry, *The Dream of the Earth*, 8–9; "The Sacred Universe," in *TSU*, 156.
109. Berry, *The Dream of the Earth*, 9.
110. Ibid., 134.

within the milieu of our ecological pathology certainly falls under Berry's critique.[112] Berry even maintains that vegetarianism is "one of the most effective things . . . we can do on an individual scale" to stymie the ecological degradation of the natural world.[113] In my view, the intensity of Berry's critique would reach deep into the magisterial documents of the Catholic Church. Berry never uses the word "gift" (and certainly not "resource"!) to describe the nonhuman creation with reference to humanity. He replaces this unilateral language by claiming that humans and nonhumans participate in "a constant exchange of gifts to each other."[114]

Berry's critique notwithstanding, reverence is not necessarily opposed to killing just as beauty is not opposed to violence. To the point: only as part of the natural order, within its ebb and flow, can humans ethically use the nonhuman creation.[115] As Deane-Drummond writes, "Human care for the earth stems from a cosmic caring that is embedded in evolutionary processes." Thus, the justification for practices such as hunting and meat-eating is not based on a unique spiritual dignity deriving from human transcendence. In fact, the justification is based on the opposite, human immanence within a cosmos that is macroanthropos. As I will note in chapter 6, Orthodox theologians (and many others) claim that humanity is the microcosm of the universe—and here Berry agrees. But Berry goes further in claiming that humanity does not transcend the cosmos. Such is the meaning and significance of the cosmos as macroanthropos. Humanity is a unique concentration of the many

111. Berry, "Loneliness and Presence," 6.
112. See Berry, *The Dream of the Earth*, 203.
113. See Thomas Berry, "Every Being Has Rights," available online at http://www.gaiafoundation.org/sites/ default/files/documents.
114. Berry, "Loneliness and Presence," 8.
115. Deane-Drummond, *Eco-Theology*, 41.

facets of the universe. But the universe is itself a vast amplification of these facets. Thus, in *The Great Work*, Berry defines humans as

> a mystical quality of the Earth, a unifying principle, and integration of the various polarities of the material and the spiritual, the physical and the psychic, the natural and the artistic, the intuitive and the scientific. We are the unity in which all these inhere and achieve a special mode of functioning.[116]

Humans engage in the mechanisms of evolution, including predation, because we are participants in the integral order of the cosmos, an order that requires violence. I thus view Berry's position on, for instance, hunting, to be that of other environmental ethicists such as Aldo Leopold who maintain that hunting is a means of placing humanity in the context of the natural order.[117] This engagement is good and therefore not in need of redemption. It requires reverence, wonder, awe. But it does not require the cessation of violence in all its forms. For, in the words of McDougall, "The primary intention of life is neither one of peace nor conflict, but creativity."[118]

Cosmocentric Conservation in Summation

This exploration into the work of Thomas Berry provides a concrete example of the eco-theological paradigm I label cosmocentric conservation. While many other scholars from across denominational lines and hermeneutical emphases including creation spiritualists, liberation theologians, and ecofeminists, do not share the exact claims of Berry, his eco-theological vision nonetheless provides a broad

---

116. Berry, *The Great Work*, 174–75.
117. See Marc R. Fellenz, *The Moral Menagerie: Philosophy and Animal Rights* (Chicago: University of Illinois Press, 2007), 164–166.
118. McDougall, *The Cosmos as Primary Sacrament*, 22.

framework into which many such writers fit. Within this framework, there are six central tenets. The first four pertain to cosmocentrism while the other two pertain to conservation.

First, the cosmos is a community of subjects in mysterious interconnectedness. Second, each member of this community participates in the goodness and mystery of the whole and thereby is due the reverence of a common dignity. Third, human beings are no longer the transcendent ones, unique in the possession of psyche, spirit, soul, or even the *imago Dei*. Rather, humans are members of the cosmic community, kin to all living creatures, and participants in the pervasive mystery of existence. Fourth, only as members of this community can humans properly engage the cosmos, engagements that must balance a gracious "letting be" with a reverential "living-with" fellow members of the community, including the earth.

Fifth, the earth community is good and ordered as it is, and is therefore in no need of an eschatological redemption that fixes or changes nonhuman nature. Sixth, because humans await no eschatological redemption, human engagement of the earth must derive from the laws of nature evident in the emerging temporal cosmos. These laws do not negate use or predation, for each of these dimensions of existence is part of the good and ordered cosmos. Rather, the laws mandate humility in such use, recognizing that human benefit does not constitute the primary purpose of the nonhuman cosmos.

6

Anthropocentric Transfiguration

Cosmocentric conservation provides a critique to its anthropocentric counterpart for an overemphasis on the importance of humans in history. Anthropocentric transfiguration critiques its conservationist counterparts for an under-emphasis on the import of nonhumans in the eschaton. In this paradigm, the whole of the cosmos is destined for transfiguration, which denotes an eschatological participation in God's eternal life. However, the nonhuman creation's participation in the eschatological community is primarily—if not solely—for the sake of the divine-human drama. That is, the cosmos serves both historically and ultimately as a sacrament the divine-human rapport. John Haught is thus correct in his acknowledgement that referring to nature as a sacrament that will be eschatologically transfigured does not necessitate the abandonment of a value-based anthropocentrism.[1]

Anthropocentric transfiguration is best represented in Eastern Orthodox theology.[2] However, not all Orthodox theologians

1. John Haught, *God after Darwin: A Theology of Evolution*, second edition (Washington, DC: Georgetown University Press, 2008), 167.

explicitly uphold its fundamental tenets.[3] Some are unclear regarding whether or not the nonhuman creation will share in God's life for its own sake or for the sake of humans. Others seem to suggest that the cosmos will be included for its own sake, advocating something more akin to the paradigm of cosmocentric transfiguration. While it would thus be inaccurate to classify all of Orthodox theology as an example of anthropocentric transfiguration, it is nonetheless the case that this paradigm finds it clearest expression from within Orthodox thought. Therefore, establishing concrete examples of the paradigm will require an exploration of Orthodox theology. I begin this exploration with an overview of Maximus the Confessor. I then trace the transfigurative and anthropocentric strands of Orthodox theology.

The Theology of Maximus the Confessor

While Augustine and Aquinas exclude most of the nonhuman creation—including plants and nonhuman animals—from the eschatological community, other voices in Christian history explicitly deny this exclusion.[4] In this vein John Meyendorff states, "The patristic doctrine of creation is inseparable from eschatology—the goal of created history, of time itself, is oneness in God."[5] One important proponent of this inclusive eschatological vision is Maximus the Confessor, who, in the words of Elizabeth Theokritoff, "remains to this day the single most important figure in Orthodox cosmological thought."[6] Similarly, Meyendorff writes, "Maximus can

2. On Roman Catholic representation, see William C. French, "Subject-centered and Creation-centered Paradigms in Recent Catholic Thought," *The Journal of Religion*, 70/1 (January 1990), 48–72.
3. Here, my emphasis will be on the Orthodox school of neo-patristic synthesis as opposed to Russian sophiology.
4. See McLaughlin, *Christian Theology and the Status of Animals*, chapter 4.
5. Meyendorff, "Creation in the History of Orthodox Theology," 29–30.

be called the real father of Byzantine theology."[7] His work on creation provides "criteria for all later Byzantine thought."[8] As this authority, Maximus provides the developed foundations for contemporary Orthodox theologians and, in turn, anthropocentric transfiguration.

For Maximus, the entire created order participates in God as material instantiations (plasticized *logoi*) of the divine *logoi*.[9] In the words of Celia Deane-Drummond, these instantiations are "the principles and ideas in the sensory world as we know it in different manifestation, but which ultimately express their source in the divine Logos."[10] The divine *logoi* are, in Theokritoff's words, "exemplars in the divine will for created things, 'blueprints' in accordance with which the actual creature comes into being."[11] Plasticized *logoi* are created things in a nascent form of what God ultimately desires them to be. They are the "ontological becoming of God's ideas."[12]

All plasticized *logoi* have a natural mode of existence by which they move toward the divine intention for them. This movement is their *tropos*—the proper dynamic orientation of a created entity.[13] The *tropos* of all creation is ultimately directed toward God.[14] In other

6. Elizabeth Theokritoff, "Creator and Creation," in *The Cambridge Companion to Orthodox Christian Theology*, eds. Mary B. Cunningham and Elizabeth Theokritoff (New York: Cambridge University Press, 2008), 66.

7. John Meyendorff, *Christ in Eastern Christian Thought* (Washington, DC: Corpus Books, 1969), 99.

8. Meyendorff, "Creation in the History of Orthodox Theology," 29.

9. Elizabeth Theokritoff, *Living in God's Creation: Orthodox Perspectives on Ecology* (Crestwood, NY: St Vladimir's Seminary Press, 2009), 53–54.

10. Celia Deane-Drummond, *Eco-Theology* (Winona, MN: Anselm Academic, 2008), 61.

11. Theokritoff, *Living in God's Creation*, 54.

12. Daniel Munteanu, "Cosmic Liturgy: The Theological Dignity of Creation as a Basis of an Orthodox Ecotheology," *International Journal of Public Theology* 4 (2010), 334.

13. See Maximus the Confessor, *Ambigua*, 7, 42. Sections from *Ambigua* are taken from *On the Cosmic Mystery of Jesus Christ*, trans. Paul M. Blowers and Robert L. Welken (Crestwood, NY: St Vladimir's Seminary Press, 2003). See also Radu Bordeianu, "Maximus and Ecology: The Relevance of Maximus the Confessor's Theology of Creation for the Present Ecological Crisis," *Downside Review* 127, no. 447 (2009), 104–107; Meyendorff, *Christ in Eastern Christian Thought*, 101–102.

words, all actual created entities—living and nonliving—naturally move toward the divine intention for them, which is a participation in God.[15]

Human beings, unique in the possession of the image of God—and destined for their own divine *logoi* as the likeness of God through divination—have the ability to decipher the *logoi* of creation and therefore bear the responsibility to facilitate their *tropos* through a synergistic cooperation with the divine.[16] As humanity engages in this deciphering, the nonhuman creation functions as a sacrament for humanity, revealing the divine wisdom and facilitating the divine-human drama. Human beings are well-suited for their task because, as both material and spiritual, they are microcosms of the created order. As such they are able to gather up all dimensions of the cosmos in their own being, which we then bring to God.[17]

This gathering, for Maximus, constitutes the role of humanity. Humans are priests of the sacramental world, the ones called to unite the cosmos with the divine.[18] Maximus describes this priestly role more specifically as a uniting of the five divisions in the cosmos: "uncreated and created, intelligible and sensible, heaven and earth, paradise and the world, male and female."[19] The gathering of all creation into humanity constitutes the movement of the cosmos toward the divine. This movement leads to its transfiguration in

14. Maximus, *Ambigua*, 7; Meyendorff, "Creation in the History of Orthodox Theology," 29.
15. The natural dynamism in Maximus's cosmology strikes against the Platonism of Origen. See Meyendorff, *Christ in Eastern Christian Thought*, 99–101.
16. Meyendorff, *Christ in Eastern Christian Thought*, 103–105; Andrew Louth, "Between Creation and Transfiguration: The Environment in the Eastern Orthodox Tradition," in *Ecological Hermeneutics: Biblical, Historical and Theological Perspectives*, eds. David G. Horrell, Cherryl Hunt, Christopher Southgate and Francesca Stavrakopoulou (New York: T & T Clark, 2010), 217–219.
17. Vladimir Lossky, *The Mystical Theology of the Eastern Church* (Crestwood, NY: St. Vladimir's Press, 1976), 108–109.
18. Maximus, *Ambigua* 41, taken from Bordeianu, "Maximus and Ecology," 117.
19. Bordeianu, "Maximus and Ecology," 111. See also Meyendorff, *Christ in Eastern Christian Thought*, 105; Theokritoff, "Creator and Creation," 66–67.

which it becomes what God intended it to be, a transparent revelation of the divine in eternity.[20]

Thus, for Maximus humanity plays a crucial role in the transfiguration of the cosmos.[21] In turn, the cosmos, as the sacrament of divine presence, plays a crucial role in the transfiguration of humanity. "The relationship between humanity and the world is mutual: humans sanctify creation, and creation helps us in our salvation."[22]

Humanity strayed from its role, derailing the *tropos* of creation.[23] Such is the cosmic dimension of the fall. In the present state of nature, "a disorderly kind of movement is perpetuated" because "the movement of Adam determines the direction in which the rest of creation moves."[24] As humans bear the responsibility of facilitating the proper *tropos* of the cosmos, when humans stray from the path to God, the cosmos follows them.

Human priesthood has been compromised by sin, leaving the cosmos in disarray. Yet, in Christ the task has been realized; for, in Christ the divisions of the created order are overcome.[25] Thus, the incarnation enables humans to return to their proper role and in turn draw the cosmos back to its *tropos*, the path to transfiguration. Humanity, functioning properly as priests, can detect the *logoi* of created reality and, through cooperation with the divine, correct the corrupted *tropos* of the cosmos.[26]

20. See Louth, "Between Creation and Transfiguration," 215–216; Alexander Schmemann, *For the Life of the World: Sacraments and Orthodoxy* (Crestwood, NY: St Vladimir's Seminary Press, 1973), 102.
21. Meyendorff, *Christ in Eastern Christian Thought*, 105; Bordeianu, "Maximus and Ecology," 110–111. For a critique of this viewpoint, see David Clough, *On Animals* (New York: Bloomsbury, 2014), 68–70.
22. Bordeianu, "Maximus and Ecology," 117. Also Meyendorff, *Christ in Eastern Christian Thought*, 105.
23. Maximus, *Ambigua*, 8.
24. Bordeianu, "Maximus and Ecology," 109.
25. Lossky, *The Mystical Theology of the Eastern Church*, 110.

Contemporary Orthodox Thought

Contemporary Orthodox theologians have appropriated Maximus as a powerful Christian response to improper attitudes concerning the nonhuman creation.[27] While there are definite nuances among these voices, there are also consistent similarities. The most prominent similarity is the cosmic dimension of transfiguration. Another similarity, while less prominent, is a theocentrically-couched anthropocentrism in which this cosmic transfiguration is for the sake of the divine-human drama.

Transfiguration

To understand the import of transfiguration for Orthodox theology, it is imperative to place this term in the larger theological context of creation, fall, and redemption. [28] The doctrine of creation in Orthodox theology begins with the fundamental tension between divine transcendence and immanence.[29] Orthodox theologians express this tension with the distinction between the divine essence and divine energies.[30] As Lossky notes, this distinction is neither a division within God nor a distinction between God and not-God:

> We . . . recognize in God an ineffable distinction, other than that between His essence and His persons, according to which He is, under different aspects, both totally inaccessible and at the same accessible. This distinction is that between the essence of God, or His nature, properly co-called, which is inaccessible, unknowable and incommunicable; and the energies or divine operations, forces proper to and inseparable from

26. Bordeianu, "Maximus and Ecology," 109.
27. See ibid., 103–126.
28. See John Chryssavgis, "The Earth as Sacrament: Insights from Orthodox Christian Theology and Spirituality," in *The Orthodox Handbook of Religion and Ecology*, ed. Roger S. Gottlieb (New York: Oxford University Press, 2006), 98–99.
29. Theokritoff, "Creator and Creation," 64.
30. See Lossky, *The Mystical Theology of the Eastern Church*, chapter 4.

God's essence, in which He goes forth from Himself, manifests, communicates, and gives Himself.[31]

It is within this distinction that God can create (an act of absolute freedom deriving from the divine nature enacted through the divine energies) and remain unchanged (in the divine nature).

This distinction also permits an aporetic tension between divine immanence and transcendence vis-à-vis the creation. On the one hand, the creation is the product of the divine energies carrying out the divine will without being ontologically the same as those *uncreated* energies. Thus, the cosmos is other than God, a point consistent with the Orthodox emphasis on *creatio ex nihilo*.[32] Though, Kallistos Ware qualifies this view: "Rather than say that [God] created the universe out of nothing, we should say that he created it out of his own self, which is love."[33] At any rate, as Meyendorff notes, God's transcendence will remain even in the oneness of "the ultimate eschatological union."[34] Cosmic transfiguration and union with the divine does not end the particularity of the cosmos as an "other" before God.

On the other hand, the divine *logoi*—which according to Lossky exist in the divine energies but derive from the *Logos*, the second hypostases of the Trinity—are in some sense present in the created order itself.[35] Hence, "every created thing has its point of contact with the Godhead; and this point of contact is its idea, the reason or *logos* which is at the time the end toward which it tends."[36] Or, as Kallistos

31. Ibid., 70.
32. See Lossky, *Mystical Theology*, chapter five.
33. Kallistos Ware, *The Orthodox Way*, revised edition (Crestwood: St. Vladimir's Seminary Press, 1995), 44. See also Chryssavgis, "The Earth as Sacrament," 101–104.
34. Meyendorff, "Creation in the History of Orthodox Theology," 30.
35. See Meyendorff, "Creation in the History of Orthodox Theology," 28–29; Theokritoff, *Living in God's Creation*, 54.
36. Lossky, *The Mystical Theology of the Eastern Church*, 98. See also, Meyendorff, *Christ in Eastern Christian Thought*, 102.

Ware states, "The whole universe is a cosmic Burning Bush, filled with the divine Fire yet not consumed."[37] In Ware's panentheistic view, "God is *in* all things as well as *above and beyond* all things."[38] Likewise, within the tension of transcendence and immanence, Chryssavgis can claim that the Holy Spirit "safeguards the intrinsically sacred character of creation" without lapsing into pantheism.[39]

The pervasive tension of divine transcendence and immanence in Orthodox cosmology establishes two key theological points. First, with regard to transcendence, the creation was not created complete. The very real distance between God and the world suggests that the latter was created *in via* toward its divinely intended telos. Thus, even before the fall, there was a "not yet" of the created order, a distance between what it is and what God ultimately intends it to be. Says Lossky, "The primitive beatitude was not a state of deification, but a condition of order, a perfection of the creature which was ordained and tending towards its end."[40]

Second, with regard to immanence, the sharp distinction between nature and grace dissolves.[41] Within this dissolution, the entire cosmos, as an expression of the divine *logoi*, becomes a sacrament.[42] It is the revelatory means of communion with the divine.[43] The sacramental dimension of the entire nonhuman creation is not exhausted in history—as was the case with Aquinas. Rather, the cosmos will be the final sacrament, necessary for the divine-human drama even in eternity.[44] Thus there is an irrevocably cosmic dimension to human existence, now and always.[45]

37. Ware, *The Orthodox Way*, 118.
38. Ibid., 46.
39. Chryssavgis, "The Earth as Sacrament," 97.
40. Lossky, *The Mystical Theology of the Eastern Church*, 99.
41. Meyendorff, *Christ*, 87; Lossky, *The Mystical Theology of the Eastern Church*, 101.
42. Schmemann, *For the Life of the World*, 14–15.
43. Ware, *The Orthodox Way*, 42; Schmemann, *For the Life of the World*, 44–45.

Within the order of the good and sacramental cosmos, humanity has an essentially unique role. Following Maximus, Orthodox theologians consistently use the images of priest and microcosm to describe this role.[46] On this point, Alexander Schmemann is worth quoting at length:

> The only *natural* (and not "supernatural") reaction of man, to whom God gave this blessed and sanctified world, is to bless God in return, to thank Him, to *see* the world as God sees and—in this act of gratitude and adoration—to know, name and possess the world. All rational, spiritual and other qualities of man, distinguishing him from other creatures, have their focus and ultimate fulfillment in this capacity to know, so to speak, the meaning of the thirst and hunger that constitutes his life. "*Homo sapiens*," "*homo faber*" . . . yes, but, first of all, "*homo adorans*." The first, the basic definition of man is that he is *the priest*. He stands in the center of the world and unifies it in his act of blessing God, of both receiving the world from God and offering it to God—and by filling the world with this eucharist, he transforms his life, the one that he receives from the world, into life in God, into communion with Him. The world was created as the "matter," the material of one all-embracing eucharist, and man was created as the priest of this cosmic sacrament.[47]

The nonhuman cosmos is a sacramental gift from God to humanity. Humans act as priests of the sacramental cosmos by offering it back to God as a return gift in worship.[48] In this act of offering, the cosmos becomes communion between God and humanity.[49] As the object of gift exchange that facilitates communion, the nonhuman cosmos itself is drawn into the divine life.[50]

44. Andrew Louth, "Eastern Orthodox Eschatology," in *The Orthodox Handbook of Eschatology*, Jerry L. Walls, editor (New York: Oxford University Press, 2008), 212–213.
45. Lossky, *Mystical Theology*, 110.
46. This position is the central subject of John Zizioulas's lectures at King's College. These lectures appeared later in *King's Theological Review*. On this point, see also Radu Bordeianu, "Priesthood Natural, Universal, and Ordained: Dumitru Staniloae's Communion Ecclesiology," *Pro Ecclesia* 19, no. 4 (2010), 409.
47. Schmemann, *For the Life of the World*, 15.
48. Zizioulas, "Preserving God's Creation," Part I, 1–5; Ware, *The Orthodox Way*, 49–50.
49. Ware, *The Orthodox Way*, 54.

This priestly role of humanity has been corrupted by human sin, which bears a strong ecological component.[51] In conjunction with this corruption, the movement along the path (*tropos*) to the transfiguration of the cosmos, dependant as it is in some sense on the role of humanity, is derailed.[52] The cosmos is fallen. As such, "We cannot simply look at the actual states of the world and read off the Creator's original and ultimate will for creation."[53] Indeed, Theokritoff notes, "It is precisely for this reason that the Fathers see a fall, a dislocation in God's original plan, as affecting the whole created order."[54] In the words of Meyendorff, "The fall of man, who had been placed by God at the center of creation and called to reunify it, was a cosmic catastrophe that only the incarnation of the Word could repair."[55]

Thus, the transfiguration of the cosmos is thwarted in the fall and reestablished in the incarnation, which constitutes the historical realization of its destiny: union with the divine.[56] This realization enables humanity to return to the position of priest and thereby redirect the cosmos toward the divine.[57] This redirection of the cosmos requires a synergistic effort between God and humanity.[58] In this act of cooperation, which is essentially a gift exchange between the divine and the human, there is both a remembrance of the protological past and a prolepsis of the inaugurated future.[59]

---

50. Dumitru Staniloae, *The Experience of God: Orthodox Dogmatic Theology*, trans. and eds. Ioan Ionita and Robert Barringer (Brookline, MA: Hold Cross Orthodox Press, 2000), 2:21–22; Ware, *The Orthodox Way*, 53–55; Lossky, *Mystical Theology*, 111.
51. Meyendorff, *Christ*, 87, 106–108; Schmemann, *For the Life of the World*, 16–18, 61; Staniloae, *Creation and Deification*, 65, 185–187; Ware, *The Orthodox Way*, 59–63.
52. See Deane-Drummond, *Eco-Theology*, 61.
53. Theokritoff, *Living in God's Creation*, 58.
54. Ibid.
55. Meyendorff, *Christ*, 108.
56. Louth, "Between Creation and Transfiguration," 216.
57. Meyendorff, *Christ*, 88–89; Staniloae, *Creation and Deification*, 3, 65.
58. Chryssavgis, "The Earth as Sacrament," 99; Schmemann, *For the Life of the World*, 23.

The heart of eschatological transfiguration lies at the intersection of creation and the fall. The entire cosmos is the necessary sacrament for the divine-human drama. This role constitutes its destiny.[60] Without the cosmos, humans cannot commune with God. Humans are not only irrevocably embodied; we are irrevocably encosmosed.[61] Thus, regarding the eschatological community, contemporary Orthodox theologians consistently maintain that the entire cosmos will be transfigured in the eschatological consummation.[62] (Though, Meyendorff states that deification is "proper to man only."[63] Lossky rejects this claim.[64])

According to Lossky, the creation "can have no other end than deification."[65] Ware writes, "In the 'new earth' of the Age to come there is surely a place not only for man but for the animals: in and through man, they too will share in immortality, and so will rocks, trees and plants, fire and water."[66] The participation of the sacramental nonhuman cosmos in eternity requires its transfiguration, in which it will become that which God always intended it to be. The task of humanity is to "transform the whole earth into paradise."[67] Thus, Lossky claims, "In his way to union with God, man in no way leaves creatures aside, but gathers together in his love the whole cosmos disordered by sin, that it may at last be transfigured by grace."[68]

---

59. See Theokritoff, "Creator and Creation," 70; Chryssavgis, "The Earth as Sacrament," 100; Louth, "Eastern Orthodox Eschatology," 237.

60. Schmemann, For the Life of the World, 120.

61. This term is my own. However, see John Zizioulas "Ecological Asceticism: A Cultural Revolution," Sourozh 67 (1997), 24.

62. Ware, The Orthodox Way, 136–137; Louth, "Eastern Orthodox Eschatology," 237–238.

63. Meyendorff, Christ, 97.

64. Lossky, Mystical Theology, 99–101.

65. Ibid., 101.

66. Ware, The Orthodox Way, 137.

67. Lossky, Mystical Theology, 109.

68. Ibid., 111.

Such a transformation of the cosmos distinguishes anthropocentric transfiguration from its conservational variants. Zizioulas in fact critiques Augustine on this very point, claiming that under his influence "the human being was singled out from nature as being not only a higher kind of being but in fact the sole being that mattered eternally."[69] This rejection of the eternal significance of the cosmos, in Zizioulas's view, led to Descartes's sharp distinction between the thinking subject and the non-thinking machine.[70] Based on such claims, Zizioulas maintains that Lynn White's accusation against Christianity is accurate in the case of Western theology.[71] At any rate, it is evident that, on account of an affirmation of the transfiguration of the cosmos, Orthodox theologians differ from advocates of anthropocentric conservation.

The disparity between the cosmos as it is now and as it will be in eternity leads many Orthodox writers to critique a purely conservationist framework. Schmemann denounces a blithe acceptance of death.[72] Staniloae maintains that humanity can improve the static laws of nature.[73] Of particular import is Radu Bordeianu's critique of the biocentrism of both Deep Ecology and Thomas Berry.[74] In Bordeianu's view, Maximus would reject the cosmic-centered position of Berry:

> Biocentrism and geocentrism cannot be the solutions to the ecological crisis; on the contrary, they are precisely the cause, or at least part of the cause of today's environmental destruction, since Adam looked for stability in creation and thus regarded it as the purpose of his movement, when in fact only God can offer stability and purpose.[75]

69. Zizioulas, "Preserving God's Creation," Part I, 3.
70. Ibid., 3–4.
71. See Zizioulas "Ecological Asceticism," 22.
72. Schmemann, For the Life of the World, 97–101.
73. Staniloae, Creation and Deification, 45–52, 65.
74. Bordeianu, "Maximus and Ecology," 106–107, 114–115.
75. Ibid., 115. See also Theokritoff, Living in God's Creation, 65–66.

In defense of Berry, his view is developed within a theocentric cosmology, as is Thomas Aquinas's. Appeals to theocentrism in the face of anthropocentrism remain a categorical error, in my view.

Without specifically naming Berry or any other potential representatives of cosmocentric conservation, Zizioulas critiques the foundations of cosmocentric conservation. He even goes so far as to equate its manner of recovering the sacredness of the cosmos with paganism:

> The pagan regards the world as sacred because it is permeated by divine presence; he therefore respects it (to the point of worshipping it explicitly or implicitly) and does not do damage to it. But equally, he never worries about its fate; he believes in its eternity. He is also unaware of any need for transformation of nature or transcendence of its limitations: the world is good as it stands and possesses in its nature all that is necessary for its survival.[76]

Granted, Zizioulas's claim that the pagan does not worry about the fate of the world because it has no beginning or end could not be farther from Berry's work. That point aside, every other emphasis in the quote seems in complete disagreement with Berry's environmental theology. Berry does emphasize divine immanence in the cosmos. He does accept the nonhuman world is good as it is. He would also disavow a functional anthropocentrism that voids meaning of the nonhuman creation in the absence of humanity. In short, Zizioulas offers what amounts to a rejection of Berry's position.

Anthropocentrism

If the transfigurative dimension of Orthodox thought is clear, the anthropocentric dimension is more complicated. On the one hand,

---

76. Zizioulas, "Preserving God's Creation: Three Lectures on Theology and Ecology," *King's Theological Review* 12 (1989), Part III, 5.

Orthodox writers are consistent in affirming a functional anthropocentrism in which humanity performs a central role—that of microcosm and priest—in the transfiguration of the cosmos.[77] Thus Zizioulas states, "The solution of the problem [of the survival of the cosmos] lies in the creation of Man."[78] On the other hand, they maintain that any form of anthropocentrism divorced from a theocentric anthropology is untenable.[79]

Here, however, my question regards specifically whether or not the nonhuman cosmos, including particular nonhuman animals, exists primarily (or exclusively) for the sake of humanity in relation to God and as such bears only indirect moral standing. With regard to Orthodox theology the question is not whether or not the cosmos is included in the eschatological community. It is. The question is *why* it is included. More poignantly: does the nonhuman cosmos exist, and will it be included in the eschatological community, only to facilitate the gift exchange between God and humans?

Orthodox theologians provide a gamut of answers to this question. Furthermore, at times the answers seem ambiguous. According to Lossky, the world was "created that it might be deified."[80] Lossky furthermore posits a sacramental view of the cosmos in which "revelation for theology remains essentially geocentric." However, such revelation is "addressed to men."[81] It thus appears that the deification of the cosmos is connected to the geocentric nature of revelation—even in the eschaton—which is in turn for humanity in relation to God.

---

77. Meyendorff, *Christ*, 105–106.
78. Zizioulas, "Preserving God's Creation," Part III, 1. Also, Louth, "Between Creation and Transfiguration," 214.
79. On this point, see Zizioulas's critique of Augustinian anthropocentrism. Zizioulas, "Preserving God's Creation," Part I, 3. Also Theokritoff, "Creator and Creation," 71–73.
80. Lossky, *Mystical Theology*, 101.
81. Ibid., 105.

From a liturgical perspective, Schmemann states that the earth is a gift to humanity for communion with God: "In the Bible the food that man eats, the world of which he must partake in order to live, is given to him by God, and it is given as *communion with God*."[82] Humanity's (or more accurately "man's"[83]) role as priest is to "know, name and possess the world." In doing so the human creature is "receiving the world from God and offering it to God."[84] Schmemann's words later in the same work are revealing. The cosmos is "an essential means both of knowledge of God and communion with [God], and to be so is its true nature and its ultimate destiny."[85] Thus, the inclusion of the nonhuman creation in the eschatological community is anthropocentric inasmuch as "its true nature and its ultimate destiny" are exhausted by being the necessary sacrament that facilitates the divine-human drama.

Zizioulas does not deny the superiority of human beings, only that such superiority rests in the quality of rationality. Rather, it rests in humanity's tending toward that which is beyond the creation that is "given": communion with God, which entails "freedom."[86] Zizioulas rejects an anthropocentrism in which humans, as individuals, engage in utility of the cosmos for the sake of "self-satisfaction or pleasure."[87] However, he affirms a doxological anthropocentrism in which the human encounters the cosmos and—as a person within it—offers it back to God. In this approach, "man would still use creation as a source from which he would draw the basic elements necessary for his creation as a source of life, such as food, clothing, building of houses, etc. But to all this he would give a dimension which

---

82. Schmemann, *For the Life of the World*, 14.
83. For Schmemann's seemingly androcentric view of natural priesthood, see ibid., 85.
84. Ibid., 14–15.
85. Ibid., 120.
86. Zizioulas, "Preserving God's Creation," Part I, 2; Part III, 2–3.
87. Ibid., Part III, 4; "Ecological Asceticism," 22.

we could call *personal*."[88] In Zizioulas, use becomes reverential or liturgical, drawing creation into the communion between humanity and God.[89] In this sense, humanity is not the end of the nonhuman creation—which was also true of Aquinas's theology. Rather, in the priesthood of humanity the cosmos finds its teleological aim: a means of communion. "A human is the priest of creation as he or she freely turns it into a vehicle of communion with God and fellow human beings."[90] Note that communion with the creation itself is not part of this equation. Zizioulas states that when we receive back what we have offered to God (e.g. in the formal celebration of the Eucharist), "we consume them no longer as death but as life."[91]

Meyendorff's anthropocentrism is at times obvious. He writes, "The ultimate aim of the divine plan is . . . *man's* deification."[92] On the other hand, at times his affirmations are ambiguous. Citing Maximus, he claims, "All creatures are destined for communion with" God.[93] Though again, citing Maximus he writes that only "in the case man" does God grant "an eternal existence."[94] This ambiguity notwithstanding, the question is whether or not "all creatures are destined for communion" with God for their own sake. Or, do they simply facilitate a sacramental role for the divine-human drama?

Meyendorff claims that Orthodox theology finds common ground in a "theocentric anthropology" and an "anthropocentric cosmology."[95] The former claim denotes that, even as *imago Dei* and whatever attributes that implies, humanity is only truly human in relation to God, and ultimately in deification.[96] For Meyendorff, "the

---

88. Zizioulas, "Preserving God's Creation," Part III, 4.
89. Zizioulas "Ecological Asceticism," 23.
90. Ibid.
91. Zizioulas, "Preserving God's Creation," Part III, 5.
92. Meyendorff, *Christ*, 109; emphasis mine.
93. Meyendorff, "Creation in the History of Orthodox Theology," 29.
94. Meyendorff, *Christ*, 104.
95. Meyendorff, "Creation in the History of Orthodox Theology," 34–37.

'theocentricity' of man makes it inevitable that the whole of creation be considered as anthropocentric."[97] Meyendorff continues:

> Man—and man alone—if liberated by baptism from his fallen state of dependence upon nature, possesses in himself a restored image of God. This changes his entire relationship with created nature. The ancient Orthodox liturgical tradition is very rich in various sacramental acts through which nature is "sanctified." However, all these acts affirm the lordship and responsibility of man, exercised *on behalf of* the Creator. The eucharistic bread and wine become the body and blood of Christ because they are *human* food. Baptismal water—or water sanctified on other occasions—is holy because it serves as means of cleansing and drinking. Oil is blessed as an instrument of healing. Examples here can be multiplied. They all point to the restoration, in the Church of God, of the original, paradisiac plan of relationships between God and creation, with man serving as mediator, as servant and as friend of God.[98]

Thus, anthropocentrism does not mean that human beings are all that matter in creation. In fact, Meyendorff's central point is that it as human *creatures*, as material subjects, that humans matter (as opposed to as the impersonal notion of human nature). In other words, value is not, for Meyendorff, relegated to humanity's incorporeal dimensions.

Meyendorff's anthropocentrism is first and foremost functional. It regards humanity's role in the cosmos.[99] And yet this point entails a position in which, in a manner ironically similar to Aquinas's position, the nonhuman creation matters to God *through human beings*. Humans sanctify the nonhuman creation and thereby mediate the proper relation between it and God by *using it* properly.[100] In this vein, Meyendorff detects a "double movement" of salvation. The first is God's movement to humanity through the world. The second is

96. Ibid., 35.
97. Ibid., 36.
98. Ibid.
99. Meyendorff, *Christ*, 104–105.
100. Ibid., 109.

humanity's movement to God in the world. Meyendorff goes as far as to claim that a "positive" achievement of "the modern scientific and technological revolution" is that it entails "the reaffirmation, more explicit than ever, of man's rule over creation."[101]

Even more so—or at least explicitly more so—than the above authors, the position of Dumitru Staniloae, the Romanian theologian persecuted under a Communist regime, evinces anthropocentrism. On this point, Staniloae is unapologetic: "The world as nature is created for the sake of human subjects and has an anthropocentric character."[102] In his view, nature is "an object or . . . succession of objects." Furthermore, "God creates this ensemble of objects . . . *for the sake of a dialogue with humans. Otherwise, their creation would have no point.*"[103] Elsewhere, Staniloae makes the same claim regarding nonhuman animals: if the rationality evident in these creatures "did not have as its purpose the service of man, it, too, would be without meaning."[104]

Still, Staniloae is clear that the nonhuman cosmos participates in deification: "Nature as a whole is destined for the glory in which men will share in the kingdom of heaven."[105] Likewise, humanity experiences deification through the cosmos.[106] Says Bordeianu, "Staniloae refers to the sacramentality of creation in the sense of visible sign and instrument through which grace is communicated."[107] This sacramental role of the nonhuman creation will continue in the eschaton; and, it is for this reason that it is included.[108] The nature of nonhuman participation in the

101. Meyendorff, "Creation in the History of Orthodox Theology," 36.
102. Staniloae, *Creation and Deification*, 20.
103. Ibid., 14; emphasis added.
104. Ibid., 28.
105. Ibid., 3, 18–19, 25, 58–59.
106. See Bordeianu, "Priesthood," 410.
107. Ibid., 409.
108. Ibid.

eschatological community is indirect. It always remains for the sake of divine-human drama.[109] Staniloae believes this view is rooted in Maximus.[110] Perhaps ironically, Staniloae and Aquinas (and Maximus?) only disagree about the eschatological community with regard to degree. That is, the main difference is *how much* of the nonhuman creation is included in the eschaton. Concerning the *why* of its inclusion, they are nearly identical: for the divine-human rapport.

For Staniloae, the nonhuman cosmos "finds it meaning in" humanity.[111] It is an object of gift-exchange that facilitates love between God and humanity and among humans.[112] In a manner that is strikingly similar to Aquinas, Staniloae writes, "The rationality of things has this double purpose: first, to be useful to man in maintaining his biological existence; second, and equally, to foster human spiritual growth through the knowledge of meanings."[113]

Ultimately, for Staniloae, the world is "only a framework," a "field" created so that humanity "might raise the world up to a supreme spiritualization, and *this to the end that human beings might encounter God within a world that had become fully spiritualized through their own union with God.*"[114] In other words, the transfiguration of the cosmos remains anthropocentric in that it is for the sake of the divine-human drama. In short, the world is the necessary and eternal sacrament *for humanity.*[115]

Theokritoff defends both Meyendorff and Staniloae against the charge of anthropocentrism, qualifying their use of the term.[116]

---

109. Staniloae, *Creation and Deification*, 1.
110. Ibid., 20; Bordeianu, "Priesthood," 407–408.
111. Staniloae, *Creation and Deification*, 13.
112. Ibid., 21–27, 71; Bordeianu, "Priesthood," 410.
113. Staniloae, *Creation and Deification*, 40.
114. Ibid., 62–63; emphasis added.
115. Ibid., 77–78, 212–213; Bordeianu, "Priesthood," 409.
116. Theokritoff, "Creator and Creation," 70–71.

Ultimately, she suggests that the Orthodox position is thus: "If the world exists 'for humanity', it is no less true that humanity exists for the sake of the universe."[117] Indeed, "Man the microcosm—made of the same stuff as the mosquito—receives the divine inbreathing *for the sake of the world*."[118] These claims are significant. However, they are difficult to maintain in light of Staniloae's comment: "Nature itself proves itself to have been made for the sake of consciousness, not consciousness for the sake of nature."[119] David Clough's claim is here germane: "If God's purpose in creating the universe was to establish a relationship with human beings and all other-than-human parts of creation are intended by God to prepare and provide for the human, then everything else is scenery."[120]

At any rate, my point is not to classify all Orthodox theology. Indeed, the appreciation for the aporetic mystery of the divine-world drama within Orthodox thought resists a sharp categorization.[121] I only maintain that, based on my explorations, *some* Orthodox theologians evince a concretized form of anthropocentric transfiguration.

A Nonhuman Ethics of Anthropocentric Transfiguration

What does an eco-theological ethics of anthropocentric transfiguration look like in practice? Answering this question is difficult, as Deane-Drummond notes that Orthodox theologians

117. Ibid., 73.
118. Theokritoff, *Living in God's Creation*, 67.
119. Staniloae, *Creation and Deification*, 6; see also 20.
120. Clough, *On Animals*, 3.
121. For a thoroughly non-anthropocentric Orthodox view, see Issa J. Khalil, "The Orthodox Fast and the Philosophy of Vegetarianism," *Greek Orthodox Theological Review* 35, 3 (1990), 237–259.

resist the construction of a system of ethics.[122] Still, a humble effort must be made here.

First and foremost, such an ethics would be grounded in the notion that one ought to treat the sacramental cosmos in a manner akin to how one treats the elements of the Eucharist itself. In this vein, Ware states that humanity's "vocation is not to dominate and exploit nature, but to transfigure and hallow it."[123] Chryssavgis suggests living by a "sacramental principle, which ultimately demands from us the recognition that nothing in this life is profane or unsacred."[124] For Zizioulas, any engagement of the nonhuman creation that violates its sacramentality constitutes a sin. Such actions are sins because they constitute "disrespect towards a divine gift" and the obstruction of human fulfillment.[125] To treat the world as a sacrament is to celebrate the inbreaking of the eschaton in the resurrection of Christ, a point that Chryssavgis sees in liturgical prayers of Orthodoxy.[126] Thus, he states: "There is . . . no greater estrangement from the world than in its use in a manner that fails to restore the correct vision of the world in the light of the resurrection."[127]

But what does this vision entail? It cannot be separated from the notion of creation itself. Louth's words are illuminating here:

> The doctrine of creation . . . means that our created environment is touched by the hand of God, is a place where we can encounter God, and still in some way bears the traces of the paradise of delight that God intended his creation to be. Human sin obscures our perception of this, and encourages an attitude to the created order that ceases to take seriously the fact that it is created, seeing it rather as a resource to be exploited for our own purposes. As we do that we begin to misconstrue the world around us, our attitude becomes destructive, we cease to see

---

122. Deane-Drummond, *Eco-Theology*, 56. See Zizioulas, "Preserving God's Creation," Part I, 1–5.
123. Ware, *The Orthodox Way*, 54.
124. Chryssavgis, "The Earth as Sacrament," 92–93.
125. Zizioulas, "Ecological Asceticism," 24.
126. Chryssavgis, "The Earth as Sacrament," 108–110.
127. Ibid., 110.

the world as a gift, and instead begin to compete with one another in fashioning our own worlds, which encroach on one another, so that it becomes a matter of contention whether this is mine or yours, as we forget that it is God's—and so both mine and yours, as a gift to share, or neither mine nor yours, as a possession to grasp and hold.[128]

Louth's comment maintains the reverential respect for the cosmos. Yet, at the same time it highlights another dimension of this paradigm: the manner in which we hallow that cosmos. The world is *not* a resource for the human community to abuse for self-gratification. However, the world *is* a gift to the human community.

In Zizioulas's estimation, reverencing the cosmos implies a world-affirming or ecological asceticism.[129]

An "ecological asceticism" . . . always begins with deep respect for the material creation, including the human body, and builds upon the view that we are not masters and possessors of this creation, but are called to turn it into a vehicle of communion, always taking into account and respecting its possibilities as well as its limitations.[130]

Such asceticism demands that humans—and more accurately, contemporary humans influenced by modernity's mechanistic understanding of nature—reevaluate our "concept of quality of life."[131] In short, it requires a simple living in which we do not take more than we need. And what we do take, we must take reverentially. Thus Chryssavgis states that asceticism "is a communal attitude that leads to the respectful use of material goods."[132]

In this sense, the ethical consequence of anthropocentric transfiguration is a reverential use of the material cosmos. All matter becomes liturgical in the hands of human priests, who engage it

128. Louth, "Between Creation and Transfiguration," 213.
129. Zizioulas, "Preserving God's Creation," Part I, 5.
130. Zizioulas, "Ecological Asceticism," 24.
131. Ibid., 24.
132. Chryssavgis, "The Earth as Sacrament," 110.

humbly and always with ultimate reference to God. Such engagement entails a use of creation in which it is transformed into communion with God and within the human community.[133]

Anthropocentric Transfiguration and Individual Nonhuman Animals

Where do individual nonhuman animals fit into this ethics? Schmemann claims that the sacramentality of the cosmos recovers a reverence for eating. Yet food is still food.[134] Do animals fall into this category of that which humans both reverence and eat? Chryssavgis suggests that humanity's proper relation to the environment is evident in Adam's naming of the animals, which entails "a loving and lasting personal relationship."[135] Yet this notion implies that the sacramental eating of plants is not at odds with such a relationship.

Zizioulas notes how hagiographies depict compassion of saints to animals, even weeping over their death. He continues, "Even today on Mount Athos one can encounter monks who never kill serpents, but co-exist peacefully with them—something that would make even the best Christians among us shiver and tremble."[136] Likewise, Lossky quotes Isaac the Syrian, who maintains that the "merciful heart" weeps over the suffering of all creatures, as the Eastern Orthodox view of the cosmos.[137]

There is, then, the possibility of a non-violent response to nonhuman animals as a reverent appreciation of their goodness. Indeed, Issa Khalil notes that the Orthodox faithful are vegan for more than half the year on account of liturgical fasts. Furthermore,

---

133. Staniloae, *Creation and Deification*, 2–3, 44, 48–49, 82; Zizioulas, "Ecological Asceticism," 23.
134. Schmemann, *For the Life of the World*, 15–16.
135. Chryssavgis, "The Earth as Sacrament," 105.
136. Zizioulas, "Preserving God's Creation," Part I, 5.
137. Lossky, *Mystical Theology*, 110–111.

Orthodox monks are vegetarian for most of the year.[138] Khalil notes that the Orthodox foundation for this fast is not primarily the sentience of the animals; rather, it is self-control. However, he also notes a "deeper theological meaning of the fast." It is "an act of repentance towards the animals, as well as an act of reconciliation, prefiguring life in paradise where the lamb shall lie with the wolf and not be hurt, and especially lie with the worst predator of all, and not be eaten."[139] I am not convinced Orthodox theologians like Meyendorff and Staniloae would accept this claim.

These notions notwithstanding, for many Orthodox theologians individual nonhuman animals are subject to reverential use for the sake of the human-divine rapport. And such a use does not seem to reject the possibility of killing individual nonhuman creatures. For example, in Staniloae's theological view, the nonhuman animal is part of the sacramental world and thus part of the "succession of objects" that facilitates "the dialogue of the gift" between God and humanity.[140] At the very least, I maintain that an eco-theological ethics of anthropocentric transfiguration more easily tends toward a permissiveness to harming individual animals than its explicitly cosmocentric counterpart, which I explore in subsequent chapters.

Anthropocentric Transfiguration in summation

This exploration through the work of various Orthodox theologians teases out the possibility of a paradigm of eco-theological ethics that I label anthropocentric transfiguration. It would be a misnomer to identity all Orthodox theology with this particular paradigm. Nonetheless, the theological foundations of anthropocentric

138. Khalil, "The Orthodox Fast," 257.
139. Ibid., 259.
140. Staniloae, *Creation and Deification*, 20, 22.

transfiguration are most evident in concrete form in the work of certain theologians within the Orthodox tradition.

These foundations include the following: first, an affirmation of the sacredness or sacramentality of the entire cosmos, which in turn renders the nonhuman creation necessary for temporal and ultimate human fulfillment; second, an inclusion of the cosmos in the eschatological community through humanity; third, an emphasis on the purpose of the nonhuman world as existing in order to facilitate the divine-human drama through a gift-exchange.

The picture arising from these foundations is one in which humans use the creation reverentially, offering it back to God in worship. While the created order is not merely a machine for human pleasure, neither does it have a purpose or integrity separate from its benefit to humanity. Ultimately, the cosmos is the eternally necessary sacrament for humanity in relation to God. Its inclusion in the eschatological community is ultimately for that relationship.

Part I Conclusion

I have considered three of the four paradigms of my proposed taxonomy of nonhuman theological ethics. My exploration provides concrete examples of these paradigms within Christianity. Among the most important differences between the paradigms are the role and status of the human being (anthropology), the role and status of the nonhuman creation (cosmology), and the scope of the eschatological community (eschatology). At this intersection, one senses the real contrast among nonhuman theological ethics.

Table IC.1 summarizes this contrast:

Table IC.1			
Tensions of the Three Paradigms			
	Anthropocentric Conservation	Cosmocentric Conservation	Anthropocentric Transfiguration
Anthropology: Central Status/ Role of Human Beings	Essentially unique moral dignity; Subject of ultimate divine concern	Enhanced dignity; Member of creation community	Essentially unique moral dignity; Microcosm, co-creator, and priest
Cosmology: Central Status/ Role of the Nonhuman Creation	Network of good and ordered resources/gifts for human well-being	Good and ordered interconnected community of intrinsic value	Necessary and ultimate sacrament for divine-human drama
Scope of the Eschatological Community	God and humanity; Angels and elements/matter	Eschatology de-emphasized in favor of current order of world and its goodness	Cosmos (human and nonhuman)
The Primary Unity of Moral Consideration (General or Particular)	Particular humans; General nonhumans	General	Particular humans; General nonhumans
Ethical Human Engagement of the Nonhuman Creation	Proper use *in via* toward uniquely human *telos*	Balance of a "letting be" and a reverential "living-with"	Reverential use as sacramental gift that facilitates communion with others and God
Some Representatives	Augustine; Thomas Aquinas; Roman Catholic Magisterium	Thomas Berry; Matthew Fox; Rosemary Radford Ruether	John Meyendorff; Dumitru Staniloae

The differences between these paradigms underline the possibility for a fourth. Note the fundamental categories. On the one hand, a paradigm can be either anthropocentric—understood as claiming only humans have intrinsic value before God—or cosmocentric—understood as the entire cosmos including both human and nonhuman having intrinsic value before God. On the other hand, a paradigm can be either conservational—understood as the preservation of the current good and natural order—or transfigurative—understood as the movement of a fallen and/or incomplete creation toward its eschatological telos. Thus a fourth paradigm naturally forms, as is evident in table IC.2:[1]

Table IC.2			
Space for another Paradigm			
		Why does creation have value/dignity?	
		Utility to human beings	*Intrinsic value*
What is the responsibility of human beings toward creation?	*Preserve the goodness and order of the unfallen cosmos.*	Anthropocentric conservation	Cosmocentric conservation
What is the responsibility of human beings toward creation?	*Guide the fallen and/or eschatologically incomplete cosmos toward its telos.*	Anthropocentric transfiguration	???

I naturally label this fourth paradigm as cosmocentric transfiguration. Although underdeveloped, in my view this paradigm represents a promising path forward as a theologically grounded Christian ethics.

1. I am grateful to Brenda Colijn for drawing up this chart.

Because cosmocentric transfiguration is underdeveloped, my next task is to explore two concrete examples of the theological foundations for it in depth. First, I engage the thought of the Lutheran theologian of hope, Jürgen Moltmann. Second, I examine the work of the premier animal theologian, Andrew Linzey. Comparing and contrasting these two Christian thinkers and placing them in dialogue with the three paradigms developed in this chapter provides an opportunity to point toward the construction of a developed nonhuman theological ethics of cosmocentric transfiguration.

Cosmocentric Transfiguration in the Theologies of Jürgen Moltmann and Andrew Linzey

Part II Introduction

Part II will develop basic parameters of cosmocentric transfiguration by critically engaging and comparing the work of Jürgen Moltmann and Andrew Linzey. While Moltmann and Linzey are contemporaries, there is very little engagement between them. To my knowledge Moltmann never engages Linzey's work. Linzey does engage Moltmann, but very rarely and never in any great detail.

This lack of engagement is lamentable as Moltmann and Linzey complement one another well. Moltmann thrives in theological ingenuity but is rather non-concrete (and inconsistent) in his ethics. Linzey's ethics are, more often than not, specific and definite. However, he tends to be less developed in his theological explorations than Moltmann. Collectively, they provide a solid theological and ethical vision of cosmocentric transfiguration.

A brief overview of each thinker here will introduce part II.

Jürgen Moltmann

"If I have theological virtue at all, then it is one that has never hitherto been recognized as such: curiosity."[1] This sentence provides

---

1. Jürgen Moltmann, *The Coming of God: Christian Eschatology*, trans. Margaret Kohl (Minneapolis, MN: Fortress Press, 1996), xiv.

an insight into Jürgen Moltmann's (b. 1926) methodology, which is unapologetically subjective, personal, dialogical, and experimental.[2] Even so, Moltmann's influence on the landscape of theology in the twentieth century and today can hardly be overstated. His seminal work, *Theology of Hope*, launched him into international recognition, and his following works have not disappointed in their ingenuity.

Moltmann's first three works—*Theology of Hope* (1965),[3] *The Crucified God* (1973), and *The Church in the Power of the Holy Spirit* (1975)—each "look at theology as a whole from one particular standpoint."[4] In his later six volume set, he seeks to make contributions to theological themes pertinent to systematic theology without constructing a concrete system.

> I now viewed *my "whole" as a part* belonging to a wider community, and as my contribution to theology as a whole. I know and accept the limits of my own existence and my context. I do not claim to say everything.[5]

This set of contributions includes, in order of publication, *Trinity and the Kingdom* (1980), *God in Creation* (1985), *The Way of Jesus Christ* (1989), *The Spirit of Life* (1991), *The Coming of God* (1995), and *Experiences in Theology* (2000). Moltmann has of course written many other works, the most recent of which, *Ethics of Hope* (2010), he refers to as "the close of my contributions to theological discussions."[6]

Moltmann's influences are vast and diverse.[7] He is quite impacted by Jewish thought, both in thinkers like Ernst Bloch, Franz

---

2. See Jürgen Moltmann, *Experiences in Theology: Ways and Forms of Christian Theology*, trans. Margaret Kohl (Minneapolis, MN: Fortress Press, 2000).

3. These parenthetical dates reflect the year of the original German publication.

4. Jürgen Moltmann, *The Trinity and the Kingdom: The Doctrine of God*, trans. Margaret Kohl (Minneapolis, MN: Fortress Press, 1993), xi.

5. Moltmann, *Trinity and the Kingdom*, vii.

6. Jürgen Moltmann, *Ethics of Hope* (hereafter *EH*), trans. Margaret Kohl (Minneapolis, MN: Fortress Press, 2012), xi.

7. For more extensive considerations, see Richard Bauckham, *Moltmann: Messianic Theology in the Making* (Basingstoke, UK: Marshall Pickering, 1987).

Rosenzweig, Martin Buber, and Abraham Heschel; and in Kabbalism. His affiliation with Bloch evinces Moltmann's debt to Karl Marx—a debt further evident by his affinity with the Frankfurt School.[8] He was instructed by both Karl Barth and Karl Rahner. His biblical scholarship bears the marks of Gerhard von Rad.[9] His works evince dialogue with contemporary theologians such as Wolfhart Pannenberg and Hans Urs von Balthasar.[10] In later works especially, he is heavily influenced by Eastern Orthodox theology.[11] Finally, it must be said that Moltmann has been influenced by his own life experience, including his stint as a German soldier in World War II.[12] Ultimately, Moltmann's theology is an experiential and thus subjective contribution amidst the great community of theologians and thinkers to whom he acknowledges his indebtedness.

Andrew Linzey

Throughout his career, Linzey acknowledges that his work entails a "continued wrestling" that requires ongoing development.[13] Those who read individual works of his without referring to other installments in his extensive corpus often miss these developments along with nuances of his thought.[14] I do not pretend to engage everything Linzey has written. I do, however, take close account

8. See Jürgen Moltmann, *The Crucified God: The Cross of Christ as the Foundation and Criticism of Christian Theology*, trans. R. A. Wilson (Minneapolis, MN: Fortress Press, 1993), 5. On the Frankfurt School, see Gerald L. Atkinson, "About the Frankfurt School," available online at http://frankfurtschool.us/history.htm.

9. See Geiko Müller-Fahrenholz, *The Kingdom and the Power: The Theology of Jürgen Moltmann*, trans. John Bowden (Minneapolis, MN: Fortress Press, 2001), 47–48.

10. Richard Bauckham, *Moltmann: Messianic Theology in the Making* (Basingstoke, UK: Marshall Pickering, 1987), 93–96.

11. Moltmann's *History and the Triune God* is dedicated to Dumitru Staniloae.

12. For considerations, see Müller-Fahrenholz, *The Kingdom and the Power*, 15–39; Jürgen Moltmann, *A Broad Place: An Autobiography*, trans. Margaret Kohl (Minneapolis, MN: Fortress Press, 2008).

13. See Andrew Linzey, *Christianity and the Rights of Animals* (New York: Crossroad, 1987), 2–6.

of the major works he has authored.[15] These works include *Animal Rights* (1976), *Christianity and the Rights of Animals* (1987), *Animal Theology* (1994), *After Noah* (1997), *Animal Gospel* (1998), *Creatures of the Same God* (2007), and *Why Animal Suffering Matters* (2009).[16]

Linzey has many influences. He acknowledges his debt to the animal welfare movement in general.[17] He is also influenced by particular ethical and theological voices, including Rosalina Godlovitch, whom Linzey suggests may be "the intellectual founder of the modern animal movement"[18]; Karl Barth, whose theology constituted the center of Linzey's dissertation; Albert Schweitzer, whose "reverence for life" Linzey describes as "the most penetrating contribution made to our subject [i.e., animal rights] by a person from within the Christian Tradition"[19]; Dietrich Bonhoeffer, to whom Linzey credits the genesis of his notion of theos-rights[20]; Tom Regan, whose "intellectual grasp" regarding issues surrounding the rights of nonhuman animals, is, for Linzey, "without rival in the movement."[21] Linzey also draws upon central thinkers of the Christian tradition, though mostly from the East.[22]

Linzey currently holds the International Fund for Animal Welfare's Senior Research Fellowship at Mansfield College, Oxford, which is directed specifically toward Christian theology and animal welfare.

---

14. Andrew Linzey, *Creatures of the Same God: Explorations in Animal Theology*, (New York: Lantern Books, 2009), 55–56.

15. On Linzey's "important works," see See Andrew Linzey, "The Divine Worth of Other Creatures: A Response to Reviews of *Animal Theology*," in *Review and Expositor*, 102 (Winter 2005): 124, n. 12.

16. These parenthetical dates represent the original publication dates.

17. Andrew Linzey, *Animal Rights: A Christian Assessment* (London: SCM, 1976), viii.

18. Andrew Linzey, *Why Animal Suffering Matters: Philosophy, Theology, and Practical Ethics* (New York: Oxford University Press, 2009), 158.

19. Linzey, *Animal Rights*, 42.

20. See Andrew Linzey, "C. S. Lewis's Theology of Animals," *Anglican Theological Review* 80/1 (Winter 1998): 60–81.

21. Linzey, *Christianity and the Rights of Animals*, ix.

22. See ibid., 17–18, 32.

His post is the first of its kind. He also is the founder and director of the Oxford Centre for Animal Ethics, "an international and multi-disciplinary center at Oxford dedicated to the ethical enhancement of the status of animals through academic research, teaching, and publication."[23] While mainly an animal theologian/ethicist, Linzey has also published on child rights, human violence, embryonic research, and justice for homosexuals.[24]

23. Linzey, *Creatures of the Same God*, xix
24. Ibid., xiii.

7

Moltmann on God, Creation, and the Fall

I begin my examination of Moltmann with his Trinitarian framework, which provides the contours for his cosmology. The history of the cosmos is also the history of the divine community. The two impact one another. All that happens in the history of the world happens in the history of the triune God. In this chapter, I explore Moltmann's social doctrine of the Trinity and how that doctrine impacts cosmology, including the fall.

The Social Trinity's History with the World

Moltmann begins to develop his thoughts on the Trinity in his earlier works. In *Theology of Hope* and *The Crucified God*, he focuses mainly on the relationship between the Father and the Son and its significance for Christian thought and practice. In *The Church in the Power of the Holy Spirit*, he more clearly brings the pneumatology that was latent in those previous works into the forefront. However, it is with *The Trinity and the Kingdom* that he fully focuses on the doctrine of the Trinity and delineates his social understanding of it.

The Social Trinity

In Moltmann's view, two forms of emphases on divine oneness have dominated Western thought. The first is substantialistic. This view "was given by Greek antiquity, continued to be given in the Middle Ages, and still counts as valid in the present-day definitions of the Roman Catholic Church."[1] The divine persons share in a common substance that underlies them. This substance vouchsafes the divine unity and logically precedes it. Thus, writers in the West tend to begin with the attributes of God (i.e., qualities that belong to the divine substance and are thus shared by all the persons) and only afterwards discuss the Trinitarian persons.

The second form emphasizes God's subjectivity. This view develops in the wake of the metaphysical shift in anthropology beginning with Immanuel Kant.[2] Based on the modern notion of "person" as a sovereign subject, advocates of this position claim that it is no longer appropriate to think of Father, Son, and Spirit as persons. Moltmann identifies his mentor Karl Barth as one of the promulgators of this view.[3] Barth argues that sovereignty belongs to the whole of the divine—to "God"—not individually to its persons.[4]

Moltmann claims that both of these approaches to Trinitarian thought miss the complexity of the biblical view of the divine by surrendering the doctrine to H. Richard Niebuhr's "radical monotheism."[5] Such views are reductionist for Moltmann because

---

1. Jürgen Moltmann, *The Trinity and the Kingdom: The Doctrine of God* (hereafter *TKG*), trans. Margaret Kohl (Minneapolis, MN: Fortress Press, 1993), 10.
2. Ibid., 13–15.
3. Ibid., 63–64.
4. Ibid.

they do not give primacy to God as Trinity and therefore do not do justice to the self–disclosure of God in history.[6] They prioritize abstract considerations of God's nature according to reason (general revelation) over God's acts in history (special revelation).[7] In this critique, Moltmann is similar to Karl Rahner.[8]

In response to these emphases on God's oneness, Moltmann turns to the Eastern Fathers who focused on the relationships of the Trinitarian persons.[9] In line with this thinking, he seeks "to start with the special Christian tradition of the histo y of Jesus the Son, and from that to develop a historical doctrine of the Trinity" (*TK*, 19). Within this framework, Moltmann argues that God's eternal existence is always and already a Trinitarian existence of mutual love. Drawing on the imagery of perichoresis developed by John Damascene, Moltmann maintains that God's oneness originates in the intimacy of the persons with and in one another.[10] "God is a community of Father, Son, and Spirit, whose unity is constituted by mutual indwelling and reciprocal interpenetration" (*TK*, viii; also 174–75). It is the perichoretic union of the divine community of persons that vouchsafes God's oneness.[11] Neither a common

---

5. See Jürgen Moltmann, *The Crucified God: The Cross of Christ as the Foundation and Criticism of Christian Theology* (hereafter *TCG*), trans. R. A. Wilson (Minneapolis, MN: Fortress Press, 1993), 215. On Niebuhr, see H. Richard Niebuhr, *Radical Monotheism and Western Culture—with Supplementary Essays* (Louisville, KY: Westminster/John Knox, 1970).

6. Jürgen Moltmann, *History and the Triune God: Contributions to Trinitarian Theology* (hereafter *HTG*), trans. John Bowden (New York: Crossroad, 1992), 84–85.

7. Moltmann, *TKG*,17; *HTG*, 82–84; Geiko Müller-Fahrenholz, *The Kingdom and the Power: The Theology of Jürgen Moltmann*, trans. John Bowden (Minneapolis, MN: Fortress Press, 2001), 142.

8. See Karl Rahner, *The Trinity*, trans. Joseph Donceel (New York: The Crossroad Publishing Company, 2005), 15–21. On further similarities, see Richard Bauckham in *The Theology of Jürgen Moltmann* (Edinburgh: T&T Clark, 1995), 156.

9. Moltmann, *TKG*, 19; *HTG*, xi–xii. John Meyendorff approvingly reviews Moltmann's view with reference to the Cappadocian Fathers. See "Reply to Jürgen Moltmann's 'The Unity of the Triune God," *St. Vladimir's Theological Quarterly*, 28/3 (1984): 183–188. He differs in claiming that each person perichoretically shares an intellect, will, and immutable nature.

10. Moltmann, *TKG*, 174.

substance nor a single subjectivity is required in the face of perichoresis.[12]

In line with Eastern thought, Moltmann appears to advocate the monarchy of the Father.[13] Based on this appearance, Timothy Harvie argues that Moltmann upholds an essential similarity in substance among the divine persons.[14] However, Harvie's claim falters in the face of Moltmann's self-understanding. In *The Way of Jesus Christ*, Moltmann summarizes his effort in *Trinity and the Kingdom* as an attempt "to free the Christian doctrine of God from the confines of the ancient metaphysics of substance."[15] The monarchy of the Father does not necessitate a divine substance underlying and preceding the divine persons.

At any rate, for Moltmann the Trinitarian union is what John means when he writes, "God is love" (1 John 14:16).[16] This communitarian view of God correlates to the kind of union that God desires for the created order.[17] Moltmann maintains that radical monotheism is dangerous in that it leads to oppression in the natural and political spheres through an emphasis on the sovereignty of a singularity over the community.[18] Contrarily, the social Trinity, in

---

11. Jürgen Moltmann, *The Coming of God: Christian Eschatology* (hereafter *CoG*), trans. Margaret Kohl (Minneapolis, MN: Fortress Press, 1996), 298.

12. Moltmann, *TKG*, 175.

13. See ibid., 162–70.

14. Timothy Harvie, *Jürgen Moltmann's Ethics of Hope: Eschatological Possibilities for Moral Action* (Burlington, VT: Ashgate, 2009), 113–17.

15. Jürgen Moltmann, *The Way of Jesus Christ: Christology in Messianic Dimensions* (hereafter *WJC*), trans. Margaret Kohl (Minneapolis, MN: Fortress Press, 1993), xv.

16. See Moltmann, *TKG*, 57–60. For a summary of Moltmann's view, see Bauckham, *The Theology of Jürgen Moltmann*, 173–82.

17. See Jürgen Moltmann, *God in Creation: A New Theology of Creation and the Spirit of God* (hereafter *GC*), trans. Margaret Kohl (Minneapolis, MN: Fortress Press, 1993), 16–17; *CoG*, 301–02.

18. Jürgen Moltmann, *God for a Secular Society: The Public Relevance of Theology* (hereafter *GSS*), trans. Margaret Kohl (Minneapolis, MN: Fortress Press, 1999), 97–98; Moltmann, *TKG*, 191–202.

safeguarding the uniqueness of the divine persons in relation to one another, prioritizes community without dissolving individuality.[19]

The Open Trinity

If the Trinity is a community, it is not a closed-gate community. The relational life of God is open to that which is other than God—namely, the creation. God desires to share God's life with the cosmos.

The Trinity's openness takes two forms for Moltmann. First, cosmologically, the Trinity opens a space "in God" for creation to be itself. I address this aspect in the current chapter. Second, eschatologically (and soteriologically), the Trinity is open to perichoretic union with the created order.[20] I address this aspect in the next chapter.

God's openness to the world means that the history of the world is simultaneously the history of the Trinity.[21] God lets the world in and is affected by it. The events between the God and the world are absolutely meaningful to both. It is within history—as part of it—that God desires the world and seeks its companionship.[22] This seeking is only possible because the Trinity opens itself to cosmic history. Within this framework, the doctrinal facets of the economy of salvation, including creation, evil, christology, pneumatology, and eschatology, are all expressions of the Trinity's dynamic history with the world. This economy impacts the life of the created order and the life of the triune God by constituting the history of each.[23] In this

---

19. Moltmann, *TKG*, 191–222; Müller-Fahrenholz, *The Kingdom and the Power*, 147–50.
20. See Moltmann, *HTG*, 86–87. On soteriology, see Joy Ann McDougall, *Pilgrim of Love: Moltmann on the Trinity and Christian Life* (New York: Oxford University Press, 2005), 122–25.
21. See Richard Bauckham, *Moltmann: Messianic Theology in the Making* (Basingstoke, UK: Marshall Pickering, 1987), 106–10; Bauckham, *The Theology of Jürgen Moltmann*, 58–60.
22. See Müller-Fahrenholz, *The Kingdom and the Power*, 137–47.

sense, the Trinity's openness to the cosmos frames Moltmann's entire theological project, from theology proper to the protological creation to the eschaton.

The Creation as Dynamic and Teleological

"A new doctrine of creation had been on my agenda ever since I wrote *Theology of Hope* in 1964" (GC, xi). This statement suggests that Moltmann understood the cosmological implications of hope from the beginning of his work, even though these implications do not receive attention until later. In these later works, Moltmann distinguishes between three phrases of creation: *creatio originalis*, *creatio continua*, and *creatio nova*.[24] Here, I use this structure to consider the dynamic community of creation and its eschatological orientation.

The Dynamism of God's Creation

Historically, the doctrine of creation tends toward an understanding of the "six days" of God's creative work.[25] Moltmann views this tendency as reductionist in three manners. First, *creatio originalis* is itself preceded by a divine decree and act. Moltmann adapts the traditional notion of *creatio ex nihilo* by addressing what the presence of "nothing" means. Drawing on the kabbalistic notion of *zimzum*, Moltmann maintains that the nothing within which the created order takes shape is necessarily preceded by God's decree to withdraw the

---

23. See Jürgen Moltmann, *The Church in the Power of the Spirit: A Contribution to Messianic Ecclesiology* (hereafter CPS), trans. Margaret Kohl (Minneapolis, MN: Fortress Press, 1993), 50–65; Bauckham, *Messianic Theology*, 110–13.
24. See Moltmann, GC, 208; Bouma-Prediger, *The Greening of Theology*, 110–14.
25. See Moltmann, GC, 55.

divine presence in order to create space for the cosmos.[26] Before God creates *something*, God makes space (*nothing*) for the something to occupy.

This claim leads naturally to Moltmann's dismantling of divine passibility, which is one of the central tenets of his theology.[27] In order to create, God must first be passible, able and willing to suffer the space necessary for the created order's integrity.[28] Thus, not only *can* God suffer, but, in order for creation to exist in genuine rapport with the divine, God *must* suffer. Yet, contra the tenets of process theology, this suffering is God's own doing: "Only God can limit God."[29] Because God embraces God's own passibility in order to give creation its own space, God's suffering is "part of the grace of creation" (*CoG*, 306). That is, it is God's suffering that makes a genuine rapport with creation possible.

Because creation is preceded by the Trinity's willingness to suffer creation its own space, Moltmann can say that *creatio ex nihilo* is simultaneously *creatio ex amore Dei*.[30] "God loves the world with the very same love that he himself is in eternity" (*TK*, 57). Thus, the act of creation is both an act of freedom and one of nature (i.e., love), a point consistent with Moltmann's panentheistic view of the cosmos.[31] In creating the world out of love, God creates the world out of

---

26. Ibid., 86–89; *CoG*, 297; *TKG*, 109; Harvie, *Moltmann's Ethics of Hope*, 65–67.

27. For a critique, see Daniel Castelo, "Moltmann's Dismissal of Divine Impassibility: Warranted?" *The Scottish Journal of Theology* 61/4 (2008): 396–407.

28. See Moltmann, *TKG*, chapter 2; Bauckham, *The Theology of Jürgen Moltmann*, 58–61; Müller-Fahrenholz, *The Kingdom and the Power*, 77–79.

29. Jürgen Moltmann, "God's Kenosis in the Creation and Consummation of the World" (hereafter "GKC") in *God and Evolution: A Reader*, ed. Mary Kathleen Cunningham (New York: Routledge, 2007), 279.

30. Moltmann, *GC*, 75–76; Jürgen Moltmann, *Ethics of Hope* (hereafter *EH*), trans. Margaret Kohl (Minneapolis, MN: Fortress Press, 2012), 122. For criticism, see Alan Torrance, "*Creatio Ex Nihilo* and the Spatio-Temporal Dimensions, with Special Reference to Jürgen Moltmann and D. C. Williams," in *The Doctrine of Creation: Essays in Dogmatics, History and Philosophy*, ed. Colin E. Gunton (New York: T&T Clark, 1997), 89.

31. See Moltmann, *TKG*, 106–8; *GC*, 79–86.

God's self. Based on this view of creation, Moltmann notes that God's self-limitation of omnipotence and omnipresence is simultaneously a delimitation of God's goodness.[32] In a manner of speaking, by withdrawing the divine presence in suffering love—the very love that God is—God is supremely present.

Second, Moltmann claims that a strict six-day understanding of God's creative work neglects the actual crown of the original creation: God's sabbath rest.[33] I develop this point in the following chapter. Here, it is sufficient to note that the sabbath day of rest is an act of creation, not simply an appendix to that which precedes it.

Third, God's creative activity does not cease with the sabbath. Moltmann rejects any relegation of the doctrine of creation to *creatio originalis*. In his view, this relegation would constitute a reduction of the doctrine's significance for both the created order and God.[34] The act of creation in the beginning is only one stage of creation. It is followed by *creatio continua*, God's ongoing creative engagement with the world. Furthermore, creation is aimed toward *creatio nova*, the new creation. For Moltmann, the term "creation" must embrace *creatio originalis, creatio continua, and creatio nova* in order to be truly messianic.[35]

Creatio continua has two components. First, the created order has a dynamic self-development within the space and time God has ceded to it.[36] It has randomness and unpredictability, which are dimensions of its integrity. In divine withdrawal, God has set the creation free to be itself outside of the realm of absolute divine control. The evolutionary emergence of the cosmos, including the development

---

32. *TKG*, 119.
33. Moltmann, *GC*, 187. Müller-Fahrenholz, *The Kingdom and the Power*, 156–58.
34. Moltmann has in mind here Scholastic theology and its legacy. Moltmann, *GC*, 55.
35. Ibid.
36. Moltmann, *GC*, 198–200.

and organization of life into increasingly complex life forms, occurs within this freedom.[37]

Second, God remains involved in the created order. God remains other than the world so that the world might be genuinely other than God. Nonetheless, God remains present in the world as the affirmation of life in all living things. This paradox of divine transcendence and divine immanence is all for the wake of the world.[38] God's transcendence is necessary for the created order's integrity. God's immanence is necessary for the created order's life and well-being.

In the unfolding narrative of *creatio continua*, creation's integrity has meaning for God. While *creatio originalis* is an act of both divine will and nature that is constitutive for the created order, it is also, in some sense, constitutive for God inasmuch as it requires divine self-limitation. This reciprocation continues with *creatio continua* because the Trinity's own history is now a history with and within the unfolding of the created order—an "other" with its own integrity.[39] The Trinity is caught up in the world for the world.

The Community of God's Creation

Just as God is not the monad of radical monotheism but rather a community of persons in perichoretic union, so also the cosmos is an interconnected community. As such, humanity cannot be isolated from the nonhuman creation.[40] In the beginning, God creates humanity *within* the world. In the end, God will not redeem humanity *without* the world. On this point Moltmann adjusts

---

37. Ibid., 200–207.
38. On this paradox, see Bouma-Prediger, *The Greening of Theology*, 114–19.
39. Bauckham, *The Theology of Jürgen Moltmann*, 58–60.
40. Moltmann validates this point both theologically and scientifically. See Moltmann, *GC*, 185–90.

Cyprian's famous quip as follows: "*nulla salus sine terra*" (*CoG*, 274). The nonhuman creation is essential for human creation, existence, and salvation. Based on the intrinsic relationality of the cosmos and the ontological significance of that relationality for human identity, John Haught concurs with Moltmann on this point.[41]

Moltmann's vision of the community of creation bears three significant corollaries. Humans are embodied, em-personed, and en-cosmosed.[42] Humans cannot truly exist, either now or in eternity, without bodily form.[43] There is no immortal soul underneath the flesh.[44] The human being "shall die *wholly*" and "rise *wholly*" (*CoG*, 67). The only persistence of a being upon death is a *relational persistence* in which a person's Gestalt "remains in God's relationship to that person" (*CoG*, 76).

As em-personed, human beings are intrinsically relational—that is, always and already in relation with others. This point is solidified in Moltmann's relational interpretation of the *imago Dei*. This doctrine is "first of all God's relationship to the human being, and then the relationship of human beings, women and men, to God" (*CoG*, 72). This understanding of the *imago* corresponds to Moltmann's dynamic and relational ontology.[45] Humans are not the *imago Dei* as isolated monads, but rather as a community.[46] In this manner, humans are the image of Trinitarian love, or the "image of [God's] inward nature" (*GC*, 241).[47] With this claim Moltmann establishes a Trinitarian *imago*—a "social image of God" in which no one can

---

41. John Haught, *God after Darwin: A Theology of Evolution*, second edition (Washington, DC: Georgetown University Press, 2008), 169–70.
42. "Em-personed" and "en-cosmosed" are my terms.
43. Moltmann, *GC*, 244–47.
44. Moltmann, *CoG*, 58–60.
45. See Moltmann, *GC*, 230–34.
46. Moltmann, *EH*, 68.
47. Müller-Fahrenholz, *The Kingdom and the Power*, 160–63. The *imago* also has an eschatological dimension in which humans become *imago Christi* and finally *gloria Dei*.

embody the *imago* outside of the human community—in contrast to Augustine's emphasis on the individual as the *imago trinitatis*.[48]

Moltmann's relational understanding of the image of God also embraces the nonhuman creation. Human beings are not the *imago Dei* as a community isolated from creation, but rather as part of the cosmic community.[49] Humans are both *imago Dei* and *imago mundi*.[50] As the former, they are meant to bring peace to the cosmos.[51] Humans "stand before God on behalf of creation, and before creation on behalf of God" (*GC*, 190). This functional dimension reveals that, for Moltmann, the *imago* has meaning for God, humanity, and the nonhuman creation.[52]

The significance of the *imago* for the nonhuman creation adumbrates that embodied and em-personed human beings are also en-cosmosed. Humans exist always and only as part of the community of creation.[53] In this community, there is a sacramental reciprocity between humans and the nonhuman world. The creation is sacramental for humanity in that it makes possible humanity's relationship with the divine—though this sacramental role exhausts neither its purpose nor its value. Humans are sacramental to creation because they reveal God's eschatological hope to the cosmos. Thus, the creation of the cosmos precedes (and makes possible) humanity and the redemption of humanity precedes (and, in some sense, makes possible) the redemption of the cosmos. In this sense, "creation has its

---

48. See Stanley J. Grenz, *The Social God and the Relational Self: A Trinitarian Theology of the Imago Dei* (Louisville, KY: Westminster John Knox, 2001), 154–57. On the difference between this view and Moltmann's see Moltmann, *HTG*, 60–63; *GC*, 234–40; McDougall, *Pilgrim of Love*, 115–16.
49. Moltmann, *GC*, 29–31.
50. Ibid., 185–86.
51. Ibid., 29–31, 187–88.
52. Ibid., 77–78, 188–90.
53. Moltmann, *GC*, 31.

meaning for human beings, and human beings have their meaning for the community of creation" (GC, 189).[54]

This affirmation of the cosmic community correlates to an affirmation of the intrinsic value of the nonhuman creation.[55] Value is not born with Adam. The community has its own integrity within which humans fit and in which humans participate. This value leads Moltmann to affirm that all members of the community have a right to a life for their own sakes.[56] Such a view shatters modern expressions of anthropocentrism, which Moltmann consistently claims are detrimental to the cosmos.[57]

The Teleological Nature of God's Creation

Moltmann's cosmology is "messianic" in that it "sees creation together with its future—the future for which it was made and in which it will be perfected" (GC, 5). It does not isolate the realities of *creatio continua* from the hope for *creatio nova*. Thus, the community of creation is not simply all created things existing at any particular time. It encompasses all creation from all times. The present creation, both human and nonhuman, is united as a community in part because it suffers together the contradictions of its current state while longing together for *creatio nova*.[58]

A messianic cosmology cannot consider the cosmos solely "as it is," isolated from its eschatological destiny, which is "the perfected *perichoretic* unity of God and world" (SRA, 30). Thus, for Moltmann the hope of cosmic christology cannot simply be the

---

54. Ibid., 189.
55. Ibid., 11.
56. Moltmann, GSS, 111–13; GC, 289–90.
57. See Moltmann, CoG, 92–93; GSS, 94–101.
58. Jürgen Moltmann, *Sun of Righteousness, Arise! God's Future for Humanity and the Earth* (hereafter SRA), trans. Margaret Kohl (Minneapolis, MN: Fortress Press, 2010), 70–71.

supposedly existing 'harmony of the world', for its starting point is the reconciliation of all things through Christ; and the premise of this reconciliation is a state of disrupted harmony in the world, world powers which are at enmity with one another, and threatening chaos. (*WJC*, 278)

It is this eschatological dimension of his cosmology that stands in stark contrast with theologians like Thomas Berry.[59]

The messianic trajectory of creation leads Moltmann to reject the notion of a perfect original creation. He adheres to an Irenaean cosmology in which God creates the entire cosmos in an infancy requiring development.[60] The creation is meant to grow into its telos—or, more properly, to encounter the advent of that telos within its history. Thus, for Moltmann, eschatology is not a return to a protological state.[61] It is a process, one in which God "suffers the contradiction of the beings he has created" and continues to work in creation by "opening up the systems that are closed in on themselves" (*GC*, 210–11).

On account of this teleological view of the cosmos, Moltmann establishes a stark contrast between the notions of "nature" and "creation."[62] The former is that which one can observe in *creatio continua*. Says Moltmann, "Theologically, we call 'nature' the state of creation which is no longer creation's original condition, and is not yet its final one" (*CoG*, 91). As it is, "nature" is "full of beauties and full of catastrophes" (*SRA*, 68). As it is, "nature…knows no sabbath" (*GC*, 6). For these reasons, nature *requires* redemption in order to become creation.

---

59. See Moltmann, *GC*, 7. However, Moltmann also offers a positive evaluation to cosmic spirituality. Moltmann, *GSS*, 101–106.
60. On Irenaeus's cosmology, see Matthew Craig Steenberg, *Irenaeus on Creation: The Cosmic Christ and the Saga of Redemption* (Boston: Brill, 2008), 145–49.
61. See Moltmann, *TCG*, 261; Moltmann, *CoG*, 296–308.
62. Moltmann, *GC*, 37–40; *WJC*, 253.

Unlike "nature", the term "creation" refers to the historical *and* eternal scope of the cosmos, thus including its eschatological transfiguration. This view of creation does not accommodate God to nature (i.e., defining God according to the way things are), but rather understands creation (understood teleologically) according to God's promises.[63]

The messianic understanding of the world is the true natural theology. In the messianic light, all earthly things and all living beings can be discerned in their forfeiture to transience and in their hope for liberation to eternity. (GC, 60)

This understanding is messianic in part because it depends on Christ's return: "the coming of Christ in glory is accompanied by a transformation of the whole of nature into its eternal discernible identity as God's creation" (*WJC*, 280). In the meantime, nature is embedded within the cycles of suffering, predation, and death, all of which for Moltmann constitute evils.

Evil as Suffering and Death

Moltmann defines evil as "the perversion of good, the annihilation of what exists, the negation of the affirmation of life" (GC, 168). Consistent with this definition, Moltmann's understanding of evil tends to center on transience, in particular suffering and death. Here I consider how Moltmann understands transience, including evolution, vis-à-vis the original creation, the ongoing creation, and the new creation.

Moltmann commonly refers to the current state of the created order (i.e. "nature") as disrupted.[64] He accepts some form of its "fallenness."[65] However, this fallenness takes the form of a (*pre-human*)

---

63. Moltmann, *GC*, 53.
64. Moltmann, *WJC*, 281. See also *HTG*, 71–72.
65. Moltmann, *SRA*, 67.

straying from the path towards the telos of the dynamic cosmos rather than a singular event that shatters protological harmony.[66] The corruption entailed by creation's straying is systemic, affecting every particle of the cosmos.

What is the effect of this corruption? Do the darker mechanisms of evolution, such as suffering and death, burgeon out of the cosmic straying? Or, are they the result of divine ordination? These questions present a great difficulty for Moltmann. He engages biblical material with reference to this question but finds an ambiguity therein. Death at times appears the negative result of sin. Elsewhere it is the natural end of life.[67] This ambiguity is reflected in Moltmann's own thought.

Moltmann wants to take seriously the findings of science, which suggest that neither suffering nor death can have originated with human disobedience.[68] "Did the dinosaurs become extinct because of the sin of the human beings who did not yet exist?" (*CoG*, 83) Implicitly then, death is not the result of human sin, for animals die long before the dawn of humanity.[69] For Moltmann, even human death is not the result of human sin.[70]

In line with these claims, Moltmann maintains that death is, in some sense, "natural."[71] He frequently refers to the biblical image of a grain of wheat that brings forth fruit, thus suggesting a positive dimension to death when it is not isolated from the vast sweep of created existence.[72] Elsewhere, he states that death is neither the

---

66. Moltmann, *CoG*, 261–67; Richard Bauckham, "Eschatology in *The Coming of God*," in *God Will Be All in All: The Eschatology of Jürgen Moltmann*, ed. Richard Bauckham (Minneapolis, MN: Fortress Press, 2001), 17.

67. Moltmann, *CoG*, 78–83.

68. Moltmann, *GC*, 22; "GKC," 273; John Polkinghorne, "Jürgen Moltmann's Engagement with the Natural Sciences," in *God's Life in Trinity*, ed. Miroslav Volf and Michael Welker (Minneapolis, MN: Fortress Press, 2006), 61–62.

69. Moltmann, *CoG*, 90.

70. Ibid., 90–91.

71. Ibid., 90.

72. Moltmann, *GC*, 269; *SRA*, 64–65; *WJC*, 248–49.

salvation of the soul from the body nor the separation of the human from God; it is rather the necessary point of transformation from transient life to eternal life.[73] "Death de-restricts the human being's spirit in both time and space" (*CoG*, 77). These passages suggest a positive role of death in the cosmos.

Indeed, Moltmann highlights many positive dimensions of the evolutionary process. It produces higher forms of life. It requires a level of cooperation in the cosmos. It suggests an openness to the future.[74] Thus, creation and evolution are not opposing concepts per se.[75] In *God and Creation*, Moltmann even suggests that God is the author of evolution: "There is a creation of evolution, because evolution is not explicable simply in terms of itself" (*GC*, 19). He also writes, "The Spirit is the principle of evolution" (*GC*, 100).[76]

These positive dimensions of evolution notwithstanding, Moltmann does not explicitly pinpoint God as the author of death. Indeed, he does not want to accept that suffering and death are part of God's good creation. "The living God and death are irreconcilable antitheses" (*SRA*, 81). Furthermore, neither suffering nor death pertains to the eschatological future of creation. Indeed, "New creation is new from the root up only if it issues from the cosmic annihilation of the death of created being" (*WJC*, 252). Thus, to the extent that death is "natural," it is also the enemy in juxtaposition to resurrection hope.[77] Says Moltmann,

> Even if death is part of temporal creation, it does not have to be called 'natural' in the sense of being self-evident of a matter of course; and if it is called natural, this 'nature' by no means has to be taken as final. If we

73. Moltmann, *WJC*, 249–50.
74. Moltmann, *GC*, 100, 196–97; *SRA*, 218; *EH*, 126–27.
75. Moltmann, *GC*, 19.
76. Also, Moltmann, *SRA*, 207; *EH*, 122–23.
77. Moltmann, *CoG*, 65–66; Bauckham, "Eschatology in *The Coming of God*," 18.

turn back from the end to the beginning, then the death of all the living is a sign of the first, temporal and imperfect creation. (*CoG*, 91)

Because death stands in contrast to the divine intention for the cosmos, blithely embracing it is an affront to Christian cosmology. Death should elicit grief and protest (as it did for Christ on the cross, evinced in the cry of dereliction).[78] Thus, Moltmann claims that death "is a fact that evokes grief and longing for the future world and eternal life" (*CoG*, 92). Why? Because "all life is intended to live and not to die" (*WJC*, 253).

Thus, Moltmann's affirmation that death is "natural" must be read in light of his differentiation between "nature" and "creation." Inasmuch as "nature" is disrupted creation, death is natural. Inasmuch as "natural" depicts God's design of the world, death is unnatural: In this sense, Moltmann writes, "The death of all the living is neither due to sin nor is it natural" (*CoG*, 92).[79]

What is clear is that Moltmann consistently claims that evolution can exhaust neither the divine aim for creation nor the means of realizing that aim. Evolution has too many victims.[80] Thus, only "Christ brings human beings into harmony with God's good creation. Orientation toward the forces of nature, which are themselves in need of redemption, does not help" (*SRA*, 68). Bauckham notes here a "sharp rejection of Teilhard de Chardin's thorough-going identification of the evolutionary process with salvation history."[81] This rejection implicitly applies as well to Berry.

Because neither suffering nor death is an acceptable condition for the created order, Moltmann maintains that at the eschaton the

---

78. Jürgen Moltmann, *The Spirit of Life: A Universal Affirmation* (hereafter *SL*), trans. Margaret Kohl (Minneapolis, MN: Fortress Press, 1992), xii.

79. See also Müller-Fahrenholz, *The Kingdom and the Power*, 206.

80. Moltmann, *WJC*, 294; *SRA*, 223.

81. Bauckham, *The Theology of Jürgen Moltmann*, 194. See also Moltmann, *WJC*, 293–97; *SRA*, 209.

entire cosmos will be freed from its corrupted state.[82] While there is a positive dimension to evolution in which the Spirit is at work, because evolution as it occurs in nature requires suffering and death—and gratuitously so!—it cannot be the final word on the doctrine of creation. Even the Spirit's participation as the principle of evolution is nuanced inasmuch as this is part of the divine "sighing" for redemption: "The evolutions and the catastrophes of the universe are also the movements and experiences of the Spirit of creation. That is why Paul tells us that the divine Spirit 'sighs' in all created things under the power of futility" (GC, 16). In short, evolution is not redemptive; it must be redeemed.

But the question remains: Did God ordain the darker mechanisms of evolution? If not, what is their origin? In his earlier works, Moltmann seems to suggest that there can be no answer to these questions.[83] The only response he offers is that, in the face of suffering and death, God, through the incarnation, engages in compassion—co-suffering and even co-death.[84] In the Spirit, too, God suffers alongside the cosmos.[85]

In later works, however, Moltmann seems to suggest that the forces of annihilation in the created order result from the integrity of the space and time that God allots to the world.[86] Already in *Trinity and the Kingdom* he writes, "God creates the world by letting his world become and be in *himself*: Let it be!" (*TK*, 109) In his later *Sun of Righteousness*, he specifically links this "letting be" to the existence of evil:

82. Moltmann, *CoG*, 90–91.
83. Moltmann, *TKG*, 50–51; Bauckham, *The Theology of Jürgen Moltmann*, 82–91. For the context of Moltmann's "eschatological theodicy," see ibid., 71–82.
84. Moltman, *TCG*, 146–53; Eugene B. Borowitz, *Contemporary Christologies: A Jewish Response* (New York: Paulist, 1980), 83–84.
85. Moltmann, *SL*, 51; *GC*, 96–97.
86. See Moltmann, *GC*, 164–69.

Why is this creation of God's threatened by chaos and why has it fallen victim to annihilation? Because the creator is by no means 'the all-determining reality' of what he has created—in that case creation would be itself divine—but because he has conferred on creation its own scope for freedom and generation. (*SRA*, 205)

The space of creation includes its freedom and generation. This space also necessitates the possibility of disruption, even *before humans arrive*.[87] In this vein Moltmann writes, "We even have to talk about the 'sin' of the whole creation, which has isolated itself from the foundation of its existence and the wellspring of its life, and has fallen victim to universal death" (*WJC*, 283). The fall may thus be interpreted as the straying *of the nonhuman creation*, both in randomness and, much later, in will, from the path toward eschatological consummation. Human sin, then, can be interpreted not as the cause of the fall, but rather as both the embracing of it and, in this embrace, the intensifying of cosmic straying.

This point, I believe, counters Tim Chester's critique that Moltmann advocates a Hegelianism in which evil is necessary to the becoming of God.[88] Evil is potential in the history of God in relation with a world to which God permits its own time and space. Such a view finds its roots in Irenaeus, not Hegel.[89] Though, in my reading, Moltmann differs from Irenaeus because the potentiality of evil is at risk of coming to fruition from the beginning of creation on accounts of its integrity, which entails randomness. Suffering and death pertain to the transient stage of the creation—*creatio continua*—not because God ordains them but because God withdraws to give creation its own space. In this space, suffering and death become "characteristics

---

87. For this position, see Moltmann, "GKC," 273–83.
88. Chester, *Mission and the Coming of God*, 46–48.
89. See John Hick, "An Irenaean Theodicy," in *Encountering Evil: Live Options in Theodicy*, ed. Stephen T. Davis (Louisville, KY: Westminster John Knox Press, 2001), 40–42; Celia Deane-Drummond, *Eco-Theology* (Winona, MN: Anselm Academic, 2008), 172.

of a frail, temporal creation which will be overcome through the new creation of all things for eternal life" (*CoG*, 78). I develop this view in greater detail in Part III.

At any rate, Chester's criticism highlights a tension in Moltmann's thought—a tension also acknowledged by Richard Bauckham in his comparison of *God in Creation* and *The Way of Jesus Christ*.[90] On the one hand, Moltmann highlights the randomness of evolution and its negative dimensions that will be transfigured in the eschaton. On the other hand, he claims that the Spirit is the working principle in evolution and affirms positive dimensions of it, which at times seem to include death. The obvious questions: How must randomness and negativity? How much divine ordination and positivity?

This ambiguity detracts from Moltmann's evolutionary theodicy inasmuch as the etiology of evolution remains unclear.[91] This lack of clarity has led to justified critiques.[92] Deane-Drummond suggests that Moltmann shifts his pneumatology regarding the question of evolution between *God and Creation* and *The Way of Jesus Christ*.[93] I partly concur with this assessment. However, I believe Bauckham is correct in interpreting Moltmann's positive assessment of evolution within the boundaries of its requiring redemption.[94] That is, Moltmann's intention in *God in Creation* is best interpreted in light of his thought in *The Way of Jesus Christ*. Even the beauty of nature requires redemption in order for nature to become creation.

---

90. See Bauckham, *The Theology of Jürgen Moltmann*, 190–98.
91. Celia Deane-Drummond, *Christ and Evolution: Wonder and Wisdom* (Minneapolis, MN: Fortress Press, 2009), 46–47.
92. See Jeremy Law, "Jürgen Moltmann's Ecological Hermeneutics," in *Ecological Hermeneutics: Biblical, Historical and Theological Perspectives*, ed. David G. Horrell Cheryl Hunt, Christopher Southgate, and Francesca Stavrakopoulou (New York: T&T Clark, 2010), 235; Deane-Drummond, *Eco-Theology*, 107.
93. Deane-Drummond, *Eco-Theology*, 132–33.
94. Bauckham, *The Theology of Jürgen Moltmann*, 194.

Conclusion

To this point, I have delineated Moltmann's vision of God, the cosmos, and the existence of evil. The cosmos reflects the freedom and relationality of the Trinity and is able to do so because God withdraws the divine presence to provide creation its own space and integrity. God suffers the creation its own space to be and to become in its own way. While Moltmann is ambiguous concerning how evil—and most particularly suffering and death—arises within this unique space of creation, he nonetheless is adamant that no aspect of the transient nature of the cosmos constitutes part of God's eternal intention for it. Said differently, the suffering and death that are both pervasive and inevitable in the unfolding saga of creation are part of what God seeks to overcome. They are not redemptive. They require redemption. This claim leads into Moltmann's eschatological vision of redemption in which transience is transfigured by the cosmos's participation in the Trinity's perichoretic communion.

8

Moltmann on Redemption and Mission

In the previous chapter, I explored Moltmann's understanding of God, the creation, and the fall. God, who is a community of love, chooses to create—and thereby suffer the existence of—a world that is other-than-God. This world has its own communal integrity, which entails negative dimensions of transience such as suffering and death. However, the divinely intended telos of the world is a participation in the perichoretic love of the Trinity, which entails the transfiguration of transience. To understand the nature and extent of this transfiguration in Moltmann's theology, I here examine his Christology, pnuematology, eschatology, and mission-oriented ecclesiology.

Christ as the Eschatological Turning Point

Christology is arguably the central theological theme of Moltmann's work.[1] Even his emphasis on eschatology is fundamentally derivative of Christology.[2] Here, I examine the function of the cross and resurrection in Moltmann's theology and the relationship between these events and the evolutionary history of the cosmos.

The Cross as Trinitarian Contradiction

Cosmologically, the Son is the Logos of creation, its wisdom.[3] However, in the incarnation, the Son becomes the concrete divine assumption of the world's contradictions. This assumption climaxes at the cross, where Jesus takes on the entirety of nature's corrupted condition.[4] He experiences the abysmal depths of suffering, the pain of God-forsakenness, and ultimately the sting of death.[5]

As Moltmann's social doctrine of the Trinity begins with the persons in communion as opposed to the oneness of God's substance or subjectivity, he can claim that the cross reveals the passibility of God.[6] It is the cross that calls for "the revolution needed in the concept of God" (TCG, 4) in which the Trinity revealed therein replaces the Hellenistically derivative immutable deity of "theism."[7] For Moltmann, the cross constitutes a real "death in God" (TCG,

1. See Richard Bauckham in *The Theology of Jürgen Moltmann* (Edinburgh: T&T Clark, 1995), 4–5.
2. Jürgen Moltmann, *Theology of Hope: On the Ground and Implications of Christian Eschatology* (hereafter *TH*), trans. James W. Leitch (London: SCM Press, 1967), 178–81; Richard Bauckham, "Eschatology in *The Coming of God*," in *God Will Be All in All: The Eschatology of Jürgen Moltmann*, ed. Richard Bauckham (Minneapolis, MN: Fortress Press, 2001), 2–10.
3. Jürgen Moltmann, *Sun of Righteousness, Arise! God's Future for Humanity and the Earth* (hereafter *SRA*), trans. Margaret Kohl (Minneapolis, MN: Fortress Press, 2010), 30–31.
4. Jürgen Moltmann, *The Crucified God: The Cross of Christ as the Foundation and Criticism of Christian Theology* (hereafter *TCG*), trans. R. A. Wilson (Minneapolis, MN: Fortress Press, 1993), 246.
5. Ibid., 146–53.
6. Ibid., 204–5. Also, Bauckham, *The Theology of Jürgen Moltmann*, 47–49, 60–65; Ryan A. Neal, *Theology as Hope: On the Ground and the Implications of Jürgen Moltmann's Doctrine of Hope* (Eugene, OR: Pickwick Publications, 2009), 45–50; Tim Chester, *Mission and the Coming of God: Eschatology, the Trinity and Mission in the Theology of Jürgen Moltmann and Contemporary Evangelicalism* (Eugene, OR: Wipf & Stock Publishers, 2006), 36–37.
7. Moltmann, *TH*, 127–28; *TCG*, 207–219.

207)—Moltmann's Trinitarian resolution of the monotheistic phrase "death of God."[8] It is in this manner that the central contradiction of creation (i.e., life and death) becomes a contradiction *within* the Trinity. The *entirety* of one of the persons of the Trinity—the *Logos*—dies on the cross.[9] Furthermore, the Father uniquely suffers the experience of the death of the Son[10] while the Spirit protests this unprecedented separation between the Father and the Son.[11] Hence, all of the suffering of the created order is taken into the perichoretic union of the Trinity.[12]

However, the suffering of the Trinity at the cross is not the end. For Moltmann, the cross is a dialectic event with the resurrection.[13] The cross reveals the present state of creation; the resurrection reveals its eschatological hope.[14] In his incarnation, life, and death, Jesus takes on the fullness of nature's condition. In his resurrection, he heals it.[15] Thus, "the transfiguration of Christ's dead body is the beginning of the transfiguration of all mortal life" (*WJC*, 251). It is in this sense that Ryan Neal notes, "The ground of Moltmann's hope is the dialectic of the cross and the resurrection."[16] God becomes the world not for the sake of divine experience but rather for the sake of transfiguring it. Without the resurrection, the incarnation has no salvific import.

---

8. See Moltmann, *TCG*, 200–207.

9. Ibid., 193, 205–06.

10. Ibid., 243.

11. For the inclusion of the Spirit, see Jürgen Moltmann, *The Trinity and the Kingdom: The Doctrine of God* (hereafter *TKG*), trans. Margaret Kohl (Minneapolis, MN: Fortress Press, 1993), 80–83; *SL*, 60–73.

12. Moltmann, *TCG*, 244–47; Jürgen Moltmann, *The Way of Jesus Christ: Christology in Messianic Dimensions* (hereafter *WJC*), trans. Margaret Kohl (Minneapolis, MN: Fortress Press, 1993), 157; Jürgen Moltmann, *The Spirit of Life: A Universal Affirmation* (hereafter *SL*), trans. Margaret Kohl (Minneapolis, MN: Fortress Press, 1992), 75–77.

13. Moltmann, *TCG*, 178–87; *TH*, 210–15; Bauckham, *The Theology of Jürgen Moltmann*, 32–33.

14. Moltmann, *TH*, 6; Bauckham, *The Theology of Jürgen Moltmann*, 34.

15. Moltmann, *WJC*, 44–45; *TCG*, 182–86.

16. Neal, *Theology as Hope*, 1.

Hence, Moltmann writes, "Christianity stands or falls with the reality of the raising of Jesus from the dead" (*TH*, 152).

The Resurrection as Eschatological Promise

The concept of promise is significant for Moltmann's messianic theology.[17] "It is from promise that there arises that element of unrest which allows of no coming to terms with a present that is unfulfilled" (*TH*, 89). The promises of God constitute hope and all hope rests on God's promises. Promise opens history to a new future.[18]

In the resurrection, the messianic promises of God regarding the future of creation come to fruition.[19] Christ "is the pioneer and leader of the life that lives eternally" (*CoG*, xi). The resurrection is the concrete realization of God's eschatological promise—the burgeoning of a new creation in which death is no more.[20] In this sense, Christ is the eschatological turning point in history. His resurrection "is the first day of the new creation" (*HTG*, 77)—that point in which the power of death falters in its encounter with the divine affirmation of life.[21]

As the eschatological turning point of history, Christ's resurrection is more than an interruption of history. It is the actual advent of the eschaton.[22]

17. For a good reflection on this function of promise in Moltmann's thought, see Harvie, *Moltmann's Ethics of Hope*, 13–22, 151; Neal, *Theology as Hope*, 12–15; Hans Schwarz, *Eschatology* (Grand Rapids, MI: William B. Eerdmans Publishing Company, 2000), 147–48.

18. See *TH*, 103–4.

19. See Jeremy Law, "Jürgen Moltmann's Ecological Hermeneutics," in *Ecological Hermeneutics: Biblical, Historical and Theological Perspectives*, eds. David G. Horrell Cheryl Hunt, Christopher Southgate, and Francesca Stavrakopoulou (New York: T&T Clark, 2010), 226.

20. Moltmann, *TCG*, 171; Harvie, *Moltmann's Ethics of Hope*, 20.

21. Jürgen Moltmann, *Ethics of Hope* (hereafter *EH*), trans. Margaret Kohl (Minneapolis, MN: Fortress Press, 2012), 55–56.

22. See Jürgen Moltmann, *The Coming of God: Christian Eschatology* (hereafter *CoG*), trans. Margaret Kohl (Minneapolis, MN: Fortress Press, 1996), 25–29; Geiko Müller-Fahrenholz, *The Kingdom and the Power: The Theology of Jürgen Moltmann*, trans. John Bowden (Minneapolis,

> If Christ has been raised *from* the dead, then he takes on proleptic and representative significance *for* all the dead. . . . The process of the resurrection of the dead has begun in him, is continued in 'the Spirit, the giver of life', and will be completed in the raising of those who are hid, and of all the dead. (*CoG*, 69)

The resurrection constitutes a "conquest of the deadliness of death" (*TH*, 196). This conquest happens in history, as history, to history.[23]

Christ is the beginning of the fulfilled promise for new creation. Yet, this promise was given to the "old" creation. Thus, in order for the promise to be fulfilled, there must be continuity between *creatio continua* and *creatio nova*. Christ is the fulfillment of promise at just this point: the new creation of his resurrection is as continuous with the present creation as the resurrected Christ is with the crucified God.[24] For Moltmann, "the risen Christ *is* the historical and crucified Jesus, and *vice versa*" (*TCG*, 160). However, the risen Christ bears a radical newness. He is *transfigured*.[25] The resurrection of Christ is thus the concrete occurrence of the world's destiny: transience transfigured.

Christ's Future as the Redemption of Evolution

In his earlier works, Moltmann does not emphasize the importance of Christology vis-à-vis the doctrine of creation. His later developments are implicit in some cases and germinal in others. The full development of this line of thought does not surface explicitly until later works such as *God in Creation* and *The Coming of God*.

Moltmann contrasts his own position with that of Teilhard de Chardin by claiming that Christ cannot be merely the pinnacle

---

MN: Fortress Press, 2001), 50–51. On the distinction between Moltmann and Pannanberg here, see Neal, *Theology as Hope*, 8–12.

23. Moltmann, *WJC*, 252–53.
24. See Moltmann, *TH*, 184–85; *CoG*, 84–85.
25. Moltmann, *TCG*, 126–27; *CoG*, 28–29.

product of evolution. He also rejects the notion of an "omega point" in which the evolutionary process comes to an historical head.[26] Evolution has too many victims to be redemptive.

Furthermore, as noted in the previous chapter, the positive outcomes of the evolutionary process do nothing to redeem the suffering of those left in its wake. Those like Teilhard de Chardin and Berry seem to accept that all suffering is redemptive inasmuch as it contributes to the upward movement of the cosmic community through participating in its evolutionary emergence.[27] Such is also the view of secular ethicists like Holmes Rolston III, who writes, "The question is not whether the world is, or ever was, a happy place. Rather, the question is whether it is a place of significant suffering through to something higher."[28] For Moltmann, the question is not whether or not all suffering is redemptive in the sense that it is the seed for something greater, but rather whether or not all suffering is redeemed for suffering individuals.[29] Says Bauckham,

> In identifying with the godforsaken the crucified God does not sanction their suffering as part of his purpose, because the dialectic of the cross and resurrection still remains. God's purpose is liberation from suffering, promised in the resurrection.[30]

If any of the victims of evolution are left in their graves, then their suffering is not redeemed.[31]

---

26. See Moltmann, *WJC*, 293–97.
27. On de Chardin, see Celia Deane-Drummond, *Christ and Evolution: Wonder and Wisdom* (Minneapolis, MN: Fortress Press, 2009), 45.
28. Holmes Rolston III, "Does Nature Need to be Redeemed?" *Zygon* 29 (1994), 218.
29. Moltmann, *WJC*, 302–3. I believe Eugene Borowitz misses this point in his criticism of Moltmann's dialectics of the cross. See Eugene B. Borowitz, *Contemporary Christologies: A Jewish Response* (New York: Paulist, 1980), 90–94.
30. Bauckham, *The Theology of Jürgen Moltmann*, 87. Also, Celia Deane-Drummond, *Eco-Theology* (Winona, MN: Anselm Academic, 2008), 172.
31. Moltmann, *WJC*, 296.

Thus, in contradistinction to Teilhard de Chardin, Moltmann describes Jesus not as the apex of evolution, but rather as its ultimate victim.[32] Jesus cannot be the apex of evolution because the incarnation does not *evolve* naturally in history; it is something new, a crossing of God into creation's space. In this newness, Christ suffers the fate of all the victims of evolution, human and nonhuman.[33] Through his resurrection he becomes the new beginning in which the divine promise of messianic redemption actualizes in history.[34] "Christ died the death of all the living in order to reconcile them all (Col. 1.20) and to fill them with the prospect of eternal life" (*CoG*, 92–93). Christ's death gathers up the death of the entire cosmos. Likewise, his resurrection will gather up the life of the entire cosmos, drawing it into God's own triune life. Any less extensive Christology is, for Moltmann, too anthropocentric.[35] Moltmann carries this christological dismantling of anthropocentrism into his pneumatology, maintaining that the Spirit, in various modes of relation to the cosmos, draws all creation into the life of the divine.

Pneumatology as Divine Immanence and Eschatological Advent

Before *The Church in the Power of the Holy Spirit*, discussion of the Spirit was somewhat limited in Moltmann's thought—a point that opened him to critique.[36] His later work on the Spirit is, like his cosmology, nascent in his earlier works.[37] His development of the

32. Ibid.
33. Ibid., 255.
34. Ibid., 253.
35. Moltmann, *WJC*, 45; *CoG*, 92–93.
36. Richard Bauckham, *Moltmann: Messianic Theology in the Making* (Basingstoke, UK: Marshall Pickering, 1987), 110.
37. See Bauckham, *The Theology of Jürgen Moltmann*, 151–57.

social doctrine of the Trinity in *Trinity and the Kingdom* provides further engagement with the Spirit as a personal member of the Trinity.[38] However, his clearest exploration in pneumatology is his originally unplanned addition to his contributions to systematic theology, *The Spirit of Life.*

The Spirit as Divine Immanence

Cosmologically, Moltmann maintains that the Spirit "has to do with life and its source" (*SL*, 7). The Spirit, as the breath of God, is the principle of life present in all living things.[39] To establish this position, Moltmann draws on the linguistic connection of the Hebrew *ruach*, which translates as breath, wind, and/or spirit.[40]

> Everything that is, exists and lives in the unceasing inflow of the energies of and potentialities of the cosmic Spirit. This means that we have to understand every created reality in terms of energy, grasping it as the realized potentiality of the divine Spirit. Through the energies and potentialities of the Spirit, the Creator is himself present in his creation. He does not merely confront it in his transcendence; entering into it, he is also immanent in it. (*GC*, 9)

The Spirit is thus active in the protological act of creation as the initial principle of life. The Spirit is also present and active in *creatio continua*, preserving the cosmos as its ongoing principle of life.[41]

As the presence of God in the unfolding history of creation, the Spirit is the manner in which God suffers the fate of the created

---

38. On the personhood of the Spirit, see Moltmann, *TKG*, 125–26.
39. Moltmann, *SL*, 35.
40. Ibid., 40–43; *HTG*, 72–75. Also, Harvie, *Moltmann's Ethics of Hope*, 63; Müller-Fahrenholz, *The Kingdom and the Power*, 184–86.
41. Moltmann, *HTG*, 75–77; Jürgen Moltmann, *God in Creation: A New Theology of Creation and the Spirit of God* (hereafter *GC*), trans. Margaret Kohl (Minneapolis, MN: Fortress Press, 1993), 10.

order.[42] As the immanence of God in a world subjected to the futility of evolution, the Spirit is *"God's empathy*, his feeling identification with what he loves" (*SL*, 51). Thus, the Spirit is within all sighing in the cosmos—all longing for redemption.[43] This sighing is the openness of all creatures in *creatio continua* to *creatio nova*.[44]

Furthermore, it is pneumatological immanence that constitutes the community of creation.[45] The Spirit "indwells both every individual creature and the community of creation," which entails that all things have a "self-transcendence" (*GC*, 101). The divine Spirit thus entails a commonality between humanity and the nonhuman creation:

> To experience the fellowship of the Spirit inevitably carries Christianity beyond itself into the greater fellowship of all God's creatures. For *the community of creation*, in which all created things exist with one another, for one another and in one another, is also *the fellowship of the Holy Spirit*. (*SL*, 10)

In this sense, pneumatology negates a value-based anthropocentrism.[46]

The Spirit as Prolepsis of God's Future

If the Spirit is the immanent divine presence in the cosmos from the onset of creation and through its ongoing existence, what is the significance of Pentecost? Moltmann delineates three modes of the Spirit's indwelling presence to answer this question: cosmic, reconciling, and redemptive.[47] I have already noted the Spirit's creative and sustaining role, evident in the Spirit's presence as the

---

42. Moltmann, *SL*, 51; *GC*, 96–97.
43. Moltmann, *SRA*, 206; *TKG*, 111.
44. Moltmann, *SRA*, 207.
45. Moltmann, *GC*, 11.
46. Moltmann, *SL*, 37.
47. Moltmann, *GC*, 12.

principle of life in all things. The reconciling and redemptive roles of the Spirit entail rendering the new creation present within history and ultimately consummating the cosmos in its eschatological telos. Thus, the same Spirit is present and active both cosmologically and eschatologically.[48]

Moltmann develops the Spirit's reconciliatory role in his pneumatological Christology (and christological pneumatology).[49] The Spirit is present in the life, death, and resurrection of Christ and infuses the world in a new manner through that same life, death, and resurrection.[50] In Bauckham's words,

> The Spirit, whose mission derives from the event of the cross and resurrection, moves reality towards the resolution of the dialectic, filling the God-forsaken world with God's presence and preparing for the coming kingdom in which the whole world will be transformed in correspondence to the resurrection of Jesus.[51]

Because Christ's death and resurrection constitute, on the one hand, the contradictions of the world being taken into the very life and history of the Trinity and, on the other hand, the new creation burgeoning into the very life and history of the world through the healing of those contradictions, Moltmann associates the Spirit's presence with the new creation. The Spirit is a "sacrament of the kingdom."[52] In the redemption that pours out from the life of Christ, the Spirit becomes the principle of *new* life—eternal life—for the entire created order. In this sense, the Spirit pertains to both the sustaining of the cosmos and its transfiguration. Imbued the Spirit,

48. Moltmann, *SL*, 9.

49. On this link between pneumatology and christology, see ibid., 17–18.

50. Moltmann, *GC*, 95–96; *EH*, 38.

51. Bauckham, *The Theology of Jürgen Moltmann*, 5.

52. See Jürgen Moltmann, *The Church in the Power of the Spirit: A Contribution to Messianic Ecclesiology* (hereafter *CPS*), trans. Margaret Kohl (Minneapolis, MN: Fortress Press, 1993), 199–206.

the entire created order is already drawn into the life of the Trinity. The Spirit's presence is thus the prolepsis of the new creation within history—the "advance pledge of foretaste of the coming kingdom of glory" (*SL*, 74). In the Spirit, God is more than a conservationist.[53] The Spirit does not merely preserve the cosmos; the Spirit opens the new possibilities of its transfiguration.

Finally, the Spirit's eschatological role is not relegated to the present. The Spirit will bring to consummation the indwelling of God in the cosmos.[54] It is by the Spirit that the resurrection and transfiguration of the cosmos are completed.[55] Thus the Spirit preserves creation in its groaning, draws it proleptically into its future, and will ultimately consummate that future eschatologically. In the end, the Spirit "will make petrified conditions dance" (*SL*, 74).

Moltmann's Christology and pneumatology both highlight that the eschaton is that event in which all of creation, even the systems of life themselves, will be transfigured into the life of Christ through the Spirit. It is the transfiguration of creation, the healing of its wounds and its perichoretic union with the divine. It is a maximally inclusive panentheism.

Eschatology as a Maximally Inclusive Panentheism

In *Theology of Hope*, Moltmann views the entire scope of Christian theology through the lens of eschatology vis-à-vis the resurrection of Christ. He writes, "From first to last, and not merely in the epilogue, Christianity *is* eschatology, is hope, forward looking and forward moving, and therefore also revolutionizing and transforming the present" (*TH*, 16). Yet, Moltmann's eschatology diverges from

---

53. Moltmann, *GC*, 209; *HTG*, 77–79; Bauckham, *The Theology of Jürgen Moltmann*, 188–89.
54. Moltmann, *GC*, 149–150.
55. Moltmann, *TKG*, 123–24.

the traditional "last things."[56] Here, I explore this divergence in three dimensions: first, the import of Sabbath and Shekinah for Moltmann's eschatology; second, the scope of the eschatological community; and third, the categories of *adventus* and *novum* in relation to phenomenological time.

The Redemption of Time and Space

Already in *Theology of Hope*, Moltmann writes about an "all-inclusive eschatology which expects . . . a new being for all things" (*TH*, 190). He develops this view in *The Coming of God* in which he argues that such an eschatology must include both time and space. I here consider each inclusion in turn.

The subject of time is a complex dimension of Moltmann's thought on account of the relationship between phenomenological time and eternal time.[57] Phenomenological time is the "time of creation." In the act of creation, "God withdrew his own eternity into himself in order to take time for his creation and to leave his creation its own particular time" (*GC*, 114). This time is specific to creation. Yet, favor of Boethius's view, Moltmann claims that eternity is not the absence of time but its fullness—all time gathered together.[58] Eternity is thus a qualitative qualifier of time, not a quantitative one.[59] Thus, God's eternity is not without time.[60]

---

56. Hans Schwarz, *Eschatology* (Grand Rapids: William B. Eerdmans Publishing Company, 2000), 149.
57. For a good summary, see Richard Bauckham, "Time and Eternity," in *God Will Be All in All: The Eschatology of Jürgen Moltmann* (Minneapolis, MN: Fortress Press, 2001), especially 158–73.
58. For a summary and critique of Boethius's view, see Garrett J. DeWeese, *God and the Nature of Time* (Burlington, VT: Ashgate, 2004), 134–45. On Moltmann's view, see Moltmann, *SRA*, 62–63; *CoG*, 280–81, 291.
59. Moltmann, *EH*, 58.
60. On this tension, see Harvie, *Moltmann's Ethics of Hope*, 147–48.

Time entails change. Eternal time thus entails divine mutability. Likewise, phenomenological time requires cosmic mutability, which endows the cosmos with an openness for the new future God desires for it.[61] Bauckham refers to this openness as the positive side of historical time. However, unlike eternal time, phenomenological time risks a negative side: transience. As such, creation's mutability is neither fully identical with time nor fully antithetical to God's eternity.[62] Phenomenological time is open to "eternal time." The latter constitutes the destiny of the former. In this destiny, "there will be time and history, future and possibility, and these to an unimpeded degree." Yet, the mutability entailed by future and possibility in eternal time necessitates "change without transience, time without past, and life without death" (*GC*, 213). Based on this claim, Bauckham suggests that "time without past" could (and should) mean the possibility of newness (i.e., future) without the transient threat of nothingness (i.e., past).[63] The future pours into the present and gathers there without ever being lost to the past. The eternal present is the insatiable sponge that soaks in and retains the future.

Moltmann's concept of eternal time adumbrates the priority he ascribes to the future.[64] Following Georg Picht and Bloch, Moltmann claims the past is that which is complete and unalterable—realized being. The future is that which may actualize within history—potential being. The present is that moment of "now" in which potential becomes real and unalterable (i.e., it happens) or becomes unrealized (i.e., it does not happen)—actual being.[65] This flow of time gives priority to the phenomenological future.[66]

---

61. Moltmann, *CoG*, 283; *GC*, 197–214.
62. See Bauckham, "Time and Eternity," 173, 183.
63. Ibid., 162–63, 183–86.
64. See Moltmann, *GC*, 118–24. Müller-Fahrenholz, *The Kingdom and the Power*, 202–3.
65. Moltmann, *CoG*, 286.
66. See Jürgen Moltmann, "The Bible, the Exegete and the Theologian," in *God Will Be All in All: The Eschatology of Jürgen Moltmann* (Minneapolis, MN: Fortress Press, 2001), 228.

If reality is real-ized potentially, then potentiality must be higher ontologically than reality. If out of the future there is past, but out of past there is never again future, then the future must have pre-eminence among the modes of time. (*CoG*, 287)

This move permits Moltmann to give absolute precedence to the eternal future. This future "is the transcendent possibility of time in general" (*CoG*, 287). It is the source of phenomenological time and that for which this time is destined. It is its destiny because eternal time is God's time, which God has opened to phenomenological time. It is its source because the past comes from the future and the eternal future is the future of all phenomenological time, including the phenomenological future.

The Trinity's openness to cosmic time is also costly for God. In the unfolding history of the world, phenomenological time is a time of transience—of suffering and death. The divine openness to phenomenological time entails that its darker sides will affect God in eternity. This cost is evident both in the Spirit who suffers the contradictions of history and in the Son's death of the cross. God's willingness to bear this cost renders possible the inclusion of the transient cosmos in eternity. God lets phenomenological time in, bearing its cost in order to transfigure it.

The transfiguration of time is foreshadowed in the Sabbath, the true crown of God's created work in which the entire created order shares in God's rest, the pure enjoyment of life. For Moltmann, the historical Sabbath is the proleptic link between *creatio continua* and the *creatio nova* of eschatological consummation.[67] "The sabbath opens creation for its future. On the sabbath the redemption of the world is celebrated in anticipation" (*GC*, 276). This anticipation is evident

---

67. Moltmann, *WJC*, 119–22; Jürgen Moltmann, "The Liberation of the Future and Its Anticipations in History" (hereafter LTF), in *God Will Be All in All: The Eschatology of Jürgen Moltmann*, ed. Richard Bauckham (Minneapolis, MN: Fortress Press, 2001), 279–80.

in the first creation account in which the Sabbath has no night.[68] The divine rest thus encompasses the scope of time within it.[69] The Sabbath also evinces the Trinity's openness to time; for, God does not begrudge his creatures a share in Trinitarian rest. Indeed, God actively seeks to include them in it.

What about space? Because God is the Creator, nothing created can fall away in the new creation. Thus, not only time, but also all space must be drawn into God's life. Just as the Trinity opens itself to time, so also it opens itself to space.

I have already explored the Trinity's openness to space in the cosmological exploration of Moltmann's appropriation of *creatio ex nihilo*. As with time, the divine openness to space is adumbrated in the first creation narrative in which God withdraws in order to make space (i.e., *nihilo*) for the created order to fill. This withdrawal necessitates a distance between God and the cosmos.[70] The distance between God and creation is for the sake of the divine-world rapport. Only with this distance can the world be a genuine other with which God can seek communion.

Yet, God remains with the world. Moltmann describes this tension between immanence and transcendence with the notion of God's Shekinah, which he appropriates from rabbinic and kabbalistic thought.[71] The term denotes a division within God that allows God to be both present in the created order and transcendent to it. In the words of Franz Rosenzweig, "God cuts himself off from himself. He gives himself away to his people."[72] Moltmann states, "The same thing is true in its own degree of the indwelling of God in the creation of his love: he gives himself away to the beings he has

---

68. Moltmann, *GC*, 277.
69. See Law, "Jürgen Moltmann's Ecological Hermeneutics," 230–31.
70. Moltmann, *CoG*, 296–97.
71. He is here particularly influenced by Rosenzweig. See Moltmann, *GC*, 15.
72. Rosenzweig, *Der Stern der Erlösung*; quoted in Moltmann, *GC*, 15.

created, he suffers with their sufferings, he goes with them through the misery of the foreign land" (Moltmann, *GC*, 15). Moltmann links the Shekinah specifically to the Spirit.[73] He goes as far as to say that, as the Spirit/Shekinah, God is in exile with the created order, suffering is separation from God.[74] In this sense, Moltmann maintains that God is open to the creation in both opening the divine space to make a unique space for the created order and in cutting God's own self off in order to share that cosmic space with the creation without obliterating its integrity.

Just as the Sabbath proleptically evinces God's openness to share God's eternal time with the created order, so also the Shekinah proleptically evinces God's openness to share with it the divine space.[75] Hence, the distance between God and the world is not the final destiny of the creation. If the redemption of phenomenological time is the dismantling of transience through the perichoretic union of phenomenological time and eternity, the redemption of space is the traversing of the distance implied by cosmic space through the perichoretic union of the Trinity and the cosmos. The eschatological telos of the cosmos is a perichoretic indwelling with the Triune God. This mutual indwelling occurs when God comes to dwell in the spaces of the world.[76] As the persons of the Trinity interpenetrate each other in a perichoretic union, so also the Trinity and creation will interpenetrate one other in the eschaton.[77] The world becomes *"God's eternal home country."* Conversely, God becomes *"the eternal home of everything* he has created."[78]

---

73. See Moltmann, *GC*, 15, 96; *SL*, 47–51.
74. Moltmann, *GC*, 97.
75. Moltmann, *CoG*, 283.
76. Ibid., 306.
77. Jürgen Moltmann, *In the End, the Beginning: A Life of Hope* (hereafter *IEB*), trans. Margaret Kohl (Minneapolis, MN: Fortress Press, 2004), 103.
78. Ibid., 157–58.

In Moltmann's view, the original divine self-limitation implied by *creatio ex nihilo* corresponds to an eschatological de-limitation in which God comes to earth in order to be at home.[79] God surrenders space in the beginning and gains something new at the end. The divine traversing of the original distance between God and creation—which is literally the negation of the original "nothing" of creation—obliterates neither the uniqueness of the Trinity nor the world: "In the consummation, everything in its unique character (and therefore without losing itself) will dwell within the Deity beyond" (*IEB*, 158).

The Eschatological Community of Creation

As noted, the scope of Moltmann's eschatology includes not only time and space, but all the times of all spaces. According to Moltmann's cosmology, the creation is allotted its time and space by divine withdrawal. Time and space are then filled with life infused with the Spirit. This life, too, is the subject of God's redemptive scope.

Eschatology thus embraces all things. Bauckham notes this all-inclusive eschatology has three underlying foundations.[80] First, God is both Creator and Redeemer; therefore, all creation must be redeemed. Creation and redemption, cosmology and eschatology, are intricately and irrevocably linked. For Moltmann, "without cosmology, eschatology must inevitably turn into a gnostic myth of redemption" (*CoG*, 260). Second, Christ died for all; therefore his resurrection must apply to all.[81] Thus, Moltmann's eschatology establishes a link between his cosmology and Christology: "Unless

---

79. Moltmann, *GC*, 88–89.
80. Bauckham, "Eschatology in *The Coming of God*," 12–13.
81. On this claim, see Moltmann, *CoG*, 69–70; *WJC*, 193–94.

the whole cosmos is reconciled, Christ cannot be the Christ of God and cannot be the foundation of all things" (*WJC*, 306).[82] Third, all creation is interconnected; therefore, the resurrection of part of the creation implies the resurrection of the entire creation.

Regarding humanity, Moltmann's inclusive eschatology has two key facets. First, humans are saved as embodied.[83] As already noted, Moltmann rejects the notion of the immortality of the soul in favor of the notion of the resurrection of the flesh. Second, Moltmann's theology naturally gravitates toward a universalism in which Christ redeems both the victimized and the victimizer.[84] "As the crucified one, the risen Christ is there 'for all'. In the cross of the Son of God, in his abandonment by God, the 'crucified' God is the human God of all godless men and those who have been abandoned by God" (*TCG*, 195). This claim leads Moltmann to critique juridical interpretations of eschatological judgment. For Moltmann, judgment is "not retaliatory justice . . . that gives everyone their 'just deserts'" (*CoG*, 250), but rather the divine setting right of all that has gone astray.[85] In judgment, nothing will be left behind or unredeemed. In Hans Schwarz's words, "There are no dark spots left on the landscape."[86] A universal resurrection is essential to the very idea of justice, for neither the victimized nor the victimizers can be left in their graves.[87] For the sake of judgment, "all the disrupted conditions in creation must be put right so that the new creation can stand on the firm ground of righteousness and justice, and can endure to eternity" (*SRA*, 141). This putting right "embraces the *universal*

---

82. See Chester, *Mission and the Coming of God*, 16–17.
83. Ibid., 16.
84. Moltmann, *SL*, 129–37; *SRA*, 136–37; *HTG*, 44–53; *CoG*, 251.
85. Moltmann, *CoG*, 235–37, 250–51; *SRA*, 4. For an overview, see Harvie, *Moltmann's Ethics of Hope*, 47–51.
86. Schwarz, *Eschatology*, 151.
87. Moltmann, *SRA*, 41; *WJC*, 296–97.

reconciliation of human beings and the *bringing again of all things* into the new eternal creation" (*SRA*, 141). If all is not set right, then judgment is not complete. Thus, God's "'Last Judgment' has no 'double outcome', but serves the universal establishment of the divine righteousness and justice, for the new creation of all things" (*CoG*, 243).[88]

Moltmann's claim that humans will be saved only as embodied is coupled with his claim that they will be saved only as en-cosmosed. "There is no resurrection of the dead without the new earth in which death will be no more" (*CoG*, 69). Regarding the nonhuman creation, then, Moltmann maintains that eschatological consummation and the transfiguration of the cosmos, including its systems of development, are irrevocably connected. Furthermore, he emphasizes that *all flesh* will experience resurrection and redemption.[89] He is explicit that the word "all" includes nonhuman animals.[90] Not simply all species of animals, but every individual animal that has ever lived will participate in God's eternity without losing its individual particularity.[91]

Moltmann's eschatology is more inclusive still. Not only will each individual creature be resurrected, but all times of each creature will be resurrected and experienced by that creature diachronically into a totality of being. Bauckham refers to this eternal existence as Moltmann's "novel concept of resurrection" in which "all creatures as they are diachronically in the process of their history and in all their temporal relationships with other creatures, will be resurrected and transfigured in eternity."[92]

---

88. See also Jürgen Moltmann, "The Logic of Hell," in *God Will Be All in All: The Eschatology of Jürgen Moltmann*, ed. Richard Bauckham (Minneapolis, MN: Fortress Press, 2001), 43–47.
89. Moltmann, *CoG*, 69–70.
90. Moltmann, *WJC*, 335.
91. Moltmann, *CoG*, 306–8.
92. Bauckham, *The Theology of Jürgen Moltmann*, 210.

Thus, for Moltmann, the resurrection is the resurrection of all the times of "all the living."[93] Nothing less suffices. "If we were to surrender hope for as much as one single creature, for us God would not be God" (*CoG*, 132). This resurrection "will also bring 'the deification of the cosmos' through the unhindered participation of all created beings in the livingness of God" (*CoG*, 92).

Moltmann's emphasis on the resurrection of all flesh derives from his christological claim that Jesus is the ultimate victim of evolution. In his death, Christ dies the death of all the victims of evolutionary emergence.[94] Likewise, his resurrection is the hope for a new future for all of those victims. Redemption thus "runs counter to evolution" as "the divine tempest of the new creation, which sweeps out of God's future over history's fields of the dead, waking and gathering every last created being" (*WJC*, 303). In running counter to evolution, redemption actually encompasses evolution within it; for "the forces of nature . . . are themselves in need of redemption" (*SRA*, 68).

The nature of Christian resurrection hope thus constrains "every personal eschatology . . . to press forward to ever-widening circles to cosmic eschatology."[95] The scope of eschatological redemption includes all the times of all spaces and individual instantiations of life. The effect of Jesus's resurrection is so extensive that it includes "plants, stones, and all cosmic life-systems" (*WJC*, 258) in the hope for eternal existence. Even the beautiful needs redemption in its relation to that which is not beautiful. For example, the cooperation of nature needs redeemed in the face of nature's bloody competition.

So maximally inclusive is Moltmann's notion of eschatological redemption, even God is included in it inasmuch as God's "exiled Shekinah" is finally able to come to rest in proper relationship with

93. Moltmann, *CoG*, 69–70.
94. See Moltmann, *CoG*, 69–70; *WJC*, 193–94.
95. Moltmann, *CoG*, 70.

the created order.[96] Because God suffers the creation its own space, "the deliverance or redemption of the world is bound up with the self-deliverance of God from his sufferings" (*TK*, 60). In this sense, there is nothing, neither creation nor God, that is not swept up in the hope for redemption.[97]

Novum and Adventus

Moltmann does not develop his eschatology in a vacuum. He is affected by the historical millenarianism of Constantinian Christianity and the 19th century Christian optimism that he rejects and in contrast to which he affirms eschatological millenarianism.[98] He is likewise affected by the general recovery of eschatology from Albert Schweitzer to Karl Barth.[99] Yet, he distances his own view from theirs. Moltmann writes,

> In dispute with consistently futurist eschatology and the absolute eschatology of eternity, I propose to follow the line taken in *The Theology of Hope*, and put forward *Advent* as an eschatological category, and the category *Novum* as its historical reverse side. (*CoG*, 6)

A futurist eschatology, represented by both Albert Schweitzer and Oscar Cullmann, transports eschatology into time, thus rendering it merely a "not yet" of the "already."[100] An absolute eschatology of eternity risks surrendering the significance of history in the crisis entailed by a wholly other eternity breaking into time.[101] In

96. Moltmann, *CoG*, 305–6; *SL*, 48–49. See also, Neal, *Theology as Hope*, 124–28.
97. For a critique, see John Polkinghorne, *The God of Hope and the End of the World* (New Haven: Yale University Press, 2002), 122–23.
98. See Moltmann, *CoG*, 146–202; Harvie, *Moltmann's Ethics of Hope*, 45; Schwarz, *Eschatology*, 150–51; Bauckham, "Eschatology in *The Coming of God*," 21–22. For a summary and critique of Moltmann's view, see Müller-Fahrenholz, *The Kingdom and the Power*, 207–13.
99. See Moltmann, *TH*, 23–81; Bauckham, "Time and Eternity," 155–57, 174–78.
100. Moltmann, CoG, 7–13.
101. Moltmann, *CoG*, 13–14. On both accounts, see Bauckham, "Time and Eternity," 157.

contradistinction to these two positions, Moltmann suggests that "the eschaton is neither the future of time nor timeless eternity. It is God's coming and his arrival" (CoG, 22). By this claim, Moltmann intends to distinguish eschatology from phenomenological time and thereby emphasize its genuine newness. The eschaton neither develops naturally out of the flow of history nor has no connection to the flow of history. To explicate this position, he offers the related notions of *novum* and *adventus*.[102]

Novum is that which is genuinely new and thus cannot burgeon wholly out of the latencies of history.[103] It must meet history from the future, permitting "eschatological surprise."[104] Because *novum* meets history, the new must not discard the "old." That is, *novum* cannot obliterate history in its coming. It must meet history within history and transfigure it.

Novum comes from *adventus*, which Moltmann juxtaposes to *futurum*. *Futurum* is that which develops out of and within the flow of historical time.[105] *Adventus*, on the other hand, is the eschatological future that comes to phenomenological time and encounters it. It is "*God's* future . . . the future of time itself."[106] In its encounter with God's future (*adventus*), the entirety of the "old" is transfigured into the genuinely "new" (*novum*) without losing its identity.[107]

Adventus makes *novum* possible within history. Thus, there can be genuine proleptic experiences of it in history. However, these experiences are only anticipations that "correspond to the future

---

102. The following discussion derives from Moltmann, CoG, 25–29. See further David Beck, *The Holy Spirit and the Renewal of All Things: Pneumatology in Paul and Jürgen Moltmann* (Eugene, OR: Pickwick Publications, 2007), 121–26. For the influence of Ernst Bloch at this point, see Neal, *Theology as Hope*, 27–32.

103. Harvie, *Moltmann's Ethics of Hope*, 21.

104. Beck, *The Holy Spirit and the Renewal of All Things*, 126.

105. Moltmann, CoG, 25; Bauckham, "Time and Eternity," 163–64.

106. Moltmann, LTF, 265.

107. Moltmann, GC, 132–33.

of the coming God," for the kingdom is not a matter of human effort in history, of *futurum*.[108] This hope for genuine newness and its *anticipations* even within the ebb and flow of history permit Moltmann to avoid, on the one hand, a mere conservation of the world as it is and, on the other, efforts to progressively complete the kingdom within history.[109]

As an example of *novum*, Moltmann refers to the resurrection.[110] The resurrected Christ does not evolve naturally from the crucified Jesus. People do not resurrect as a matter of course. However, the resurrected Christ is no one other than the crucified Jesus transfigured.[111] Thus, the new is not bound to the unfolding sequence of the old. Neither is the old obliterated with the coming of the new.[112] In Bauckham's words, "Historical time cannot produce [the eschatological future], but nor is it unrelated to historical time: it comes to time to transform it."[113] Such is the image of God's coming to the created order. *Adventus* enables *novum*, which implies transfiguration—"a glorifying and a transformation" (*TK*, 123)—but never a replacement.

Ecclesiology as Hope and Mission

How does eschatology impact the present? One of the clearest ways is the work of the Spirit within the church. Thus it is pertinent to consider briefly Moltmann's ecclesiology.

---

108. Moltmann, LTF, 289. See also Bauckham, *The Theology of Jürgen Moltmann*, 104–6; Harvie, *Moltmann's Ethics of Hope*, 23; Müller-Fahrenholz, *The Kingdom and the Power*, 93.
109. See Moltmann, LTF, 276–79.
110. Moltmann, *CoG*, 28–29.
111. See Moltmann, *TH*, 206–7; *TCG*, 160; *TKG*, 123.
112. See Bauckham, "Eschatology in *The Coming of God*," 5–7.
113. Bauckham, "Time and Eternity," 157.

Between his understanding of what constitutes the church and his vision of the relationship between the church and Israel, Moltmann's ecclesiology is complex.[114] My aim here is not a comprehensive overview. I seek only to establish Moltmann's general understanding that the church is the community of hope that witnesses proleptically to the eschatological future. The church is "the agent of eschatological unrest."[115]

In the wake of the resurrection, the Spirit works to draw all creation from the suffering of the cross into the glory of the resurrection.[116] In this sense, the creation is not statically awaiting eschatological redemption. It is rather immersed in the burgeoning of that redemption by the presence of the Spirit.[117] For Moltmann, humanity, and most visibly the church, is to proclaim in word and deed the new creation in the present.[118] The church's

> universal mission is to prepare the way for this future. Christianity prepares for it now by already drawing everything into its worship of God, and by respecting everything, each in its own right, in 'reverence for life.' (SRA, 32)

Bauckham succinctly summarizes Moltmann on this point:

> Christian eschatology is the hope that the world will be different. It is aroused by a promise whose fulfilment can come only from God's eschatological action transcending all the possibilities of history, since it involves the end of all evil, suffering and death in the glory of the divine presence indwelling all things. But it is certainly not therefore without

---

114. For competent summaries of Moltmann's ecclesiology, see Bauckham, *The Theology of Jürgen Moltmann*, 119–50; Müller-Fahrenholz, *The Kingdom and the Power*, 80–106; Veli-Matti Karkkainen, *An Introduction to Ecclesiology: Ecumenical, Historical and Global Perspectives* (Downers Grove, IL: Intervarsity Press, 2002), 126–33.

115. Bauckham, *The Theology of Jürgen Moltmann*, 102.

116. See Moltmann, *TKG*, 89; *SL*, 234.

117. The Spirit is present in nascent form in Moltmann's earlier works. See *TH*, 211–12; *TCG*, 244–46.

118. Moltmann, *CPS*, 76–84, 189–96; *TH*, 20–22; Bauckham, *The Theology of Jürgen Moltmann*, 13–14.

effect in the present. On the contrary, the resurrection set in motion a historical process in which the promise already affects the world and moves in the direction of its future transformation. This process is the universal mission of the church.[119]

The church is centered on the notion of hope, which makes eschatology the subject of advent. There is no real hope without ethics.[120] As such, eschatology is always a combination of hope and praxis.[121] As eschatological agents, Christians must be converted to "the anticipation of life in the kingdom of God in the conditions of the old world" (*WJC*, 102).[122]

If this anticipatory life of hope is true of the Christian, it is also true of the church: "The church in the power of the Holy Spirit is not yet the kingdom of God, but it is its anticipation in history" (*CPS*, 196). Because the church is not yet—nor can it be—*the* kingdom, it must anticipate the kingdom by suffering the contradictions of the world as an exiled community.[123] In these contradictions, it endures the fellow-suffering of the entire created order in love. This solidarity with all creation drives the church to act as a herald of the eschatological future.[124] In this manner, "the *pro-missio* of the kingdom is the ground of the *missio* of love to the world" (*TH*, 209). Such is the church's essentially "eschatological orientation" (*TH*, 309).

The church's eschatological witness entails contradicting the world by alleviating the suffering of creatures. "Those who hope in Christ

119. Bauckham, *The Theology of Jürgen Moltmann*, 10; also, Moltmann, *SL*, 230–31.

120. Moltmann, *TH*, 18.

121. This combination is at the heart of *Theology of Hope*. Moltmann, *TH*, 16; Bauckham, *The Theology of Jürgen Moltmann*, 6.

122. For a good reflection on the function of the phrase "kingdom of God" in Moltmann's thought, see Harvie, *Moltmann's Ethics of Hope*, 39–55.

123. See Bauckham, *The Theology of Jürgen Moltmann*, 146–50; Harvie, *Moltmann's Ethics of Hope*, 31–36; Chester, *Mission and the Coming of God*, 77–85.

124. See Jürgen Moltmann, *God for a Secular Society: The Public Relevance of Theology* (hereafter *GSS*), trans. Margaret Kohl (Minneapolis, MN: Fortress Press, 1999), 105; Neal, *Theology as Hope*, 78–85.

can no longer put up with reality as it is, but begin to suffer under it, to contradict it" (*TH*, 7). Moltmann draws on the Orthodox notion of humans as priests of creation as a way of discussing this role of alleviating suffering.[125] In the Spirit, members of the church are led "into solidarity with all other created things. They suffer *with* nature under the power of transience, and they hope *for* nature, waiting for the manifestation of liberation" (*GC*, 101). This fellow-suffering of the church also pertains to death.

> *Faith* may be able to free us from the religious fear of death, if that means fear of judgment. . . . But *love* brings us into solidarity with the whole sad and sighing creation. We die into the earth, which is need of redemption and awaits it. *Hope*, finally, means that we cannot come to terms with dying at all, or with any death whatsoever, but remain inconsolable until redemption comes. (*CoG*, 93)

Hope for a future without death leads the church to be the life-embracing witness to that future.[126] But what does this witness entail? In part, "resistance against the forces of death and unconditional love for life" (*EH*, 55). In a world of death, the church is a proleptic witness to the eschatological future of the world evident in the resurrection of Christ. In its life-affirmation in the Spirit, the church's hope is transformative for the world.[127]

Conclusion

For Moltmann, with the incarnation of the Son the Trinity welcomes the whole of the cosmos, including the transience of every last speck, into the perichoretic union of the divine life and thereby provides the means of its transfiguration. The Spirit, who is the breath of

125. See Moltmann, *GC*, 189–90; *WJC*, 307–12.
126. Moltmann, *TH*, 17.
127. Ibid., 311–12; *CPS*, 191–96; Harvie, *Moltmann's Ethics of Hope*, 89.

all the living, facilitates this new life within history. While the consummation of creation's telos remains an eschatological affair, the Church nonetheless bears the mission of witnessing to the values of the eschatological kingdom within history. Such is the effect of hope. Given this theological vision, how should the Church engage the nonhuman creation within history? What are the contours of Moltmann's nonhuman theological ethics? It is to these questions that I now turn.

9

9

Moltmann's Nonhuman Theological Ethics

In the previous two chapters, I offered an explication of dimensions of Moltmann's theology pertinent to my thesis. In this chapter, I delineate Moltmann's ethics of cosmocentric transfiguration, both with regard to the whole and individual nonhuman animals. I also suggest why I believe his ethics is inconsistent with the theological foundations I have outlined.

Holistic Ethics

The holistic dimension of Moltmann's ethics burgeons out of his affirmation of the cosmic community. This community is one of law, which entails cosmic rights. The nature of these rights is unclear as they exist in a tension between conservation and transfiguration.

Cosmocentrism and the Cosmic Community

Moltmann specifically targets anthropocentrism as a central culprit in the ecological crisis.[1] He furthermore acknowledges (Western) Christianity's part in this philosophical legacy.[2] The radical monotheism of Western theology validates hierarchal views of the world in which nature becomes merely the object of human use. It is just this human-centered worldview that Christianity must shed if it is to have anything relevant to say in its current context. Moltmann reviews both creation spirituality and the Gaia hypothesis positively inasmuch as they both move toward this aim.[3] Humans must learn about other creatures not for the sake of domination, but rather to know how best to love them for their own sakes.[4] The shedding of anthropocentrism begins with the social Trinity, which replaces the rule of the one with the community of the many.[5]

Moltmann's rejection of anthropocentrism in favor of a cosmic community is similar to Berry's position.[6] This rejection in no way lessens concern for human well-being.[7] Moltmann is adamant: "The dignity of human beings is unforfeitable" (GC, 233). However, the

---

1. Jürgen Moltmann, *Sun of Righteousness, Arise! God's Future for Humanity and the Earth* (hereafter *SRA*), trans. Margaret Kohl (Minneapolis, MN: Fortress Press, 2010), 190–92; Jürgen Moltmann, *God for a Secular Society: The Public Relevance of Theology* (hereafter *GSS*), trans. Margaret Kohl (Minneapolis, MN: Fortress Press, 1999), 96–101; Jürgen Moltmann, *The Spirit of Life: A Universal Affirmation* (hereafter *SL*), trans. Margaret Kohl (Minneapolis, MN: Fortress Press, 1992), 29–31; Jürgen Moltmann, *The Way of Jesus Christ: Christology in Messianic Dimensions* (hereafter *WJC*), trans. Margaret Kohl (Minneapolis, MN: Fortress Press, 1993), 271–72; Jürgen Moltmann, *Ethics of Hope* (hereafter *EH*), trans. Margaret Kohl (Minneapolis, MN: Fortress Press, 2012), 61.
2. Moltmann, *GSS*, 98; *SL*, 36–37; *EH*, 135–36.
3. See Moltmann, *GSS*, 101–110; *EH*, 109–11.
4. Jürgen Moltmann, *God in Creation: A New Theology of Creation and the Spirit of God* (hereafter *GC*), trans. Margaret Kohl (Minneapolis, MN: Fortress Press, 1993), 69–70.
5. Moltmann, *EH*, 68.
6. Moltmann is very close to Berry's "New Story" of the cosmos in *WJC*, 246–47.
7. Moltmann, *SRA*, 144–46; Timothy Harvie, *Jürgen Moltmann's Ethics of Hope: Eschatological Possibilities for Moral Action* (Burlington, VT: Ashgate, 2009), 181–87.

dignity of humanity is not *categorically* unique. It is a manifestation of the dignity of the created order. In the cosmic community, each individual member has its own intrinsic dignity as part of the whole. The individual is not dissolved into the whole. Neither is the whole disregarded on account of the individual. Rather, each member is drawn into the other members in a manner of love that reflects God's communal existence.[8] Everything has worth in itself. But everything is related as a whole; and the whole also has worth in itself.[9]

Despite this notion of the cosmic community, Moltmann does not explicitly embrace cosmocentrism—which he seems to understand only in its pre-industrial context.[10] Rather, he claims that Christianity must recover its theocentrism.[11] However, while Moltmann is critical of cosmocentrism divorced from theocentrism,[12] his description of theocentrism matches what I have defined as cosmocentrism within a theocentric framework.[13] That is, God has given all creatures value apart from their utility to one another. Such is the theological and ethical significance of the Sabbath.[14] Moltmann writes, "Life is an end in itself...it is beyond utility or uselessness" (*EH*, 59). No creature is simply a chain in evolutionary emergence.[15] No creature is merely a resource for human use. Thus, Moltmann can write: "It is not the human being that is at the center of the earth; it is life" (*EH*, 61-62). This biocentric statement is grounded by his theocentrism: "If this earth, together with all living things, is *God's creation*, then its

8. Moltmann, *EH*, 68, 137.

9. On holistic value, see Moltmann, *GSS*, 101.

10. See Moltmann, *GSS*, 130.

11. Moltmann, *GC*, 30–31, 139; Richard Bauckham in *The Theology of Jürgen Moltmann* (Edinburgh: T&T Clark, 1995), 189–90, 93; Steven Bouma-Prediger, *The Greening of Theology: The Ecological Models of Rosemary Radford Ruether, Joseph Sittler, and Jürgen Moltmann* (Atlanta, GA: Scholars Press, 1995), 231.

12. See Moltmann, *WJC*, 271–72.

13. See Bauckham, *The Theology of Jürgen Moltmann*, 158, 200–3; Moltmann, *WJC*, 46–47, 276.

14. Moltmann, *GC*, 286.

15. Moltmann, *SRA*, 222–23; *EH*, 128.

dignity must be respected for *God's* sake, and its continued existence must be protected for its *own* sake" (*GSS*, 111). Whereas for Aquinas the nonhuman creation exists for God by existing *for humanity*, for Moltmann the nonhuman creation, including each individual creature, exists for God *for its own sake*.[16]

(Conservationist) Law and the Cosmic Community

Moltmann's theocentrically based cosmocentrism bears legal ramifications. His affirmation of a community of creation in which all individual members bear a unique dignity coupled with his dismantling of anthropocentrism places him firmly in the cosmocentric category as I have delineated it. There is one cosmic community. But community relies on law, which safeguards the integrity of its members. Law is especially necessary for creatures that cannot make formal legal protests themselves. Thus, Moltmann calls for a legal solidification of the rights of the various parts of the cosmos for their own sakes.[17]

This law certainly entails conservation. Humanity cannot live by destroying the world.[18] Humans must use nature conservatively and, in some sense, let nature be nature. Moltmann makes this appeal with reference to the Sabbath:

> In the sabbath stillness men and women no longer intervene in the environment through their labour. They let it be entirely God's creation. They recognize that as God's property creation is inviolable; and they sanctify the day through their joy in existence as God's creatures within the fellowship of creation. The peace of the sabbath is peace with God first of all. But this divine peace encompasses not merely

---

16. Moltmann, *GSS*, 104; *EH*, 127–28.
17. Moltmann, *GSS*, 112–13; Moltmann, *GC*, 289–90. On human rights, see Bauckham, *The Theology of Jürgen Moltmann*, 113–17.
18. Moltmann, *GC*, 46–47.

the soul but the body too; not merely individuals but family and people; not only human beings but animals as well; not living things alone, but also, as the creation story tells us, the whole creation of heaven and earth. (GC, 277)

In line with this sabbatical letting-be, Moltmann offers general boundaries and guidelines for the law of the cosmic community.[19] The Sabbath laws imply a peace in the cosmic community. But they also demand compassion within the human community itself. Thus Moltmann's theology mandates a balance with regard to utilization of the earth between first and third world nations.[20] He is also adamant about the rights of individual humans, human communities, and future humans.[21] This balance includes a law of compensation for the sake of the entire cosmic community:

> The first ecological law is that for every intervention in nature there must be a compensation. If you cut down a tree you must plant a new one...If your city builds a power station, it must plant a forest which produces just as much oxygen as the power plant uses up. (GSS, 94)

Thus Moltmann advocates conservationism; for "every intervention in nature which can never be made good again is a sacrilege" (GSS, 105).

In addition to Sabbath laws, Moltmann also highlights the significance of divine immanence. Because Christ is the wisdom of creation, "the person who reverences Christ also reverences all created things in him, and him in everything created." Correspondingly, then, "what we do to the earth, we do to Christ" (GSS, 103). Likewise, a recognition of the presence of the Spirit in

---

19. On these guidelines, see also Jürgen Moltmann, "The Liberation of the Future and Its Anticipations in History" (hereafter LTF), in *God Will Be All in All: The Eschatology of Jürgen Moltmann*, ed. Richard Bauckham (Minneapolis, MN: Fortress Press, 2001), 280–89.
20. Moltmann, *GSS*, 92–95.
21. See ibid., 110, 117–29.

the cosmos "leads to a cosmic adoration of God and an adoration of God in all things" (GSS, 104).

In line with these sabbatical principles and the affirmation of divine immanence, in *Ethics of Hope* Moltmann delineates four general rights of the inanimate creation.[22] First, it has the right to existence, which Moltmann defines as "preservation and development." Second, it has the right to the integrity of its ecosystems. Third, it has the right to its own development apart from human intervention with the exception of justified and legitimate cases. Concerning the criteria of justification and legitimacy, Moltmann states that interventions

> are only permissible if the conditions for the intervention have been established in a democratically legitimate proceeding and with regard to the rights of nature, if the concern behind the intervention is weightier than the concern for an undiminished preservation of the rights of nature, and if the intervention is not excessive.[23]

Furthermore, "after any damage, nature must be restored once more whenever possible."[24]

Finally, for Moltmann rare ecosystems are under absolute protection. These rights pertain to the eschatological future of the cosmos as the temple of God's Shekinah.[25]

Transfiguration and the Cosmic Community

The cosmic community is a community of law. Yet, for Moltmann the present existence of the cosmos cannot be isolated from the totality of its existence, including the future hope of *creatio nova*. Thus there is a tension within the law of the community between the law

22. The following is from Moltmann, *EH*, 144–45.
23. Ibid., 144.
24. Ibid.
25. Ibid., 150.

of nature (as we encounter them in our experience of *creatio continua*) and the law of creation (which is revealed as *novum* in the advent of God's eschatological future). I here explore the tension Moltmann's eschatology causes for his ethics.

Law, Nature, and (New) Creation

For Moltmann, one of the tasks of theology is to "show how nature is to be understood as God's creation" (*GC*, 38). Here again is the distinction between "nature" and "creation." Nature cannot be theologically discarded; for "the present world is a real symbol of its future" (*GC*, 56).[26] However, "nature" is both distorted and open to the eschatological future.[27] Therefore, an understanding of "creation" cannot be wholly based on the laws and cycles of observable nature. To subsume creation into nature isolates what is (*creatio continua*) from what will be (*creatio nova*) and is thus theologically myopic. Therefore—to use my own categories—the law of *nature* cannot be the ultimate law of *creation*. This claim has ethical import; for "Christian ethics are eschatological ethics" (*TLF*, 289).

In Christ, "resurrection has become the universal 'law' of creation" (*WJC*, 258). The resurrection permits humanity to see nature anew, according to its eschatological destiny of transfiguration. Christ's resurrection reveals nature as creation. Because the entire cosmos is included in the hope for the eschatological resurrection, "all those who hope for a resurrection [are] under an obligation to remain true to the earth, to respect it, and to love it as they love themselves" (*SRA*, 72). Thus, the law of creation (i.e., resurrection) establishes a new community of creation—the community of *creatio nova* in which

---

26. On the relationship between natural and revealed theology, see *GC*, 57–60.
27. Moltmann, *WJC*, 251; *GC*, 63, 197–206.

"mutual destruction is replaced by a community of peace in which all created being are there for one another, with one another and in one another" (*WJC*, 255).

Moltmann does not relegate the law of creation to a transcendent future. This new future already breaks into history as *adventus* with the redemptive presence of the Spirit in the wake of the Christ event. The inbreaking future opens the entire community of creation to proleptic moments of *novum* in the unfolding of history.

Yet, Moltmann's eschatology makes it clear that the eschatological kingdom is not a matter of human effort. One cannot discard the law of nature and attempt to systematize *creatio nova* in the midst of *creatio continua*. There is thus a tension, not so much between the "already" and the "not yet" but rather between *creatio continua* and *creatio nova*. Moltmann resolves this tension by maintaining that the law of creation challenges the law of nature (again, my categories) by way of *anticipation*:

> The hope for God's eschatological transformation of the world leads to a transformative ethics which tries to accord with this future in the inadequate material and with the feeble powers of the present and thus anticipates it. (*EH*, xiii)

In the midst of *creatio continua*, there exists a "*creatio anticipavita*" (*GC*, 209), the prolepsis of *creatio nova* in the presence of the Spirit. While Moltmann is careful to distinguish anticipation from fulfillment, anticipation is nonetheless "already the presence of the future in the conditions of history" (*CPS*, 193).

The Law of (New) Creation and Historical Practice

It is clear that Moltmann's notion of a cosmic community governed by law cannot be limited to conservation of "nature." Indeed, Moltmann is critical of such ethics, writing,

> Deep respect for 'the good earth' does not mean that we have to give ourselves up for burial with the consolation that we shall live on in worms and plants. It means waiting for the day when the earth will open, the dead will rise, and the earth together with these dead will 'be raised' for its new creation. (*CoG*, 276–77)

While this critique is directed at Rosemary Radford Ruether, it applies to those like Teilhard de Chardin and Berry as well.

In contradistinction to these views, Moltmann consistently claims along with Eastern theologians that the eschatological telos of the cosmos is transfiguration.[28] Thus, conservation in the present does justice to the community of nature, but not the community of *creation*. Moltmann's ethics moves, at least in theory, beyond conservation to incorporate transfiguration. Conservation and preservation remain important.[29] They pertain to a realistic worldview. But they do not exhaust human responsibility to the cosmos, which includes witnessing to new possibilities in hope through proleptic, transforming action.[30]

The transfigurative dimension of Moltmann's ethics is qualified by his theocentric cosmocentrism. In this way, his position differs from many Orthodox writers. Though he cites Dumitru Staniloae frequently, he especially differs from him. Moltmann does not define

---

28. Moltmann, *WJC*, 47–48, 302; Jürgen Moltmann, *The Coming of God: Christian Eschatology* (hereafter *CoG*), trans. Margaret Kohl (Minneapolis, MN: Fortress Press, 1996), 267–79.

29. See Moltmann, *GSS*, 92–101.

30. Moltmann, *EH*, 3–5; Jürgen Moltmann, *The Church in the Power of the Spirit: A Contribution to Messianic Ecclesiology* (hereafter *CPS*), trans. Margaret Kohl (Minneapolis, MN: Fortress Press, 1993), 191–96.

creation's eschatological inclusion according to an anthropocentric sacramental role.[31] On the contrary, in the eternal kingdom "God will be directly and universally manifest through himself, and creation with all created things will participate directly and without any mediation in his eternal life" (GC, 64). The nonhuman creation's participation in eternity is not predicated upon the facilitation of the divine-human drama. Rather, every instantiation of life, every particle of matter, participates in God's communal life *for its own sake*.

This ethics of cosmocentric transfiguration suggests that the human role is to witness to the eschatological kingdom of God, which Moltmann defines as "God in all things and all things in God" (SRA, 32). It is in this manner that Moltmann writes, "Creation is to be redeemed through human liberty" (GC, 69). The nonhuman creation experiences redemption here and now through humanity's Spirit-enabled witness to the perichoretic communion of the eschatological future. This human role is not predicated upon creation's sacramentality, but rather upon God's desire for the creation for its own sake. Humans do not love the creation in order to love God; they love God by loving the creation for its own sake. God desires the human being to be *for the created order for its own sake*.

Individual Nonhuman Animals

My delineation of Moltmann's holistic ethics points toward how that ethics would affect humanity's relation to individual nonhuman animals. Animals are part of the cosmic community. God desires them for their own sake. They share a destiny *with humanity*: transfiguration and a perichoretic indwelling with the Trinity. Here, I seek to examine more closely Moltmann's engagement with

31. Moltmann, GC, 69–71.

nonhuman animals and critically suggest where his ethics *should go* based on his theological framework.

Human Uniqueness; Human Responsibility

The affirmation of a cosmic community in which all living creatures participate does not entail that all creatures are the same. There are important commonalities—especially regarding the telos of life—but there are also differences.[32] Moltmann's anthropology maintains that "human beings must neither disappear into the community of creation, nor must they be detached from that community" (GC, 190).

For Moltmann, humanity's central uniqueness is expressed in the doctrine of the *imago Dei*. (He also views humans as unique with reference to awareness of death and, as a result, desire to sin.)[33] However, unlike much of the substantialistic tradition before him, for Moltmann this difference does not afford humans a unique privilege over and against animals.[34] He is explicit that the *imago Dei* denotes neither despotism nor dominion.[35] In conjunction with relational interpretations of the *imago*, Moltmann maintains that humans exist *with and before* God. In conjunction with functional interpretations of the *imago*, he maintains that humans exist *with and before* the created order. Humans have a "priestly calling." We "stand before God on behalf of creation, and before creation on behalf of God" (GC, 190). This priestly function is, at least in part, for the sake of creation.

---

32. For a general overview, see Bouma-Prediger, *The Greening of Theology*, 223–30.
33. See Moltmann, *CoG*, 54, 91, 93.
34. See Douglas John Hall, *Imaging God: Dominion as Stewardship* (Grand Rapids, MI: William B. Eerdmans Publishing Company, 1986), 90.
35. Moltmann, *EH*, 67–68.

To understand the nature of this function, it is pertinent to remember that Moltmann's anthropology is Irenaean.[36] While *imago Dei*, human beings are called to *become* the *imago Christi* in the world.[37] Thus, the *imago* is both a reality and calling. Functioning as the *imago* bears different ethical meanings for animals than it does for the earth. Says Moltmann:

> The prophetic visions of the messianic kingdom of peace (Isa. 11.6ff) give sublime and ultimate form to [the] initial peaceful order between animals, human beings and the plants of the earth. But the beginning teaches that human lordship over the animals has to be distinguished from human subjection of the earth for the purposes of nourishment, and distinguished more clearly than is the case in the traditional theological doctrine of the *dominium terrae*; for this doctrine throws the two together and intermixes them, with disastrous consequences for the world. (*GC*, 224)

For humans bearing the *imago*, subduing the earth means "nothing but the injunction to eat vegetable food." But for animals it is different: "there is no mention at all in the creation accounts of enmity between human beings and beasts, or of a right to kill animals. Human beings are appointed as 'justices of the peace'" (*GC*, 188).

On a few occasions Moltmann references—at least within the symbols of biblical mythology—the vegetarian diet of protological humans.[38] While he rejects the historicity of this Edenic state, he nonetheless accepts that it provides a prolepsis of the eschatological future. The peaceful vision of creation in Genesis 1 envisions the eschatological kingdom of Christ. It is to this kingdom that humans

---

36. See Matthew Craig Steenberg, *Irenaeus on Creation: The Cosmic Christ and the Saga of Redemption* (Boston: Brill, 2008), 101–52.

37. See Moltmann, *GC*, 225–28; Harvie, *Moltmann's Ethics of Hope*, 172–74.

38. Moltmann, *GC*, 29–31, 187–88, 224.

must witness. Thus, with regard to nonhuman animals, the priestly role of humanity implied by the *imago* is one of reverential service that reflects Christ's own eschatological ministry.

Moltmann's understanding of the *imago* suggests that not only do animals *not* exist for the sake of humans—as both Aristotle and Aquinas maintained—but humans exist functionally for their well-being. Anything less is an affront to the God whose image humanity bears:

> As the image of the Creator, human beings will love all their fellow creatures with the Creator's love. Otherwise, far from being the image of the Creator and lover of all the living, they will be his caricature. (*GSS*, 132)

The human task in creation is to function as *imago*. In this sense, the *imago* does not remove nonhumans from the realm of dignity. Indeed, the greater dignity humanity bears, the greater dignity one may ascribe to the creation because humans are called to function on its behalf. In this sense, there can be no talk of human dignity apart from the cosmos. "We can talk about special human dignity if the premise is our recognition of *the creation dignity* of all other creatures—not otherwise" (*GSS*, 132).

The difference between humans and animals is thus not that proposed by modern anthropocentric followers of Immanuel Kant. Moltmann is extremely critical of the distinction between "person" and "thing" with regard to nature generally, but especially with regard to animals.[39] "An animal is not a human 'person', but it is not a 'thing' or a 'product' either. It is a living being, with its own rights, and it requires the protection of public law" (*GSS*, 131).[40]

---

39. Moltmann, *GSS*, 129–30.
40. Ibid., 131.

The recognition of such rights is part of the priestly and eschatological role of humanity. In it, human beings witness to a deeply significant commonality between humans and animals: Christ died for both. This claim draws all creatures into a common telos and a common dignity.

> If Christ has died not merely for the reconciliation of human beings, but for the reconciliation of all other creatures too, then every created being enjoys infinite value in God's sight, and has its own right to live; this is not true of human beings alone. If according to the Christian view the uninfringeable dignity of human beings is based on the fact that 'Christ died for them', then this must also be said of the dignity of all other living things. And it is this that provides the foundation for an all-embracing reverence for life.[41] (*WJC*, 256)

On account of Christ's death and resurrection, "every created being" has "infinite value" and "its own right to live." Thus, the theological grounding of creation's dignity leads to a political dimension of humanity's priestly role vis-à-vis nonhuman animals: animal rights.

(Individual) Nonhuman Animal Rights

Moltmann claims that "a Universal Declaration of Animal Rights should be part of the constitutions of modern states and international agreements" (*GSS*, 131).[42] Yet, like many of his ethical claims Moltmann is vague in his description of animal rights. He maintains that these rights must include a prohibition on factory farming and GMOs.[43] He wavers on animal experimentation, calling for reduction through the development of alternative methods, but not cessation.[44]

---

41. Moltmann borrows the terms "reverence for life" from Albert Schweitzer. Moltmann, *SL*, xiii; *WJC* 256.
42. See also Moltmann, *WJC*, 256, 307–8.
43. Moltmann, *GSS*, 131; *EH*, 156–57.
44. Moltmann, *GSS*, 131.

He does not—nor could he—reject that humans can "use" animals.[45] However, use is qualified by this eschatological caveat: "God wants all he has created to live in peace with one another 'each according to its kind'" (*WJC*, 311).

Moltmann's vagueness derives partly from an agnosticism:

> It is not yet fully clear what it means to withdraw from human beings the right of disposal over the creatures which they are in a position to dominate. But it quite certainly includes the protection of species. (*WJC*, 311)

It seems to me that Moltmann is clear about the conservationist side of ethics (protection of species). In *Ethics of Hope*, he claims that all animals have the right to "preservation and development of its genetic inheritance" and "a species-appropriate life" (*EH*, 144). His vagueness—which I maintain is a hesitancy to follow his own theological thought to conclusion—seems to arise with reference to what individual nonhuman animals, who have "*infinite value*" and a "*right* to live" (*WJC*, 256), are due in actual praxis. It is here that I will critique Moltmann's ethics.

Humanity as the Proleptic Witness to a Particular Eschatological Hope

While Moltmann embraces, however vaguely, the notion of animal rights in a conservationist sense, I submit that his eschatological theology mandates that he go further in order to be consistent with his own framework. That is, while his theology relies heavily on the notion of cosmic transfiguration—including every instantiation of life that has ever lived—his ethics toward nonhuman life is at times astonishingly conservationist. Here, I aim to delineate what I believe

---

45. Ibid., 112.

to be ethical principles that are consistent with Moltmann's theology. I then argue that Moltmann's own ethics are inconsistent in light of these principles.

The Church Revisited (for Nonhuman Animals)

As already noted, for Moltmann it is humans who, in Christ, are able to see the world as a new cosmic community of peace that reflects resurrection as the new "universal 'law' of creation" (*WJC*, 258) for all life. Trevor Hart refers to this notion as the imagination of humanity set loose by the Spirit.[46] More specifically, it is the church that is meant to be the heart of this new community in history. It becomes as such by opening itself to the suffering of others within the contradictions of the world:

> When the weaker creatures die, the whole community of creation suffers. If the church sees itself as representing creation, then it will feel this suffering of creation's weaker creatures as conscious pain, and it will have to cry out in public protest. (*GSS*, 105)[47]

In this reference, Moltmann is engaging creation spirituality and is most likely referring to the "weaker creatures" in a general sense (i.e., the loss of a species). At any rate, the church is to represent the new creation and the new law of resurrection by embracing the suffering of all life as its own and lamenting death, whether human or nonhuman. This fellow-suffering leads to protest—to action on behalf of those that suffer. It is a refusal to become numb to nature's law of death. Says Moltmann:

We have got used to death, at least the death of other creatures and

---

46. Trevor Hart, "Imagination for the Kingdom of God? Hope, Promise, and the Transformative Power of an Imagined Future," in *God Will Be All in All: The Eschatology of Jürgen Moltmann*, ed. Richard Bauckham (Minneapolis, MN: Fortress Press, 2001), 61–76.
47. Also, Jürgen Moltmann, *Theology of Hope: On the Ground and Implications of Christian Eschatology* (hereafter *TH*), trans. James W. Leitch (London, UK: SCM Press, 1967), 183.

other people. And to get used to death is the beginning of freezing into lifelessness oneself. So the essential thing is to affirm life—the life of other creatures—the life of other people—our own lives…the people who truly affirm and love life take up the struggle against violence and injustice. They refuse to get used to it. They do not conform. They resist. (SL, xii)

Therefore, while ultimate justice remains eschatological, the church, in hope, willingly suffers and protests in the midst of the contradictions of history. In that suffering, the church becomes a prolepsis of the future. And that future is the reverse of the suffering itself:

Anyone who lives in necessary contradiction to the laws and powers of 'this world' hopes for a new world of correspondences. The contradiction suffered is itself the negative mirror-image of the correspondence hoped for. (CoG, 200)

Witness to the eschatological future entails becoming the "mirror-image" of the contradictions that creatures suffer in history. Thus is the eschatological mission of the church. But what should this "mirror-image" look like with reference to nonhuman animals?

The New Law of Resurrection and Transfigurative Ethics

Given Moltmann's position regarding the new law of resurrection and the new community it establishes, it seems quite accurate to claim that Christians ought to live in such a way as to protect all creatures from suffering and death and also attempt to shape public policy along these lines. Surely this protection ought to take the shape of a deeply transfigurative ethics.[48] After all, Christ reveals that neither suffering nor death pertain to the eschatological future of

---

48. Harvie's *Moltmann's Ethics of Hope* offers very little by way of nonhuman ethics.

any individual creature. If such is the case, then no one can justify killing by appealing to the *naturalness* of death. There is a new law—a law of life. There is a new community—a community of peace. This community includes all creation and entails a cosmic sympathy—a suffering together that "banishes fear and the struggle for existence from creation" (*GC*, 213).

Therefore, the suffering and death of any and every creature should cause lament. Such transience is antithetical to God's kingdom, of which the church is a proleptic witness. Because every life is part of the community and sighs for redemption, every life taken out of necessity should elicit a "metaphysical sadness," which Moltmann defines as "a feeling for the tragedy of history" (*EH*, 75).[49]

Yet even more can be said when one adds Moltmann's understanding of eternity to his christological eschatology and the new cosmic community it entails. For Moltmann, eternity is the fullness of time—all time gathered up into an eternal present. As such, a nonhuman animal's participation in eternity entails that the totality of its cosmic times be gathered up into God's life. The entire history of that creature is gathered into the eternal present.[50] But this point suggests that *every moment of time of every creature's life bears eternal significance*. Each moment of every individual creature's life is sacred. Therefore, to cause one creature even a moment of suffering is to embrace the order of transience. While at times such actions might be necessary, it seems to me that they should never be considered good.

---

49. Moltmann is here discussing medical ethics and focusing on humanity. Still, I believe the point is consistent with his understanding of all victims of suffering and death.
50. Moltmann, *CoG*, 75.

Moltmann's Inconsistency:
The New Law of Resurrection and Meat-Eating

Moltmann's theology provides the grounds for a radical ethics of cosmocentric transfiguration. Yet, whether or not Moltmann adheres to such an ethics with regard to nonhuman animals is unclear. In fact, his ethics seems to suffer from a lack of consistency vis-à-vis his theological framework. This inconsistency is evident in his views on vegetarianism.

If the eschatological future is seriously a category of *novum*, then every proleptic witness to it is simultaneously an act of rebellion toward some reality pertaining to the present—a "mirror-image" of the "contradiction suffered" (*CoG*, 200). So, if "an ethics of hope sees the future in light of Christ's resurrection" and "points the way to transforming action so as to anticipate as far as possible, as far as strength goes, the new creation of all things" (*EH*, 41); if this new creation entails a cosmic peace between humans and animals that precludes predation; and if so many humans on the planet today eat meat out of luxury and not necessity; then it seems an inevitable conclusion that vegetarianism is a higher form of proleptic witness than meat-eating. The same reasoning that Moltmann applies elsewhere (e.g., regarding fair trade prices) applies here. Just prices in a global economy are not "already the kingdom of God itself; but...they correspond to the kingdom more closely than unjust prices" (*TLF*, 288). It seems to me that, following the same logic, vegetarianism better corresponds to the eschatological kingdom—in which peace will reign and death will be no more—than meat-eating.[51]

---

51. This conclusion only applies to those who are contextually able to live without meat. On Moltmann's balance between amorphous and rigid ethics, see Moltmann, *EH*, 74.

Moltmann does not make this link between the eschatological future and vegetarianism explicitly. He does claim that vegetarianism is a better way to live; but, like Berry, this claim seems more about preservation than eschatological witness.

> It is…useful not to eat the goods which top the food chain but to move away from meat to vegetarian dishes. How much grain has to be used in order to produce one kilo of meat? It is not just cheaper to eat vegetarian food but fairer too, and healthier in addition. No one must suddenly become a vegetarian if his body cannot cope with the changeover to vegetarian food, but everyone can reduce his consumption of animal food to some extent, as long as this is not distasteful. (*EH*, 157)

The qualification of "as long as this is not distasteful" strikingly undermines any notion that vegetarianism is optimal for Christian living. It makes sense for Moltmann to suggest that people hindered by health issues should not "suddenly" switch to vegetarianism.

Even so, for Moltmann, one *does not even have to "reduce his consumption" of meat if it is "distasteful" to do so!* The weakness of this claim is certainly confusing in light of Moltmann's Christology. He states,

> Unless *the whole* cosmos is reconciled, Christ cannot be the Christ of God and cannot be the foundation of all things. But if he is this foundation, then Christians cannot encounter other creatures in any way other than the way they encounter human beings: every creature is a being for whom Christ died on the cross in order to gather it into the reconciliation of the world. (*WJC*, 307).

How can one encounter an animal in the same way "they encounter human beings" and eat it simply because the alternative is "distasteful"? Moltmann's position takes the form of a half-hearted suggestion that aims not to offend. At the same time, it in surprisingly inconsistent with his theology.

In Sum

Moltmann's vague ethics of nonhuman animals can be summed up consistently with his theology as follows. All members of the community of creation should be protected under law. Each animal is a member of the community that is meant to reflect the perichoretic love of the Trinity. Each sighs under the chains of evolutionary emergence—under the transience of death. Each is imbued with the Spirit that awakens its life and opens it to the eschatological future. Each is the subject of Christ's redemptive action on the cross and in the resurrection. Each will have all of the moments of its life gathered up into the fullness of eternal life at the resurrection. Each will participate in God's eschatological kingdom of interpenetrating love. For all of these reasons, each individual animal has its worth and dignity and therefore has the right to live. Every violation of the eschatological destiny of all creatures requires some form of justification. Humans do not have the right to kill animals; they have the responsibility to serve them as proleptic witnesses of a future in which all the negatives in history will be negated in the coming of God.

Conclusion

Moltmann's theological vision as it pertains to my thesis may be summarized as the history of the triune God and the world. The beginning of this history is the self-limitation of God, which is an outpouring of the eternal love that constitutes the unity of the social Trinity. This limitation enables the space and time within which the created order develops in its own integrity. The ongoing nature of this history is the dynamism in which God moves in and toward the cosmos—which is in some sense both corrupted and incomplete (i.e., it is "nature")—from the eschatological future. The ultimate telos of this history is an eschatological panentheism in which the Trinity and the totality of the created order perichoretically indwell one another in eternity. Within this history, the Son and the Spirit act in unique manners in order to bring the created order to its telos. The Son is both the wisdom of the created order and, in the incarnation, the historical concretization of its telos. The Spirit is the principle of life and the reinvigorating principle of new life. Because the Spirit and the Son (through the Spirit) continue to be active in the history of the created order in a redemptive fashion, the eschatological consummation continues to move toward the world in history, making it new without obliterating it. The church is the proleptic community of this movement, bearing witness to the genuine newness of the inbreaking kingdom of God. Humanity's experience of redemption calls them to participate in proclaiming eschatological hope by living in solidarity with all who suffer and engaging in efforts to alleviate that suffering. The picture Moltmann envisions is a perichoretic community of creation analogous to God's own communal life. Because all life constitutes the community, the division between community and resource dissolves.

Based on this theological vision, Moltmann's nonhuman theological ethics fits in the category of cosmocentric transfiguration. It cannot bear anthropocentrism. Nor can it bear mere conservationism. Human beings should act as proleptic witnesses to the eschatological future in which all creatures will participate together in the Trinity's communion and will thereby live in eternity. The dimensions of transience that pertain to the present order of creation—death and suffering—will be no more in the kingdom of God. Because it is *this kingdom* to which humanity is called to be a witness, because it is *this kingdom* they render proleptically present through anticipation, the manner of mission must be life-affirmation. This affirmation pertains to humans, nonhuman animals, and the earth itself.

10

Linzey on Creation, Fall, and Redemption

"For me the choice has always been between theism and nihilism. There is either reason to hope or nothing to hope for; good news or no news at all."[1] This claim evinces the import of religion for Andrew Linzey. However, his first work, *Animal Rights*, is much less theologically explicit than his later works.[2] He acknowledges a development in his appreciation for the Christian tradition. In self-critique, he states that his early work "failed to grapple sufficiently with the theological tradition about animals that we have inherited" and thereby offered "moral critique with insufficient theological understanding."[3] Turning more thoroughly to the Christian tradition in his second work he writes, "The best the Christian tradition has to offer cannot . . . be bettered elsewhere" (*CRA*, 5).[4] Linzey's

---

1. Andrew Linzey, *Animal Gospel* (hereafter *AG*), (Louisville, KY: Westminster John Knox, 1998), 1. Hereafter, quotes from Linzey's work will be cited parenthetically in the text.
2. Andrew Linzey, *Animal Rights: A Christian Assessment* (hereafter *AR*), (London: SCM, 1976).
3. Andrew Linzey, *Christianity and the Rights of Animals* (hereafter *CRA*), (New York: Crossroad, 1987), 5.
4. See especially Andrew Linzey, *After Noah: Animals and the Liberation of Theology* (hereafter *AN*), (Herndon, VA: Mowbray, 1997), 62–113.

237

theological emphasis continues into *Animal Gospel,* in which he claims: "I believe that without faith in the Gospel we are inexorably led to a fundamental kind of despair about animal suffering" (*AG,* 2).[5] Given this development, in this chapter and the next I seek to delineate key features of Linzey's theology that provide the foundation for his ethics, which I address in chapter 12. To begin, I examine Linzey's theology proper and the narrative of creation, fall, and redemption in his work.

The Trinity of Suffering Love

In *Animal Gospel,* Linzey concludes his introduction with a personal credo. It affirms God as the Creator of all, Jesus as the "Word made flesh," and the Spirit as the animator of all life.[6] He ends with a Trinitarian prayer: "May God the Holy Trinity give me strength to live out my commitment to this day" (*AG,* 8). This creed evinces the Trinitarian roots of Linzey's theology. He derives three important points from this doctrine: (1) God's nature is love and is open to the created order; (2) this love grounds rights; and (3) God's openness is the ground for eschatological hope.

God's openness to creation is fundamentally predicated upon Trinitarian love. "God is *for* creation. I mean by that that God, as defined by Trinitarian belief, cannot be fundamentally indifferent, negative or hostile to the creation which is made."[7] God's Trinitarian nature, which is love, opens itself to creation, thereby allowing

---

5. Michael Hauskeller, though not a theist, concurs with Linzey's assessment, claiming that without some religious framework there can be no intrinsic value of all creatures. Michael Hauskeller, *Biotechnology and the Integrity of Life: Taking Public Fears Seriously* (Burlington, VT: Ashgate Publishing, 2007), 77–90.

6. Linzey, *AG,* 7.

7. Andrew Linzey, *Animal Theology* (hereafter *AT*), (Chicago: University of Illinois Press, 1994), 24.

creation to be itself. But this space is ultimately meant to be overcome, evident in the incarnation: "The Trinity is that community of love which has already taken creation to itself, to bind it, and heal it, and make it whole" (*AN*, 77).

For Linzey, God's Trinitarian love establishes rights for the created order.[8] Thus, Linzey's view of animal rights is, especially in his later works, predicated upon the rights of the Creator as opposed to the creation itself, a view to which he refers to as theos-rights. It is the Trinity's shared narrative with the world in the economy of salvation that permits Linzey to extend his understanding of rights to nature.

The Trinity's nature, as love, also grounds the economy of salvation for the created order, including its eschatological hope. Said differently, the ultimate hope of the created order is predicated upon God's story with it, a story in which the Trinity works toward the eschatological consummation of all things. Says Linzey:

> God the Father gives life; God the Son in his passion, death, and resurrection rescues this life from its own folly and wickedness, thereby reconciling it again to the Father; and God the Spirit indwells in this life preserving it from dissolution, working towards the redemption and consummation of all created things. (*CRA*, 71)[9]

Thus, the Trinity grounds both the creation's current existence and its eschatological hope. Only because the Trinity is open to the suffering of the entire cosmos can there be any hope that "*all* suffering can be transformed by joy" (*CRA*, 45). In this manner, the Trinity is imperative for Linzey's theology, his understanding of animal rights, and his hope for the future.

Because the Trinity's love is a suffering love, God must be passible. In *Animal Theology*, Linzey writes that the

---

8. Ibid., 24, 95.
9. See also Andrew Linzey, *Creatures of the Same God: Explorations in Animal Theology* (hereafter *CSG*), (New York: Lantern Books, 2009), 53.

'for-ness' of God toward creation is dynamic, inspirational, and costly. It is dynamic because God's affirmation of creation is not a once-and-for-all event but a continual affirmation otherwise it would simply cease to be. It is inspirational because God's Spirit moves within creation—especially within those creatures that have the gift of a developed capacity to be. It is costly because God's love does not come cheap. (*AT*, 25)

Evident in this quote is Linzey's position that the original act of creation is a risk for God inasmuch as it entails the inauguration of an ongoing dynamism that is at least in part free from divine control.[10] In a manner similar to Moltmann, Linzey maintains that creation necessitates a God who is willing to suffer the cosmos its own integrity. Creation must begin with an act of kenosis. This kenosis continues throughout creation's narrative because the Trinity continuously safeguards the integrity of the cosmos. God continues to suffer in this narrative, particularly with reference to sin and redemption.[11]

For Linzey, this scope of God's co-suffering with the creation is maximal. God's suffering is open to all suffering.[12] Thus, the Trinity encompasses the travails of individual nonhuman animals—at least the travails that are bound up in the notion of sentience, which Linzey defines as "sense of perception *and* the capacity to experience pain" (*AR*, 26). In later works, he refers to this combination of attributes as "suffering," which also includes the psychological effects when animals are denied "some aspect or condition of their natural life without ameliorating compensation" (*CRA*, 110).[13]

---

10. Linzey, *CRA*, 12.
11. Linzey avoids the question of how God's suffering might be reconciled with attributes like omnipotence or impassibility. Linzey, *AT*, 50.
12. See ibid., 52.
13. For a more detailed description, see Andrew Linzey, *Why Animal Suffering Matters: Philosophy, Theology, and Practical Ethics* (hereafter *WASM*) (New York: Oxford University Press, 2009), 9–10, 47.

The divine openness to suffering ultimately shapes Linzey's theology of animals: "Only the most tenacious adherence to the passibility of God may be sufficient to redeem us from our own profoundly arrogant humanistic conceptions of our place in the universe" (*AT*, 57). In this manner, God's ability to suffer—and God's willingness to suffer with and for animals—is central to Linzey's theological concern for the well-being of nonhuman animals.

The Creation that Belongs to God

For Linzey, God's suffering love is evident in the act of creation itself. God is the one who risks both creating and loving creation. The corollary of this claim is that the creation belongs first and foremost to God, not humans.

Linzey maintains that one of the most pressing issues for animal theology is to help humans to understand "properly the nature of the creation around us and our part within it" (*CRA*, 7). Essential in this understanding is the dismantling of a value-based anthropocentrism. In *Christianity and the Rights of Animals*, Linzey makes a case for this dismantling based on the theological notion of blessing: "To affirm the blessedness of creation is to affirm an independent source of its worth. In this sense *all* creation has an irreducible value" (*CRA*, 8). As the Creator, God establishes value—and God has blessed all things.

This claim highlights a unique dimension of Linzey's animal rights. The *intrinsic* value of all creatures is grounded *relationally* through every creature's relationship to God. Lisa Kemmerer misses this point when she argues that Linzey denies the intrinsic value of all creatures in favor of a claim that only God has value.[14] Linzey's theos-rights entails that the whole of creation has intrinsic value to God. This

---

14. Lisa Kemmerer, *In Search of Consistency: Ethics and Animals* (Boston: Brill, 2006), 270–271.

point is clear in *Christianity and the Rights of Animals*, where Linzey establishes three definitive facets of theos-rights. First, "God as Creator has rights in his creation"; second, "Spirit-filled, breathing creatures, composed of flesh and blood, are subjects of inherent value to God"; and third, "these animals can make an objective moral claim which is nothing less than God's claim upon us" (*CRA*, 69). In short, "All creation, large and small, intelligent and unintelligent, sentient and non-sentient, has worth because God values it" (*CRA*, 9). The intrinsic value and rights of individual creatures do not derive from some unchanging *esse*, but rather from their relational existence as God's creatures.[15]

Significantly, theos-rights are not grounded in a contractualism that requires an equal capacity for duties on all parties involved. The community of life is important. It is where rights bear meaning. However, "while rights are grounded in the existence of Spirit-filled lives, what constitutes their rights is the will of God who desires that they should so live" (*CRA*, 75). It is therefore not capacity that grounds dignity, but rather a creature's being before God. (However, Linzey does accept that the capacity to suffer grounds rights in a unique manner.)[16]

It is the combination of Linzey's emphasis on God as Creator and his relational view of rights that entails the rejection of anthropocentrism. All creation belongs not to humanity, but to God. It is therefore *God's rights in creation that are protected by animal rights.*[17] For this reason, "Christians are precluded from a purely humanistic, utilitarian view of animals." Humans cannot be the measure of value because "God alone is the source of the value of all living things" (*AG*, 37).

---

15. Linzey, *AT*, 23–25. Also, Kemmerer, *In Search of Consistency*, 232–235.
16. See Linzey, *WASM*, 10–11.
17. Linzey, *CRA*, 55.

One might ask: In line with Aquinas, could it not be that God created a hierarchical world of values? After all, evolutionary biology suggests that the stronger have always advanced, at least in part, through the suffering of the weaker. Is such a world compatible with Linzey's claim that animal rights are predicated on the notion that "God desires that [animals] should so live"? If God desires animals to live, why are suffering, predation, and death biologically necessary? Linzey addresses this problem by appealing to nature's disruption.

Protological Peace and the Fall

Although Linzey is adamant that creation is good and blessed by God, he is equally as adamant in claiming that the entire cosmos is, in some sense, fallen and incomplete.[18] In *Christianity and the Rights of Animals*, he juxtaposes the goodness of creation, represented by the aforementioned notion that creation is blessed, with the corruption of that good creation, which Linzey represents with the notion of curse.[19] This latter notion sums up for Linzey the meaning of cosmic fallenness, which I critically examine here.

The Essentiality of the Fall

Linzey maintains that the fall is a "vital key" in Christian theology. In particular, "Classical Christian theism teaches that the wickedness of man throws the system of intending order into disorder, harmony becomes engulfed in meaninglessness and teleology lapses into futility" (*CRA*, 11). So vital is the fall that Linzey posits it as a dividing feature between Christian and non-Christian thought:

18. Linzey, *CRA*, 33.
19. See Linzey, *CRA*, chapter one.

Here, we reach another parting of the ways between Christians and non-Christians. For the latter, there is no Fall, either of human or anything else. The world is simply 'as it is,' and we must be reconciled to it as it is. But the Gospel truth is that we do not have to accept the world as it is. We must distinguish creation from nature. (*AG*, 15)

Linzey's refusal to accept the world "as it is" dramatically expresses the difference between his own position and that of advocates of cosmocentric conservation. In fact, Linzey explicitly develops his thought in juxtaposition to "anti-Fall theologians" (*AG*, 30).[20] Included in this camp are Richard Cartwright Austin and Matthew Fox.[21] Accurately and dramatically, Linzey describes their position: "Life eating life is not some unfortunate aspect of the natural world to be tolerated in the meantime between creation and consummation. Rather, God actually wills and blesses a self-murdering system of survival. God's will *is* death" (*AT*, 119).[22]

In *Creatures of the Same God*, Linzey links a rejection of cosmic fallenness to an emphasis on holistic ethics by marking a sharp differentiation between eco-theologians and animal theologians. He rightly qualifies his distinction: "Not all ecologists are anti-animals and vice versa" (*CSG*, 37). He furthermore acknowledges that these groups overlap in their rejection of anthropocentrism, which correlates to a recognition of the larger community of creation, a community that is not divided into subjects and resources.[23] It is just this similarity that I intimate by the term "cosmocentrism." Nonetheless, Linzey notes a stark distinction:

Ecologists invariably look upon the system of predation as God-given

---

20. See also Andrew Linzey, "C. S. Lewis's Theology of Animals" (hereafter CSLTA), *Anglican Theological Review* 80/1 (Winter 1998): 70–71.
21. See Linzey, *CSG*, 33. Linzey also includes process theologian Jay B. McDaniel (33–35) and feminist theologian Rosemary Radford Ruether (53) in this camp.
22. See also, Linzey, *CSG*, 15–16. "Self-murdering" refers to the death of individuals.
23. Linzey, *CSG*, 30.

and care more for 'the whole' than they do for individual animals. Animal theologians, on the other hand, see 'nature' as we now know it as incompatible with the good creation that God originally made. Nature is fallen and has a tragic quality; and individual sentients count—not just the system as a whole. (*CSG*, 29)[24]

Two important and correlative points arise here. First, for many environmental theologians, the suffering of individual animals exists for the common good of the larger system. This goodness in some ways nullifies the apparent evil itself, rendering the suffering part of the good system.[25] Second, because suffering is part of the good system, there is no reason to speak of the fallenness of creation. To this latter point, Linzey adds the corollary that there is no need for redemption if there is no fallenness. Given these tensions, Linzey writes, "There is, I believe, no easy way to harmonize these perspectives," which are separated by a "deep theological cleavage" (*CSG*, 44).

For Linzey, the position on the other side of this divide is untenable for Christian theology. In line with this belief, he lists four problems that would arise should the doctrine of the fall disappear from theology.[26] First, "predation and parasitism [become] either morally neutral or, even worse, positive aspects of nature to be tolerated or even emulated" (*AG*, 28).

Second, there is no longer any need for the eschatological redemption of the nonhuman world.[27] For Linzey, the absence of this need is an issue on account of Jesus's eschatological message.[28] A rejection of the fall does not do justice to the centrality of eschatology for Christian thought. Christopher Southgate retorts Linzey on this

---

24. Linzey engages Annie Dillard to highlight this point. See Linzey, *CSG*, 30–32.
25. See Holmes Rolston III, "Does Nature Need to be Redeemed?" *Zygon* 29 (1994): 205–229.
26. Linzey, *AG*, 28–31; CSLTA, 70–71.
27. Linzey, *AG*, 29.
28. Linzey, *AT*, 123.

point, writing, "There is no reason to believe that just because God used a long evolutionary process to give rise to the biosphere we know, God may not have inaugurated a redemptive movement that will heal that process."[29] In Southgate's reading, such is the view of Moltmann, whom he juxtaposes to Linzey. As chapter 8 indicates, I am not in agreement with his reading of Moltmann.

Third, humans are not ethically obliged to witness against the mechanisms of evolution, but rather should participate in the "one inexorable law of the universe," which is "eat and be eaten" (*AG*, 30). Finally, "to reject absolutely the possibility of a transformed new heaven and earth in which all sentients will be redeemed is logically tantamount to denying the possibility of a morally good God" (*AG*, 31).

I will revisit the significance of the fall for theology proper below. First, it is prudent to examine more closely Linzey's rejection of nature as a moral guide for human action.

The Fall and the Law of Nature

In Linzey's estimation, the rejection of the fall (or at least the cosmic dimension of it) that often accompanies conservationist paradigms entails the theologically deficient identification of the current state of nature with God's intention. He prefers to understand nature in light of its eschatological telos—that is, as creation. The corollary of this rejection is that the present state of creation cannot "simply be read as a moral textbook" (*CRA*, 61); for the creation "it is both glorious and bestial" (*CRA*, 20).

For Linzey, the darker side of creation must be accounted for both theologically and ethically. He makes this point early on: "Suffering

29. Christopher Southgate, *The Groaning of Creation: God, Evolution, and the Problem of Evil* (Louisville, KY: Westminster John Knox, 2008), 179, n. 1.

is an integral part of the natural world and, moreover, often caused through non-moral beings" (*AR*, 70). Creation *is* good, glorious, and blessed because it was created by a good and loving God. At the same time it is *also* "bestial."[30] By the term "bestial" Linzey intimates something negative. He laments that this term is often used derogatively with references to animals.[31] Thus, Linzey maintains that what a nonhuman animal is *not* (a "beast") the collective system of evolutionary emergence *is* ("bestial"). While it is appropriate for humanity to seek to emulate and participate in creation's goodness, it is at the same inappropriate for humanity to justify causing suffering, engaging in predation, or killing other creatures simply because that is nature's way of operating.

Linzey cannot accept the conservationist view in which "we are supposed to glory in the economy of existence whereby one species devours another with consummate efficiency" (*AT*, 85). Natural law, as a means of adjudicating moral propriety, cannot be established merely by appeals to the current state of nature.[32] Rather, true natural law is better understood as "trans-natural law"—a law that accounts for God's eschatological intention for nature.[33] Such a law recognizes that creation remains unfinished "until all violence is overcome by love" (*AN*, 76). Indeed, "It is violence itself within every part of creation that is the preeminent mark of corruption and sinfulness" (*AT*, 127).[34] A trans-natural law recognizes that there is real evil in nature—*natural evil*. Given this cosmology, the law of fallen nature cannot be the moral code of human beings.

---

30. Linzey, *AN*, 78.
31. Linzey, *WASM*, 44.
32. Neil Messer makes a similar point in his discussion of Aquinas's appropriation of Aristotelian biology: Neil Messer, "Humans, Animals, Evolution and Ends," in *Creaturely Theology: On God, Humans and Other Animals*, ed. Celia Deane-Drummond and David Clough (London: SCM, 2009), 215.
33. Linzey, *AT*, 83–84.
34. Also, Linzey, *AG*, 148.

The Etiology of Nature's Corruption

Linzey's affirmation of nature's fallenness is clear. Less clear is his answer to the difficult question regarding the etiology of nature's darker qualities. How did God's good creation become so ambiguous?

Linzey acknowledges that this question is a difficult one. Its difficulty is evident in the ambiguity of his answer, which he develops somewhat amorphously throughout his writings.[35] In *Christianity and the Rights of Animals*, Linzey writes, "Humans alone are properly responsible" for the curse, including "suffering and predation," apparent in the present condition of nature (*CRA*, 18). This claim makes it seem as if Linzey adheres to the notion of an historical Eden absent of death. Yet, in the same work he also acknowledges that evolutionary suffering, which includes predation, "seems almost essential to" creaturely life (*CRA*, 61). Hence, while he maintains that there is "some connection between human sin and creaturely corruption" (*CRA*, 61), the nature of this connection is undefined.

In *Animal Theology*, Linzey appears to soften his emphasis on protological harmony and the fall. He still maintains that, according to Genesis, "parasitical existence is incompatible with the original will of God" (*AT*, 80). He further argues that the Genesis narrative presents God as accommodating a distorted creation by both permitting and limiting killing. However, he refers to both the fall and flood narratives as "the great symbols of why humanity can no longer live at peace either with themselves or with other creatures" (*AT*, 81). The word "symbol" adds a level of ambiguity to his view. Was there ever an historical state of existence absent of predation? Was there an actual historical "fall" from such a state? If not, did

---

35. Also, Linzey, *CRA*, 11.

God ordain predation, contra the language of Genesis 1? Linzey summarizes the apparent dilemma:

> Either [we] can accept that God did not ordain a just state of affairs, in which we can no longer postulate a loving, just deity; or, otherwise [we] have to accept that God is not—as claimed—the sovereign Creator of all things. (*AT*, 81)

Linzey argues that this dilemma is a false one, advocating an alternative possibility; namely, "that the world is really *creation*" (*AT*, 81). Creation, because it is by definition other-than-God, requires growth and development. It is "incomplete, unfinished, imperfect" (*AT*, 81). Thus, he seems to back away from the image of the human corruption of an historical edenic state. Creation is incomplete; but this term is not synonymous with fallen. In line with this thought, Linzey notes the positive elements of evolutionary emergence (e.g., cooperation and symbiosis).[36]

Still, Linzey does not abandon the notion that the darker mechanisms of evolutionary emergence betray a corruption of nature. In conjunction with his appeal to the incompleteness of creation, he cites E. L. Mascall's musing that the evolutionary process resulted from an angelic fall prior to human existence.[37] Linzey acknowledges that this view, while one of the "many theories that have been expounded" to explain the current state of the cosmos, has not "found complete assent within the Christian tradition" (*AT*, 98). Even so, in his later thought he gives this view preference over others, suggesting that evolution is in fact the result of an historical fall, but one that predates humans.[38] Linzey is here influenced by C.

---

36. Linzey, *AT*, 120.
37. See ibid., 167, n. 8.
38. See Linzey, CSLTA, 70; *AN*, 106. For more considerations on an angelic fall, see Robert N. Wennberg, *God, Humans, and Animals: An Invitation to Enlarge Our Moral Universe* (Grand Rapids, MI: William B. Eerdmans Publishing Company, 2003), 327–330.

S. Lewis, approving his reasons for appealing to an angelic fall: (1) human sin cannot account for the suffering of dinosaurs in a post-Darwin worldview and (2) "Lewis cannot resign himself to predation, carnivorousness and pain as the result of God's direct will" (CSLTA, 64).

In *Animal Gospel*, Linzey remains ambiguous about the historical nature of the fall. He suggests that the world described in Genesis 1 reflects the eschatological hopes of Israel evident in Isaiah's vision of the peaceable kingdom rather than a past historical reality.[39] He furthermore clarifies what he holds to be the "complex truth" underlying the doctrine of the fall. This truth includes

> the dual recognition that God as the Creator of all things must have created a world which is morally good—*or at least justified in the end as a morally justifiable process*—and also the insight that parasitism and predation are unlovely, cruel, evil aspects of the world ultimately incapable of being reconciled with a God of love. (*AG*, 27–28; emphasis mine)

Significantly, Linzey here accepts the possibility that the present state of existence, including the mechanisms of evolutionary progress, may be *justifiable* (which, for Linzey, is not necessarily the same as "good"). Such a justification, ultimately eschatological, would be necessary in the face of God's love and justice. At any rate, the truth behind the doctrine does not seem to necessitate a human fall from Eden. But it does require the disavowal of any identification of suffering, predation and death with the goodness of the created order.

In *Creatures of the Same God*, Linzey's ambiguity intensifies. On the one hand, he maintains his position that "creation is good, even 'very good,' yet it is also incomplete and unfinished" (*CSG*, 36). On the other hand, he appears to reject his own earlier "third option" to

39. Linzey, *AG*, 81.

the false dilemma of nature and evil: "Either parasitical nature is or is not evil. Either God wills a self-murdering system of survival or God does not. There really is not a third way" (*CSG*, 53).[40] This dilemma leads Linzey to suggest that, while the exact nature of the fall, and most significantly its origin, is problematic, the doctrine is necessary because "the alternative is dire beyond words" (*CSG*, 54).

In Sum

Linzey's ambiguity notwithstanding, he is consistent in his claim that whatever the etiology of creation's current state of predation and suffering—whether an angelic fall exacerbated by human sin or merely a natural outpouring of cosmic finitude—the eschatological hope for creation calls humans to a higher ethics than nature reveals. He is adamant that the world of suffering and predation presents a problem with regard to the affirmation of a good and loving God. There can thus be no unadulterated affirmation of the goodness of nature. Nature does not yet bear the fullness of the good qualities God intends for it. There is a greater future for the cosmos—one that cannot be derived from its current state. In this sense, Linzey's view of fallenness corresponds to his understanding of eschatology.

The Sentient-Inclusive Peaceable Kingdom

Linzey is adamant about avoiding three reductions in eschatology. First, it cannot be discarded by way of the claim that creation is not in need of redemption. Second, eschatology cannot be limited to the human creature. Third, eschatology cannot be relegated to a

40. Also, Linzey, CSLTA, 71.

transcendent future that bears no direct meaning for history. Here, my aim is to develop these three positions in Linzey's thought.

Creation and Redemption

Even in his earliest thought, Linzey notes that anything less than cosmic redemption renders the travail of nature incoherent and pointless.[41] The exhaustive extent of cosmic fallenness corresponds to an exhaustive need for redemption. Because all of creation "is radically estranged from God," it "cries out for redemption" (*CRA*, 40). Thus, Linzey argues, "the act of reconciliation must . . . include *all* that is fallen, *all* that was previously unreconciled" (*AT*, 98). Whether or not animals have sinned, they are affected by sin—drawn into its consequences. Therefore, redemption from sin (and its consequences) must bear relevance for animals, thought it will look different than it does for humans.[42]

Linzey believes the fallenness of nature is evident in predation and suffering. God's will is the negation of this fallenness—"a redeemed creation free from parasitism" (*AT*, 76). It is this view that grounds his criticism that "much ecotheology issues in a non-redeeming God and therefore a non-God, at least as traditionally understood" (*CSG*, 128, n. 10). Contrarily, Linzey argues that divine justice renders the redemption of animals necessary.[43] The eschatological future is necessary for the gospel: "Gospel hope in the future is not some optional extra to moral endeavor." Rather it is "its essential basis" (*AG*, 152). This view represents an absolute break with those like Thomas Berry who reject cosmic redemption as a pertinent dimension of Christian theology. For Linzey, there can be no good

41. Linzey, *AR*, 75.
42. See Linzey, *AT*, 98–99; *CSG*, 52.
43. Linzey, *CSG*, 53.

news if there is not good news for all creatures who suffer and die in the unfolding process of evolutionary development. The cosmic dimension of eschatology, which Linzey rightly notes is well-attested in both Jewish and Christian history,[44] is essential to Christianity.[45]

Sentient-Inclusive Eschatology

While Linzey is distinct from conservationists, he also differs from many who embrace the notion of a cosmically eschatological redemption, including many Orthodox theologians. This difference is two-fold. First, he maintains that all *individual* sentient creatures must be redeemed. Second, he maintains that these creatures are redeemed *for their own sake*.

In *Animal Gospel*, Linzey's creed states: "I affirm the hope of the world to come for all God's creatures" (*AG*, 7). This confession suggests that all individual creatures will in some manner, as individuals, participate in the eschatological redemption of the cosmos. This individually-inclusive eschatological redemption derives from his cosmology.

> Nothing that God has made can be omitted in the moment of completion. Christians may be questioning and agnostic as to the precise details of this hope, but it cannot but follow from a God who creates, incarnates, and reconciles that *everything* will be made new. . . . It must also follow that each and every hurt and harm in creation (both human and animal, in so far as each is capable of being hurt or harmed) will be made good, and that all the suffering of the present time is not worth comparing to the glory yet revealed. (*AT*, 99–100)

---

44. See Linzey, *CRA*, 33, 49; *AR*, 74–75. Linzey also notes the cosmic eschatology evident in non-canonical literature. Linzey, *AN*, 62–70; *AG*, 26–27.
45. Linzey, *CSG*, 50.

This quote links Linzey's individually-inclusive eschatology to his christology.[46] For Linzey, the incarnation constitutes God's "triumph over death" and is therefore "the hope for all creatures" (*AR*, 130). The passage also reveals that, for Linzey, redemption complements (and completes) creation.

Like the import of cosmic eschatology in general, Linzey notes that the inclusion of animals in redemption is not without precedence in Christian thought. Engaging the thought of both John Wesley and C. S. Lewis, he writes, "Some form of eternal life for animals has found serious advocates within Christianity" (*AT*, 100).[47] Based on this tradition, Linzey maintains that, at the very least, the belief in the resurrection and eternality of individual nonhuman animals "can be supported by [doctrines of] orthodox Christian belief" and, much stronger, that "these doctrines taken together require such an affirmation" (*AT*, 100–101).

It is this form of reasoning that leads Linzey to his own affirmation "that all sentient beings will be redeemed in a way that compensates them for the injustice and suffering that they have had to undergo." Linzey adds, acknowledging the need for caution: "*How* precisely that will be done, I am happy to leave to the Almighty" (*CSG*, 133, n. 13).[48] But *that* it happens "is required by the doctrine of a just God" (*CSG*, 133, n. 13); for a God who does not redeem the suffering of individual creatures has not acted righteously with regard to those creatures.[49]

Linzey's eschatological inclusion of all individual sentient creatures for the sake of divine justice highlights his break from what I have labeled anthropocentric transfiguration. These creatures are not

---

46. Linzey, *CSG*, 14.
47. On Lewis, see Linzey, CSLTA, 64–66.
48. Also, Linzey, *WASM*, 26–27.
49. Linzey, CSLTA, 65, 74; *AN*, 82–84.

included as a sacrament of communion between humanity and God. Rather, the recompense they receive for their suffering is their own. It is for their sake in relation to God; for "God enjoys creatures" (*AN*, 104) in and of themselves.

Eschatology, History, and Ethics

Linzey's eschatology, particularly the inclusion of all individual sentient creatures in the redemption from the darker mechanisms of evolution, corresponds to a theological ethics with regard to nonhuman animals. To establish this claim, it is first pertinent to examine the somewhat unclear nature of the relationship between eschatology and history in Linzey's thought. What does eschatology have to do with the present?

Neil Messer is not misguided when he writes that "Linzey's language of 'approximating' the peaceable kingdom has its dangers, because it tends to obscure [the] distinction between witnessing to and establishing the kingdom."[50] Indeed, Linzey writes that the Isaianic vision of the peaceable kingdom is, by the Spirit, a "realizable possibility" (*CRA*, 104). Does his mean that this eschatological peace is achievable within history via political programs? He runs the risk of this interpretation when he goes on to write that humanity's "impossible commission to make peace" in the cosmos "is made possible" by the Spirit (*CRA*, 104). Linzey's eschatology at times seems in danger of appearing to be one that is realizable within history.

50. See Messer, "Humans, Animals, Evolution and Ends," 224. Messer does, however, misread Linzey's affirmation of the complexity of the world and the moral ambiguity that accompanies that complexity. See 222–226. Southgate provides a better reading of Linzey than Messer on this point in Southgate, *The Groaning of Creation*, 120–121.

However, in the same work Linzey also maintains that eschatological redemption, while calling for humanity's participation and witness, is ultimately a divine activity. All creatures, including humans, "await the world that is to come" (CRA, 35).[51] There is thus a restriction on human activity. Living in a fallen world that is not yet redeemed impedes the experience of redemption within history. In this manner, Linzey recognizes the limitations of constructing the kingdom. This limitation notwithstanding, he writes, "Christians should never say that this world as it is, is all that we have to contend with and that God is satisfied that we stay as we are" (CRA, 50). As long as one maintains that the world is not as God desires it to be, the embrace of the present reality of nature can never be without qualification.

In line with this refusal to embrace the goodness of nature as it currently exists, Linzey draws on the dynamism of creation to dismantle appeals to the status quo of nature. God is working within the created order to direct it toward its eschatological telos.[52] Limitation is thus coupled with possibility. "Human striving cannot . . . by itself achieve the dream [of universal peace], but we cooperate with God's Spirit in the realization of the divine dream" (AG, 71).[53]

It is here that Linzey's ambiguity is evident. Humans cannot construct the kingdom through their own striving. But is it possible for the eschatological future to develop *fully* within history when human striving cooperates with God's grace? Or, does the eschatological future—the fullness of the kingdom—require a decisive break with history such that even humans cooperating with grace cannot realize it now? Even in Linzey's later work, in which he more explicitly emphasizes the need for divine intervention to establish

51. See Linzey's discussion of Stanley Hauerwas in Linzey, CRA, 50.
52. Linzey, CRA, 50.
53. Also, Linzey, CSG, 50.

the peaceable kingdom, whether or not this intervention can happen fully within history or requires a decisive break with the laws of natural history is unclear.[54]

At any rate, Linzey neither relegates eschatology to a fully transcendent future nor subsumes it into mere human effort. Eschatology informs both what will be in the ultimate future and what a witness to redemption should look like within history. For Linzey, "Christian ethics is essentially eschatological . . . The God of Isaac, of Jacob, of Abraham, and of Jesus is not limited by what we know of elementary biology" (*AG*, 17).[55] He makes this point by juxtaposing, in my words, conservation and transfiguration: "If 'eat and get eaten' is the moral law of the universe, or if predation is 'beautiful,' there can be no moral imperative to live without injury" (*AG*, 31). However, if there is a hope for the resurrection and eternal life of individual sentients, then living without injury as much as possible is a Christian ideal. To act otherwise is to embrace the fallenness of the world:

> Whatever the difficulties in conceiving a world without predation, to intensify and heighten—without any ethical necessity—the parasitical forces in our world is to plunge creation further into that darkness from which the Christian hope is that we shall all, human and animal, be liberated. (*AT*, 114)

Thus, the eschatological inclusion of individual nonhuman animals entails meaning for them even in the present. As will become evident in Linzey's anthropology, through humanity's moral interaction with animals, these creatures already experience a prolepsis of their eschatological telos.

---

54. Linzey, *CSG*, 51, 53.
55. Christopher Southgate concurs on this point. See Southgate, *The Groaning of Creation*, 116–117.

Conclusion

For Linzey, this world is God's world because God created it. It is good. However, its goodness is distorted in some manner. Creation longs for redemption from its current state, entrenched as it is in the mechanisms of evolutionary emergence. Its redemption is nothing short of a reversal of these mechanisms, the end of all suffering, predation, and death in the resurrection of all creatures. This eschatological vision grounds practices of peace toward sentients in history. When humans see God's future, they witness to it. These claims are further explicated in Linzey's Christology, pneumatology, and anthropology. These theological loci constitute the subject of the next chapter.

11

Linzey on Christ, the Spirit, and Anthropology

In the previous chapter, I examined the role that theology proper, creation, the fall, and eschatology play in Linzey's theological framework. The good creation is fallen, evident in the ubiquity of suffering and death. The creation longs for redemption from these mechanisms through the eschatological inbreaking of the divine kingdom. In this chapter, I explore how Linzey's Christology, pneumatology, and anthropology speak further to creation's longing.

Christology as Cosmic Redemption

Linzey's theology is decidedly christocentric: "For me Jesus is the way, the truth, and the life. What is given in Jesus is, in my view, determinative of our understanding of the nature of God".[1] His

---

1. Andrew Linzey, *Animal Gospel* (hereafter *AG*), (Louisville, KY: Westminster John Knox, 1998), 47. However, Linzey is an inclusivist, not an exclusivist.

Christology, like his eschatology, provides a stark challenge to both anthropocentrism and conservation. Here, I seek to explicate the manners in which Christ's life, death, and resurrection bear meaning for Linzey's animal theology.

Incarnation as God's Cosmic Eschatological Embrace

For Linzey, Christ is far more than merely the savior of humans. Christ is the embodiment of the cosmic messianic hope found in Judaism.[2] As the Logos, he "is the origin and destiny of all created things."[3] This Logos becomes the creation in the incarnation.

Such claims lead Linzey to critique Barth's Christology as anthropocentric.[4] The incarnation cannot simply be "God's 'Yes'" to humanity. Rather, "since the *ousia* assumed in the incarnation is the *ousia* of all creaturely being, it is difficult to resist the conclusion that what is effected in the incarnation for man is likewise effected for the rest of the non-human creation" (*CRA*, 34).[5] For Linzey, "The incarnation is God's love affair with all fleshy creatures" (*CSG*, 14).

God affirms creation in the graciousness of the decision both to create that which is other than God and to become (in the incarnation) that which is other than God. Creation and Christology both reveal that "nothing God has made can be in the last resort alien to him" (*CRA*, 8–9). That is, everything that exists must come to rest in the divine community that is both Creator and Redeemer. In this sense, the covenant of Christ is as extensive as the Noahic one.[6]

---

2. Andrew Linzey, *Christianity and the Rights of Animals* (hereafter *CRA*), (New York: Crossroad, 1987), 33–34; Linzey, *AG*, 14–15.

3. Andrew Linzey, *Creatures of the Same God: Explorations in Animal Theology* (hereafter *CSG*), (New York: Lantern Books, 2009), 14.

4. See Andrew Linzey, *Animal Theology* (hereafter *AT*), (Chicago: University of Illinois Press, 1994), 31–32, 68.

5. For a similar position, see David Clough, *On Animals* (New York: Bloomsbury, 2014), 84–86. Though, Clough is more general to Barth than Linzey. See ibid., 16–17.

The incarnation thus solidifies Linzey's eschatological vision in which the creation, as ontologically other than the Creator, "is open to God" (*AT*, 97) and God to it. That is, the incarnation at once affirms the transcendence and immanence of God by acknowledging God's alterity from the world and God's at-home-ness in the world. God's becoming flesh reveals that the cosmos "is the appropriate medium for [divine] self-revelation" (*AT*, 97) and that God is the appropriate end for the entire cosmos.

The Incarnation, Suffering, and Liberation

In the incarnation, the Son not only takes on the matter of the cosmos, but also its travails, even to the point of death. Thus, Linzey can write: "What we see in Jesus is the revelation of an inclusive, all-embracing, generous loving" (*AG*, 20). Christ's suffering envelops the suffering of all sentient creatures. "The curse which Jesus Christ takes upon himself reverses the natural order of mortality not only for human beings but for the 'sad uncomprehending dark' of innocent creatures" (*CRA*, 13).[7] It is in this sense that Christ's suffering grounds the hope that "all innocent suffering will be transformed."[8]

Christ's work is primarily the work of liberation from suffering. In this emphasis Linzey bears similarities to liberation theology. He follows Gustavo Gutierrez's basic notion that "Christ's work is understood as recreating or making a new creation" (*AR*, 74). However, he differs from many liberation theologians in his answer to the key question: "What or whom is to be liberated?" (*AT*, 62) Linzey is critical of liberation theology, accusing many of its central

6. Ibid., 69–70.
7. Also Andrew Linzey, *Animal Rights: A Christian Assessment* (hereafter *AR*), (London: SCM, 1976), 76.
8. Andrew Linzey, *Why Animal Suffering Matters: Philosophy, Theology, and Practical Ethics* (hereafter *WASM*) (New York: Oxford University Press, 2009), 164.

advocates—including Gutierrez and Leonardo Boff—of a staunch anthropocentrism deriving from a "deficient christology."[9] (It should be noted that Linzey wrote *Animal Theology* before Boff's later works *Ecology and Liberation* (1995) and *Cry of the Earth, Cry of the Poor* (1997), both of which point toward a more inclusive moral paradigm.) At any rate, Linzey argues that while Boff evinces an awareness of the cosmic dimension of Christ's work, he fails "to recognize its moral dimension" (*AT*, 70). Linzey offers a similar critique of Gutierrez.[10]

In line with Linzey's critique, I content that some liberation theologians fit the paradigm of anthropocentric conservation, claiming that all creation is to be conserved and justly distributed to all peoples. In this manner, liberation theology at times excludes individual animals from the realm of liberation, accepting their suffering and death as part of the good cosmos.[11] This exclusion betrays an anthropocentrism, "albeit qualified and seemingly sympathetic to environmental concerns" (*AT*, 67).

In Sum

For Linzey, Christ's work must include every individual sentient in order to be a genuine liberation from suffering. Contra anthropocentrism, Christ's person draws in the *ousia* of all flesh into the life of God. Contra conservationism, Christ's redeeming work assumes and promises to redeem the suffering of all sentient creatures. This redemption begins already in the work of the Spirit, who makes possible both present existence and new creation.

9. See Linzey, *AT*, chapter 4; *AR*, 75. Linzey also includes Jon Sobrino in this critique. Linzey, *AT*, 68.
10. Linzey, *AT*, 64
11. Ibid., 67.

Pneumatology and Divine Immanence

Linzey's pneumatology bears two significant dimensions. First, the Spirit has a cosmological role as the vitality of all life. Second, the Spirit bears an eschatological role in the wake of the Christ event, opening new possibilities of peace between humans and animals.

In *Animal Gospel*, Linzey confesses his belief in "the life-giving Spirit, source of all that is wonderful, who animates every creature" (*AG*, 7). Elsewhere, "It is the Spirit immanent in creation that gives life and in so doing develops all beings into their particular fullness" (*CRA*, 9).[12] This presence of the Spirit in breathing creatures constitutes their unique claim of theos-rights.[13] As the breath of all sentient creatures, the Spirit draws them into a community. This commonality is evident biblically in the notion of *nephesh*, which Linzey links both to the soul of humans and animals and to the presence of the Spirit in these creatures.[14] The commonality of *nephesh* in humans and animals leads Linzey to the eschatological assertion that "whatever hope there might be for a future life for humans applies equally to animal life as well" (*CRA*, 37).

The cosmological presence of the Spirit is also the manner of divine immanence in the fallen cosmos. "Through the Holy Spirit, the giver of life and inspirer of all, God experiences the creation as it were *from the inside*, and sees and feels through all the creatures of the earth" (*CSG*, 14). The Spirit is God's manner of suffering in creation even prior to the incarnation. This presence of the Spirit is the catalyst of a dynamism in which the cosmos is open to and moving toward God's desire for it.[15]

---

12. Also, Linzey, *CSG*, xii.
13. Linzey, *CRA*, 69.
14. See Linzey, *CSG*, xii.
15. Linzey, *AG*, 141.

The Spirit's cosmological role of vitalizing, sustaining, suffering, and developing takes on new eschatological significance in light of the incarnation. It is this redemptive presence of the Spirit that enables new forms of living within the world—forms that make for peace between humanity and nonhumans.[16] The Spirit is "moving creation forward, however mysteriously, to the realization of God's hope for us and his world" (*CRA*, 103).

In light of these considerations, Linzey maintains that Christians must not dismiss Isaiah's vision of the peaceable kingdom (Is 11:6–9) either as a future or present possibility. For this vision of the cosmos "is not simply presented…as a future state, but a realizable possibility through the Holy Spirit" (*CRA*, 104). I examined the problematic language of "realizable possibility" in the previous chapter. Linzey's central point is that the Spirit enables humans to become more than "mere spectators of the world of suffering" (*AT*, 56). In the power of the Spirit, humans cooperate in the world's redemption as the continuation of God's incarnate work.[17] How do humans to this? To answer this question, I turn to Linzey's anthropology.

Human Beings as Unique Eschatological Witnesses

I wish here to address Linzey's understanding of human beings vis-à-vis the nonhuman creation. In particular, I explore his rejection of a value-based anthropocentrism and his embrace of a functional anthropocentrism, his understanding of the boundaries of humanity's role within history, and finally his claim that humans are to witness to eschatological hope in their practices.

---

16. Linzey, *AR*, 74; *CRA*, 49; *AT*, 72.
17. Andrew Linzey, *After Noah: Animals and the Liberation of Theology* (hereafter *AN*), (Herndon, VA: Mowbray, 1997), 109; *AG*, 32.

Human Uniqueness and Moral Differentiation

Linzey does not deny that there are differences between humans and nonhuman animals. However, he argues that many supposed distinctions are little more than cultural assumptions ethicists utilize to make specious justifications for human activities that harm animals.[18] According to Linzey, the two most basic assumptions are that humans are masters of nature and that animals have no valid claims to direct moral consideration.[19]

Linzey incriminates the dominant voices of Western Christianity on both of these accounts.[20] He often centers this critique on the magisterial Roman Catholic tradition.[21] Though, he also rightly acknowledges positive voices in the Roman Catholic tradition.[22] In *Animal Gospel*, Linzey engages the most recent Roman Catholic Catechism as an example of Christian thought perpetuating cruelty "because it represents in a clear and dramatic way how unenlightened official Christian teaching still is about animal welfare" (*AG*, 57).[23] He argues that the Catechism acknowledges animals as God's creatures that are due kindness but also embraces "a wholly instrumentalist understanding of their status as resources for human use" (*AG*, 61). He also maintains, "It is absolutely vital that all who care for animals make known their opposition to this *Catechism*" (*AG*, 62).

Linzey often references Pope Pius IX's refusal to open an animal protection office in Rome because of his belief that humans have no direct duties to nonhuman animals.[24] In Linzey's view, this Catholic

---

18. For a similar view of differentiation between human and nonhuman animals, see Clough, *On Animals*, chapter 3.
19. Linzey, *AR*, 4.
20. Linzey, *CRA*, 22–23.
21. See Linzey, *AR*, 5; *AT*, 12, *AG*, 34–36, 56–63; *CSG*, 11–13; *WASM*, 16–17.
22. See Linzey, *CSG*, 26; *AG*, 64–67; *WASM*, 38–39.
23. See Linzey, *AG*, 56–63.
24. See Linzey, *AR*, 9; *CRA*, 23; *AT*, 19; *AN*, 10; *AG*, 19–20.

tradition has, at least magisterially, taken up the position of Thomas Aquinas, whom he chastises more so than any other theologian on account of his Aristotelian anthropocentrism.[25] It is in this manner that Linzey claims Aquinas "leaves Christianity theology with a bitter legacy" that has "helped support years of indifference and wantonness towards animal life" (*CRA*, 27–28). Even when Linzey qualifies his critique of Aquinas, for instance acknowledging his context[26] or referring to him as "a great scholar and saint" (*AG*, 21), his ultimate aim for engagement is to critique Thomas's view on animals. In addition to Aquinas, Linzey also accuses Augustine of promulgating a "negative tradition" toward animals in Christian thought.[27]

Other Western traditions are similarly culpable.[28] In his earliest work, Linzey writes, "Very few, if any, Catholic and Protestant theologians have questioned man's right to exploit animals and to use animal life for the needs of man" (*AR*, 9). Thus, Linzey also criticizes major voices in the Protestant tradition, including Martin Luther and John Calvin.[29] Linzey notes that his criticisms of various Christian traditions have elicited "furious letters" (*AG*, 56). At any rate, these criticisms are not limited to Roman Catholicism.

Another Western religious voice Linzey frequently disparages is René Descartes, whose mechanistic view of nonhuman animals facilitates a denial of their sentience.[30] Even here, however, Linzey intimates Aquinas's accountability: "The French philosopher…carries the line of indifference to animal cruelty…already indicated by St. Thomas, to its logical conclusion" (*AR*, 12).[31] Linzey maintains that

25. See Linzey, *AR*, 10–12; *CRA*, 22; *AT*, 12–15, 17–19, 46–47; *AN*, 6–7; *AG*, 19–21; *CSG*, 11, 15; *WASM*, 14–17.
26. Linzey, *CRA*, 27.
27. Linzey, *CSG*, 26.
28. See Linzey, *CRA*, 16–17; *AG*, 56.
29. See Linzey, *AR*, 9; *AN*, 7–8 *CSG*, 11.
30. See Linzey, *AR*, 12–14; *AN*, 8–10.
31. See also, Linzey, *CRA*, 62.

the Cartesian rejection of animal suffering has been adopted by Western Christian thought.[32] Though he notes exceptions to his critiques, Linzey ultimately judges that Christianity is "arguably one of the most anthropocentric of all world religions" (*WASM*, 108).

This anthropocentric history of differentiation begins to break down in the face of scientific inquiry, including an affirmation of the evolutionary development of humans.[33] Although, Linzey's acceptance of some of these scientific developments is at times tentative.[34] Indeed, regarding the questions of ethics he states, "Moral issues cannot be turned into scientific ones, nor subsumed under scientific categories" (*WASM*, 61). Nonetheless, he fully accepts the evidence regarding nonhuman animals' ability to suffer, which includes self-consciousness.[35] Linzey writes that there is "ample evidence in peer-reviewed scientific journals" concerning this claim (*CSG*, 5).[36] He does not, however, provide a citation for this claim.

Throughout Linzey's work, he not only attempts to confront the ingrained assumptions about what nonhuman animals lack (e.g., sentience and rationality), but also to question the moral conclusions based on these assumptions.[37] Says Linzey, "The difference-finding tendency in Western tradition has undoubtedly served to minimize the moral standing of non-human creatures, and to enable us to exploit them with a clear conscience" (*AT*, 47). While Linzey begins this critical process early on, he develops and clarifies it in later works.[38] In *Why Animal Suffering Matters*, he accepts, for the sake of argument, standard assumed differences between humans and animals

---

32. Linzey, *CRA*, 63; *WASM*, 45–47.
33. See Linzey, *AT*, 46.
34. Linzey, *AR*, 5.
35. Linzey, *AG*, 112; *WASM*, 9–10.
36. Also Linzey, *WASM*, 47.
37. See Linzey, *CRA*, 54–67.
38. For Linzey's earlier views, see *AR*, 10–19, *CRA*, 52–67.

in order to explore "whether any of the proposed differences are *morally relevant*, that is, whether any should reasonably form the basis for differential treatment of one species over another" (*WASM*, 10). Table 11.1 summarizes his conclusions:

Table 11.1 The Moral Relevance of Differentiation[39]		
Proposed Difference	*Proposed Moral Conclusion*	*Linzey's Moral Conclusion*
The world as a teleological hierarchy	In nature, the lesser are naturally slaves to the greater	In Christ, the greater exist for the sake of the lesser
Animals lack reason	Animals cannot suffer in the proper sense of the term	Lack of reason can intensity the experience of suffering, rendering it more morally significant
Animals lack language	Animals cannot participate in social contracts, which means they are not part of the moral community	Animals cannot consent to human exploitation such that "every act which makes them suffer is an act of coercion" (*WASM*, 22)
Animals are amoral	Animals cannot be part of the moral community	Animals cannot be improved by suffering as moral agents can
Animals lack an immortal (rational) soul	Animals are not of intrinsic value to God (or humanity)	Animal that suffer will not receive eternal compensation (as humans will), making their suffering more problematic
Animals lack the *imago Dei*	Humans have the right to dominate animals	Humans uniquely responsible for bearing the image of a loving God to the creation

Functional Anthropocentrism

As I have noted, Linzey challenges both the scientific validity of certain claims about human uniqueness and the ethical conclusions

39. This chart is developed from Linzey, *WASM*, 11–29.

drawn from proposed distinctions between humans and nonhuman animals. Even so, he does maintain that humans are unique in the cosmos. So what does make humanity unique?

"One crucial difference is that of capacity for moral consciousness and responsibility" (*AR*, 69).[40] Linzey's consistent claim that "there is no evidence that any other species possess [the] capacity for morality" (*AR*, 69) is too strong. There is, in fact, evidence to the contrary.[41] David Clough makes a compelling case for even applying the notion of sin to nonhuman animals.[42] At any rate, For Linzey morality does not privileging humans above the nonhuman world; rather, it is just this difference that renders humans uniquely accountable *to God for the world* (a unique accountability that would be true if this difference were only one of degree).[43] Elsewhere Linzey writes, "It has to be said that humans are freer in their relationship to God" than other creatures. This "special freedom" also means that humans "are freer in their relationship with other creatures as well" and therefore elicits a "particular responsibility" (*CRA*, 10).

Thus, Linzey's rejection of anthropocentrism intimates more specifically a rejection of an anthropomonistic view of value—that is, that only humans are of intrinsic value and therefore a matter of direct moral concern.[44] In fact, for Linzey the value of humans and the value of nonhumans are complimentary.[45] In this vein he writes, contra many suspicions,

---

40. Also, Andrew Linzey, "C. S. Lewis's Theology of Animals" (hereafter CSLTA), *Anglican Theological Review* 80/1 (Winter 1998): 77.
41. See Celia Deane-Deane-Drummond, "Are Animals Moral? Taking Soundings through Vice, Virtue, Conscience and *Imago Dei*," in *Creaturely Theology, Creaturely Theology: On God, Humans and Other Animals*, ed. Celia Deane-Drummond and David Clough (London: SCM, 2009), 190–210.
42. Clough, *On Animals*, 105–119.
43. Clough echoes this point. See ibid., 118.
44. Linzey, *CRA*, 61; *AT*, 58–59; *AG*, 49; *CSG*, 11.
45. See Linzey, *CRA*, 76; *AT*, 72.

Christian animal rights advocates are not interested in dethroning humanity. On the contrary, the animal rights thesis requires the reenthroning of humanity. The key question is, what kind of king is to be reenthroned? (*AG*, 38)

Linzey's answer to this question is perhaps most evident in his discussion on the term "dominion." He rejects the prevailing anthropocentric interpretations of dominion evident in both Aquinas and Luther.[46] Such views replace the monarchial responsibility of humanity as co-creators and co-redeemers for the well-being of the cosmos with a hierarchical status that privileges human over and against animals.[47] Kemmerer thus missteps when she writes, "Linzey maintains the traditional view of hierarchy." [48] Her point is that Linzey accepts a special place of humanity vis-à-vis the nonhuman creation. Yet, Linzey's monarchial interpretation of this place is not "the traditional view of hierarchy."[49] It is just the moral implications indicative of this traditional view that for Linzey comprises the dominant strand of Western Christian thought from Aquinas to the present—a view that is "unthinkingly anthropocentric" (*CSG*, 11).[50]

For Linzey, dominion can be neither despotic nor hierarchical for three reasons. First, exegetically, in Genesis 1, the notion of dominion includes a vegetarian mandate for humans (Gen. 1:29).[51] This limitation detracts from any tyrannical reading of dominion. In his later thought, Linzey follows the dominant strand of biblical studies experts in linking the *imago* to humanity's function for the cosmos.[52] He notes that when the doctrine of the *imago* is subsumed

46. Linzey, *CRA*, 25. See also Linzey's introduction to Part II of *Animals on the Agenda* (63–65).
47. Linzey, *CRA*, 27; *AT*, 40.
48. Lisa Kemmerer, *In Search of Consistency: Ethics and Animals* (Boston: Brill, 2006), 248.
49. Kemmerer intimates this point but does not develop it.
50. Linzey, *AT*, 64–65; *AG*, 48–50; *WASM*, 108.
51. Linzey, *CRA*, 25; *AT*, 34, 125–126. See especially *WASM*, 28–29.
52. See J. Richard Middleton, *The Liberating Image: The* Imago Dei *in Genesis 1* (Grand Rapids, MI: Brazos, 2005).

into a capacity-based and substantive notion, the exclusion of animals from moral consideration typically follows.[53] In juxtaposition to such a view, Linzey argues that the function of the *imago* "is inexorably related to the exercise of dominion and the maintaining of God's peace in creation" (*CSG*, 16).[54]

Second, because dominion is connected to the functional *imago* and the *imago* is the image of a particular God, the exercise of dominion is best informed by the divine condescension in Christ.[55] In *Animal Gospel*, Linzey expounds this nature in his creed, confessing that Jesus is "the true pattern of service to the weak," "the Crucified" in whom are "the faces of all innocent suffering creatures" (*AG*, 7). Christ expresses the nature of divine rule, which in turn expresses the intended nature of human rule. In Christ, "God's power is expressed in powerlessness, in condescension (*katabasis*), humility and sacrificial love" (*CRA*, 28). Therefore, "to stand for Jesus is to stand for animals as God's creatures, against all purely humanistic or utilitarian accounts of animals as things, commodities, resources, here for us" (*AG*, 11).[56]

In Christ's condescension, the hierarchal value system of creation is reversed, which reveals the proper moral paradigm for humanity.[57] "Where we once thought that we had the cheapest ride, we are now beginning to sense we may have the costliest responsibilities" (*CRA*, 29). Linzey connects this christic form of dominion to the *imago Dei* by claiming that Christ opens new possibilities for creation because he renews the divine image which has been "marred by human sinfulness and violence" (*AG*, 16). In this sense, the *imago* bears both

---

53. Linzey, *CRA*, 63. This view echoes that of Douglas John Hall. See *Imaging God: Dominion as Stewardship* (Eugene, OR: Wipf and Stock Publishers, 2004), 90.
54. This link is further solidified in Linzey, *WASM*, 28–29.
55. See Linzey, *AT*, 32–33.
56. Also, Linzey, *CSG*, 17.
57. Linzey, *AG*, 38–39.

moral and eschatological dimensions.[58] Christ restores—or at least begins the process of restoring—the divine image and thereby enables humans to assume their role as keepers of the peace in the cosmos.[59] In *Animal Theology*, Linzey parses this role in terms of humanity as the "servant species."[60] "From this perspective, humans are the species uniquely commissioned to exercise a self-sacrificial priesthood, after the one High Priest, not just for members of their own species, but for all sentient creatures" (*AT*, 45).

For Linzey, Christlike priesthood is for the other's sake. It is "an extension of the suffering, and therefore also redeeming, activity of God in the world" (*AT*, 52). As priests, humans follow Christ's example, sacrificing their own peace by entering into the suffering of all those who suffer. They furthermore do so for the sake of those suffering creatures. This act points toward the eschatological solidarity of all creation. In this sense, there can be no genuine human priesthood of creation that is not *for nonhuman animals*. Drawing on the extensive solidarity of Isaac the Syrian, Linzey writes, "Only when we can say that we too have entered—however fleetingly—into the suffering of Christ in the suffering of all creatures can we claim to have entered into the priestly nature of our humanity" (*AT*, 56).

Linzey's notion of priesthood bears similarities to the Orthodox notion of natural priesthood and coheres with certain interpretations of that notion. However, on this point Linzey too easily draws support from voices that are more nuanced than he acknowledges. He often uses similar terms as these other voices, but in such a different way that they may not recognize his use as valid.[61] Such is the case with his view on the natural priesthood of humanity,

58. See Linzey, *AR*, 19.
59. Linzey, *AG*, 149.
60. See Linzey, *AR*, chapter 3; *CSG*, 3.
61. For example, see Linzey, *AT*, 52–55.

which, as with the concept of the sacramentality of creation, differs from those in the category of anthropocentric transfiguration.[62] Based on my exploration of Orthodox theologians in chapter 6, I doubt Dumitru Staniloae would find Linzey's depiction of natural priesthood acceptable.

As already noted, Linzey's functional understanding of the *imago* renders humans necessary for the eschatological redemption of the cosmos.[63] This necessity highlights a third reason the *imago* cannot be despotic: both stewardship and dominion must be interpreted within the cosmic eschatology of Christianity.[64] Human beings are to act in light of God's ultimate desire for the cosmos, which entails its redemption from suffering and death. Part of the human role, which Linzey sees as evident in the monastic tradition, entails being moved by the suffering of sentient creatures and acting to alleviate such suffering.[65] When humans act peacefully toward other creatures, the eschatological future of the world becomes present by means of anticipation. "We must let the Spirit, that is the Spirit of *all* suffering creatures, pray through us so that we may become a sign of the hope for which all creation longs" (*AN*, 109). Thus, against Barth's reluctance to structure an ethics for nonhuman animals based on eschatology, Linzey proposes a balance between a realizable and a fully transcendent eschatology.[66] In his view, the doctrine of Trinity—including its economic interaction with the world—requires humans to cooperate with the redemptive movement of God within history without lapsing into a political program of completing the kingdom apart from eternity.[67]

---

62. See Linzey, *AT*, 54–55; *AN*, 94–95.
63. Linzey, *AT*, 45.
64. Linzey, *CRA*, 86–89.
65. Linzey, *CRA*, 45.
66. On Linzey's critique of Barth, see *CRA*, 93.
67. Linzey, *CRA*, 93.

Linzey's dominant argument is that humanity's great uniqueness constitutes a powerful responsibility for the sake of those creatures that do not share that uniqueness. In *Animal Theology*, he captures this responsibility with the term "generosity."

> The Generosity View rejects the idea that the rights and welfare of animals must always be subordinate to human interests, even when vital human interests are at stake. We must be quite clear about this. Acting out the Generosity Paradigm will cost human beings. (*AT*, 44)

In Linzey's view, generosity is the proper outlook at the intersection of sentience and innocence, an intersection that links animals and children.[68] Like children, animals have, in some sense, a greater moral claim than adult humans. "In my view, what we owe animals is more than equal consideration, equal treatment, or equal concern. The weak, the powerless, the disadvantaged, the oppressed should not have equal moral priority but greater moral priority" (*AG*, 39).

Possibilities and Limitations of Eschatological Witness

Linzey consistently makes the claim humanity is central to God's redemptive movement in the cosmos. In this manner, his functional anthropocentrism bears an eschatological dimension and solidifies an ontological cosmocentrism: "New creation is man-centered…but it cannot logically be man-monistic, i.e., for man only" (*AR*, 75). The new creation is centered on humanity "precisely because of [humanity's] unique ability to co-operate with the Spirit" (*CRA*, 76). On account of this ability, "humankind is essential in order to liberate animals" (*AT*, 72). This functional anthropocentricity, directed toward the well-being of the nonhuman creation for its own

---

68. On the connection between animals and children in Linzey's thought, see also Linzey, *AT*, 36–38; *WASM*, 30–34, 36–37.

sake, exists within the framework of a moral cosmocentricity. Human beings, following the example of Christ's kenotic sacrifice for the world, must embrace the value of all sentient life. In this manner Christ's death "is the basis for a contemporary Christian ministry to all creatures" (*AG*, 148).

In *Animal Rights*, Linzey intimates his (albeit nascent) position on humanity's role as proleptic witness in the saga of cosmic redemption. "By reception of the gift of redemption, by receiving the 'first fruits' of the Spirit, man stands in a unique position responsible to God for the completion of the work of redemption" (*AR*, 74). As noted in chapter 10, elsewhere Linzey writes that Isaiah's vision of the peaceable kingdom presents "a realizable possibility through the Holy Spirit" (*CRA*, 104).

The words "completion" and "realizable" are problematic in that they intimate the possibility of completing the eschatological kingdom through human effort. However, as I argued in the previous chapter, Linzey is clear that the eschaton must not be subsumed into a historical endeavor. He furthermore qualifies his position by claiming human effort must go "as far as we are enabled by the Spirit" (*CRA*, 104). His position is more clearly softened in his later work, in which he maintains that the human role in creation is both essential and limited. On the one hand, "humans cannot redeem animals (only God can do that)." On the other hand, "they can at least become anticipatory signs of the kingdom" (*CSG*, 52).

The notion that humans can (and should) become "signs of the kingdom" highlights what I believe is Linzey's central and most valuable anthropological claim. Human beings, in the power of the Spirit made available in the Christ event, are uniquely capable of witnessing proleptically to the eschatological future in which all creatures will be at peace with one another. When humans engage in this witness, acting peaceably toward sentient creatures, they become *sacraments of the eschaton* for those creatures.[69] In doing so, they render present the eschatological redemption in a limited but very real manner. They provide a "glimpse of the possibility of world redemption" (*CRA*, 36).

Based on this possibility, Linzey argues that, ethically, humans must "seek to become a living sign of the Gospel for which all creatures long" (*AG*, 7–8). Hence, dominion bears an ethical corollary. Says Linzey: "Living without killing sentients wherever possible is a theological duty laid upon Christians who wish to approximate the peaceable kingdom" (*AT*, 76). Here, he anticipates my distinction between cosmocentric conservation and cosmocentric transfiguration. For it is at just this point—the claim that humans must not only perceive themselves as part of nature but also as those with the capacity to witness to creation's eschatological telos of peace—that he acknowledges a "major cleavage between those who advance an 'ecological ethic' and those who advocate a creation-based liberation theology" (*AT*, 76). Linzey's ethics requires the exercise of eschatological imagination, which exceeds a blithe acceptance of the current state of nature.[70] "The groaning and travailing of creation awaits the inspired sons of God" (*CRA*, 104). The fallen cosmos longs for the witness of the saints who enacted peace even in the wilderness.[71]

Conclusion

Linzey's Christology is inclusive both ontologically and soteriologically. It is ontologically inclusive because Christ takes on the nature of all sentient creatures. It is soteriologically inclusive

---

69. The phrase "sacraments of the eschaton" is my own.
70. Linzey, *CRA*, 102–103.
71. Linzey, *AG*, 26–27; *AN*, 100.

because Christ's work of redemption, evident in his resurrection, applies to the breadth of creatures with whom he shares a nature. The precedence for this fellow suffering resides in the Spirit through whom God experiences creation's suffering. Furthermore, in the wake of the Christ-event, the Spirit enables genuinely new possibilities of peace between humans and animals—which is to say a fuller, though still incomplete, realization of theos rights. Such a realization is the proper form of the human role of dominion, which, modeled after Christ, is essentially kenotic. How do these theological affirmations, in conjunction with those I examined in chapter 10, translate into practice within history? The answer to this question constitutes the aim of the next chapter.

12

Linzey's Nonhuman Theological Ethics

In the previous two chapters, I explored Linzey's theological framework. In the present chapter, I examine how this framework translates into a nonhuman theological ethics. I begin with his moral position regarding the cosmos at large and non-sentient creatures. Next, I consider at length the place that individual sentient animals occupy in his ethics, including his position on practices such as hunting, experimentation, and meat-eating.

The Cosmos in General and Non-Sentient Creatures

Linzey maintains that humans are unique in the created order. However, he denies that this uniqueness constitutes an exclusion of sentient nonhuman animals from the moral community. With regard to non-sentient life, however, Linzey's position is far less morally inclusive.

Morally Relevant Gradations of Being

"All creation, large and small, intelligent and unintelligent, sentient and non-sentient, has worth because God values it"—indeed, "irreducible value."[1] This sentiment captures the extent of Linzey's concept of value regarding the cosmos. However, he also notes, "To hold the biblical principle that all life has value is not to hold that all being has the same value or to hold that there are not morally relevant distinctions between one kind of being and another."[2] More strikingly, in *Animal Gospel*, he claims that God does not love all creatures equally.[3] (I assume he means God does not love all creatures *in the same manner*.)

Linzey argues that scripture evinces both an inclusion of animals and an exclusion of plants from the moral community.[4] The inclusion of animals is evident in their similarity to humans. They "are made on the same day, recipients of common blessing, subject both to the blessing and curse of the Lord, and are both to be redeemed" (*AT*, 23).[5] Furthermore, he draws out the significance of the notion of covenant for nonhuman animals. Covenant establishes community, including moral parameters of interaction.[6] Based on these similarities, Linzey argues that it "is simply not possible to extrapolate from the biblical material the notion that God wished to create man as an *entirely* different form of life" (*CRA*, 65).[7] Humans and

---

1. Andrew Linzey, *Christianity and the Rights of Animals* (hereafter *CRA*), (New York: Crossroad, 1987), 9.
2. Andrew Linzey, *Animal Theology* (hereafter *AT*), (Chicago: University of Illinois Press, 1994), 23.
3. Andrew Linzey, *Animal Gospel* (hereafter *AG*), (Louisville, KY: Westminster John Knox, 1998), 37–38.
4. Linzey, *AT*, 34–35; Lisa Kemmerer, *In Search of Consistency: Ethics and Animals* (Boston: Brill, 2006), 229–230.
5. Also Linzey, *CRA*, 31.
6. Ibid., 31–32.
7. For a good critique, see Kemmerer, *In Search of Consistency*, 272–274.

animals belong in a common moral community that excludes plants. Succinctly: "The lilies are not to be compared with the glory of Solomon but it is the sparrows who are not forgotten by God" (*AT*, 35).

According to Linzey, both pneumatology and Christology provide a manner of differentiating between the rights of animals and the rights of non-sentient life forms. The Spirit's unique presence in certain creatures as *ruach* ("breath") coupled with the Spirit's redemptive role for individual suffering creatures permit a distinction. In addition, Christ's assumption of flesh and blood in the incarnation provides a unique vision of redemption for sentient creatures of flesh and blood.[8] While Linzey recognizes that these arguments do not provide a "watertight distinction," he nonetheless suggests that the biblical view tends toward an affirmation that "through his covenant God elects creatures of flesh and blood into a relationship with himself and humanity" (*CRA*, 80).

Based on these claims, Linzey opts for an "exclusive view" of theos-rights: "Only animals which come clearly within the definition of 'Spirit-filled, breathing beings composed of flesh and blood' have theos-rights" (*CRA*, 84). His intention here is to maximize moral concern for creatures that are clearly sentient and yet have been excluded from rights language. He furthermore seeks to avoid the caricature that animals rights activists will soon be working toward the rights of plants.[9] These considerations notwithstanding, Linzey remains cautious about his exclusivism, acknowledging that there is yet much to learn about the spiritual capacities of insects. Moreover, he maintains that, regardless of their capacities, "all living beings are subjects of value" (*CRA*, 85).

---

8. Linzey, *CRA*, 79–80.
9. Andrew Linzey, *Why Animal Suffering Matters: Philosophy, Theology, and Practical Ethics* (hereafter *WASM*) (New York: Oxford University Press, 2009), 53.

The Status of Non-Sentient, Nonhuman Life

As should already be evident, Linzey's position regarding the moral status on non-sentient life is unclear. He echoes Moltmann's view of the Sabbath, suggesting that sharing in the divine rest is the telos of all creatures, sentient or not.[10] All creatures "are to be with God. They are to enjoy their life with him according to their creaturely being" (CRA, 10). Such is the foundation of the value of all creatures.[11]

Linzey also defines creation as a "gift" (see CRA, 8) that elicits celebration. This affirmation comes somewhat close to the common Orthodox notion of cosmic sacramentality.[12] For Linzey, however, created existence itself (as an act of divine generosity) is a gift to the entire created order, rather than the nonhuman creation being a gift to humanity. Thus, the non-sentient creation is not simply a gift to the sentient creation.

At least it would seem. Yet, when Linzey addresses the issue of sealing, he offers a strikingly instrumentalist view of non-sentient plants in order to solidify concern for seals:[13]

> If seals were simply vegetables, that is, beings without sentience who could experience no pain, fear, or suffering and whose movements exhibited no complexity of awareness, then there would be no moral objection to using them and killing them. They might, like vegetables, have a kind of aesthetic value, but no one would think of mounting campaigns to protect them or worry about their rights. . . . It is because seals, like other mammals, are sentient . . . that it is right to say that they have—as individuals—'intrinsic' or 'inherent' value. . . . The value of other sentient beings in the world does not rest (as in the cases of stones or cabbages) entirely or largely in their relationship to us and the uses we may put them. (WASM, 137–138)

10. Linzey, CRA, 10–11.
11. Ibid., 9.
12. Also Andrew Linzey, *After Noah: Animals and the Liberation of Theology* (hereafter AN), (Herndon, VA: Mowbray, 1997), 78, 81–82.
13. For the larger discussion, see Linzey, WASM, chapter 5.

What is startling about this claim is that Linzey appears to deny intrinsic value to non-sentient creatures.[14] It seems that Linzey's position is that an ethics of transfiguration applies to sentient life while an ethics of conservation applies to non-sentient life. In this sense, it might be more accurate to label his paradigm as sentiencentric transfiguration. Indeed, Linzey does not reject such a label, though he defines it as "mammalocentricity."[15] At any rate, Linzey accepts that a transfigurative ethics—which entails protesting dimensions of nature such as suffering, predation, and death—is appropriate for creatures that can suffer. But this ethics does not seem to apply to non-sentient life. For such life, a conservationist ethics—which entails accepting predation and death—seems sufficient for Linzey.

Linzey and Holistic Nonhuman Ethics

Linzey is certainly interested in the protection of species. However, his primary unit of moral concern is the *individual* nonhuman animal.[16] He is adamant that a conservationism that seeks to protect a species by subordinating the rights of individual animals is problematic. Here, Linzey takes specific aim at Aldo Leopold's land ethic.[17] Holism is the "blind spot" of conservationists who do not seek to protect each individual creature from harm (*WASM*, 138). Ultimately, he maintains, "We treat animals and humans unjustly if we proceed on the assumption that their rights can normally be sacrificed to the interest of others" (*CRA*, 133).

---

14. For criticism, see Kemmerer, *In Search of Consistency*, 277–278.
15. See Linzey, *CRA*, 84–85.
16. Ibid., 109.
17. Linzey, *CRA*, 132–133. Also, *WASM*, 68, 138.

For Linzey, all *individual* "animals have an irreducible non-utilitarian value" (*AT*, 95). Thus, it is inappropriate to sacrifice the one for the sake of the many except in conditions of necessity. It would seem that this same line of thinking would apply to ecosystems as well—although, like many animal ethicists and theologians, Linzey does not really address the moral status of systems of life. The one significant exception is evolution. It is this system that Linzey refers to as "bestial" (*CRA*, 20), "self-murdering" (*AT*, 119), and incompatible with divine goodness.[18] These claims aside, it is somewhat unclear how Linzey's ethics would include larger systems of life, which depend on predation for balance. What is clear is that he refuses to subsume the value or rights of the individual into a holistic ecology.

Individual Nonhuman Animals

Linzey's entire theological project may rightly be seen as an attempt to put nonhuman animals on the agenda for theological and ethical discussion.[19] As noted above, his primary concern is for the *individual* animal—and more specifically, the individual *sentient* animal. Here, I seek to expound this concern in Linzey's thought.

Rights and (Breakable) Rules

Linzey is interested in establishing the import of law for protecting the well-being of individual sentients. He thus avoids relegating issues of animal protection to the language of welfare. While acknowledging the theological dangers and inadequacies of rights

18. See Linzey, *AT*, 81.
19. Andrew Linzey, *Animal Rights: A Christian Assessment* (hereafter *AR*), (London: SCM, 1976), vi, 1–2.

language,[20] he nonetheless maintains that such language is an essential *part* of the discussion of animal protection.[21]

In his earliest work, Linzey attempts to build a rational Christian case for the inclusion of nonhumans into the sphere or rights based on sentience.[22] In later works, however, he adjusts this Bentham-like approach in favor of the construction of a theological framework that accounts for sentience.[23] In this framework, rights cannot be based on "any capacities which may be claimed by the creature itself in defense of its own status" (*CRA*, 83); rather, they must be based on "God-given spiritual capacities" that remain only because of God's ongoing relationship to the created order.[24] Linzey adds to this theological dimension the claim that God's own passion draws all suffering, regardless of degree, into the sphere of moral concern.[25] From this standpoint, he maintains that Christian theology provides a better foundation for animal rights than secular thought, thus distinguishing himself from those like Peter Singer and Tom Regan.[26]

Linzey never abandons the rational case for animal rights. In fact, in his latest authored book, he calls for more development of it.[27] However, he acknowledges that "rational argument . . . has to begin somewhere . . . with something *given*" (*AG*, 5). In *Why Animal Suffering Matters*, Linzey's "given" is that it is wrong to harm sentient animals because of their

inability to give or withhold their consent, their inability to verbalise

---

20. Andrew Linzey, *Creatures of the Same God: Explorations in Animal Theology* (hereafter *CSG*), (New York: Lantern Books, 2009), 56–57; *AT*, viii–ix, 3–19, 41–42; *CRA*, 94–96; *WASM*, 162.
21. Linzey, *AR*, 42–46; *CRA*, 68–98; *WASM*, 160–162.
22. Linzey, *AR*, chapter 3.
23. See Linzey, *CRA*, 80–81.
24. Ibid., 83.
25. Linzey, *AT*, 51–52.
26. See Angus Taylor, *Animals and Ethics: An Overview of the Philosophical Debate*, third edition (Buffalo, NY: Broadview, 2009), 66.
27. Linzey, *WASM*, 1–3.

or represent their interests, their inability to comprehend, their moral innocence or blamelessness, and, not least of all, their relative defenselessness and vulnerability. (*WASM*, 151)

These "givens" shape Linzey's conviction that "no religion that leads us to insensitivity to suffering can be the real thing" (*CSG*, 7).

Linzey's emphasis on rights seemingly situates him in a deontological framework. Consistent with this classification, Linzey lauds the papal encyclical *Veritatis Splendor* for its "reaffirmation of the category of 'intrinsically evil acts'" along with its "utter rejection of consequentialism as an adequate basis for theological ethics" (*AG*, 66). He furthermore decries the use of violence by animal rights activists because, in his view, "rights theory, in contrast to utilitarianism, consists in its rejection of consequences as an adequate basis for ethics" (*AG*, 88). These claims suggest an affinity with deontology and a definitive break with utilitarianism.[28]

However, for Linzey, rights are neither absolute nor inviolable.[29] While he does maintain "taking pleasure from the cruel death of an animal is nothing less than morally evil" (*WASM*, 86),[30] he also acknowledges "in practice . . . we are always inevitably speaking of rights which may be overridden if there is sufficient moral justification" (*CRA*, 91). While the violation of rights may be justified, such violation still incurs guilt. We are all guilty because *evil has become a necessity in creation,* a claim which requires some notion of cosmic fallenness.[31] Thus, Linzey argues, "Circumstances, benefits, or compensating factors may limit the offense [i.e., causing animals suffering], but they can never make the practice morally licit" (*WASM*, 106). Oddly, in the same work Linzey writes, "Accepting

28. See ibid., 61, 78–83, 93, 162.
29. Linzey, *AR*, 33–34; *CRA*, 89–91, 101–102; *AG*, 48–49.
30. For Linzey, the term "cruel" denotes any form of harm caused to a sentient creature that is not for the benefit of that individual creature. See Linzey, *WASM*, 85.
31. Linzey, *AR*, 33–34; *CRA*, 89–91, 101–102; *AT*, 107–112, 129.

that animal life has value, and that it should not be destroyed without good reason, is not the same as accepting that it is always wrong to kill" (*WASM*, 159).

At any rate, Linzey's view is not quite deontological. After all, Kant simply would not have been Kant if he maintained it was acceptable to lie in cases of necessity! In my view, Linzey's view is best described as proportionalism. By this term I intimate David Kelly's definition in which proportionalism constitutes a shift "from legalism to at least a moderate form of situationalism—though it is certainly not a radical situationalism, because rules are still of great importance."[32] Of particular import is the balance of law and consequence. An act may be at once evil (i.e., it violates a good law) and yet necessary and permissible on account of the extraordinary context of the act.

Supporting my interpretation, Linzey acknowledges, "Some element of calculating the good as we see it is inevitable in moral evaluation" (*AT*, 109). Yet, he distances himself from Singer in that he refuses to appeal only to utilitarian calculations to establish proper actions.[33] He acknowledges that there are utilitarian values for animal abuse, including experimentation. He also warns, "Once our moral thinking becomes dominated by crude utilitarian calculations, then there is no right, value or good that cannot be bargained away, animal or human" (*CRA*, 120). Thus, while calculation helps one to choose the route of the lesser evil, such calculations do not render an action good in itself. Perhaps killing may be necessary and therefore rights violable; but necessity does make the action of killing good. Linzey would be better served to say, with regard at least to sentient creatures, that killing is never justified; but it is at times inevitable

32. David F. Kelly, *Contemporary Catholic Health Care Ethics* (Washington, DC: Georgetown University Press, 2004), 90.
33. Linzey, *AT*, 38; *WASM*, 152–155.

and/or necessary. For "we have no biblical warrant for claiming killing as God's will. God's will is for peace" (*AT*, 130).

Identifying and Respecting Sentience

As already noted, Linzey emphasizes sentience as a morally relevant distinction even in his later works. But how does one tell whether or not a creature is sentient? For Linzey, "this is in part a scientific question" (*AR*, 27). However, he recognizes the limits of science in establishing the sentience of certain nonhuman animals. That is, some who engage in allegedly cruel practices against nonhuman animals claim that such practices should continue until absolutely clear scientific evidence proves the sentience of these creatures.[34] Yet, for Linzey, the lack of sentiency for some life forms appears self-evident. For example, he writes that sentience "should certainly not include plant life and forms of life such as insects" because "response to stimuli . . . does not constitute sentience" (*AR*, 27).

In *Why Animal Suffering Matters*, Linzey engages five arguments that reject the significance of the sentience of nonhumans for matters of moral concern.[35] First, there is the agnostic claim that we cannot ultimately know the reality of nonhumans and therefore cannot build a case of moral concern from their experience of suffering. Linzey replies that there are some things we can know "at least *as reasonably as* we know them in the case of most humans" (*WASM*, 50). Aside from this point, it would seem rather odd indeed to default to a position of abuse where sentience seems possible on account of epistemic uncertainty. If animal rights cannot be established because of agnosticism, why can animal abuse? Second, there is the claim that

---

34. See Linzey, *AR*, 62–66. Also, *WASM*, 51.
35. See Linzey, *WASM*, 49–55.

we must wait for clearer data.[36] Linzey's response is that the appeal to complexity of suffering and self-consciousness could also apply to infants. Third, there is the claim that the ascription of human qualities to nonhumans muddles the discussion. To this claim Linzey responds that describing an animal as "unhappy" fits the animal's experience of its own natural life such that practices that deprive animals of the ability to act on their instincts by definition violates their pursuit of the good. Fourth, regarding the possibility that all things are sentient, including plants, Linzey appeals to scientific evidence that establishes a distinction. The difference is not that there is ambiguous evidence, but rather that there is no evidence that plants suffer. Finally, regarding the possibility that animal suffering is not comparable to human suffering on account of the higher mental capacities of human beings, Linzey argues that (1) scientific evidence suggests otherwise and (2) such arguments would apply to less-developed humans as well. Ultimately, Linzey maintains, in the face of scientific evidence that suggests sentiency, "we have to make ethical decisions and give animals the benefit of the doubt" (AR, 65).[37]

Right to Life for Sentients

In *Animal Rights*, Linzey suggests that the position of many animal-friendly Christians is as follows: "It is immoral to inflict suffering upon animals, but it is not wrong to kill them humanely" (AR, 29). Contrarily, Linzey assents to Rosalina Godlovitch's notion that such a position is incoherent in that it would necessitate ending all nonhuman animal life humanely inasmuch as this action would

36. See ibid., 80.
37. See also Linzey's thoughts on the burden of proof with regard to animal capacity. Linzey, *WASM*, 47.

relinquish the evil of suffering by a non-evil means (humane killing).[38] I am not convinced this logic necessarily holds primarily because it does not make the distinction between necessary and unnecessary suffering. Regardless, Linzey maintains that "issues of life and suffering are fundamental to any discussion of animal rights" (*AR*, 58). He muses that the rejection of this connection of life and suffering is likely "due to the problematic consequences of maintaining a 'no killing' principle" (*AR*, 31).

Practices of Proleptic Witness

Given Linzey's position, what will cosmocentric transfiguration look like in practice vis-à-vis individual, sentient, nonhuman animals? What actions best represent humanity's role to be a proleptic witness to the eschatological future? Here, I seek to answer these questions. I begin, however, with his caveat regarding the limits of moral practice in a fallen and sinful world.

Living in a Fallen World

Linzey recognizes the contradictions of the present state of reality.[39] "The kind of world, cursed as it is, in which we live does make it *impossible* to respect all kinds of life all the time" (*CRA*, 19–20; emphasis mine).[40] Human sin makes it so "no human being can live free of evil" (*CRA*, 101). It is this admission that leads him to disavow self-righteousness, by which he intimates the feeling of superiority of animal activists because they engage in certain actions that lessen the presence of harm in the world. For Linzey, "we are all sinners when it

---

38. Linzey, *AR*, 30; *WASM*, 158.
39. Linzey, *CSG*, 34–35.
40. For example, see Linzey's position on self-defense. Linzey, *WASM*, 24–25.

comes to animals" (*CSG*, xv). Indeed, Linzey acknowledges that even a vegan lifestyle results in the death of animals during the farming process.[41]

When discussing the issue of self-defense, Linzey maintains, "When there is a *direct* choice between the life of an individual human and an individual animal, we may rightly choose to save the human agent" (*CRA*, 138). Furthermore, it "is difficult to resist the need to kill" in situations where animals, including insects, jeopardize food supplies for the human community (*CRA*, 139). His view is therefore not that humans "can easily turn to live in some Edenite harmony with other creatures" (*AT*, 58). The tensions of a fallen world require eschatological redemption. On the path toward that redemption, humans can live in solidarity with other creatures caught up in the same "structures of disorder" (*AT*, 58). However, "there is no pure land" in a fallen world.[42] There may even be instances in which humane killing is in the best interest of creature, including humans (e.g., euthanasia).[43]

The balance Linzey seeks is, on the one hand, the recognition that life as we know it necessitates suffering and death and therefore leads to moral conflicts for someone who seeks to alleviate and prevent such realities, and, on the other hand, the call to avoid normalizing suffering and death institutionally on the basis that they are, in certain situations, necessary for either human existence or the ongoing well-being of the cosmos.[44] Said theologically, humanity's Spirit-filled and imaginative witness to the eschatological future remains a witness.[45] It is not the province of humans to construct the kingdom of God in

---

41. Linzey, *AT*, 132; *AG*, 77–79; *CSG*, xiv–xv.
42. See Linzey, *AT*, 132, *AG*, 90; *CSG*, xiv.
43. Linzey, *WASM*, 159.
44. Linzey, *AR*, 33–42.
45. Linzey, *CRA*, 35.

its fullness; but neither is it the luxury of humans to ignore its ideal for the sake of self-gratification.

Nonhuman Animal Experimentation

Even though utilitarian value does not in itself constitute moral propriety, Linzey holds that the question of necessity is crucial when discussing animal experimentation. "It is important to distinguish what human beings want and what they need"; for "many of the necessities for animal experimentation turn out not to be necessities at all" (*AR*, 53–54). An example Linzey offers is testing cosmetic products on animals.[46]

For Linzey, the justification of experimentation requires the establishment of vital necessity. And instances of such necessity are rare. Even in these cases, Linzey notes,

> some of us . . . would be as disinclined to support painful experimentation on animals as we would be disinclined to support the torture of human subjects, no matter how 'beneficial' the results might be. (*WASM*, 156)

Hunting

"Hunting represents the anti-gospel of Jesus our Predator" (*AT*, 114). This quote represents Linzey's basic position with regard to hunting.[47] However, at least in his early thought, he softens his ethics of non-suffering and non-killing on account of the fallenness of the world.

46. Linzey, *AR*, 53.
47. See Linzey, *WASM*, chapter 3.

Has man the *right to kill* animals whenever his own species or other species or the welfare of the species concerned is endangered through over-population or aggression? There is no logical reason, I believe, why such a principle should not be accepted as long as the method of killing is as humane as possible and that no persons are receiving pleasure from such activity. (*AR*, 38; emphasis mine)

Here, Linzey acknowledges the possibility of necessary killing. More importantly, he claims that such killing can be viewed as a *right*. However, he qualifies this view by stating that no pleasure should be derived from such killing, intimating that the killing itself is still an evil, albeit a necessary one.

Why is hunting evil? Because it

offends two basic moral principles. The first is that *it is intrinsically wrong to deliberately inflict suffering on a sentient mammal for purposes other than its own individual benefit* . . . But there is a second, even more fundamental principle, namely, *it is intrinsically wrong to deliberately cause suffering for the purposes of amusement, recreation, or in the name of sport*" (*WASM*, 83–84).

Such a position leads to an unequivocal rejection of hunting for sport.[48] Indeed, Linzey refers to this practice as "one of the least justifiable, and the most objectionable, of all current practices" of animal cruelty (*WASM*, 95). His position also leads to a moral challenge both to those who enjoy hunting for food and those who hunt for food where meat-eating is no longer a contextual necessity for human survival. Hunting is only "justifiable" in cases of vital human need. Thus, for Linzey, most modern practices of hunting fall under the category of "wanton injury."[49] They are not necessary for survival, self-defense, or essential benefit.

---

48. Linzey, *AR*, 39–42; *AT*, 114–118.
49. Linzey, *CRA*, 104–110; *AT*, 114–119.

In his earlier work, Linzey argues that species control is a possible justification for killing. However, he qualifies this view: "A great deal more of research needs to be conducted in this area of moral necessity for animal control" (*AR*, 38). Furthermore, we should "always reject . . . 'control' of animals when this is inspired by man's selfish interests alone" (*AR*, 39). In his later work, Linzey takes a stronger stance on this issue, arguing that the case for hunting based on control fails for three reasons. First, "nature is an essentially self-regulating system" (*WASM*, 91). Second, it is unclear what balance *ought* to look like in nature, especially when humans encroach on an ecosystem. Third, nature has a way of compensating human efforts to cull a species.

Linzey also denies that the human practice of hunting is justified because nature requires predation. Such appeals to an amoral system to establish the propriety of the actions of moral agents constitute a fallacy.[50] Indeed, that humans are moral creatures ought to open the possibility for the opposite interpretation. Contrarily, "only if parasitical nature is to be celebrated as divinely-purposed existence can hunting for amusement be justified" (*AT*, 114). Neither Linzey's eschatology nor his Christology can permit such a celebration. Hunting violates the eschatological vision of creation and the role that humans are meant to play within that vision—a role which entails that they "live free of needless misery" (*CRA*, 108). If Jesus affirmed the mechanisms of evolutionary progress as the good means of authentic development, he would have been "the butcher *par excellence*" (*AT*, 120) rather than the good shepherd who dies for his sheep.[51]

50. Linzey, *AR*, 40–41.
51. Linzey, *AT*, 120.

Fur-Trapping and Farming

Regarding the logistics of trapping, Linzey holds that "almost all methods involved are *inherently* painful" (*CRA*, 125). This argument seems to extend also to other forms of killing animals for resources.[52] Linzey thus laments that the majority of Christian voices—and all of them until very recently—that have addressed fur-trapping have defended it.[53]

For Linzey, the arguments in favor of fur-trapping, including that it protects indigenous cultures, facilitates economic well-being, and aids conservation, are all faulted. Regarding indigenous cultures, Linzey states, "Human traditions and ways of life may be generally worth defending, but not at any cost and certainly not when they depend upon the suffering of thousands if not millions, of wild animals every year" (*CRA*, 127). Indeed, few people argue that cultural practices such as human sacrifice or cannibalism should be preserved for the sake of reverencing a culture. Aside from this position, Linzey notes that there is a "distinction between what is genuinely indigenous and what are indigenous skills exploited for our [non-indigenous peoples'] benefit" (*CRA*, 127).[54] As Linzey notes in a later work, the aboriginal contribution to fur-trapping constitutes lower than 0.1 percent of global fur trade.[55] Regarding conservation arguments, Linzey notes that they tend to be directed toward human benefit in relation to the whole as opposed to any concern for the suffering of individual animals.[56]

Linzey argues that fur farming includes particular forms of deprivation of natural living for animals, including "the level of stress

---

52. For instance, see Linzey's discussion of sealing in Linzey, *WASM*, chapter 5.
53. Linzey, *AG*, 116–117.
54. Linzey, *AG*, 120–121.
55. Linzey, *AG*, 119; also *WASM*, 134–136.
56. Linzey, *CRA*, 126.

and suffering when wild animals are restricted to small, barren cages" (*AG*, 118). His view is backed by the findings of the Scientific Committee on Animal Health and Animal Welfare of the European Union in 2001, which claims that animals kept for fur are not provided suitable opportunity to follow basic instincts of well-being. Thus, Linzey writes, "It is now unreasonable to hold that fur farming does not impose suffering on animals" (*WASM*, 102). Even so, "around 50 million mink . . . and 7 million foxes . . . are bred each year to meet the world demand for their skins" (*WASM*, 97).

Linzey's dominant critique against fur-trapping and farming is that the practices do not constitute a necessity for human well-being.[57] For most humans, fur is not necessary for survival or well-being.[58] Because there is no vital justification for the practices and because they violate the hope for all sentient creatures, Linzey finds them to represent an unchristian ethics.

Vegetarianism

"Of all the ethical challenges arising from animal theology, vegetarianism can arguably claim to have the strongest support" (*AT*, 125). This support is, for Linzey, grounded in scripture and systematic theology. It furthermore challenges a majority of contemporary meat-eating practices—in which there is no vital necessity—by claiming that they fail to proclaim the gospel to sentient creatures.

Linzey notes the biblical ambiguity regarding meat-eating.[59] He maintains that the permission to eat meat in Genesis 9 is an accommodation to cosmic fallenness.[60] It is furthermore limited by

57. Linzey, *WASM*, 106–107.
58. Linzey, *AG*, 121.
59. Linzey, *CRA*, 141–142

the mandate not to take in an animal's blood, which Linzey rightly claims denotes, in the passage's original context, the animals' life. Thus, "even within this permissive tradition, human beings are not given an entirely free hand" (*CRA*, 142). Lisa Kemmerer argues well that the accommodation argument is problematic: "There is much an atheist or Hindu might say about such a God" who accommodates human sin by promulgating nonhuman suffering.[61]

In different writings, Linzey compares the human consumption of meat to vampirism—not in terms of evil, but rather in terms of nature. Drawing on Anne Rice's *Interview with the Vampire*, he notes the arguments therein in which vampires justify consuming human blood by an appeal to the natural order. Similarly, he muses whether or not vegetarians are "opposing the nature of things as given" (*AT*, 80). Yet, drawing on Genesis 1–3, he claims that God's original intent for creation was not survival of the fittest, but rather "a state of perfect Sabbath harmony within creation where humans and animals are both prescribed a vegetarian diet" (*AT*, 80).

Linzey *may* overstep exegetical bounds when he suggests that "Genesis 1 clearly depicts vegetarianism as a divine command" (*AT*, 125).[62] However, he stands on strong exegetical grounds when he writes,

> Even though the early Hebrews were neither pacifists nor vegetarians, they were deeply convicted of the view that violence between humans and animals, and indeed between animal species themselves, was not God's original will for creation. (*AT*, 126)

I also think Linzey is essentially correct when he writes, "The ideal of the peaceable kingdom was never lost sight of" in Israel (*AT*,

60. See especially Linzey, *AT*, 127–129.
61. Kemmerer, *In Search of Consistency*, 242.
62. See Ryan Patrick McLaughlin, *Christian Theology and the Status of Animals* (New York: Palgrave Macmillan, 2014), 86–87.

129). That is, the protological claim of edenic peace finds a prophetic counterpart in the Isaianic hope of the peaceable kingdom.

Eschatologically speaking, the new possibilities that Christ opens for creation and to which the Spirit enables humans to witness makes vegetarianism "an implicitly theological act of greatest significance" (*AT*, 90). Says Linzey:

> By refusing to eat meat, we are witnessing to a higher order of existence . . . By refusing to go the way of our 'natural nature' . . . by standing against the order of unredeemed nature we become signs of the order of existence for which all creatures long. (*AT*, 90–91).

Even if refusing to eat meat stands against what appears to be natural in evolutionary history, Linzey maintains, "From a theological perspective no moral endeavor is wasted so long as it coheres with God's purpose for his cosmos" (*CRA*, 146). In this sense, vegetarianism bears an "anticipatory character" (*CSG*, 38). It is a proleptic witness to a maximally inclusive eschatological hope, "an act of anticipation of the peaceable Kingdom that we seek" (*CSG*, 50).

Based on this claim, Linzey challenges Matthew Fox's "Eucharistic law of the Universe"—which embraces as good the notion that all life must eat and be eaten—by noting that Jesus's sacrifice reverses survival of the fittest. "The significance of the eucharistic meal, therefore, is not the perpetuation of the old world of animal sacrifice but precisely our liberation from it" (*AT*, 122). The Eucharist is a foretaste of eschatological hope.[63] More can be said here. The Eucharist, as the meal of communion *par excellence*, is a meal without animal meat. Christ takes the place of the main course, freeing humans to new encounters of peace with animals.

---

63. Linzey, *AT*, 122.

The aforementioned arguments notwithstanding, Linzey's position is not that meat-eating is never permissible. He contextualizes his vegetarianism, arguing that killing for food "*may be justifiable, but only when human nourishment clearly requires it, and even then it remains an inevitable consequence of sin*" (CRA, 142). Linzey further acknowledges that, "given the confusing interrelationship of light and darkness, blessing and curse, it is difficult to hold out for any truths so self-evident that people who fail to see them are somehow morally culpable" (CRA, 145). In a similar vein:

> The biblical case for vegetarianism does not rest on the view that killing may never be allowable in the eyes of God, rather on the view that killing is always a grave matter. When we have to kill to live we may do so, but when we do not, we should live otherwise. (AT, 131)

Linzey's carefulness is theologically necessary on account of Jesus, who was not vegetarian.[64] Linzey maintains that it is the concession of God to a fallen world in Genesis 9 that draws Jesus, as a person historically located in first century Palestine, to consume meat.[65] In this manner, he emphasizes the importance of acknowledging Jesus's context and the limitations implicit in that context.[66]

> God incarnates himself or herself into the limits and constraints of the world as we know it. It is true that one of the purposes of the incarnation was to manifest something of the trans-natural possibilities of existence, but no one human life can demonstrate, let alone exhaust, all the possibilities of self-giving love. (AT, 86)

---

64. On this point, and Jesus's likely participation in the sacrificial system, see Richard Bauckham, "Jesus and Animals II: What Did He Practice?" in *Animals on the Agenda: Questions about Animal Ethics for Theology and Ethics*, ed. Andrew Linzey and Dorothy Yamamoto (Chicago: University of Illinois Press, 1998), 50–54.
65. Linzey, CRA, 47–48.
66. See Linzey, AT, 134–137.

True, Jesus was apparently no vegetarian. But neither did he campaign against slavery. He was not necessarily a visionary with regard to women's welfare—in fact he derogatively referred to a Gentile woman as a dog.[67] In short, Jesus was neither a complete "accommodation to nature" nor the exhaustive answer to every moral query that arises in history. His is "a birth of new possibilities for all creation . . . the *beginning* of its transformation" (*AT*, 87; emphasis mine).[68]

At any rate, Jesus's context was very different from the context of most Western Christians today. "For the first time in history of the human race vegetarianism has become a publically viable option, at least for those who live in the Western world" (*AT*, 83–84). For most of these people, meat-eating is necessary for neither survival nor optimal health.[69] Furthermore, the mass consumption of animal protein renders other food sources unusable for humans, resulting in a net loss of available food for the human community.[70] Based on his view of the importance of sentience, Linzey maintains,

> Once it is perceived that satisfactory alternatives to animal protein exist, and are sufficiently plenteous to cope with the increased world demand for food, then vegetarianism becomes a moral necessity. (*AR*, 36)

As with most of Linzey's arguments, his promotion of vegetarianism culminates in eschatology. "Those individuals who opt for vegetarianism can do so in the knowledge that they are living closer to the biblical ideal of peaceableness than their carnivorous contemporaries." For, "to opt for a vegetarian life-style is to take one

67. See Matt. 15:21–28.
68. Bauckham seems to make similar claims in his essays on Jesus in *Animals on the Agenda* (see 59–60). Even so, Linzey is uncomfortable with Bauckham's findings (see 5–6 of the same volume).
69. Linzey, *AR*, 34–37.
70. Ibid., 35–36.

practical step towards living in peace with the rest of creation" (*AT*, 132).[71]

Letting Be

One of the most basic points of Linzey's ethics at first glance seemingly strikes against transfiguration. Humans ought to let the nonhuman creation be.[72] This "letting be" is the "*attitude* with which we begin" (*CRA*, 19). Practically, it entails "respecting at least some of the natural instincts which animals possess" (*AR*, 2–3).

The concept of "letting be" is a complicated one for Linzey. He is suspicious of conservationist efforts.

> The thinking behind attempts at conservation are often anthropocentric (i.e., human beings conserve other species not because they have recognized the value and rights of other animals but because they themselves will be deprived if some other species becomes extinct). (*AR*, 41)

This suspicion immediately separates Linzey's earliest thought from the anthropocentric conservationism I outlined in chapter 1. He furthermore separates his position from those cosmocentric voices that value the whole over the individual when he claims, "From the standpoint of theos-rights, it makes some difference but not much whether it is the very last tiger, or one of many thousands, that is gratuitously killed" (*CRA*, 109). Said differently, the value of an individual creature is never subsumed into the value of the whole.[73]

"Letting be" does not mean inactivity or refusal to interact with nonhuman nature. Linzey is adamant that humans have "*active*

71. Also Andrew Linzey, "C. S. Lewis's Theology of Animals," *Anglican Theological Review* 80/1 (Winter 1998): 76–77.
72. Linzey, *CSG*, 17.
73. For critiques of conservationist practices, see ibid., 40–42.

responsibilities to animals in particular" (*CRA*, 19). Nor does it intimate blithe participation in the mechanisms of the evolutionary process (e.g., predation). "Letting be" denotes a reverence for the blessing God has given to the nonhuman creation.[74] It means letting creation be free and significant without reference to human value.

For Linzey, one violation of "letting be" is the captivity of animals, most particularly in zoos and circuses, which entail "the curtailment or frustration of the animal's basic instincts and freedoms" (*AR*, 58).[75] Linzey categorizes such uses of animals—alongside hunting for sport—under the heading "wanton injury."[76] Also, on farms animals must be permitted to act out their natural inclinations, including appropriate sustenance and an open environment that permits natural movement.[77] Linzey later argues that the notion of theos-rights renders these permissions necessary; for "animals have a God-given right to be animals" (*CRA*, 112).[78]

Another dimension of "letting be"—and one that, in my opinion, is crucial to Linzey's view—is his claim that "human beings are not responsible for what the natural world may bequeath to animals in the forms of drought, disease and death, except perhaps to alleviate the suffering caused whenever the situation arises" (*AR*, 58). The significance of this claim suggests that peaceful actions that serve as witnesses to eschatological hope can never become scientific attempts to create Eden on earth.

74. Linzey, *CRA*, 18–21.
75. Also ibid., 130–131.
76. Ibid., 104–110.
77. See Linzey, *AR*, 64–66.
78. Such an argument would apparently apply to predatory animals as well.

Against Institutionalized Suffering

As already noted, Linzey acknowledges the necessity—indeed in many cases the inevitability—of violence. However, rare acts of violence driven by necessity are not the same as the institutionalization of violence. It is this legal justification of the common practice of causing millions of animals an immense amount of suffering that Linzey seeks first and foremost to restrict and ultimately eliminate.

In *Animal Gospel*, Linzey advocates six steps toward this end.[79] First, humans must be provided with a "space for an ethical appreciation of living creatures" (*AG*, 127). For Linzey, this step entails encouraging the childlike intuition to protect nonhuman animals. Second, advocates must bring light to cruel practices of the various forms of institutionalized suffering. Third, animal rights scholars must engage in interdisciplinary dialogues and debates concerning their positions; for "we shall not change the world for animals without also changing people's ideas about the world" (*AG*, 130). Fourth, animal advocates must seek, as consumers, "to institutionalize informed ethical choice" (*AG*, 131).[80] This step entails accurate labeling of products and transparency about how the various dimensions that go into that product come to reach the aggregate whole that consumers purchase. For instance, are eggs from free range chickens? Are the chickens genetically modified? Are the chickens permitted other natural tendencies (e.g., vegetarian feed)? These questions help consumers make informed choices concerning the animal products they purchase. Fifth, there must be legislation that is both gradual (i.e., not all or nothing for animals) and truly progressive (i.e., that entails more than cosmetic changes to

79. Linzey, *AG*, 126–139.
80. Also, Linzey, *WASM*, 66–67.

institutionalized suffering). In a later work, Linzey notes that "only changes in laws secure lasting protection" (*WASM*, 66). Sixth, though Linzey is critical of capitalism, he argues that there are enough people who would seek alternative products if they were offered.[81]

Conclusion

It seems to me that the basic question of Linzey's entire moral theology is this: "How could it be that a God who out of love creates animals would delight in their gratuitous destruction?" (*AT*, 104). The question is rhetorical. The trinitarian God whose very nature is love and whose character is most fully revealed in the Son's incarnational kenosis and the Spirit's fellow-suffering with all sentient creatures suggests that human relations with those creatures, in order to be just, must seek their well-being in the form of the alleviation of suffering and promulgation of rights. God's desire must be for peace, not predation; harmony, not bloody competition; kenotic love, not self-aggrandizing power.

This desire grounds the rights of all creatures relationally, for they are all creatures before the God who created them and seeks their well-being. The completion of the ultimate vision of God remains an eschatological hope that remains out of the reach of human striving and political programs. In world that is fallen and incomplete, there can be no edenic state. Nonetheless, that hope has broken into the history of the cosmos with the incarnation and the new loosing of the Spirit. This breaking-in opens up the possibility for humans to more fully become the *imago Dei* by practicing peace toward nonhuman animals. Forms of this practice include the culling of animal experimentation, the fur industry, hunting, and meat-eating.

81. See Linzey, *AG*, 136–137.

They also include working toward a more just society for animals through the establishment of legal protection.

In short, the rights of God are best recognized when God's desires for the creation to which God has given space are taken up and honored by humans in the power of the Spirit. When humans act in this manner, they become sacraments of the eschaton—the peaceable kingdom in which all creatures will be freed from the darker mechanisms of evolution, most notably suffering and death. Therefore, seeking the rights of sentient animals—among other forms of seeking animal welfare—constitutes a proleptic witness to cosmic eschatological hope within history. Such is the responsibility of humans in the wake of Christ's salvific movement and the Spirit's empowering presence.

13

Moltmann and Linzey

Comparison and Analysis

As far as I can tell, Moltmann never cites Linzey in his work. Linzey does infrequently cite Moltmann, though at times only to critique a perceived anthropocentric deficiency.[1] Given this dearth of interaction, I here seek to examine the convergences, divergences, and ambiguities that exist between their thought. In my view, Moltmann tends to provide a more thoroughly developed theological foundation for cosmocentric transfiguration while Linzey is far consistent in establishing how these foundations translate into practice with regard to (at least sentient) nonhuman animals. It is not my purpose here to engage criticisms of Moltmann and Linzey, a task I undertake in chapter 15.

---

1. See, for instance, Linzey's assessment of *The Crucified God* and *God in Creation*. Andrew Linzey, *Animal Theology* (hereafter *AT*), (Chicago: University of Illinois Press, 1994), 191.

Theology

Moltmann's doctrine of the social Trinity is a well-developed theological vision that draws heavily on Trinitarian conversations throughout the history of Christianity. Linzey's emphasis on God's nature as love is emblematic of Moltmann, who also maintains that God's nature is best described as love. This view grounds for both theologians the nature of God's love for creation, which includes a stark challenge to divine impassibility inasmuch as God suffers in that love.[2] Yet Moltmann's expression of the Trinity as a divine community of persons whose perfect unity is established by a self-emptying perichoretic love is much stronger theologically than Linzey's more basic appeal to God as love.[3] This strength correlates to a clearer expression of what Trinitarian love means for creation—most particularly that the divine nature is intimated in the very act of creation, which entails a divine kenosis of withdrawal in order to seek genuinely communion with that which is other than God.[4]

At any rate, both Moltmann and Linzey claim that the Trinity desires communion with the world.[5] Yet the world does not seem to reflect the perichoretic union of the divine. Rather, it reflects the mechanisms of evolutionary development which, while including dimensions of harmony, balance, and symbiosis on the level of ecosystems, still throughout history and in the lives of individual creatures entails competition, gratuitous suffering, and death.

2. On Moltmann, see Jürgen Moltmann, *The Crucified God: The Cross of Christ as the Foundation and Criticism of Christian Theology* (hereafter *TCG*), trans. R. A. Wilson (Minneapolis, MN: Fortress Press, 1993). On Linzey, see *AT*, 48–52.

3. See Jürgen Moltmann, *The Trinity and the Kingdom: The Doctrine of God* (hereafter *TKG*), trans. Margaret Kohl (Minneapolis, MN: Fortress Press, 1993).

4. See Jürgen Moltmann, *God in Creation: A New Theology of Creation and the Spirit of God* (hereafter *GC*), trans. Margaret Kohl (Minneapolis, MN: Fortress Press, 1993), 75–86.

5. Moltmann, *TKG*, 57; Linzey, *AT*, 24.

Moltmann and Linzey both evince a level of ambiguity regarding the etiology of these mechanisms—and also some tension with one another. Linzey seems more anxious to maintain the traditional doctrine of the fall, even if it must be initially relegated to an angelic corruption prior to the existence of humanity.[6] While Moltmann desires to maintain that the mechanisms of evolution cannot be the final word from God regarding the fate of the cosmos, he is more willing to discard an historical Fall that results from sin.[7] In my opinion, neither Linzey nor Moltmann are satisfactory here. Linzey contributes something important in his refusal to credit (or blame) God for the shadowy sides of evolution. Moltmann contributes something important in his refusal to attribute evolution to some evil will, such as humans or angels. I believe there is a third possibility here that includes both contributions. I will develop this option below. At this point, it is enough to note that Linzey and Moltmann are in unity in maintaining that the mechanisms of evolution constitute an issue for divine love and justice and must be remedied through eschatological redemption.[8]

As with theology proper, Moltmann's Christology is more developed than Linzey's. This point notwithstanding, both recognize the incarnation as significant for nonhuman animals, drawing on the import of Christ taking on flesh, suffering, and dying. Linzey emphasizes mainly Christ's meaning for nonhuman creatures with flesh and blood that suffer.[9] Moltmann does not neglect this

6. See Andrew Linzey, *Animal Gospel* (hereafter *AG*), (Louisville, KY: Westminster John Knox, 1998), 15; Andrew Linzey, "C. S. Lewis's Theology of Animals" (hereafter CSLTA), *Anglican Theological Review* 80/1 (Winter 1998): 106.

7. Jürgen Moltmann, *The Coming of God: Christian Eschatology* (hereafter *CoG*), trans. Margaret Kohl (Minneapolis, MN: Fortress Press, 1996), 91–92.

8. Jürgen Moltmann, *Sun of Righteousness, Arise! God's Future for Humanity and the Earth* (hereafter *SRA*), trans. Margaret Kohl (Minneapolis, MN: Fortress Press, 2010), 221; Linzey, *AT*, 81.

9. Andrew Linzey, *Christianity and the Rights of Animals* (hereafter *CRA*), (New York: Crossroad, 1987), 79–80.

dimension of the incarnation. Christ experiences their transience as well as the disposition of humans. He becomes the ultimate victim of evolution, the sufferer par excellence, and thereby draws their plight into the trinitarian life in order to secure redemption for all.[10] However, Moltmann's christology is more extensive than Linzey's, for he also stresses the import of Christ's death and resurrection for *all living things that die*. Even more generally, Moltmann claims that Christ's experience of transience bears salvific meaning for every bit of matter in the cosmos.[11] In this sense, Moltmann fits within the category of "cosmocentric" somewhat easier than Linzey, whose theology tends more toward a sentiocentrism.[12]

While Moltmann and Linzey both maintain that the Spirit bears a role as the vitalizing principle of life, as with christology, they diverge on the extent of this role. For Linzey, the Spirit's vitalizing presence is primarily located in sentient creatures of flesh and blood. The Spirit suffers with suffering creatures.[13] For Moltmann, the Spirit is the manner of divine immanence in the entire cosmos, from rocks to trees to antelopes to humans. The Spirit suffers with suffering creatures, experiences death in all life that dies, and knows the transience of all transient creation.[14] This pneumatological difference in Moltmann and Linzey correlates to a disparity regarding the eschatological presence of the Spirit in creatures. In Moltmann's framework, the Spirit renders present the advent of eternal life for all creation.[15] Linzey largely limits the redemptive presence of the Spirit to sentient creatures.[16] This difference aside, both Moltmann

---

10. Jürgen Moltmann, *The Way of Jesus Christ: Christology in Messianic Dimensions* (hereafter *WJC*), trans. Margaret Kohl (Minneapolis, MN: Fortress Press, 1993), 296.

11. Moltmann, *WJC*, 253; *CoG*, 92–93.

12. Linzey acknowledges this point. See Linzey, *CRA*, 84–85.

13. Andrew Linzey, *Creatures of the Same God: Explorations in Animal Theology* (hereafter *CSG*), (New York: Lantern Books, 2009), 14.

14. Jürgen Moltmann, *The Spirit of Life: A Universal Affirmation* (hereafter *SL*), trans. Margaret Kohl (Minneapolis, MN: Fortress Press, 1992), 51; *GC*, 96–97.

and Linzey agree that the Spirit's eschatological presence has a unique meaning for human beings in that it establishes their ability to witness to eschatological hope within the flow of history.[17] However, they differ about the nature of this witness. Linzey focuses on theos-rights, which he limits to sentients. Moltmann focuses on the rights of the entire cosmos, though at times neglecting individual in favor of the whole.

Both Moltmann and Linzey expand the traditional scope of the eschatological community. The common ground of this expansion entails the inclusion of every individual victim of suffering, human or nonhuman, that has ever lived in history.[18] Therefore, the eschaton necessitates a resurrection of every individual sentient creature that has ever graced the earth with its presence. The two thinkers diverge on the issue of non-sentient life. Linzey does not reject the possibility of their inclusion, but strongly emphasizes sentient creatures on this point.[19] For Moltmann suffering is not the only significant problem that a just God must overcome. God must also overcome transience, which includes death.[20] Therefore all *dying* life (which is to say all life) must be resurrected and freed from its transience.[21]

One major difference between Moltmann and Linzey is the issue of time. The reason for this difference is that Moltmann develops a theology of time while Linzey does not.[22] Moltmann juxtaposes

---

15. Jürgen Moltmann, *The Church in the Power of the Spirit: A Contribution to Messianic Ecclesiology* (hereafter *CPS*), trans. Margaret Kohl (Minneapolis, MN: Fortress Press, 1993), 199–206; *SL*, 74.

16. See Linzey, *CRA*, 69.

17. Moltmann, *CPS*, 196; *GC*, 101; Linzey, *CRA*, 75; *AT*, 56.

18. Moltmann, *CoG*, 69–70, 306–308; Linzey, *CSG*, 133, n. 13.

19. Andrew Linzey, *After Noah: Animals and the Liberation of Theology* (hereafter *AN*), (Herndon, VA: Mowbray, 1997), 82–84.

20. See especially Moltmann, *WJC*, 252.

21. Moltmann, *CoG*, 92.

22. On Moltmann, see Richard Bauckham, "Time and Eternity," in *God Will Be All in All: The Eschatology of Jürgen Moltmann*, ed. Richard Bauckham (Minneapolis, MN: Fortress Press, 2001), 158–73.

phenomenological time with eternal time. The latter is the gathering up of the all moments of the former into a perichoretic union of presence. Said differently, eternity renders each moment of history eternally significant.

Finally, both Moltmann and Linzey lay on Spirit-filled humanity the grace-enabled potential and responsibility to witness to eschatological hope in the present. Moltmann does so through his theological appropriation of Ernst Bloch's philosophy of hope. Linzey does so through an appeal to christology, pneumatology, and the lives of saints in history. The main tension of their thought here is how they express the relation between history and eschatology. Moltmann's creative expression of the categories of *novum* and *adventus* in conjunction with his detailed exploration of time helps to solidify both why and the manner in which eschatology informs ethics in the unfolding of history. That is, the eschatological future, which is God's coming and arrival, does not burgeon out of history but rather accosts history as that which is genuinely new (*novum*). This coming is already affecting history now, for history is in its *adventus*.[23] In the advent of God's coming and arrival, new possibilities manifest, if only as *creatio anticipativa*, within history.[24] The distinction between *creatio anticipativa* and *creatio nova* distances Moltmann from all attempts to establish the kingdom on earth via human efforts and political programs. Linzey at times struggles to achieve this distance.[25]

23. See Moltmann, *CoG*, 21–29.
24. Moltmann, *GC*, 197–206.
25. For example, Linzey, *CRA*, 104.

Ethics

Moltmann's theology grounds an ethics of transfiguration. Yet his (somewhat) concrete application of that theology is oddly conservationist. Linzey, while less theologically comprehensive than Moltmann, fares far better in my view with regard to the construction of an ethics that is consistent with his theological claims—at least with regard to sentient life.

As already noted, regarding the inanimate and non-sentient creation, Linzey remains somewhat silent. He does not deny the value of these dimensions of the cosmos.[26] Yet he does deny them theos-rights.[27] He is furthermore less concrete regarding human action in this sphere of creation. I have suggested that Linzey has no explicit ethical qualms with the death of individual non-sentient creatures—with the exception of gratuitous slaughter.[28] He thus seems to accept implicitly a conservationist ethics for all non-sentient creation.

Moltmann is adamant that the inanimate creation should have rights.[29] Here he differs from Linzey. Yet these rights, while more explicit, amount to a similar conservationist ethics. Moltmann calls for preservation, including absolute protection of endangered or rare ecosystems and respect for the integrity of natural systems, including a letting be on the part of humans.[30]

Regarding sentient nonhuman animals, Linzey and Moltmann evince a divergence. Both speak of the importance of rights for nonhuman animals.[31] Oddly, while Moltmann clearly suggests that a

---

26. Ibid., 8–9, 85.
27. Ibid., 84.
28. Linzey, *AT*, 74.
29. Jürgen Moltmann, *God for a Secular Society: The Public Relevance of Theology* (hereafter *GSS*), trans. Margaret Kohl (Minneapolis, MN: Fortress Press, 1999), 112–113.
30. Jürgen Moltmann, *Ethics of Hope* (hereafter *EH*), trans. Margaret Kohl (Minneapolis, MN: Fortress Press, 2012), 144–145.

conservationist ethics is not sufficient theologically, it is just this sort of ethics that he delineates. He hints at an eschatological ethics, but ultimately remains agnostic about its practical consequences.[32] The only concrete ethics he offers regarding sentient creatures pertains to the preservation of species, the cessation of genetic manipulation, and the promulgation of an environment that meets the natural needs and desires of nonhuman animals.[33]

With regard to sentient nonhumans, Linzey is more consistent than Moltmann with regard to praxis. His concrete ethics follows the logic of his theological foundations. If the eschatological future is breaking into the present in some manner and permitting new practices of peace, then those practices ought to reflect that future. For Linzey (and Moltmann) that future is peace—the cessation of competition and violence and the end of suffering for each individual creature. Based on this vision, Linzey suggests that rights should work towards more than preservation; they should work toward (or at the very least witness to) eschatological peace.[34] Thus, he calls for the end of institutionalized suffering and the progressive disengagement of practices such as hunting, fishing, sealing, fur-farming and trapping, experimenting on animals, and meat-eating.

Conclusion

Moltmann's theology is more developed than that of Linzey. Linzey's ethics, however, are far more consistent than that of Moltmann. For my purposes, they complement one another nicely. In an effort to

---

31. Moltmann, *WJC*, 256, 307–8; Linzey, *AT*, 19–23.
32. Moltmann, *WJC*, 311.
33. Moltmann, *EH*, 144.
34. See Linzey, *CRA*, 86–89. I make this claim partly because Linzey writes that "Christian ethics is essentially eschatological." Linzey, *AG*, 17.

systematize cosmocentric transfiguration (Part III), I draw heavily on Moltmann's theology and Linzey's ethics.

Toward an Eco-Eschatological Ethics of Preservation and Protest

14

Theological Foundations for Cosmocentric Transfiguration

In part I, I delineated three theological loci for establishing a taxonomy of nonhuman theological ethics: cosmology, anthropology, and eschatology. Correlating to these loci, both Moltmann and Linzey concur on three foundational theological claims. First, God has created a good cosmos and desires communion with every single instantiation of life therein. Second, God has appointed humanity with a special responsibility in this creation. Third, the creation, while good, has become in some sense distorted or disoriented and requires eschatological redemption. While these three claims are the central tenets of cosmocentric transfiguration, they benefit from a broader systematic framework. Having examined the convergences, divergences, and ambiguities that arise at the intersection of Moltmann and Linzey, I can now develop what this framework might look like.

Theology Proper:
God as the Community of Love

The doctrine of the Trinity may not be necessary for animal theology, but when developed in a certain manner, it is a powerful foundation.[1] While the biblical grounds for the doctrine are less than obvious, the historical appropriation of scripture is not.[2] What remains undecided in contemporary recoveries of the doctrine of the Trinity is how to navigate the perpetual tension between God as a unity and God as a community.[3] The task is important because the outcome bears implications for all of theology.[4]

Moltmann's social doctrine of the Trinity maintains that God's oneness is constituted by the perichoretic relations of the three divine persons. In this constitution, the doctrine opens the space for an appropriation of a dynamic and relational ontology as opposed to a static and substantial one. It also provides a basis for cosmology; for the love that constitutes God's unity is the catalyst for the creation of that which is other than God and the pursuit of that other for the sake of communion. On this point both Moltmann and Linzey concur.[5] This cosmology suggests that it is insufficient to claim that the Logos as divine reason is both the ground and destiny of the cosmos. Rather, the ground and destiny of the cosmos is the Logos as divine reason

1. On this point, see Catherine Mowry LaCugna's work on the Trinity. *God for Us: The Trinity and Christian Life* (San Francisco: Harper, 1993), especially 396.
2. See Franz Dünzl, *A Brief History of the Doctrine of the Trinity in the Early Church*, trans. John Bowden (New York: T & T Clark, 2007).
3. See Jürgen Moltmann, *The Trinity and the Kingdom: The Doctrine of God* (hereafter *TKG*), trans. Margaret Kohl (Minneapolis: Fortress Press, 1993), 10–20; Karl Rahner, *The Trinity*, trans. Joseph Donceel (New York: The Crossroad Publishing Company, 2005).
4. See LaCugna's *God for Us*. See also Miroslav Volf, *After Our Likeness: The Church as the Image of the Trinity* (Grand Rapids: William B. Eerdmans Company, 1998); John Zizioulas, *Being as Communion: Studies in Personhood and the Church* (New York: Crestwood, 1985).
5. See Moltmann, *TKG*, 57; Andrew Linzey, *After Noah: Animals and the Liberation of Theology* (hereafter *AN*), (Herndon, VA: Mowbray, 1997), 77.

expressed as perichoretic love. Thus, all that is created, all that exists, is the object of divine pursuit for the sake of perichoretic communion.

Cosmology:
Loving Pursuit of the Other

Metaphorically speaking, pursuit and alterity necessitate at least an initial distance. Thus, for God to create and pursue in love a cosmos that is truly other-than-God mandates a distance between God and creation, a divine transcendence. This distance means that God must be able and willing to suffer the cosmos its own integrity. For this reason, God's Trinitarian love is, in the act of creation, *suffering love.* Moltmann's creative appropriation of *creatio ex nihilo* captures just this point. This suffering love is present not only at the origin of creation but also throughout the history of the Divine-world relationship. God's love must suffer not only the integrity of creation but also the ongoing cost of that integrity, including human sin. Again, here both Moltmann and Linzey concur.[6]

The social doctrine of the Trinity combined with the affirmation that God lovingly creates and pursues that which is other than God for the sake of communion enables a vision of the cosmos that is both infused by divine love and bears genuine alterity and integrity. To draw on Moltmann's imagery, God withdraws, leaving creation its own space and time in an original act of divine kenosis. The time and space of creation is at once apart from God and infused with the presence of the Spirit, who vitalizes it for its own freedom and suffers its reality, come what may.

---

6. See Jürgen Moltmann, *God in Creation: A New Theology of Creation and the Spirit of God* (hereafter *GC*), trans. Margaret Kohl (Minneapolis, MN: Fortress Press, 1993), 198–200; Andrew Linzey, *Animal Theology* (hereafter *AT*), (Chicago: University of Illinois Press, 1994), 25.

Protology and the Fall:
Cosmic Consecration, Cosmic Isolation

Denis Edwards writes that the "problem of natural evil" is "greatly intensified" by "a new understanding of the size and scope of the problem of creaturely loss."[7] The etiology of the evolutionary mechanisms that facilitate such loss is one of the most difficult questions in contemporary theology.[8] It is also one of the most important and divisive issues in nonhuman theology.

In chapter 2 (**Table 2.1**), I suggested that the crux of this issue is best expressed in the juxtaposition of Genesis 1, the *Enuma Elish*, and a Darwinian worldview:

Table 2.1 – Creation and Divine Character			
	Divine Identity	**Creative Action**	**Cosmic Identity**
Narrative/ Myth "A" (Genesis 1:1 – 2:3)	*Elohim*	Creates through peaceful and cooperative divine fiat	A world of empowered creatures absent of predation
Narrative/ Myth "B" (*Enuma Elish*)	Marduk	Creates out of a divine war for existence	An enslaved and competitive world for divine benefit
Narrative/ Theory "C" (Darwinian Worldview)	???	???	A world that, while displaying high levels of cooperation among species, nonetheless requires suffering, predation, and death in order to function

7. Denis Edwards, "Every Sparrow that Falls to the Ground: The Cost of Evolution and the Christ–Event," *Ecotheology* 11/1 (2006), 106.

8. This point is made well by Christopher Southgate in *The Groaning of Creation: God, Evolution, and the Problem of Evil* (Louisville, KY: Westminster John Knox, 2008).

The operative question is: How does one maintain the theological identity of "God A" in the face of scientific evidence that "World A" never actually existed?

Linzey most often—though not always—does so by ambiguously maintaining some form of the historicity of "World A." However, he is unclear about how "World A" becomes "World C," whether by an angelic fall, a human fall, or by the mere finitude of creation as other-than-God.[9] Moltmann moves forward by proposing that "World A" constitutes the destiny of "World C" rather than its history.[10] Yet, Moltmann is not clear if God directly ordains "World C" or it comes about by some other manner.

I have explored responses to the tension between God's goodness and the mechanisms of evolutionary emergence. Based on the gratuitousness of suffering, predation, and death in the natural order, I concur with the assessment of David Clough: "Attempting to solve the problem of the relationship between the fall and evolution by denying the fall. . . is by no means an attractive option for Christian theology."[11] Rather, what is needed here is a view that accounts for both the scientific evidence that dismantles the historicity of "World A" and the theological significances (e.g., God's goodness) implied by the specifics of "World A" delineated in Israel's creation myths and elsewhere (e.g., the eschatological vision of the prophets). I maintain that a synthesis and development of Moltmann and Linzey, one which accepts both Linzey's refusal to trace the etiology of suffering, predation, and death to God's will and Moltmann's refusal to trace

---

9. On the angelic Fall, see Andrew Linzey, "C. S. Lewis's Theology of Animals," *Anglican Theological Review* 80/1 (Winter 1998): 70. On the human fall, see Andrew Linzey, *Christianity and the Rights of Animals* (hereafter *CRA*), (New York: Crossroad, 1987), 18. On the finitude of creation, see *AT*, 81–85.

10. Jürgen Moltmann, *The Way of Jesus Christ: Christology in Messianic Dimensions* (hereafter *WJC*), trans. Margaret Kohl (Minneapolis, MN: Fortress Press, 1993), 127–28.

11. David Clough, *On Animals* (New York: Bloomsbury, 2014), 124.

these mechanisms to angels or humans, provides a promising path forward here.

The schema of creation-fall-redemption-consummation is one of the more common categorically ordered readings of God's history with the world. This schema evinces just how significant the concept of will is in Christian thought. Every aspect of the narrative requires some movement of *intentional* will. (I am following Robert Wennberg here in juxtaposing intentional will with permissive will.)[12] Creation rests solely on the divine will. The fall requires a human and/or an angelic will. Redemption requires the divine will with (in some cases) human assent. Consummation, like creation, rests solely on the divine will.

Linzey evinces this emphasis on will in his effort to place the fall at the feet of anyone other than God. Moltmann is less adamant on identifying a willful culprit upon which to lay the responsibility for the mechanisms of evolution—though his thought is at times unclear on how these mechanisms arose outside of the will of a free agent. Even so, I believe Moltmann provides the foundation for an alternative schema that can more easily house the tensions noted above concerning "God A" and "World C," most significantly by lessening the importance of will at the stage of the fall. This lessening is facilitated by increasing the importance of creation's integrity with regard to the notion of fallenness, a strategy John Polkinghorne refers to as the "free process" defense.[13]

As I have already noted, Moltmann speaks positively of God's kenotic withdrawal in creation, which opens up a unique time and space for the creation to be.[14] Yet, this space entails a risk. God's

---

12. Robert Wennberg, *God, Humans, and Animals: An Invitation to Enlarge Our Moral Universe* (Grand Rapids, MI: William B. Eerdmans Publishing Company, 2003), 331–32.
13. John Polkinghorne, *Science and Providence: God's Interaction with the World* (West Conshohocken, PA: Templeton University Press, 2005), chapter 5.
14. Moltmann, *GC*, 86–89.

refusal to be the "'the all-determining reality' of what he has created" suggests that "he has conferred on creation its own scope for freedom and generation."[15] This space for freedom and generation is the reason that the creation has "fallen victim to annihilation."[16] The creation "has isolated itself from the foundation of its existence and the wellspring of its life, and has fallen victim to universal death."[17] Moltmann refers to this cosmic isolation as "the 'sin' of the whole creation."[18]

There are two important facets of Moltmann's thought here. First, the creation engages in "sin" prior to human existence. Second, sin and death entail *isolation*. This second point is common in Moltmann's thought. He states, "Death is the power of separation, both in time as the stream of transience, materially as the disintegration of the person's living Gestalt or configuration, and socially as isolation and loneliness."[19] Again, "Life is communication in communion. And, conversely, isolation and lack of relationship means death for all living things, and dissolution even for elementary particles."[20] As this quote suggests, for Moltmann the opposite of isolation is communion. Thus, he writes, "If the misery of creation lies in sin as separation from God, then salvation consists in the gracious acceptance of the creature into communion with God."[21] Bouma-Prediger thus correctly identifies that Moltmann's "understanding of salvation implies that sin is essentially the state of being closed off or closed down or isolated."[22]

15. Jürgen Moltmann, *Sun of Righteousness, Arise! God's Future for Humanity and the Earth* (hereafter *SRA*), trans. Margaret Kohl (Minneapolis, MN: Fortress Press, 2010), 205.
16. Ibid.
17. Moltmann, *WJC*, 283.
18. Ibid.
19. Jürgen Moltmann, *The Coming of God: Christian Eschatology* (hereafter *CoG*), trans. Margaret Kohl (Minneapolis, MN: Fortress Press, 1996), 71.
20. Moltmann, *GC*, 3.
21. Jürgen Moltmann, *History and the Triune God: Contributions to Trinitarian Theology*, trans. John Bowden (New York: Crossroad, 1992), 87.

Collectively, these points suggest that the original positive distance entailed by God's withdrawal in the act of creation—which was for creation's alterity that safeguards its status as a viable partner for communion—*becomes* something altogether different (and negative) in the unfolding of creation's integrity. The original distance becomes *isolation*. Moltmann maintains that God, most specifically in the incarnation, traverses this negative distance in order to restore the hope for communion with creation.

> *Remoteness* from God and *spatial distance* from God result from the withdrawal of God's omnipresence and 'the veiling of his face.' They are part of the *grace of creation*, because they are *conditions for the liberty of created beings*. It is only for sinners, who cut themselves off from God, that they *become the expression of God's anger towards them in their God-forsakenness*. If God himself enters into his creation through his Christ and his Spirit, in order to live in it and to arrive at his rest, *he will then overcome not only the God-forsakenness of sinners, but also the distance and space of his creation itself, which resulted in isolation from God, and sin.*[23]

In an attempt to develop and clarify Moltmann's thought in a manner that maintains Linzey's position that God not be the author of suffering and death, I here offer a revision to the traditional schema of the history of the divine-world rapport (see table 14.1) by suggesting the creation is a willful act (on the part of God) of consecration—which requires distance. The fall is the transformation of consecratory distance into isolation that results not directly from any will, but rather via chance in creation's development within its own integrity. Redemption is the concrete actuality of God's ultimate desire for the cosmos in the incarnation, which restores the space of consecratory distance and enables new movement within that space.

22. Steven Bouma-Prediger, *The Greening of Theology: The ecological Models of Rosemary Radford Ruether, Joseph Sittler, and Jürgen Moltmann* (Atlanta: Scholars, 1995), 241.
23. Moltmann, *CoG*, 306; italics mine.

Finally, consummation is the final communion—the perichoretic union between God and the creation, which was the original purpose of consecratory distance.

Table 14.1 Revised Schema of Divine-World Rapport				
Traditional Schema	Creation	Fall	Redemption	Consummation
Revised Schema	Consecration	Isolation	Restoration	Communion

As I am here dealing with the question of protology and the fall, I will focus on the first two terms, consecration and isolation. To consecrate (from the Hebrew *qdš* and Greek *hagios*) something is to sanctify it, to make it holy, to set it apart. Thus, *there can be no consecration without separation—without distance*. But this separation, evident most clearly in the sacrificial system in the Hebrew Scriptures, *is for the purpose of communion*. The broad connotation of *qdš* is "the process by which an entity is *brought into relationship* with or attains the likeness of the holy."[24] That is, the telos of consecratory distance is relationship or communion.

Isolation also denotes separation and distance. It derives out of the Latin *insulatus*, denoting making something into an island. Unlike consecration, which entails a separation for the sake of communion, isolation suggests the notion of alienation.[25] Whereas the distance of consecration has a relational telos (i.e., communion), isolation is separation for the sake of separation. It is distance aimed at separation, not communion.

Consecratory distance is an essential prerequisite for communion between God and that which is other-than-God. Without this

24. K. E. Bower, "Sanctification, sanctify" in *New Bible Dictionary*, third edition, ed. D. R. W. Wood (Downers Grove, IL: Intervarsity, 1996), 1058. Emphasis added.
25. Along with isolation, Moltmann refers to creation (or more properly "nature") as alienated from God. See Moltmann, *WJC*, 253,

distance, "creation would be itself divine."[26] Sans consecratory separation, union with the divine could only be possible as pantheism, which is not communion—the participation of *others* in union. Thus, the participation of creation as that which is other-than-God in God's Trinitarian life requires distance between God and the world. God must be willing to suffer the created order its own space and integrity if God desires communion with it.

Yet, as Moltmann notes, such a suffering entails risk. Empowering creation to be itself by divine withdrawal opens the possibility that creation's being and becoming itself will not cohere to the divine desire for creation. This point is significant because, contra Deism and Descartes, the world is not a machine of static laws, but rather a dynamic and at times volatile system of interrelated components.[27] There is no watchmaker, only one who gives birth to a dynamic creation—a mother who loses at least some control of her work when she creates it and yet remains ever present with it. It is the consecratory distance that is necessary for communion that opens creation to the risk of isolation, which is creation's embrace, anthropomorphically speaking, of its distance from God.

The world does "fall" into isolation. Though, a better image than falling would be that of wandering. Instead of moving along the path to communion within the space that God has allotted to it, creation, in its integrity, strays from that path and wanders aimlessly in its open space. The creation does not move toward communion in dynamic growth but rather meanders in a form of stasis. Moltmann captures this image of wandering in isolation with his claim that the "'time of nature' is a kind of winter of creation" in which "nature is frozen,

---

26. Moltmann, *CoG*, 301.

27. See John Polkinghorne, "The Demise of Democritus," in *The Trinity and an Entangled World: Relationality in Physical Science and Theology* (Grand Rapids, MI: William B. Eerdmans Publishing Company, 2010), 15–31; Arthur Peacocke, *Theology for a Scientific Age: Being and Becoming—Natural, Divine and Human* (Minneapolis, MN: Fortress Press, 1993), 41–70.

petrified creation. It is God's creation, *alienated* from the source of its life."[28] In this state, the consecratory distance of creation becomes isolation as the divine hope for cosmic harmony and communion gives way to the tragic inevitability of nature's laws. Thus, in isolation, the developmental space and time allotted to creation by divine withdrawal becomes transience and death. Says Moltmann: "Separation from God, the wellspring of life, leads us through our isolation to experience temporality as transience, and to see death as its universal end."[29]

The movement from consecratory distance to isolation does not entail that suffering, predation, and death were absent in some historical Eden from which humans strayed. In conjunction with Moltmann, I do not see how one can affirm such a natural history in the face of science.[30] For this reason, I accept that suffering, predation, and death can be referred to as "natural." The symbol of Eden expresses God's desire for the cosmos, not its concrete history. That is, the myth of Eden is not history but rather a poetic eschatological yearning.

Even so, it is not necessary to claim that the naturalness of evolutionary mechanisms means God has ordained them. Moltmann's de-emphasis on the divine will—at least as I am developing it—suggests that God need not be the author of the mechanisms of evolution. Contra Denis Edwards, we need not accept that "biological death has to be attributed to the Creator."[31] God has ordained a dynamic creation and set it free for the sake of communion. In its consecratory separation from God—a condition necessary for its telos of communion with God—the dynamism of the cosmos became a wandering in isolation, a system of suffering,

28. Moltmann, *WJC*, 253; italics mine.
29. Moltmann, *CoG*, 292.
30. Ibid., 83.
31. Edwards, "Every Sparrow that Falls," 107.

predation, and death in which creatures survive at the expense of others.

Dimensions of this view are evident in "free process" defenses to evolutionary theodicy.[32] According to such defenses, "God accords cosmic processes the same value and reverence that God accords to human choices."[33] This view is also emblematic of Celia Deane-Drummond's appropriation of Sergii Bulgakov's notion of "shadow sophia." Deane-Drummond maintains that the mythical symbol of the fall "has repercussions both prior to and after the appearance of humanity." The "prior to" entails that "the tendencies towards immorality were present long before [human existence], and seem to be constitutive of the possibility of creaturely sophia." However, shadow sophia "is not inherent in divine Sophia and exists as a latent possibility in creaturely sophia." Thus, the *risk* of shadow is present in the expression of divine wisdom in the created order. This risk is necessary for the "teleological goal in creaturely Sophia," which is the hope for "participation in divine Sophia."[34]

In this state, even the positive dimensions of the cosmos, including its interconnectedness and symbiosis take the form of the death and suffering of individuals. Says Moltmann: "The very powers which have been perverted into what is destructive will themselves be redeemed; for their power is created power, and is as such good. It is only their power of destruction that was evil."[35] In an interconnected cosmos wrought with relational evil, even beauty needs redeemed.

Perhaps the most significant contribution this revised schema contributes—aside from the arching theme of distance upon which it draws—is that cosmic "fallenness" is not the result of any intentional

---

32. See Polkinghorne, *Science and Providence*, chapter 5.

33. Gloria Schaab, *Trinity in Relation: Creation, Incarnation, and Grace in an Evolving Cosmos* (Winona, MN: Anselm Academic, 2012), 201.

34. Celia Deane-Drummond, *Eco-Theology* (Winona, MN: Anselm Academic, 2008), 125–28.

35. Moltmann, *GC*, 169.

movement of will, whether angelic, human, or even divine. Regarding human will, I concur with Holmes Rolston III: "Human sin did not throw nature out of joint; nature does not need to be redeemed on that account."[36] Contra Rolston, however, I maintain that creation has been distorted on account of its integrity—of randomness and chance.[37] As Polkinghorne states, "God no more expressly wills the growth of cancer than he expressly wills the act of a murder, but he allows both to happen. *He is not the puppetmaster of either men or matter.*"[38] Polkinghorne is here similar to Moltmann's claim that God is not the "'the all-determining reality' of what he has created."[39]

Contra Polkinghorne, however, it is not necessary to claim that God ordains evolution for some greater good.[40] Likewise, it is unnecessary to argue, as Sideris does, that "natural processes themselves cannot be seen as wrong, evil, or in need of redemption in an eschatological sense."[41] Finally, it is unnecessary to appeal to the principle of double effect, as does Willis Jenkins, to maintain that God ordains the goodness of creatures (e.g., the ferocity of a lion), which in turn leads (inevitably, one presumes) to an indirect "evil" effect (e.g., that the lion devours the gazelle).[42]

These views are unnecessary because there is another view that does not require the divine will to explain the origin of predation and suffering—the view that God sets the world free *prior to the formation of its laws.* God creates the world, surrenders control over it, and holds

36. Holmes Rolston III, "Does Nature Need to be Redeemed?" *Zygon* 29 (1994): 207.
37. Humans have, of course, added to this distortion through anthropogenic evils.
38. Polkinghorne, *Science and Providence*, 78.
39. Moltmann, *SRA*, 205.
40. See John Polkinghorne, *Questions of Truth: Fifty One Responses to Questions* (Louisville, KY: Westminster John Knox, 2009), 16–17; also, Southgate, *The Groaning of Creation*, 15–17.
41. Lisa Sideris, *Environmental Ethics, Ecological Theology, and Natural Selection* (New York: Columbia University Press, 2003), 200.
42. Willis Jenkins, *Ecologies of Grace: Environmental Ethics and Christian Theology* (New York: Oxford University Press, 2008), 137, 144–45.

to hope.[43] Yet, as already noted, this surrendering is not a form of deism, because God remains present in the world, suffering its fate and in some sense guiding and curbing its development through the Spirit.

What God releases is the chaotic potential in the singularity preceding the Big Bang. It is here already in the very forming of the laws of thermodynamics that consecratory distance fails to develop toward communion and instead becomes a wandering in isolation. This straying is not the direct result of God's ordination. Nor is it the result of a human or angelic sin. It is simply the negative potentiality—the "shadow sophia"—of creation's self-making alterity actualizing through randomness and chance. I do not know whether or not Moltmann would accept my claim about the Big Bang constituting a cosmic fall; but it seems to me that if there is going to be a "sin" of the cosmos (as Moltmann claims) in which it strays from the path toward communion with the divine, the structuring of the laws that *require* violence and destruction is a logical place to look.

This cosmic wandering is consecratory distance becoming isolation. In this random becoming, the shadowy side of evolution, the naturalness of suffering, predation, and death becomes necessary—but only to creation in isolation. The cosmos is adapted to its isolation such that, in the words of Denis Edwards, "suffering, death and extinction are now seen as intrinsic to the process of evolutionary emergence. They are not simply unfortunate side-effects."[44] Evolutionary emergence itself is not an "unfortunate side-effect" (that is, a *necessary* corollary of some other condition) but rather the actualized outcome of the divine risk taken in the act of creation itself. Here Edwards and I part ways, as he maintains that

---

43. On this point I bear a similarity to John Haught's kenotic notion of God and the evolutionary process. See John F. Haught, *God after Darwin: A Theology of Evolution*, second edition (Washington, DC: Georgetown University Press, 2008), 49–60.
44. Edwards, "Every Sparrow that Falls," 106.

God must be the author of biological death, which serves the purpose of rendering possible the great diversity of flourishing life, including humanity.[45]

The mechanisms of evolution—indicative as they are of creation's wandering in isolation—must be overcome in a restoration of consecratory distance. Whereas the import of will is relieved with reference to the origin of cosmic isolation, it returns in full strength with reference to eschatological redemption. Restoration necessitates the *divine* will because it overwhelms the laws of nature to which humans themselves are subject.

This refigured schema of creation-fall-redemption-consecration provides an opening to affirm both the naturalness of evolution alongside the "kernel of truth" underlying the doctrine of the fall; namely, that "parasitism and predation are unlovely, cruel, evil aspects of the world ultimately incapable of being reconciled with a God of love."[46] Nature, including the mechanisms of evolution, is not the result of human sin or some evil will. Neither is it, in its current state, the direct result of its Creator's will. Furthermore, it does not reflect God's ultimate desire. Nature is not evil; it is just not yet home. It is not fallen in the sense of some ontological deficiency (i.e., essentially "ungood"); it is *relationally distorted*, isolated from its Creator and itself. In its integrity it has strayed from the path toward communion. Creation is like a family dog that, through no fault of its own, strays into the wilderness and becomes wild. The good creation is wandering in isolation and experiencing the full effects of that disposition. Creation's disposition requires a restoration of the *telos* of its integrity—communion with the divine. Christ achieves this restoration.

---

45. Ibid., 107.
46. Andrew Linzey, *Animal Gospel* (hereafter *AG*), (Louisville, KY: Westminster John Knox, 1998), 28.

Christology:
Victory over Isolation, the Restoration of Consecration

Hans Urs von Balthasar describes the Son incarnate as the door that opens the way for creation to participate in the divine.[47] Kallistos Ware echoes a similar notion: "God's incarnation opens the way to man's deification."[48] This vision of christology coheres with cosmocentric transfiguration. The incarnation is the concrete realization of eschatological hope. It is already that communion—between God and that which is other than God—which constitutes the divine desire for the entire cosmos. Thus, the incarnation at once reveals and, in a concrete but incomplete manner, accomplishes the telos of creation. In Christ, the destiny of the world is manifested in history—the door is open.

The doctrine of the incarnation is central here because, as both Moltmann and Linzey maintain, the Son does not simply become *man* or even *human*, but rather becomes *flesh*. Clough concurs, arguing that, in order to remedy the anthropocentric understanding of the incarnation, "we will need to think bigger and affirm that 'God became an animal'." However, he goes even further: "Or, most comprehensively, 'God became a creature'."[49] Clough argues that Barth's christology, where it betrays anthropocentrism, is problematic in that it excludes other flesh from Christ's work.[50] However, Clough also recognizes a problem with the term "flesh": "The logic of the argument drawing on 'flesh' vocabulary would suggest that animals, human and non-human, should be understood as recipients of election in Christ, but other creatures such as plants

---

47. See Hans Urs von Balthasar, *The Last Act*, Theo-Drama, volume 5, trans. Graham Harrison (San Francisco, CA: Ignatius, 1988), 374–75, 442.
48. Kallistos Ware, *The Orthodox Way* (Crestwood, NY: St. Vladimir's Seminary Press, 1995), 74.
49. Clough, *On Animals*, 84.
50. Ibid., 89–100.

and rocks should be excluded." While acknowledging the important distinctions between animals and non-animals, Clough concludes, "To establish a boundary here. . . seems very likely to repeat Barth's mistake in failing to appreciate the breadth of God's purposes in relation to creation."[51] For Clough, God elects (to use Barth's nomenclature) in the cosmic Christ that which God creates.[52] In my view, the claim that God became man, human, flesh, creature, all culminates in the significant point that God *became* and in becoming opened the door for all becoming to participate in the unique becoming of the Trinity. That is, when the Son *became*, all becoming was drawn into the divine life irrevocably.

Given this emphasis on the enfleshment of the Son, what then is the significance of the cross? It is first essential to say that the cross has no significance apart from the incarnation (or apart from the resurrection). In his passion and death, Christ draws into the divine all cosmic transience. In Deane-Drummond's words, "the weight of shadow sophia is born by Christ on the cross."[53] In my own words, Christ descends into the depths of creation's wandering and becomes lost—the Isolated One. In his resurrection, he leads that which is lost to its telos and therein transfigures its transience, the manifestation of its isolation.

Linzey and Moltmann agree on this point in their own way. Moltmann goes further, reading Christ's cry of dereliction in conjunction with his descent into hell.[54] On account of Christ's forsakenness, all God-forsaken places are filled with divine presence in a new manner. Even hell is now a place of hope.[55] Thus Christ

---

51. Ibid., 96.
52. Ibid., 97–98.
53. Deane-Drummond, *Eco-Theology*, 127.
54. See Jürgen Moltmann, "The Logic of Hell," in *God Will Be All in All: The Eschatology of Jürgen Moltmann*, ed. Richard Bauckham (Minneapolis, MN: Fortress Press, 2001), 46–47.
55. Jürgen Moltmann, *Jesus Christ for Today's World*, trans. Margaret Kohl (Minneapolis: Fortress Press, 1994), 66.

draws not only transience, but also forsakenness, into the Trinitarian love and thereby opens the way to communion. When the isolated creation cannot find its way to God, God finds a way to the isolated creation.

Using the language of my own framework, the cross evinces that Christ not only enters into the wandering isolation of creation but also experiences its full sting—including both the dark mechanisms of evolution and the reality of divine forsakenness that persist when consecratory distance becomes isolation. Christ becomes the divine in isolation from the divine. Yet, as the concrete communion of eschatological hope in his very person, he opens the possibility of restoring the state of isolation to consecration. That which is restored remains separate from God, but no longer in isolation. There is distance, but no longer forsakenness. The way home is made known—the trail is blazed out of the wilderness. In the words of Southgate, "the Cross and Resurrection inaugurate a great era of redemption of the nonhuman creation leading to the eschaton." In this sense the Christ-event "begins the final phase of the creation in which the evolutionary process itself will be transformed and healed."[56]

As the crucified human, Christ draws the extent of creaturely being and its isolation into the life of the Trinity. As the crucified God, he draws the presence of the divine into creation's isolation. The Son has become the world, wandering into the darkest corners of isolation, including death and hell. In doing so, he restores consecratory distance. In this sense, Christ is the way, the path to communion.[57] In short, *Christus victor* over isolation.

---

56. Southgate, *The Groaning of Creation*, 76.
57. Ware makes a similar claim. See Ware, *The Orthodox Way*, 70.

Pneumatology:
The Sanctifying Breath of Eternal Life

Both Moltmann and Linzey affirm the Spirit as the vitalizing principle of (at least sentient) life. Moltmann's vision of the Spirit as the source of life, while problematic, is nonetheless a beautiful manner of safeguarding divine immanence, including the providential presence of God. I have particular interest in the sanctifying role of the Spirit—more specifically, the role of the *Holy* Spirit in opening creation up to the triune community of love by permitting consecratory distance.

The Spirit's sanctifying presence is significant in the original act of creation. The Spirit rests in the created order, separating it *from the divine, for the divine*. There is thus a dual movement of God away from creation in divine withdrawal and toward creation in the presence of the Spirit. Moltmann captures this image by connecting God's Shekinah with the Spirit.[58] In the Spirit, God is within the creation while remaining distant from it.[59] The Trinity experiences a sort of internal separation in order that God may be the immanent source of life for a creation that is at once genuinely other-than-God. It is the Spirit that permits consecratory distance without isolation—life that is other-than-God but not God-forsaken.

What then becomes of the role of the Spirit in cosmic isolation? The Spirit safeguards against annihilation. It is the Spirit's unique presence in the world that ensures creation can never be fully isolated from God. The Spirit remains present in the midst of the creation's wandering. The Spirit suffers in the suffering of the cosmos, sighing and groaning within the mechanisms of evolution. "The divine Spirit itself, which fills the whole world, is seized by a driving force and

58. Moltmann, *GC*, 97.
59. Ibid., 9.

torment, for it is beset by the birth pangs of the new creation."[60] In a manner of speaking, the Spirit is lost with the world. Or, as Moltmann notes concerning Israel's exile, the divine Shekinah was in exile *from God with the people*.[61] The Spirit experiences isolation from God with the world, and indeed groans for eschatological communion in that isolation.[62]

In the Christ event, the cosmos is reopened to its consecratory state in the midst of isolation. On the one hand, the Spirit-filled saints elicit a glimpse, even in the wilderness, of the future communion for which all creation longs.[63] In Moltmann's words, "The experience of the Spirit does not separate those affected by it from the 'the rest of the world.' On the contrary, their experience brings them into open solidarity with it. For what they experience is. . . the beginning of the world's future."[64] Similarly, Linzey writes that the Spirit enables humans to become "active participants" in creation's redemption.[65] On the other hand, the world remains in isolation, trapped within the cycle of suffering and death.

So the Spirit now fulfills a *triple role*. First, the Spirit remains the immanent presence of the divine, suffering cruel atrocities alongside an isolated cosmos to which restoration has been opened but not completed. Second, the Spirit consecrates those who step into the way opened in Christ. Third, the Spirit works through those who are consecrated to facilitate sacramental moments of eschatological communion in the midst of cosmic isolation. In this manner the Spirit

---

60. Moltmann, *SRA*, 206. See also Andrew Linzey, *Creatures of the Same God: Explorations in Animal Theology* (hereafter *CSG*), (New York: Lantern Books, 2009), 14.

61. Jürgen Moltmann, *The Spirit of Life: A Universal Affirmation* (hereafter *SL*), trans. Margaret Kohl (Minneapolis, MN: Fortress Press, 1992), 48–49.

62. See Moltmann, *TKG*, 60.

63. See Tim Vivian, "The Peaceable Kingdom: Animals as Parables in the *Virtues of Saint Macarius*," *Anglican Theological Review* 85, 3 (Summer 2003): 477–91.

64. Moltmann, *TKG*, 124.

65. Linzey, *AT*, 56.

facilitates the restoration of consecration in the midst of isolation. If Christ is the way, the restoration of the consecratory path toward communion, then the Spirit is the wind blowing down that path, sweeping up weary travelers and directing them home. What Christ gathers, the Spirit leads toward transfiguration.[66]

Eschatology:
Cosmic Restoration and Communion

All that God creates, God consecrates for communion through separation. The world is made other-*than*-God so that it may become the other-*with*-God. When the risk entailed by the consecratory alterity of the cosmos actualizes as isolation, restoration of that consecration becomes a necessity. While both Christ and the Spirit open the space for restoration, this space is not yet nor can it be complete restoration. The cosmos is adapted to its isolation such that natural existence is predicated upon the very mechanisms facilitated by isolation. While there is some level of ambiguity in their thought, both Moltmann and Linzey recognize this reality.[67]

It is this very world, adapted to its isolation, with which God seeks communion. The penultimate consecration of the world, which is required for communion, remains irrevocably an eschatological act. In Moltmann's terms, the penultimate restoration of consecratory separation is judgment, in which all will be set right.[68] Death will be destroyed and suffering will end. This final and definitive consecration makes possible the ultimate communion that God

---

66. Edwards, "Every Sparrow that Falls," 111.
67. Moltmann, *CoG*, 78; Linzey, *CRA*, 61.
68. Moltmann, *CoG*, 235–237; "The Logic of Hell," 43–47. On this point see also Hans Urs von Balthasar, "Some Point of Eschatology" in *The Word Made Flesh: Explorations in Theology I* (San Francisco: Ignatius, 1989), 263–64.

desires. It is in this movement that, per Moltmann's famous appropriation of Paul, God will be all in all.

Eschatology, in terms of the "last things," thus entails the completion of Christ's work—a point consistent with Karl Barth's christology.[69] It is the penultimate act of consecration and the ultimate communion between God the cosmos. This communion must either include all that God has created or, if not, must mean that God's original desire for creation will be eternally unfulfilled. As von Balthasar intimates, an eternal hell for humans entails eternal tragedy for God who desires them in love.[70] The same must be said about all creatures, every sentient and non-sentient being and every inanimate part of the cosmos. Every creature with a narrative, regardless of their awareness of that narrative, must be swept up into the divine narrative if God is the Creator who seeks communion with the creation. Keith Ward is thus correct, in my view, when he states, "Immortality for animals as well as humans is a necessary condition of any acceptable theodicy."[71] The redemption of creation requires just that—the redemption of *all* creation, including the resurrection and transfiguration of every speck of the cosmos.

However, as Moltmann and Linzey both acknowledge, the eschaton is not simply the end of history. It is, in Moltmann's words, "God's coming and his arrival."[72] Eschatology cannot remain merely a doctrine of "last things" if the communion that God seeks and for which creation longs has been concretely realized in the incarnation. Nor can it remain so if the way of consecration has been restored in Christ and the Spirit set forth in a new manner in this restoration.

69. See Karl Barth, *Church Dogmatics* IV/3/2, trans. G. W. Bromiley (Edinburgh: T&T Clark, 1962), 910–912.

70. See Nicholas J. Healy, *The Eschatology of Hans Urs von Balthasar: Being as Communion* (New York: Oxford University Press, 2005), 215.

71. Keith Ward, *Rational Theology and the Creativity of God* (New York: Pilgrim, 1982), 202.

72. Moltmann, *CoG*, 22.

New possibilities exist in history. Even so, because the cosmos remains adapted to isolation, trapped in the mechanisms of evolution, history itself must be transfigured. No amount of human striving can facilitate ultimate consecration or communion. However, those who are made holy by the Spirit can consecrate the isolated creation and witness to the future communion of all things.

To sum up these ideas: consecration is distance without forsakenness. Isolation is distance as alienation. Restoration is alienation with the possibility of consecration. Communion is alterity without distance.

The final communion between God and the creation will make the creation new—transfigured. This transfiguration does not intimate a numerically different creation.[73] However, it does denote discontinuity between the present state of creation and its state in eschatological communion. Deane-Drummond notes, "The closest analogy here is with the resurrection event itself, so that there are lines of continuity and discontinuity."[74] Because the resurrection is present now in the power of the Spirit, so also moments of proleptic witness are possible—most especially in the work of those who are already, if only incompletely, being made new.

Time and Eternity:
The Eternal Significance of Every Moment

My engagement with the notion of isolation has centered mainly on its spatial (i.e., physically relational) dimension. However, isolation bears a temporal dimension. I here draw on Moltmann to make this point.

73. Ibid., 84–85.
74. Deane-Drummond, *Eco-Theology*, 167. See also Moltmann, *CoG*, 84–85.

As noted in chapter 8, for Moltmann, God's eternity is not without time. It is rather all time gathered together diachronically into a cyclical and enduring present.[75] He also maintains that the participation of the cosmos in God's eternity entails the gathering together of all the times of creation into an eternal time.[76] This new time—the time of *creatio nova*—is one of possibility without transience. Time that is realized in the present does not then become the past but remains forever in perichoretic union with all other times in the present. The eschatological present is a sponge that loses nothing it imbibes. It is "change without transience, time without past, and life without death."[77]

The unique time of nature, however, is the "winter of creation" in which all events—including death—after occurring, slip into an irretrievable past.[78] Each time is cut off from others. Humans remember the past but cannot reclaim it. They experience the present but cannot sustain it. They anticipate the future, but it is ultimately beyond their grasp.[79]

Moltmann looks forward to "the future of time itself," which is God's future transfiguring time and drawing it into perichoretic union with itself (diachronically) in eternity.[80] His vision of time and eternity bears two significant facets. First, cosmic time (as well as cosmic space) must be understood in its totality, which includes its future redemption. Moltmann refers to this broader understanding in which one "sees creation together with its future" as "messianic."[81]

---

75. Moltmann, *SRA*, 62–63.
76. Moltmann, *CoG*, 71.
77. See Moltmann, *GC*, 213.
78. Moltmann, *WJC*, 253; *CoG*, 286.
79. See Moltmann, *CoG*, 287.
80. Moltmann, "The Liberation of the Future and Its Anticipations in History," in *God Will Be All in All: The Eschatology of Jürgen Moltmann*, ed. Richard Bauckham (Minneapolis, MN: Fortress Press, 2001), 265.
81. Moltmann, *GC*, 5.

Second, each moment of time, while fleeting in the "winter" of creation's transience, will nonetheless be resurrected and participate in God's eternity.[82]

Regarding the first point, the theological separation of creation and redemption constitutes a temporal isolation. If we unequivocally affirm the unfolding integrity of the cosmos (what Moltmann refers to as "nature"), we isolate creation from redemption. If we completely reject this integrity and flee from it, we isolate redemption from creation. In a similar manner, if we unequivocally embrace and celebrate death, we isolate it from resurrection. If we refuse to preserve the system that depends on evolution, we isolate resurrection from death. In these forms of isolation, the past, present, and future are isolated from one another. When this isolation is dismantled, the way is opened for both a preservation of the present (in light of its necessity) and a protest of it (in light of its eschatological future).

Regarding the second point, the isolation of the present from its future (and its past) translates into an isolation of the present self from totality. The self subsists in a narrative of divided moments. In this scenario, finitude becomes tragedy—the cage set against the possibility of wholeness. Likewise, death appears as the end of one's experience of the present, of one's potential for the future, and his or her inescapable relegation to a past that memory can recall only imperfectly. This temporal facet of isolation returns us to the spatial/relational dimension, for it intimates the isolation of the self from its own narrative.

The redemption of temporal isolation is well captured in Moltmann's notion that, at the eschaton, all times of creation will be gathered up diachronically into a perichoretic union.[83] It is thus time

---

82. See Moltmann, *CoG*, 75; Richard Bauckham in *The Theology of Jürgen Moltmann* (Edinburgh: T&T Clark, 1995), 210.

83. Moltmann, *CoG*, 295.

itself that is redeemed in its deliverance from temporal isolation.[84] The Trinity's enduring openness to the unique time of the cosmos ensures that this time will be delivered from its temporal isolation to a temporal communion in which time is no longer lost to the past. God's victory over the present slipping into the past is the temporal analogue of God's victory over life slipping into death.

Moltmann's view is significant for cosmocentric transfiguration because it suggests that God will overcome isolation on both the spatial and the temporal levels. Bauckham makes this point in addressing the extent of resurrection for Moltmann. He is worth quoting at length.

> All death in nature Moltmann regards not as natural, but as a tragic destiny, whose reversal at the end is anticipated in Christ's resurrection. At this point one may want to ask questions. Does death really have the same significance for every kind of creature? For elephants, who mourn their dead, it is a tragic destiny, as it is for us. But for this year's marigolds, which die in the annual cycle of death and new life that will produce next year's marigolds, is death tragic? Need we mourn the individual marigold as we certainly would the species, should it become extinct? The apparent implication of Moltmann's view that every individual creature that has ever lived—every marigold, every termite, every smallpox virus—will be resurrected in the new creation may seem bizarre, but this problem is alleviated by the novel concept of resurrection which Moltmann introduces in [*The Way of Jesus Christ*]. It is that the whole of *history* (the history of nature and human beings) will be redeemed from evil and death and transformed in the eschatological eternity in which all its times will be simultaneous. So not simply creatures in what they have become in their temporal history, but all creatures as they are diachronically in the process of their history and in all their temporal relationships with other creatures, will be resurrected and transfigured in eternity.[85]

---

84. Ibid., 287.
85. Bauckham, *The Theology of Jürgen Moltmann*, 210.

Moltmann's "novel concept of resurrection" is, in my own words, the overcoming of both spatial and temporal isolation in the perichoretic union of all creatures with themselves (diachronically) and with one another (relationally) within the divine. This vision of eschatological hope, predicated upon Moltmann's understanding of time and eternity, suggests not only that the life of every individual creature bears eternal importance, but also that *every moment of every individual creature's life is of eternal significance.*

Humans:
Priests of Restoration, Sacraments of Communion

Both Moltmann and Linzey draw on the Orthodox notion of humanity's cosmic priesthood.[86] As I have already noted, there is no single view about what this priesthood entails. For some Orthodox writers, it means offering creation back to God by utilizing it reverently to facilitate the divine-rapport. This anthropocentric image is obviously insufficient for cosmocentric transfiguration. The communion God desires extends beyond humans. Indeed, when humans use creation to achieve communion with other humans and God while at once denying communion *with creation*, they perpetuate isolation. For cosmocentric transfiguration, cosmic priesthood entails following the way of Christ in taking the presence of the divine into the depths of cosmic isolation. It is a matter of becoming, in a functional sense, the *imago Dei* in the world—becoming in creation the proleptic presence of its eschatological hope.

Humanity's cosmic priesthood thus does not fully relegate the world to its sacramental role for humanity—though it need not deny that the cosmos is sacramental. Humans do not take God where

---

86. See Moltmann, *GC*, 189–90; *WJC*, 307–12; Linzey, *AT*, 54–55; *AN*, 94–95.

God is not. It entails a sacramental reciprocity between humans and nonhumans. For humanity's part, humans are sacraments of eschatological communion. Humans are to become symbols of eschatological hope *for others—whether human or nonhuman*—by witnessing to the hope for cosmic peace within history. Such a view seems consummate with that of John Chryssavgis, who writes:

> If we reject the world of darkness and accept living in the light of Christ, then each person and each object becomes the embodiment of God in this world. The divine presence is revealed to every order and every particle of this world.[87]

When the nonhuman world encounters consecrated humans, it should sacramentally encounter peace, not terror. W. Sibley Towner asks:

> When the other creatures look upon *adam* as a royal or even god-like figure, what will they see? A tyrant, an exterminator, a satanic figure? Or will they experience the ruling hand of *adam* as something as tender and gentle as that of their Creator?[88]

Humanity's sin and ongoing participation in the mechanisms of evolution augments isolation of the cosmos. Humanity's role as priest is to be a sacrament of the eschatological peace. As such, humans "must let the Spirit, that is the Spirit of *all* suffering creatures, pray through us so that we may become a sign of the hope for which all creation longs."[89] Hence, Christian hope entails "resistance against the forces of death and unconditional love for life."[90] This resistance

---

87. John Chryssavgis, "The Earth as Sacrament: Insights from Orthodox Christian Theology and Spirituality," in *The Orthodox Handbook of Religion and Ecology*, ed. Roger S. Gottlieb (New York: Oxford University Press, 2006), 107.

88. W. Sibley Towner, "Clones of God: Genesis 1:26–28 and the Image of God in the Hebrew Bible," *Interpretation*, 59, (2005): 348.

89. Linzey, *AN*, 109.

90. Jürgen Moltmann, *Ethics of Hope*, trans. Margaret Kohl (Minneapolis, MN: Fortress Press, 2012), 55.

of death and love of life, whether it is directed toward ourselves, other humans, nonhuman sentients, ecosystems, or the land itself, is what I intimate by the notion of sacraments of eschalogical communion. When humans affirm the life of creatures and actively seek their well-being, those creatures experience the eschatological communion in the priesthood of humanity. Thus, I affirm with Paul that the redemption of humanity bears significant meaning for the nonhuman creation.[91] The consecration of humanity opens the possibility for proleptic experiences of communion.[92]

While this functional anthropocentrism bears theological and ethical significance, it also runs a danger that Clough highlights. Clough argues, rightly in my view, that nonhuman animals have both a rapport with God and a vocation in God's creation that is not predicated upon humanity. This position challenges any functional anthropocentrism that identifies humans as God's unique co-creators without whom creation would be irrevocably lost.[93] However, it is still possible to maintain, as Clough does, that humans "should seek to live in a way that reflects God's gracious purpose to all creatures, on the grounds that they are a species uniquely capable of taking a view as to what might lead to the flourishing of other creatures."[94]

Conclusion

I have offered the beginning stages of a systematic construction of cosmocentric transfiguration. The paradigm maintains that the triune God has created a world with which the Trinity desires to share its community; that this desire must overcome the wandering

---

91. See Rom. 8:18–21.
92. Moltmann, *Trinity and the Kingdom*, 124.
93. Clough, *On Animals*, 40–43.
94. Ibid., 166 (also 76).

isolation of the cosmos, including suffering, predation, and death, all of which result from the integrity God suffered the creation; that this overcoming is concretely accomplished in the incarnation of the Son, including Christ's passion, death, and resurrection and is further manifested by the burgeoning future in the presence of the Spirit; and that human beings are sacraments of the eschatological hope that the mechanisms of evolution will be overcome in communion.

15

Possible Critiques of Cosmocentric Transfiguration

In chapter 13, I compared and critically evaluated both Moltmann and Linzey. In the previous chapter, I experimentally delineated in brief a set of theological foundations for cosmocentric transfiguration. Here, I address common critiques of Moltmann and Linzey that also apply to my foundations. First, I consider the hermeneutics of cosmocentric transfiguration with regard to both scripture and tradition. Second, I examine the critique that an affirmation of fallenness and redemption denigrates science and the nonhuman creation. Third, I address the question of whether the peaceable kingdom constitutes the dissolution of certain species. Finally, I clarify the issue regarding the relationship between eschatology and history.

Cosmocentric Transfiguration as Unbiblical

In 2003, at the annual meeting of the National Association of Baptist Professors of Religion, a panel reviewed Linzey's book, *Animal Theology*, from the perspective of the Hebrews Scriptures, the New Testament, and theology in general. These reviews, along with a response offered by Linzey, appeared in *Review and Expositor* in 2005.[1]

Mark McEntire, while noting the blurry lines between eisegesis and exegesis, nonetheless concludes that "the major ideas of *Animal Theology* seem utterly foreign to the Old Testament."[2] He acknowledges that the same could be said for the abolition of slavery, but maintains that a hermeneutic against slavery is much more easily identifiable than one that justifies Linzey's agenda in *Animal Theology*.[3] David May offers positive words concerning Linzey's agenda, but pejoratively defines his use of Scripture as "a proof-text method" that does not account for "social and cultural context."[4] May ultimately claims that Linzey's work, if it is "to be recognized by biblical scholars . . . will need to find a voice that is more thorough in biblical exegesis and more biblically integrated."[5]

With reference to the present work, these reviews raise the question as to whether or not the central tenets of cosmocentric transfiguration are nothing more than agenda-based eisegesis. In

---

1. David M. May, "A Review of Andrew Linzey's *Animal Theology* from a New Testament Perspective," *Review and Expositor*, 102 (Winter 2005): 87–93; Mark McEntire, "A Review of Andrew Linzey's *Animal Theology* from an Old Testament Perspective," *Review and Expositor*, 102 (Winter 2005): 95–99; Sally Smith Holt, "A Review of Andrew Linzey's *Animal Theology* from a Theological Perspective," *Review and Expositor*, 102 (Winter 2005): 101–9; Andrew Linzey, "The Divine Worth of Other Creatures: A Response to Reviews of *Animal Theology*," in *Review and Expositor*, 102 (Winter 2005): 111–24.

2. McEntire, "A Review of Andrew Linzey's *Animal Theology* from an Old Testament Perspective," 99.

3. Ibid.

4. May, "A Review of Andrew Linzey's *Animal Theology* from New Testament Perspective," 88.

5. Ibid., 90.

conjunction with Linzey, I would not claim that the paradigm of cosmocentric transfiguration is *the* biblical view.[6] Like Linzey, I am unconvinced there is any such thing as *the* biblical view on most issues.[7] Scripture, as a collection of variegated genres written by many different authors over a period of hundreds of years and subsequently redacted, copied, and translated, presents a unique challenge of interpretation.

Even so, along with Linzey, and contra McEntire's report from the Hebrew Scriptures, I believe that there are passages that provide the possibility of developing an animal-friendly hermeneutic.[8] It is true that many biblical voices focus on human beings in relation to God.[9] However, there are also passages that echo a discontent with this focus.

Regarding cosmocentrism, animals share the sixth day of creation with humans (Gen. 1:24–31). In Gen. 2:18–19, animals are not created as resources for Adam, but rather companions *with Adam*. In Genesis 9, animals, as well as the earth itself, are included in the Noahic covenant. The psalmist claims that God saves humans and animals alike (Ps, 36:6). Jesus compares his love for his followers to a "good" shepherd who cares deeply for his sheep (John 10:1–16). Jesus does maintain that humans are worth more than sparrows—but not that sparrows have no worth (Matt. 10:29–31).

Regarding the transfiguration of the cosmos, Isaiah presents an Edenic vision of cosmic harmony (Isa. 11:1–9). Paul suggests that the entire groaning creation will participate in the glory of the liberated

---

6. See Linzey's response to critiques of his use of scripture in *Animal Theology*. Andrew Linzey, "The Divine Worth of Other Creatures: A Response to Reviews of *Animal Theology*," in *Review and Expositor*, 102 (Winter 2005): 112–13.

7. See Andrew Linzey, *Christianity and the Rights of Animals* (hereafter *CRA*), (New York: Crossroad, 1987), 141–42.

8. For two examples, see Ryan Patrick McLaughlin, *Christianity and the Status of Animals: The Dominant Tradition and Its Alternatives* (New York: Palgrave Macmillan, 2014), chapters 5–6.

9. Linzey does not deny this reality. Linzey, "The Divine Worth of Other Creatures," 114.

children of God (Rom. 8:18–22). The cosmic Christologies of Col. 1:15–20 and Eph. 4:4–10 portray a cosmic reconciliation.[10]

These passages exist *despite* the dominantly human-centered context in which they arose. Linzey notes this point well with reference to the vegetarian diet implied by Gen. 1:29–30:

> It is remarkable that people who were not pacifists, vegetarians or opponents of capital punishment, felt so keenly the incongruity between violence and their belief in a holy, loving Creator—so much so that they conceived that God must have created a world free of it.[11]

True, the above passages require further exegetical exploration to establish the extent of their validity regarding cosmocentric transfiguration. While such an effort would constitute a separate project,[12] for now I can say that they at least reveal that scripture is not unambiguously unfriendly toward the value of animals and their participation in redemption. Thus, the central tenets of cosmocentric transfiguration, while not *the* biblical view, nonetheless have biblical support. What cosmocentric transfiguration needs is a thorough critical retrieval of the strands of scripture that offer such support. Such an effort would bear similarities to hermeneutical keys employed by liberation and feminist theologians.[13]

10. See Celia Deane-Drummond, *Eco-Theology* (Winona, MN: Anselm Academic, 2008), 100–107.
11. Linzey, "The Divine Worth of Other Creatures," 114.
12. For projects that move in this direction, see Richard Bauckham, *Bible and Ecology: Rediscovering the Community of Creation* (Waco, TX: Baylor University Press, 2010); Norm Phelps, *The Dominion of Love: Animal Rights According to the Bible* (New York: Lantern Books, 2002).
13. See Leonardo Boff and Clodovis Boff, *Introducing Liberation Theology* (Maryknoll, NY: Orbis Book, 1987); Rosemary Radford Ruether, *Sexism and God-Talk: Toward A Feminist Theology* (Boston: Beacon Press, 1983), chapter 1 (especially 17–33).

Cosmocentric Transfiguration as a Rejection of Tradition

As far as I can tell, cosmocentric transfiguration as I am describing it in conjunction with Moltmann and Linzey is nowhere explicit in the early Christian tradition. This tradition is, in my reading, dominantly anthropocentric with regard to value and divided with reference to the extent of eschatological redemption. It is thus appropriate to anticipate the critique that cosmocentric transfiguration entails a rejection of tradition. Indeed, regarding the resurrection of nonhuman animals—one of the central tenets of cosmocentric transfiguration as I am delineating it—Moltmann acknowledges: "It is true that the patristic church's acknowledgement of 'the resurrection of the flesh' (or body) was *always* reduced to human beings alone."[14]

Moltmann's claim may be overstated. There are minority traditions from the beginning of Christian history that challenge anthropocentrism and suggest that the nonhuman world will participate in the eschaton.[15] Such voices provide an opportunity to engage in a critical retrieval of a largely patriarchal and anthropocentric tradition that is consummate with cosmocentric transfiguration. This retrieval is further solidified in the hagiographies of many saints.

The consistently theocentric framework of the Christian tradition has grounded an anthropocentric worldview. Irenaeus claims that "creation is suited to [the wants of] man; for man was not made for its sake, but creation for the sake of man."[16] Augustine assigns animals value inasmuch as they aid humanity's progress toward God.[17] I

---

14. Jürgen Moltmann, *The Coming of God: Christian Eschatology* (hereafter *CoG*), trans. Margaret Kohl (Minneapolis, MN: Fortress Press, 1996), 70; italics mine.
15. Such is the premise of my *Christianity and the Status of Animals*.
16. Irenaeus of Lyons, *Irenaeus: Against Heresies*, Ante-Nicene Fathers, volume 1, ed. A. Roberts and J. Donaldson (Grand Rapids, MI: Willliam B. Eerdmans, 1996), 5.29.1.
17. Augustine, *City of God*, Basic Writings of Saint Augustine, ed. W. J. Oats (New York: Random House, 1948), 1:20; Augustine, *Teaching Christianity* (I/11), ed. John E. Rotelle, trans. Edmund

have already discussed Aquinas at length on the issues of both anthropocentrism and conservationism. Here I will only note that the magisterial teachings of the Catholic Church maintain his theocentric anthropocentrism.[18]

The tension between conservation and transfiguration with regard to the cosmos is more ambiguous in the Christian tradition. Both Augustine and Aquinas reject the presence of animals in the eschaton.[19] Irenaeus, however, accepts their presence.[20] Indeed, as I showed in chapter 6, the Orthodox tradition traces its hope for the transfiguration of the cosmos through the Christian tradition. The presence of animals in the eschaton is evident even in Orthodox iconography.[21] This alternative tradition has been taken up by many contemporary theologians.[22] John Wesley, in a sermon based on Rom. 8:19–22, writes "The whole brute creation will then, undoubtedly, be restored, not only to the vigour, strength, and swiftness which they had at their creation, but to a far higher degree of each than they ever enjoyed."[23] C. S. Lewis accepts the possibility (and indeed likelihood) of animals at the eschaton.[24] Stanley

Hill (New York: New York City Press, 1996), I.4; Augustine, *Miscellany of Eighty-Three Questions*, The Works of Saint Augustine, Part I Volume 12, ed. Raymond Canning, trans. Boniface Ramsey (New York: New York City Press, 2008), XXX .

18. McLaughlin, *Christianity and the Status of Animals*, chapter 2.

19. On Augustine, see *Miscellany of Eighty-Three Questions*, XXX; *Augustine on Romans*, ed. P. F. Landers (Chico, CA: Scholars Press, 1982), 23.

20. See Irenaeus, *Against Heresies*, 5.33.4.

21. See Esther D. Reed, "Animals in Orthodox Iconography," *Creaturely Theology, Creaturely Theology: On God, Humans and Other Animals*, ed. Celia Deane-Drummond and David Clough (London: SCM Press, 2009), 61–77

22. See David Clough, *On Animals* (New York: Bloomsbury, 2014), 133–72. Also *Animals and Christianity: A Book of Readings*, ed. Andrew Linzey and Tom Regan (Eugene, OR: Wipf and Stock, 1990), Part 3.

23. John Wesley, "The General Deliverance," available online at http://wesley.nnu.edu/john-wesley. See also Thomas C. Oden, *John Wesley's Scriptural Christian: A Plain Exposition of His Teaching on Christian Doctrine* (Grand Rapids, MI: Zondervan Publishing House, 1994), 126–29; Clough, *On Animals*, 133–137.

24. Linzey, "C. S. Lewis's Theology of Animals," *Anglican Theological Review*, 80 (Winter 1998), 60–81.

Hauerwas and John Berkman also accept this possibility and derive ethical import from it.[25] In her thought experiment on the cosmos as the body of God, Sallie McFague writes,

> We live with the hope against hope that defeat and death are not the last word, but that even the least body in the universe, the most insignificant, most vulnerable, most outcast one will participate in the resurrection of the body.[26]

Hans Urs von Balthasar critiques Aquinas's rejection of the presence of animals at the eschaton:

> This cruel verdict contradicts the Old Testament sense of the solidarity between the living, subhuman cosmos and the world of men (Ps 8; Ps 104; Gen 1, and so on), the prophetic and Jewish ideas of divine salvation in images of peace among the animals (Is 11:6–9; 65:25).[27]

What remains more difficult with regard to the tradition is the hope for the resurrection of *all individual* animals *for their own sake*. Yet, even here a retrieval of the tradition from its anthropocentric tendencies in conjunction with an emphasis on cosmic eschatology opens the door for the possibility of such a claim. If God cares for all creatures for their own sakes and seeks to redeem the cosmos from the mechanisms of evolutionary development, the hope entailed in cosmocentric transfiguration is the logical outcome.

What about the ethical claims of cosmocentric transfiguration? Is it a slight of tradition to claim that eschatological hope should inform how we engage animals in history? I do not think so. Indeed, the kind of transfigurative ethics I am espousing is evident in the

25. Stanley Hauerwas and John Berkman, "A Trinitarian Theology of the 'Chief End' of 'All Flesh'" in *Good News for Animals? Christian Approaches to Animal Well-Being*, ed. Charles Pinches and Jay B. McDaniel (New York: Orbis Books, 1993), 62–74

26. Sallie McFague, *The Body of God: An Ecological Theology* (Fortress Press: Minneapolis, 1993), 201–202.

27. Hans Urs von Balthasar, *The Last Act*, *Theo-Drama*, Volume 5, trans. Graham Harrison (San Francisco: Ignatius Press, 1988), 420–21.

hagiographies of many saints.[28] Saint Isaac of Nineveh writes that Christ has returned the possibility of peace between humans and animals.[29] He further suggests that the merciful heart

> is not able to bear hearing or examining injury or any insignificant suffering of anything in creation. And therefore even in behalf of the irrational beings . . . at all times he offers prayers with tears that they may be guarded and strengthened.[30]

Isaac suggests that, in Christ, the "humble man" and the "merciful heart" are drawn to *see creation differently*.[31] This new vision is evinced by the countless narratives of saints experiencing miraculous harmony with animals.[32] Such narratives lead Tim Vivian to write:"Although monks lived in close proximity with spiders, snakes, scorpions, jackals, wolves, and lions, most of them appeared to have lived quite peaceably with their animal companions in the desert." With such peaceful practices, "the monks can guide us toward the possibility of a peaceable kingdom, one created by God in the Garden and reenvisioned by the prophets.[33]

Based on these various factors, my anticipated critique that cosmocentric transfiguration entails a rejection of the Christian tradition is unconvincing. It is without doubt a critical retrieval of the tradition. However, a retrieval of a tradition is not tantamount to its rejection.

28. For some considerations, see Clough, *On Animals*, 157–58.

29. *The Ascetical Homilies of St. Isaac the Syrian*, ed. Dana Miller (Boston: Holy Transfiguration Monastery, 1984), p. 383.

30. Isaac of Nineveh, *Mystic Treatises*, trans. A. J. Wensinck (Wiesbaden: 1969), LXXIV.

31. On the import of seeing, see Linzey, *Creatures of the Same God*, chapter 4.

32. For a good collection of narratives about saints and animals, see Jame Schaefer, *Theological Foundations for Environmental Ethics: Reconstructing Patristic & Medieval Concepts* (Washington, DC: Georgetown University Press, 2009), chapter 6.

33. Tim Vivian, "The Peaceable Kingdom: Animals as Parables in the *Virtues of Saint Macarius*", *Anglican Theological Review* 85, 3 (Summer 2003): 479.

Fallenness and Eschatology as a Rejection of Science
and Denigration of Nature

Lisa Sideris, following Holmes Rolston, argues that a rejection of the goodness of evolutionary mechanisms such as suffering, predation, and death entails a rejection of scientific evidence and a denigration of nature. She writes, "Rolston's rejection of redemptive, eschatological improvements to nature is one of the chief strengths of his position, both scientifically and theologically."[34] Similarly, she argues that eschatological "hopes for nature are misguided when they distort our understanding of what nature is; more important, they obscure the issue of how much and what sort of responsibility humans have toward nature."[35]

Sideris is extremely critical of Moltmann on this point: "The denial of the given order in Moltmann's argument in favor of a new creation (established by the spirit of God who dwells in creation) expresses his preference for a world devoid of evolutionary forces that produce struggle and strife."[36] Furthermore, Moltmann's eschatology reveals both his anthropocentrism and his "inadequate and incomplete understanding of natural processes such as evolution."[37] Thus, it seems that anything supernatural or eschatological is by default anthropocentric and scientifically incorrect because it does not embrace the mechanisms of evolution as fully good. Sideris continues, "Although the desire to heal environments whose health has been compromised by human actions points to a worthy imperative, natural processes themselves cannot be seen as wrong, evil, or in need of redemption in an eschatological sense."[38] Oddly,

---

34. Lisa Sideris, *Environmental Ethics, Ecological Theology, and Natural Selection* (New York: Columbia University Press, 2003), 189.
35. Ibid., 200.
36. Ibid., 213.
37. Ibid.
38. Ibid., 200.

while Sideris seems to decry Moltmann's negative view of the world, she also decries his overly positive view of it: "In positing a direct involvement for God in 'creation,' Moltmann tends to deemphasize evil and suffering, interpreting nature as predominantly harmonious."[39]

Similarly, Willis Jenkins maintains that Moltmann's theological schema is problematic in that it creates a "discontinuity between nature as it is and nature as God would have it." This discontinuity elicits three issues. First, what Moltmann wants to save is not nature as it is, but nature as it is intended to be. This disparity places a greater emphasis on special revelation to the detriment of general revelation. Second, emphasizing such a discontinuity "may unwittingly evince some restless distaste for our present environment." Third, Moltmann offers no hermeneutic of adjudicating appropriate action in nature based on the hope for God's coming and the new creation.[40] Ultimately, Jenkins suggests, "Even though Moltmann insists natural science and revealed theology do not compete, his practical response to earth relies much more upon theological experience than natural science."[41]

In line with these critiques, theologians and ethicists whom I classify under the paradigm of cosmocentric conservation often argue that the Christian emphasis on the need for the redemption of nature desacralizes or denigrates the cosmos.[42] To claim that nature needs to be redeemed is to criticize the very reality that enables life, including human life, to exist. These critiques concur that the notion of fallenness and the hope for eschatological transfiguration in terms

39. Ibid., 92. This claim seems quite erroneous, even within Sideris' own work.
40. See Willis Jenkins, *Ecologies of Grace: Environmental Ethics and Christian Theology* (New York: Oxford University Press, 2008), 73–74.
41. Ibid., 73.
42. See Thomas Berry, *The Dream of the Earth* (San Francisco: Sierra Club Books, 1990), 25.

of overturning the darker mechanisms of evolution amount to the denigration of nature.

In contradistinction to this critique, I have suggested that the "fallenness" of the cosmos is not located in the distortion of some ontological substance but rather a relational disposition—a wandering in isolation.[43] Yet, it is the *good* creation that wanders in isolation. There is no denigration of any single creature or species in nature—such as predators—for all creatures are bound in this isolation. What is *not good*—what is incomplete and still requires the grace that perfects—are the mechanisms of the system that gratuitously sacrifices its individual components. Predators, as individuals and species, are not evil. They are, like their prey, caught up in a system bound to laws structured in isolation from its Creator. Creation (including its consecratory distance) is good; however, its state of wandering in isolation and the dispositional effects of that wandering are not good. Based on these claims, I believe Sideris misses the mark when she contends that theologians, including Moltmann, are "often deeply ambivalent about science, both critiquing and embracing it as suits their purposes."[44] For many theologians, the question is not whether or not to embrace the *findings* of science, but rather whether or not to accept that the "is" that science reveals constitutes either a moral "ought" or the divine will for the world.[45]

And why should such a position entail the denigration of either science or nature? It seems to me that Sideris's claim to hold the high ground here constitutes a logical leap. In conjunction with Gustafson's critique of Moltmann, Sideris claims, "Moltmann's God . . . is expected to reorder creation in ways that better conform

43. Ware offers such a view of original sin in his work, Kallistos Ware, *The Orthodox Way*, revised edition (Crestwood, NY: St. Vladimir's Seminary Press, 1995), 62–63.
44. Sideris, *Environmental Ethics*, 92.
45. See Peter J. Bowler, *Evolution: The History of an Idea*, revised edition (Los Angeles: University of California Press, 1989), 223.

to human hopes."[46] Thus, Sideris maintains that anything contrary to the "is" of current nature constitutes a wishful-thinking "ought" of human sensibilities. Yet, it is unclear why her own thinking is not also a presupposition demanding God to conform to human sensibilities. After all, theologically it is unclear why either a value judgment about evolution's mechanisms or a hope for a supernatural transfiguration of nature in line with Christ's own supernatural resurrection from the dead constitutes an "inadequate or incomplete understanding of natural processes such as evolution."[47] Both Moltmann and Linzey affirm the reality of the mechanisms of evolution without lapsing into an unbridled affirmation of their goodness. I wonder if James Gustafson's caution that "those who argue from various observations about nature tend to think they have captured the essence of the Deity in their concepts" might apply to the certitude that Sideris evinces regarding the impropriety of theological concepts such as eschatology.[48]

At any rate, Sideris's critique about nature and wishful thinking seems inconsistent to me. She refuses to apply the same line of thinking to humans. Following Rolston, she states that there is a stark ethical distinction between culture and nature.[49] She thus contends, as does Rolston, that an ethical analogy between human communities and ecological communities does not hold because "environmental ethics cannot ensure the well-being of each individual member of the community, regardless of those beings' degree of sentience or mental sophistication."[50] Does this claim not hold true in human communities as well? What human community can guarantee the

46. Sideris, *Environmental Ethics*, 212.
47. Ibid., 213.
48. James Gustafson, *Ethics from a Theocentric Perspective* (Chicago: University of Chicago Press, 1981), 1:34.
49. See Sideris, *Environmental Ethics*, 252–61; Holmes Rolston III, *Environmental Ethics: Duties to and Values in the Natural World* (Philadelphia: Temple University Press, 1988), 181–82.
50. Sideris, *Environmental Ethics*, 179; Rolston, *Environmental Ethics*, 59–62.

well-being of all its members? In the best of human societies, people still die young and in horrible fashions. Indeed, nature reaches into the human community. There is no sharp divide between culture and nature. Even if the community has laws and welfare programs to protect individuals from other humans and economic strife, it cannot stop disease in all cases and for all of its members. It cannot guarantee safety for all individuals from pestilence, drought, earthquakes, and hurricanes.

Furthermore, it seems because such activity is "natural," there is no reason why, in Sideris's logic, humans should not simply accept this suffering and death for individuals. Why work toward curing cancer? Why eliminate smallpox and other viruses? Are not these occurrences examples of predation of the nonhuman upon the human? This question also exists on the level of law. Social order protects one individual from others by law and thus is different from nature. But is such an exhaustive ethics for individuals conducive to evolutionary development? After all, Sideris notes that "the struggle for existence is the most severe among members of the same species."[51]

To respond to this dilemma, Sideris aligns herself with Rolston in claiming that humans occupy a "post-evolutionary position" and are thus "no longer subject to the same selection pressures from nature that wild animals are."[52] This argument, in my view, makes very little sense. Are not humans still evolving? If they are not still pressured by natural selection, why do mutations like cancer continue to haunt the species? Why are humans still preyed upon by microorganisms? In reaction to this predation, could not another species arise still? At any rate, is not creating a special moral category for creatures that are "post-evolutionary" simply another criteria for the limits of an extensionist ethics—at least with regard to a form of that ethics?

51. Sideris, *Environmental Ethics*, 295, n. 13.
52. Ibid., 192. For an instance of Rolston's position, see *Environmental Ethics*, 335–41.

Furthermore, Sideris accepts Gustafson's claim that "the source and power and order of all nature is not always beneficent in its outcomes for the diversity of life and for the well-being of humans as part of that."[53] Yet, it is unclear how claiming concern for all individual humans based on their "post-evolutionary" status is in harmony with Gustafson's position. This problem is confounded when Sideris makes the accusation that "Moltmann's account of the stages of creation assumes that God necessarily shares his particular hopes for the casting out of all forces that create struggle and strife in human and nonhuman life."[54]

It seems to me that Sideris is wildly inconsistent here. First, Moltmann is as aware of his context and finitude as Gustafson. Second, Sideris seems to assume that God necessarily shares her particular vision that the forces of struggle and strife are completely good. To disagree with this position is, it seems, tantamount to denying theocentrism.[55] The only reason she considers her assumption better than Moltmann's (or rather *not an assumption at all*) is that it is based on empirical observation of nature. Moltmann's presuppositions are no doubt experimentally (that is, subjectively) grounded. However, his vision also finds affirmation in scripture (which Sideris acknowledges). Yet, Sideris maintains that this biblical ground is insufficient.[56] Inexplicitly, then, she approvingly notes Gustafson's claim that humans ought to be concerned about the rights and wellness of individual humans because these concerns are biblically grounded![57]

---

53. James Gustafson, *A Sense of the Divine: The Natural Environment from a Theocentric Perspective* (Cleveland, OH: The Pilgrim Press, 1996), 47; Sideris, *Environmental Ethics*, 203–4.
54. Sideris, *Environmental Ethics*, 214.
55. Ibid., 228.
56. See, for instance, ibid., 189–91.
57. Ibid., 214. See also 192.

Criticisms concerning the denigration of nature based on wishful thinking, if it does apply to cosmocentric transfiguration, apply elsewhere as well. Acknowledging the necessity of death for biological existence does not require the denial of resurrection and transfiguration. If it did, Jesus would still be in the grave. If hope for a cosmic resurrection and transfiguration entails the denigration of nature, then so does the resurrection of Jesus. For all the positive aspects of Sideris' work, she ultimately offers a false dilemma: reject science and nature or embrace suffering, predation, and death as good.

The Resurrection and Eternity
of Individual Animals as Nonsensical

Christopher Southgate says of his creative engagement with evolutionary theodicy: "When I have presented the thesis of this book in various places it is always the eschatological dimension of the argument, in particular the notion that there might be animals (and even dinosaurs) in some version of 'heaven,' that has attracted the most controversy."[58] This controversy would surely be augmented with Moltmann's claim that *all life* must be resurrected at the eschaton.[59] Such controversy is not without warrant. After all, what would a dragonfly do with eternity? Where should one draw the line for individual resurrection—at humans, mammals, vertebrates, arthropods, bacteria, protozoa? Robert Wennberg notes that the issue of drawing a line applies also to humans. What about infants,

---

58. Christopher Southgate, *The Groaning of Creation: God, Evolution, and the Problem of Evil* (Louisville, KY: Westminster John Knox Press, 2008), 78–79.
59. Indeed, Moltmann does receive critique on this point. See John Polkinghorne, *The God of Hope and the End of the World* (New Haven, CT: Yale University Press, 2002), 122–23. Bauckham, *The Theology of Jürgen Moltmann*, 211.

miscarriages, a "newly fertilized ova . . . that perishes", and the severely mentally handicapped?[60]

Such questions intimate the critique that most nonhuman creatures, as individuals, are not fit for eternal existence.[61] As John Polkinghorne writes,

> What are we to expect will be the destiny of non-human creatures? They must have their share in cosmic hope, but we scarcely need suppose that every dinosaur that ever lived, let alone all of the vast multitude of bacteria that have constituted so large a fraction of biomass throughout the history of terrestrial life, will have its own individual eschatological future.[62]

Southgate similarly concedes,

> Simple organisms may possess little distinctive individual experience and agency, and they may be represented in the eschaton as types rather than individuals. However, to assume that that is the situation of all creatures, including higher animals, runs the risk of not doing full justice either to the richness of individual animal experience, or to the theodicy problems that evolutionary creation poses.[63]

The issue is less complicated for advocates of anthropocentric transfiguration. If the inclusion of the nonhuman creation, including animals, in the eschaton is for the sake of humanity's relationship with God, it does not require the animal's awareness or appreciation of its inclusion. However, if cosmocentric transfiguration maintains that every individual animal will participate in the resurrection and eternal life for their own sakes, it faces the critique that such a claim is nonsensical.

---

60. Robert Wennberg, *God, Humans, and Animals: An Invitation to Enlarge Our Moral Universe* (Grand Rapids, MI: William B. Eerdmans Publishing Company, 2003), 323–24.
61. See ibid., 322.
62. Polkinghorne, *The God of Hope*, 122.
63. Southgate, *The Groaning of Creation*, 84.

But what exactly makes the claim nonsensical? First, regarding animals that are not self-aware and thus, though they may experience the stimulus of pain, do not suffer (but still die), what significance would a participation in eternity have for them? If a creature lacks self-awareness, how can it appreciate eternal life? David Clough speaks well to this question in addressing C. S. Lewis's dismissal of non-selves from eternity. He does so by challenging the notion that animal redemption is one of *mere* compensation. That is, the inclusion of a "non-self" is not simply a matter of setting right wrongs done to an "I." It is rather the inclusion of all which God creates in divine life in eternity. This argument dispels Lewis's claim that redemption means nothing to creatures that are not self aware. "If the basis for redemption is not one of compensation, Lewis's objection loses its force: if God has reason to redeem what God has reason to create, the experience of being a redeemed newt is beside the point."[64]

A second reason the claim appears nonsensical is the belief that, even though some sentient nonhuman animals are self-aware and experience both suffering and death, they do not have the necessary facilities to appreciate eternity. Would animals that are self-aware but do not seem to be able to appropriate and interpret universal concepts understand their presence in eternal life? What would eternity be like for such creatures? Linzey responds to such claims when he argues that Christians must accept the possibility that, because grace perfects nature rather than destroys it, all creatures will find their eschatological place in a manner consummate with their *transfigured* being. Humans also require transfiguration to be fit for eternal life. Why then not also animals? Says Linzey:

All that is vital is that Christians do not eclipse the possibilities for the

---

64. Clough, *On Animals*, 146.

non-human creation by insisting that while God can transform human existence, he is sadly incapable of doing the same to animal existence. . . . We do not know precisely how God in Christ will restore each and every creature. But we must hold fast to the reality witnessed in Christ that our creaturely life is unfinished reality—that God is not yet finished with us.[65]

Thus, Linzey advocates an inclusive eschaton while remaining agnostic about the details of how various creatures will be included as those creatures.[66]

I find this line of reasoning promising. After all, is not some agnosticism required in the face of a human resurrection? Concerning the future hope of humans, John writes, "What we will be has not yet been revealed" (1 John 3:2). Aquinas acknowledges that humans require grace to be fit for eternal life.[67] The notion of the transfiguration and deification of humanity has a long tradition in Orthodox thought.[68]

The point is that humans require a change in form (a *trans-formation*) in order to be fit for eternity. Regarding just this point, Paul states that all flesh "will be changed. For this perishable body must put on imperishability, and this mortal body must put on immortality" (1 Cor. 15:52–53). Wolfhart Pannenberg states,

> The participation of creatures in the eternity of God is possible . . . only on the condition of a radical change, not only because of the taking up of time into the eternal simultaneity of the divine life but also and above all because of the sin that goes along with our being in time, the sin of separation from God, and of the antagonism of creatures among themselves.[69]

65. Linzey, *Christianity and the Rights of Animals*, 62.
66. Andrew Linzey, *Creatures of the Same God: Explorations in Animal Theology* (hereafter *CSG*), (New York: Lantern Books, 2009), 133, n. 13.
67. See Jean Porter, *The Recovery of Virtue: The Relevance of Aquinas for Christian Ethics* (Louisville, KY: Westminster/John Knox Press, 1990), 53.
68. See Norman Russell, *The Doctrine of Deification in the Greek Patristic Tradition* (New York: Oxford University Press, 2004).

Given these radical transfigurative claims, it is important to acknowledge the limits of human knowledge regarding both the extent and nature of the eschatological community—both human and nonhuman. These limits should not facilitate a view that tends to discredit maximally inclusive eschatologies, which is often the case.[70] For instance, Edwards claims that the "redemptive fulfillment of any creature . . . will be one that fits the nature of each creature." Thus he concludes, "While I think it can be argued that the fulfillment of a human being will necessarily be a personal one, the fulfillment of a mosquito may be of a different order."[71] Yet, it is unclear why the "transformation" (the term Edwards uses) of a creature, if it truly entails a *trans*-formation (i.e., a radical change in form or nature), must fit "the nature [or form] of each creature" that is being radically changed. Why must the change in form (i.e., the *trans*-formation) adhere to the form that is being changed? Why should we question—and here "question" really takes the connotation of *doubt*—"whether bodily resurrection is necessarily the most appropriate fulfillment for bacteria or a dinosaur" based on those creature's natures if it exactly those natures that are transformed?[72]

Granted, there must be continuity between original nature and transformed nature, as Moltmann maintains. Furthermore, I concur with Southgate's claim that a "scientifically informed eschatology must try to give some sort of account of what might be continuities and discontinuities between this creation and the new one."[73] It must also

69. Wolfhart Pannenberg *Systematic Theology*, trans. Geoffrey W. Bromiley (Grand Rapids, MI: William B. Eerdmans Publishing Company, 1991), 3:607.
70. See, for instance, Denis Edwards, "Every Sparrow that Falls to the Ground: The Cost of Evolution and the Christ-Event," *Ecotheology* 11/1 (2006): 117–19; Deane-Drummond, *Eco-Theology*, 173.
71. Edwards, "Every Sparrow that Falls," 119.
72. Ibid.
73. Southgate, *The Groaning of Creation*, 81.

try and relate the great final transforming act of God, of which the resurrection of Christ is usually regarded as the beginning, not just to continuities and discontinuities in human life but also to our understanding of God's relation to living creatures other than human beings.[74]

It seems to me that the best path forward is a cautious use of the Christ-event as the hermeneutical key of new creation. Christology must be the litmus test of eschatological assertions. There is here a disparity between Moltmann and Linzey's eschatological hermeneutic and that of Karl Rahner. For Rahner, eschatology begins with theological anthropology, which in turn, within the confines of salvation and grace, provides the proper hermeneutic to adjudicate eschatological assertions. Says Rahner, "We do not project something from the future into the present, but rather in man's experience of himself and of God in grace and in Christ we project our Christian present into its future." [75] For Rahner, the future must cohere with humanity's experience of salvation in the present. For Moltmann, Christ is the future concretized in history: "If we look at nature from the perspective of Christ's resurrection, then the sphere in which nature is experienced moves into the horizon of expectation of its new creation."[76] Contra Rahner, then, eschatology is the projection of the future into the present; for Christ is the future breaking into the present to redeem history itself.

I thus find Edwards's claim that the "future of creation remains obscure and shrouded in mystery" overextended on account of his Christology. He claims, "The future of creation is not something about which we have information. What we have in the resurrection

74. Ibid., 81–82.
75. Karl Rahner, *Foundations of Christian Faith: An Introduction to the Idea of Christianity*, trans. William V. Dych (New York: The Crossroad Publishing Company, 1998), 432.
76. Jürgen Moltmann, *The Way of Jesus Christ: Christology in Messianic Dimensions* (hereafter *WJC*), trans. Margaret Kohl (Minneapolis, MN: Fortress Press, 1993), 252.

of Jesus Christ is a promise. The promise does not give a clear view of the future."[77] In line with Moltmann's critique of Pannenberg, the resurrection is not simply a promise—it is the *fulfillment* of a promise and the continual unfolding of that fulfillment.[78] As such, the resurrection of Christ from the dead reveals the future of the cosmos: resurrection from death. Bacteria, dinosaurs, and plants all die *as individuals*. Why should Christ's victory in resurrection not have literal meaning for these creatures?

At any rate, it seems to me an anthropocentric hubris to argue that human existence is fit for eternity while nonhuman existence is not. It is not the place of humans to exclude creatures from eschatological life based on philosophical and scientific distinctions. We do not know the nature of these creatures' relationship with God.[79] Neither do we know the extent to which divine grace might transfigure their existence and make them fit for eternity. If we can recognize the human need for transfiguration, then why not accept the possibility that other creatures can be made fit for eternity through the same process? In Clough's words: "If the new creation will be so transformed that human beings can live happily in peace with one another, the change necessary to allow dinosaurs and bacteria bodily resurrection seem of little consequence."[80] Insisting on the opposite betrays an anthropocentric bias through the application of reason to the resurrection of nonhumans (i.e., the resurrection of some is nonsensical) while offering a gracious appeal to mystery regarding the resurrection of humans.

Hoping for the resurrection of all individual creatures does not negate mystery. Indeed, it more thoroughly embraces it than does schemas of eschatology that exclude creatures based on human

---

77. Edwards, "Every Sparrow that Falls," 117.
78. See Moltmann, *The Coming of God*, 195.
79. Edwards, "Every Sparrow that Falls," 117–18.
80. Clough, *On Animals*, 170.

reasoning by recognizing that it is theologically inappropriate for humans to reject the resurrection of an ant because we fail to see the logistics of an ant's appreciation of eternity. Here we have more than an appeal to mystery; here we have an appeal to the absolute gratuity of divine grace. Clough captures this point well:

> We must . . . respect Edward's point about the final mystery of the redemption God will bring, but if we are to hope for the promised redemption of all things in Christ, it seems to me that we should hope for a place for each creature within God's unending graciousness, rather than invent distinctions in advance in order to make sure an omnipotent and bounteous God can manage an appropriate relationship between this world and the next.[81]

In the meantime, science reveals that certain creatures suffer. Basic sense perception makes us aware of the reality that all creatures, both sentient and not, die. If Christ overcomes in his passion the suffering of the sentient by drawing their unique pain into the Godhead and healing it; if Christ overcomes death by dying the death of all the living and defeating the "last enemy"[82] in his resurrection; then it seems theologically viable to claim that neither suffering nor death can be the final word for any creature.[83] In Christ "the experiences of life's transience and the unceasing suffering of all living things no longer end only in grief, but also already lead to hope. . . . This eschatological reinterpretation of transience has to be concentrated on a single point: death; for death is the end of all the living."[84]

81. Ibid.
82. See 1 Corinthians 15:26.
83. Moltmann, *The Coming of God*, 132.
84. Moltmann, *The Way of Jesus Christ*, 252.

The Hope for Vegetarian Lions as the Dissolution
of the Lion Species

"Were the wolf tamed or the lion pacified, it would no longer intelligibly be wolf or lion but something else, perhaps a new species or maybe just a simulacra of something lost."[85] With this claim, Willis Jenkins echoes a common criticism that certainly applies to advocates of cosmocentric transfiguration.[86] The critique is present in C. S. Lewis's *The Problem of Pain*, in which he writes:

> I think, under correction, that the prophet [Isaiah] used an eastern hyperbole when he spoke of the lion and the lamb *lying down* together. That would be rather impertinent of the lamb. To have lions and lambs that so consorted . . . would be the same as having neither lambs nor lions.[87]

The criticism is this: even granting the continuity and discontinuity of creaturely existence in transfiguration, how much discontinuity can a creature or species bear without becoming something else altogether? Would a vegetarian lion still be a lion?[88] Or, would being vegetarian deny a lion its true "heaven"? As Lewis states, "If the earthly lion could read the prophecy of that day when he shall eat hay like an ox, he would regard it as a description not of heaven, but of hell."[89] Moule, engaging the vision of the peaceable kingdom in Isaiah 11:6–9, polemically raises this critique:

> No one with a grain of sense believes that . . . Isa. xi is intended literally, as though the digestive system of a carnivore were going to be transformed into that of a herbivore. What blasphemous injury would be done to great poetry and true mythology by laying such solemnly

---

85. Jenkins, *Ecologies of Grace*, 144.
86. For a response to Jenkins view that mirrors my own, see Clough, *On Animals*, 161–62.
87. C. S. Lewis, *The Problem of Pain* (New York: HarperCollins, 1996), 147.
88. See Clough's recognition of this question among critics of cosmic eschatology. Clough, *On Animals*, 158–62.
89. Ibid.

prosaic hands upon it! If we believe at all in God as Creator, and in the evolution of species as part of his design, it seems we must accept universal predation as integral to it. Indeed, it would be a catastrophic dislocation of the whole ecology if the lion did begin to eat straw like the ox—or, for that matter, if the microscopic defenders within the body gave up attacking the invaders which may cause disease.[90]

In a similar fashion, Lisa Sideris critiques Northcott's eschatological outlook, writing,

> An environmental ethic that seeks harmonious and peaceful relations among all beings surely cannot take seriously the particular needs, the specific ways of life, of animals—take for example the needs of predators, whose means of survival [and, as others would argue, their flourishing] will apparently be revoked when the original goodness of creation is restored.[91]

Linzey responds to such critiques by stating, "It is not animality itself that is to be destroyed by divine love, rather animal nature in bondage to violence and predation."[92] It is in this sense that grace perfects rather than destroys nature: "It is against the order of nature, we may say, for one species to trust another in a world that is fallen and disordered, and yet we do well to remember that grace perfects nature."[93] Grace restores the nature of predatory animals to the state that God originally intended for them. It is as if, for Linzey, the lion and the gazelle are *both* victims of predation. The gazelle is eaten. But the lion is bound to its need and desire to eat the gazelle. In this sense, both are in need of redemption. This point is similar to Moltmann's claim that divine justice must redeem both the victim and the victimizer.[94]

90. Moule, *Man and Nature in the New Testament*, 12.
91. Sideris, *Environmental Ethics*, 88.
92. Linzey, *After Noah*, 75. See also, for a rebuttal, Wennberg, *God, Humans, and Animals*, 295.
93. Linzey, *After Noah*, 100.
94. See Jürgen Moltmann, *The Spirit of Life: A Universal Affirmation* (hereafter *SL*), trans. Margaret Kohl (Minneapolis, MN: Fortress Press, 1992), 129–37.

Many environmental theologians, including Thomas Berry, would find little satisfaction in Linzey's appeal to true nature over and against distorted nature.[95] Is there another way forward? I offer three responses to the issue.

First, it seems to me that the critique that a lion would no longer be a lion if it did not hunt is a rather reductionist view of a lion's being. It relies on a Platonic or Aristotelian (or perhaps simply materialistic) reduction of lion to some *esse* (which is predation of all things!) that cannot be overcome without the dissolution of the lion-ness of the lion.[96] Such forms of "species essentialism," as Marc Fellenz terms them, are common in Western thought.[97] The critique also assumes that *trans*-figuration (again, the radical change of a creature's nature) cannot entail any change in its digestive system or predatory instincts. But if such were the case, could not the same critique be applied to the hope for human transfiguration? Will humans eat in eternity? Will they experience sexual drives? Will they sleep? Will they defecate?

Polkinghorne suggests that "the 'matter' of [the] resurrected world will be the transformed matter of this dying universe. . . . It will have new properties, consistent with the end of transience, death and suffering."[98] If this new matter enables any of the above dimensions of human existence to be overcome in transfiguration, would a human still be a human? If the "perishable body must put on imperishability" (1 Cor. 15:53), is it the same species? If so, then it seems the same argument for continuity could apply to vegetarian lions. If not, then

---

95. See Thomas Berry, *The Christian Future and the Fate of the Earth*, ed. Mary Evelyn Tucker and John Grim (Maryknoll, NY: Orbis Books, 2009), 39.

96. See, for example, Jenkins, *Ecologies of Grace*, 120.

97. See. Marc R. Fellenz, *The Moral Menagerie: Philosophy and Animal Rights* (Chicago: University of Illinois Press, 2007), 37–40.

98. John Polkinghorne, *Scientists as Theologians: A Comparison of the Writings of Ian Barbour, Arthur Peacocke, and John Polkinghorne* (London: SPCK, 1996), 54.

the continuity of human identity is as questionable as that of lions with regard to eternal life.

Thus, Southgate is somewhat inconsistent when he writes,

> It is very hard to imagine any form of being a predator that nevertheless does not 'hurt or destroy' on the 'holy mountain' of God. . . . What could the life of a predator look like in the absence of the second law of thermodynamics, and the imperative of ingesting ordered energy to ward off the ever-present slide of decay?[99]

Why would such issues not also apply to humans, who are currently predators themselves?

Or again, Southgate notes that the notion that carnivores will eat straw is "most difficult of all for the biochemically minded."[100] But are not common images of transfigured humans also biochemically problematic? Why should the transfiguration of a nonhuman animal from carnivore to herbivore pose such vast problems when the transfiguration of a human does not?

Clough picks on just this point in his criticism of Southgate's claim, based on the poem "The Heaven of Animals" by Jame Dickey, that predation may continue for immortal creatures in the eschaton. Clough asks why it would not also be legitimate to consider that human/human violence will continue in the eschaton. "There is no shortage of literary celebrations of a heroic warrior class of human beings."[101] Given the nature of some humans, "we would need a happy hunting ground where soldiers continue to develop their murderous skills" for their heaven.[102]

Obviously very few theologians will accept such a view of the human resurrection. Yet, this refusal again betrays the guise of an

99. Southgate, *The Groaning of Creation*, 88.
100. Ibid., 89.
101. Clough, *On Animals*, 159.
102. Ibid., 160.

anthropocentric bias in theology. While humans embrace the transformation of the violent (and natural!) tendencies of their own bodies, many simply will not extend such a possibility to animals. Says Clough:

> The transformation required to fit human beings for life in the new creation is hard to imagine while still preserving personal identity, if the human life I know best is anything to go by. Yet the biblical and later Christian traditions encourage us to entertain the audacious hope that even creatures like us could find a place in the peaceable kingdom. Surely if such transformations can be wrought in vicious human beings, it is a failure of imagination to consider that leopards cannot find their own perfection once released from the necessity of killing in order to survive.[103]

Perhaps some environmental theologians would respond that the notions of transfiguration and eternal life are altogether incoherent for all creaturely life, including humans.[104] To its credit, this reply is consistent. However, if one wants to maintain that humans will experience eternal life, the issue of continuity in the midst of transfiguration (including the alteration of biological factors such as digestion) poses as much a problem here as it does for nonhumans. A vegetarian lion is no more an oddity than a human who neither defecates nor dies. If the advocate of eternal life for humans appeals to mystery or remains agnostic about the exact manner of continuity and discontinuity in the midst of human transfiguration, the animal theologian should be offered the same courtesy without ridicule.[105]

---

103. Ibid.
104. Ruether seems to go in this direction. See *Sexism and God-Talk*, 257–258.
105. On the inconsistency of some thinkers on this point, see Clough, *On Animals*, 154–55. Clough notes that one question he was asked after a lecture on an animal resurrection concerned what would happen with the extra excrement of the resurrected animals. For Clough, such speculations are unhelpful. However, I think they reveal a bias, since these questions tend not to be asked about a general human resurrection.

Second, the question of the continuity of a lion's nature seems to be predicated upon the prominence of the lion species over and against the individual lion. The advocate of cosmocentric transfiguration has an advantage here in emphasizing the importance of the individual creature. If one emphasizes the species, then the potential loss of the general notion of "lion," including its carnivorous nature, is tragic. If one emphasizes the individual, then the resurrection of all lions and the transfiguration of their individual bodies ensure the continuity of that creature even if the qualities that humans identify as "lion nature" are transfigured.

While some who affirm cosmic transfiguration are satisfied with the notion that a generic representation of each species will endure in eternity,[106] they have less concern for the continuity of individual creatures in their idiosyncrasies. What matters is that the qualities of the species be preserved by means of some eschatological representative as opposed to the individual instantiations of the species.[107] Wennberg refers to this position as *creatio de novo*. That is, God does not resurrect creatures that once lived, but creates a new individual creature that will represent the entire species in eternity. Whereas all the lions that actually existed in history are not resurrected, a *new* lion is created to maintain the presence of lion-ness in eternal life.

If this new representative eschatological lion had two legs, ate straw, and enjoyed playing chess, then the critique that such a representative fails vis-à-vis the species of lion would hold. Such a creature could hardly represent all the individual lions that actually lived in history but are left in their graves. However, for those who affirm the resurrection of every instantiation of flesh, the continuity of a species is preserved in the common continuity of all individual

106. Polkinghorne, *The God of Hope*, 122–123.
107. See Wennberg, *God, Humans, and Animals*, 321–24.

instantiations of that species. Just like an exhaustive resurrection of individual humans who no longer suffer or sleep and who can teleport (see John 20:19, 26) is not tantamount to the dissolution of the human species—but rather its transfiguration—so also the exhaustive resurrection of all lions as vegetarians is not paramount to the dissolution of the species of lion. As Webb writes, "Just as Christians believe that humans will be fully transformed in the afterlife, our proclivity for violence being washed away as we are made into the image of Christ, animals too will be liberated from their habits of aggression and violence."[108]

Finally, this critique highlights another question of ontology. What is it that safeguards the continuity of an individual creature throughout its existence? Is it some static *esse* buried underneath its accidental qualities? Or is it the narrative of a creature's body-self? It seems to me that the shift to a dynamic and relational ontology renders the issue of the lion-ness of a lion less viable with regard to eschatological existence; for it is the very same body-self that is transfigured.[109] Moltmann makes this claim with regard to Jesus's resurrection. In the resurrection, Jesus is at once the same body-self who was crucified (continuity) but without suffering, anxiety, and the fear of looming death (discontinuity). It is the transfiguration of a body-self that permits radical discontinuity alongside radical continuity. Just as Jesus can be resurrected as immortal and beyond suffering without losing his identity as human, so also could a lion be resurrected as vegetarian without losing its identity as lion.

---

108. Stephen Webb, "Ecology vs. The Peaceable Kingdom: Toward a Better Theology of Nature," *Soundings* 79/1–2 (Spring/Summer 1996): 245.
109. On this view, see Clough, *On Animals*, 161.

Eschatological Ethics as a Social Program Doomed to Failure

The final critique I wish to address is the tension between eschatology and history, specifically with regard to ethics. Karl Barth writes that eschatological vegetarianism may "represent a wanton anticipation of what is described by Is. 11 and Rom. 8 as existence in the new aeon for which we hope."[110] While Barth seems here to resonate with this critique inasmuch as "it aggravates by reason of inevitable inconsistencies, its sentimentality and its fanaticism," he also cautions: "for all its weaknesses we must be careful not to put ourselves in the wrong in face of it by our own thoughtlessness and hardness of heart."[111]

Barth's eschatology grounds such a critique because history is thoroughly divorced from an ultimately transcendent eschaton.[112] This divorce makes anticipations of that eschaton unfeasible. It furthermore renders the killing of animals a "priestly act of eschatological character" that "can be accomplished with a good conscience" if it is done with a penitence that acknowledges such killing is only permissible within the confines of a history subjected to futility.[113]

Sideris also critiques eschatological vegetarianism. Contra Barth, she does so from the perspective of a complete rejection of cosmic transfiguration. "An environmental ethic must be rooted in biological realities. We cannot hope to change nature by engaging it as though it were, or could become, a perfect ecological community."[114] Thus,

110. Karl Barth, *Church Dogmatics*, trans. A. T. Mackay, T. H. L Parker, Harold Knight, Henry A. Kennedy, John Marks (Edinburgh: T & T Clark, 1961), III/4:355–356.
111. Ibid.
112. See Moltmann, *The Coming of God*, 13–16; Joseph Ratzinger, *Eschatology: Death and Eternal Life*, second edition, trans. Michael Waldstein (Washington, DC: The Catholic University of America Press, 1988), 47–48.
113. Barth, *Church Dogmatics*, III/4, 355.
114. Sideris, *Environmental Ethics*, 83.

any form of eschatological ethics is extremely problematic, especially regarding ecology.[115]

However, Sideris' critique of eschatological ethics is frequently grounded in misunderstanding. She seems unable to separate the hope for eschatological redemption from the belief in an historical Eden. She also consistently fails to grasp the tensions within eschatology concerning its relationship to both history and ethics. Her exploration of Moltmann highlights this deficiency.[116] I would venture to say that Sideris's critique of eco-theology's inadequate understanding of evolutionary science applies equally to her own understanding of eschatology. Her criticism of eschatological ethics thus loses credibility.

In response to Barth's criticism, I favor Moltmann's notions of *adventus* and *novum*, both of which permit a proleptic *creatio anticipativa* without lapsing into attempts to construct the kingdom. It is not simply individual creatures within time that require redemption, but time itself. It is not merely the victims of evolution that require transfiguration, but evolution itself. Eschatology is neither a progression within history nor a fully transcendent ahistorical future; it is rather God's eschatological future that happens *to history*.[117] Because time exists in the *adventus* of the coming God and that God's future, it is open, as history, to *novum*. This *novum* is nothing other than *creatio anticipativa* of the *creatio nova*, which is the very transfiguration of history itself.

Human beings cannot control the *adventus* of God's coming. They cannot construct the *creatio nova*. However, they can embrace the *creatio anticipativa* by witnessing to eschatological hope. This witness is by the very nature of history's disposition incomplete and

---

115. See ibid., 189–93.
116. See ibid., 191.
117. Moltmann, *The Coming of God*, 22.

imperfect. It is indeed doomed to "inevitable inconsistencies." But these inconsistencies do not negate the validity of the witness itself. Indeed, perhaps a world engulfed in evolutionary struggle should not elicit an ethics devoid of inconsistencies or tensions. At any rate, eschatological ethics are only doomed to failure if they seek to construct the eschaton. Proleptic anticipation is another matter altogether.[118]

Conclusion

I have offered responses to potential tensions and critiques that might arise concerning cosmocentric transfiguration. I do not find critiques that the paradigm is not biblical satisfactory as the paradigm is commensurable with particular passages that point to the potential of a hermeneutic that favors it. Nor do I find the critique that the paradigm constitutes a denial of the tradition satisfactory as a critical retrieval of the tradition helps support its main tenets. Suspicions that cosmocentric transfiguration amounts to the denial of science or the denigration of nature are not necessarily true given my reinterpretations of protology and the Fall. The claim that an individual animal or plant resurrection is nonsensical loses its strength once the necessity of humanity's transfiguration is considered. Likewise, the force of the claim that the resurrection of predators as non-predatory constitutes the dissolution of the species is mitigated by the hope for continuity of humanness amidst the discontinuity entailed by transfiguration. Finally, the criticism that eschatological ethics are doomed to failure does lose strength when such ethics are framed as proleptic anticipation rather than efforts to construct the kingdom in its fullness.

118. On this point, see Clough, *On Animals*, 154, 172.

16

Cosmocentric Transfiguration

An Eco-Eschatological Ethics of Preservation and Protest

Given all that has been said to this point, what are the logistics of cosmocentric transfiguration? What I offer here is nothing more than suggestions of how one might move toward answering this question. I make no claims to comprehensiveness as such a task would require another book (one which I hope to write). Here, my thoughts should be understood as a place to begin—a direction for future research.

I begin by considering the tensions of temporal existence and the qualifications I believe these tensions mandate. I then explore how cosmocentric transfiguration might translate into practices toward individual sentient nonhuman animals. Next, I address the concrete application of cosmocentric transfiguration for individual non-sentient life forms. Finally, I examine how the ethics might be applied to the cosmos at large. In the end, I conclude that cosmocentric transfiguration is best understood as an eco-eschatological ethics that exists within the tension between the preservation and the protest of the world as it is.

The Tensions of a Creation *in Via* and the Ethics that Pertains to It

In a good creation that wanders in isolation, there can be no perfect living. In Linzey's words, "There is no pure land."[1] In the world as we experience it, suffering, predation, and death are necessary. Without these aspects, the biosphere and all of its eco-systems would fail. Our present existence could not endure the dissolution of the mechanisms of evolution without a transfiguration of time, space, matter, and energy.

There must therefore be the recognition that all transfigurative ethics are anticipatory in nature. They facilitate sacramental moments of the eschaton without constituting its definitive arrival. For this reason, I am hesitant to translate transfigurative ethics into rights. It is not simply that these ethics must be violated on occasion, but rather that participation in the mechanisms of evolution—and more often than not non-volitionally— is the *norm* of human existence in this morally ambiguous and complex world.[2] However, transfigurative ethics, in assenting to a particular telos of all creatures, does ground certain legal protections for them. To better understand the nature of these protections, I first explore the notion of necessity and the ethics of proportionalism.

---

1. Andrew Linzey, *Animal Gospel* (Louisville, KY: Westminster John Knox, 1998), 90.
2. See Robert Wennberg, *God, Humans, and Animals: An Invitation to Enlarge Our Moral Universe* (Grand Rapids, MI: William B. Eerdmans Publishing Company, 2003), 51–54; William C. French, "Subject-centered and Creation-centered Paradigms in Recent Catholic Thought," *The Journal of Religion*, 70/1 (January 1990): 70.

What Does "Necessity" Mean?

Linzey argues that only genuine human need can justify the violation of another creature's theos-rights. For him, genuine need denotes that which a human cannot live without and that which humans can obtain by no other means than by the violation of said rights.[3] Thus, if a human cannot survive by any other means than eating meat, as is the case in certain contexts even today, then the violation of a creature's right to life is justified. Moltmann seems to hold a similar position. While he maintains that individual nonhuman animals have "*infinite value*" and a "*right* to live,"[4] he also accepts that this value and right can be violated in cases such as animal experimentation and consumption of meat.[5]

This line of thinking—that the well-being of nonhuman animals and plants can be violated in the case of necessity—seems almost ubiquitous in environmental and animal ethics. Michael Northcott writes, "The moral problem is not in the eating of animals but in the avoidance of unnecessary cruelty, indignity and pain."[6] Note it is acceptable to kill and eat animals provided no *unnecessary* cruelty is inflicted. Christopher Southgate's evolutionary theodicy maintains that suffering and death are *necessary* in order to achieve the kind of world of diverse and complex life that God desired to create.[7] Jame Schaefer recovers from early and medieval Christian thought the "admonitions that Christians should use God's creation moderately to provide the necessities of life."[8] Based on these admonitions and in

3. See Andrew Linzey, *Animal Theology* (Chicago: University of Illinois Press, 1994), 145.
4. Jürgen Moltmann, *The Way of Jesus Christ: Christology in Messianic Dimensions* [hereafter *WJC*], trans. Margaret Kohl (Minneapolis, MN: Fortress Press, 1993), 256.
5. See chapter 9.
6. Michael Northcott, *The Environment and Christian Ethics* (New York: Cambridge University Press, 1996), 101.
7. Christopher Southgate, *The Groaning of Creation: God, Evolution, and the Problem of Evil* (Louisville, KY: Westminster John Knox, 2008), 40–48.

conjunction with more recent ecclesial statements, Schaefer argues, "The faithful will distinguish between necessary and unnecessary uses of other animals and plants, land, and waters. They will choose to use only what they need to sustain their temporal lives as they aim for eternal life with God."[9] Note here that necessity is better defined, taking on the meaning of the necessities to sustain temporal life. Finally, the most recent Catechism of the Roman Catholic Church states that humans, as stewards, must show animals kindness. However, animals "may be used to serve the just satisfaction of man's needs."[10] These needs include food, clothing, domestication for work and leisure, and "medical and scientific experimentation" provided it "remains within reasonable limits and contributes to caring for or saving human lives."[11]

What is true in all of these examples, from Linzey to the Catechism, is that *need* either establishes the good (i.e., it is good to kill animals if it serves human need) or justifies a violation of the good (i.e., it is permissible to kill an animal to save a human life provided there is no other manner of achieving this end). In my view, the notion of need is more complicated than these assessments acknowledge. To further clarify this point, and by way of suggesting a path forward in adjudicating the propriety of violations of the tenets of cosmocentric transfiguration in the face of the inevitable contradictions of history, I here offer a more thorough reflection on need.

8. Jame Schaefer, *Theological Foundations for Environmental Ethics: Reconstructing Patristic & Medieval Concepts* (Washington, D.C.: Georgetown University Press, 2009), 197.

9. Ibid., 213.

10. *The Catechism of the Catholic Church: With Modifications from the* Editio Typica (New York: Doubleday, 1995), 2457.

11. Ibid., 2417.

Necessity, at least as it appears in these ethical conversations, is always both contingent and teleological. Necessities are only necessary to achieve some end. Such is the *formula of contingent need*:

Humans *need*	(X)	*in order to*	(Y)

The (X) here represents that which is necessary. Contingent necessity always points toward a (Y), the result sought that makes (X) a necessity.

Inasmuch as any one individual creature or even any one individual species or ecosystem (or perhaps any one particular planet) is not *essential* to the functioning of the cosmos at large or the life of the divine, it is not *unconditionally* necessary.[12] However, it is contingently necessary for some telos, some "in order to."

For instance, consider the following variables:

Humans *need*	the earth's atmosphere (Xa)	*in order to*	survive (Ya)

The cosmos *needs*	human survival (Xb)	*in order to*	survive (Yb)

This first claim is accurate. Without earth's atmosphere, biological human life as we know it would not be possible. The validity of the second claim is another issue. If all humans died, the cosmos would likely continue on largely undisturbed.

These claims suggest that the appropriate question in adjudicating ethics vis-à-vis the contradictions of history is not whether or not something is "necessary." *Anything* can be necessary by way of a near tautology:

---

12. Indeed, perhaps only God is needed in this manner—that is, non-contingently.

I *need*	wealth (Xc)	*in order to*	be rich (Yc)

One could also say:

I *need*	to eat meat (Xd)	*in order to*	be fully satisfied with my meal (Yd)

In both of these cases, the (X) itself might warrant a negative response (e.g., "You do not *need* to eat meat"). However, once the (Y) is added ("in order to be fully satisfied with my meal"), contingent necessity is established; for the (X) is, at least in theory, *needed* in order to obtain the (Y).

Because necessity is contingent in this manner, attempts to establish nonhuman theological ethics based on necessity alone fail. It is not enough to claim that necessity justifies. If it were, then the formula of contingent need would be followed by a simple "therefore, (X) is good and/or justified." But such is surely not the case. For example, surely environmental theologians would not accept the following claim of a hunter:

I *need*	to kill an endangered creature (Xe)	*in order to*	complete my taxidermy collection (Ye)
Therefore, killing the endangered creature is good and/or justified.			

There should be no doubt that the formula of contingent need is valid. But who could accept that the action is justified? The point is that *need does not in itself justify.* The primary issue is *not* necessity, but rather (1) whether or not the end (Y) coheres with a particular notion of the good and (2) if so, whether or not the (X) is the *only* means of procuring the (Y). That is, the important thing to establish is *both* necessity and the good that is implied by the necessity. Consider a more complicated claim:

Humans *need*	to kill animals (Xf)	*in order to*	eat meat (Yf)
Therefore, killing animals is good and/or justified.			

Without the possibility of laboratory-created meat, taking bites out of live animals, or eating carrion, it holds that killing animals is necessary in order to eat meat. But does eating meat cohere with the good? Of course the answer here depends upon one's view of the good. Inasmuch as the good is a teleological term, the answer in this case must be predicated upon the telos of both humans and animals. For cosmocentric transfiguration, the ultimate telos of both humans and animals is participation in the divine life, which entails peace (including the lack of predation) among all creatures. This telos is breaking into history. In doing so, it creates a new temporal telos for humans: becoming sacraments of the eschaton by witnessing against the shades of transience that will be overcome in eschatological communion. Thus, human actions should, to whatever extent possible, adhere to this eschatological good within history.

The phrase "to whatever extent possible" brings me back to the issue of contingent necessity. Yes, humans *need* to kill animals *in order to* eat meat. But why is eating meat necessary? What is the "in order to" of the necessity of meat consumption?

It depends. The "in order to" could be, as was the case with (Yd), a higher degree of satisfaction. But there could be other (Y's) as well. Furthermore, because in this world we inevitably kill and we will inevitably die, the various teloi of creatures are bound to clash. Thus, there could be a (Y) that is in fact good while also predicated upon an (X) which constitutes a violation of the good of another creature. For example:

Humans *need*	to eat meat (Xg)	*in order to*	survive (Yg)
Therefore, eating meat is good and/or justified.			

(Xg) is not true of all humans; but it is true of some. I have already noted that, according to the teloi established by cosmocentric transfiguration, eating meat is a violation of the eschatological good God desires for all the creatures eaten inasmuch as it entails their death. However, human survival is good. So, here we have a conflict of teleological necessities and an *inevitable violation of the good*. If humans eat meat, thus killing a creature and probably causing it suffering, they violate God's desire for that creature. If they do not eat meat (assuming conditions in which doing so is necessary for their survival) they will die from lack of care for their own body, which violates God's desire for them. At this juncture, a violation of the good is inevitable.

Proportionalism and Virtuous Violations of the Good

Two important questions arise here. First, how does one adjudicate which good is to be violated in such cases? Second, in what manner should the good be violated?[13]

Regarding the first question, I believe proportionalism provides the best form of ethics for cosmocentric transfiguration. By proportionalism, I intimate David F. Kelly's description of it as a shift "from traditional (deontological) method to proportionality . . . from legalism to at least a moderate form of situationalism—though it is certainly not a radical situationalism, because rules are still of great importance."[14] According to this definition, proportionalism maintains the laws of deontology while recognizing the complexity of contexts and the importance of consequences. It introduces the

---

13. This section is far from exhaustive and actually only scratches the surface of the issues it addresses. It is meant only as a reflection on the way forward vis-à-vis my reflection on necessity.

14. David F. Kelly, *Contemporary Catholic Health Care Ethics* (Washington, DC: Georgetown University Press, 2004), 90.

possibility that a violation of the law is acceptable if that violation is necessary to produce some equal or greater good.

In my language, when dealing with a valid formula of contingent need in which the (X) represents a violation of the good and the (Y) represents a proportionately greater good that cannot be achieved by means other than the (X), it is acceptable to choose the lesser evil for the greater good. However, significantly, the goodness of the (Y) does not alter that the (X) is a violation of the good. The (Y) renders the (X) permissible, but it does not render it good.

How does one make such a decision within cosmocentric transfiguration? Richard Bauckham argues that Moltmann's theological ethics fails just here. His "theological basis is plainly inadequate for the ethical distinctions that need to be made. . . . It makes death as such an undifferentiated evil in the face of which all creatures have the right to life."[15] As will be evident, I disagree with Bauckham's assessment. To claim that death is a common evil for all life does not necessitate that the death of one creature could not be more tragic than the death of another. It simply means that all death is tragic.

I believe my proportionalist approach may help at this point. Consider:

Humans *need*	to eat meat (Xg)	*in order to*	be more satisfied with their meals (Yg2)
Therefore, killing animals (to procure meat) is good and/or justified.			

Whereas survival (as is the case with Yg1) constitutes a good that is at the very least proportionately equal to the violation of the good in (Xg), this case cannot be made about greater satisfaction (Yg2) within the framework of cosmocentric transfiguration. Therefore,

---

15. Richard Bauckham in *The Theology of Jürgen Moltmann* (Edinburgh: T&T Clark, 1995), 211.

given variables (Xg) and (Yg2) in the formula of contingent need, killing animals, while necessary, is not only not good and/or justified, it is *not acceptable*.

What about the second question: In what manner should the good be violated? Stephen Pope notes the teleological nature of Aquinas's virtue ethics, in which "to understand anything, humanity included, depends on comprehending its end or purpose."[16] In Aquinas's estimation, which reflects Aristotle's understanding of virtue, to act virtuously is to act in a manner that reflects the telos of humans and the world.[17]

My discussion of necessity and the good in which each is predicated upon teleology suggests the influence of virtue ethics. Taking my lead from Aquinas, I maintain that a virtue is not established merely with reference to the end. Indeed, for Aquinas the end does inform the status of an action as good or evil, but only in conjunction with the action's genus, object, and circumstance.[18] In this sense, the end expresses how a virtue ought to be manifested. One's journey is not justified by the end one achieves; rather, the end proper to one's nature informs how one ought to engage in taking the journey. In short, the end does not justify the means; the end makes clear the distinction between virtuous and vicious means. To undergo the journey in a manner unbefitting one's nature (and thus one's telos) is already a violation of virtue—a vice.

This point leads to a qualification of my proportionalism. Robert Wennberg considers "how the morally good person should respond to those tragic elements in our world and in our life, about which we

16. Stephen J. Pope, "Overview of the Ethics of Thomas Aquinas," in *The Ethics of Aquinas*, ed. Stephen J. Pope (Washington, DC: Georgetown University Press, 2002), 32.
17. See Thomas Aquinas, *Summa Contra Gentiles*, ed. Joseph Kenny (New York: Hanover House, 1955–57), III.148.
18. See Thomas Aquinas, *Summa Theologica*, trans. Fathers of the English Dominican Province (Benziger Brothers, 1947), I–II, Q 18 A 4.

and others can do absolutely nothing."[19] There is a radical difference between one who, in the face of procuring a greater good, violates the good of a creature with ease or joy and one who violates the good with grieving and sorrow. This point is similarly stated by Karl Barth:

> A good hunter . . . will differ from the bad in the fact that even as they are engaged in killing animals they hear this groaning and travailing of the creature, and therefore, in comparison with all others who have to do with animals, they are summoned to an intensified, sharpened and deepened diffidence, reserve and carefulness.[20]

In a similar fashion, Wendell Berry writes: "To live, we must daily break the body and shed the blood of creation. When we do this knowingly, lovingly, skillfully, reverently, it is a sacrament. When we do it ignorantly, greedily, clumsily, destructively, it is a desecration."[21] (The difference between Berry and Barth—and between Berry and Moltmann, Linzey, and me—is whether or not this breaking of creation's body is part of the goodness of the cosmos.)

The point is that proportionalism benefits from virtue. There is a courageous manner, a *virtuous* way, of violating the good when such a violation is necessary—one in which the violator is steeped in lament and compassion. There is also a cowardly manner of violating the good in valid necessity—one in which the violator derives pleasure from the actions or refers to the action itself as good. Thus, it is not merely the interplay of act and consequence that establishes the good; it is also the character of the agent who acts. I thus concur with Linzey's early thought in which he claims that killing can be *permissible* in cases of *vital* necessity "as long as the method of killing

---

19. Wennberg, *God, Animals, and Humans*, xiii (see also 50).
20. Karl Barth, *Church Dogmatics*, trans. G. W. Bromiley (Edinburgh: T&T Clark, 1962), III/4:355.
21. Wendell Berry, *The Gift of Good Land: Further Essays Cultural and Agricultural* (San Francisco: North Point, 1981), 281.

is as humane as possible and that no persons are receiving pleasure from such activity."[22]

I believe this approach to ethics and the issue of necessity is the most promising path forward for cosmocentric transfiguration. I have barely blazed a trail here. I only suggest that every violation of a creature's eschatological telos is also a violation of the good. These violations are never justified; but they may be necessary in order to procure a proportionately greater good, and therefore lamentably permissible.

Preservation and Protest:
Living Cosmocentric Transfiguration

Having examined necessity and proportionality, it is now possible to suggest how cosmocentric transfiguration might translate into concrete praxis. I begin with what the ethics might mean for individual sentient animals, both humans and nonhumans. I then consider individual non-sentient life forms such as insects and plants. Lastly, I explore the meaning of the ethics for holistic cosmic structures. Collectively, my explorations yield a tension between proleptic witness, which entails a *protest* of the larger systems of death by protecting individual creatures, and letting-be, which entails the preservation of the very systems of death that elicit protest.

In each area, I take as my launching point four theological claims germane to cosmology, anthropology, and eschatology that arise out of my synthesis of Moltmann and Linzey:

1. The triune God has created a world with which the Trinity desires perichoretic communion.

22. Andrew Linzey, *Animal Rights: A Christian Assessment*, (London: SCM, 1976), 38.

2. This desire must overcome the isolation of the cosmos and the dispositional effects of that isolation (e.g., suffering, predation, and death).

3. This overcoming is concretely accomplished in the incarnation of the Son, including Christ's passion, death, and resurrection and is further manifested by the burgeoning future in the presence of the Spirit.

4. In the Spirit, human beings become sacraments of the eschatological hope that the mechanisms of evolution will be overcome in communion.

Individual Sentient Creatures

Because a good practice is one that respects the teloi of creatures—and because the telos of individual sentient creatures is, on the one hand, freedom from suffering, predation, and death, and on the other hand freedom for communion—the following fundamental guideline can be formulated: Any practice that witnesses to the hope of freedom from suffering, predation, and death is good while any practice that embraces suffering, predation, and death is not good. Thus, regarding sentient creatures, both human and nonhuman, the following is clear:[23]

1. Allowing a creature to live is good. Taking a creature's life is not good.

2. Alleviating the suffering of a creature is good. Harming a creature is not good.

3. Permitting a creature its own space and way of life is good. Denying a creature its own space and way of life is not good.

23. I am here indebted to Linzey's work.

4. Letting a creature live in peace is good. Hunting a creature is not good.

5. Allowing a creature to live out its natural life is good. Slaughtering a creature for meat is not good.

6. Healing a sick creature is good. Experimentation that elicits suffering is not good.

7. Permitting a creature the sustenance it needs for self-maintenance is good. Trapping or farming a creature for fur is not good.

8. Protecting a creature from harm is good. Procuring animal products (e.g., dairy and eggs) by methods that are painful or disruptive to the creature's well-being is not good.

9. Living in harmony with a creature is good. Keeping a creature in a manner that causes suffering by denying its natural inclinations is not good.

These claims follow from the fundamental guideline above. However, that guideline must be qualified by the following caveat: *An action can be both necessary for witnessing to the telos of one creature while at the same time witness against the telos of another.* Such actions are never justified—that is, good—but they are permissible if the good they procure is proportionately greater than the good they violate. In this manner, in certain circumstances humans can participate in evil out of inevitability and necessity without calling that evil good.

The heart of the issue with regard to concrete ethics is then the question of how to adjudicate greater goods and lesser evils. Such a project is not possible in this work. My point here is to say that, within the paradigm of cosmocentric transfiguration, *the good is always the promotion of life and the alleviation of suffering.* Whenever this good is violated even for a proportionately greater good that renders the violation necessary, that violation must be acknowledged as evil. It must be accompanied by a groaning with the creation that yearns for redemption. And if that good is violated for a good that is disproportionate to the evil, it requires repentance and conversion.

It is therefore possible for an advocate of cosmocentric transfiguration to hunt for food and eat meat where there is no other option.[24] Such actions remain a violation of the good, but are necessary to procure an (at the very least) equal good. Hunting for sport and eating meat for pleasure, however, cannot be commensurable with cosmocentric transfiguration. Harmful experimentation—even when it is necessary—will always be evil and unjustifiable. But it may procure a proportionately greater good that could not be procured otherwise. In such cases it would be permissible with virtuous lament. However, if the good procured through such practices could be procured otherwise but is not on account of profitability or some other paltry good, the means cannot be commensurable with cosmocentric transfiguration.

Individual Non-Sentient Life

For Moltmann, death is the ultimate reality that God must overcome.[25] For Linzey, it is suffering. What remains unclear in Linzey's thought is the theological and ethical significance of Christ's resurrection from death for creatures that lack sentience but nonetheless die. I believe Northcott's critique of Tom Regan applies to Linzey: Animal rights advocates often struggle to establish the rights of "non-mammalian species such as earthworms or non-sentient species such as trees." Indeed, such approaches "can give no moral value to collectivities or communities of life, such as ecosystems or the biosphere."[26] Too strong an emphasis on sentience entails that

---

24. Wennberg, *God, Humans, and Animals*, 55.
25. Moltmann, *WJC*, 252.

"an ecosystem consisting only of plants and nonsentient organisms would have no intrinsic value."[27] What remains unclear in Moltmann's thought is how the killing of any individual creature—whether sentient or not—is not a violation of eschatological hope.

The four theological claims I made above, when placed in conjunction with the fundamental guideline in which a practice is good if it witnesses to the hope of freedom from suffering, predation, and death, suggest that it is not good to kill any organism, whether sentient or not. If Christ's death is the death of all the living and his resurrection reveals the eschatological destiny of those life forms, then the promotion of insect and plant life is good. The killing of insects and plant organisms is not good.

To further make this point, I turn to Lisa Kemmerer's attempt to retrieve Linzey's "Generosity Paradigm" from an alleged hierarchy—by which she means Linzey's exclusion of non-sentient creatures from theos-rights. She states that this paradigm, when retrieved from its sentiocentric hierarchy, "suggests that Christians ought to approach all of creation with an attitude of service and self-sacrifice." This vision "does not require *equal* treatment for a crystal, a chrysanthemum, a bacterium, a katydid, and a capybara, only equal *regard* for each, out of duty to God."[28]

The significance of Kemmerer's point is crucial. If Christ's suffering and resurrection reveal that the telos of sentient creatures is freedom from suffering, then proper regard for those creatures means working to alleviate their suffering. But if Christ's death and resurrection *also* reveal that the telos of living things is eternal life,

---

26. Northcott, *The Environment and Christian Ethics*, 102.
27. Wennberg, *God, Humans, and Animals*, 38.
28. Lisa Kemmerer, *In Search of Consistency: Ethics and Animals* (Boston: Brill, 2006), 278.

then proper regard for those life forms entails promoting their lives and avoiding killing them.

Said differently, I would not strive to protect the freedom of speech for a cockroach. Neither would I do so for a human in a catatonic state. I would not strive for a tree's escape from pruning on account of its suffering. But I *would* strive to protect the life of the cockroach, the comatose patient, and the tree. Most generally, then, I am saying that to the extent that something which exists (whether rocks, plants, insects, fish, elephants, or humans) is capable of receiving my witness to the eschatological future that is breaking into history, my regard for their existence entails that I ought to so witness when I am able. David Clough moves along these lines but, on account of his focus on animals, does not develop it. Though his *On Animals* aims to expand the circle of direct moral concern to include nonhuman animals, he also acknowledges that there is need for a larger circle, "one containing all creaturely life including vegetation, and then by a circle that includes the ecosystems and geological structures that enable life on the planet earth, and so on in relation to solar system, galaxy, and universe."[29]

Based on the logic of my theological foundations, the inevitable thrust of the theological foundations for cosmocentric transfiguration as I have delineated them suggests the best dietary approximation of the kingdom is neither vegetarianism nor veganism. It is rather fruitarianism. This term has multiple meanings, so to clarify I intend by it a diet that consists of foods (typically seed-bearing) that do not result in the direct death of the host organism (i.e., never eating roots).[30] It is just this point—that the eating does not necessitate the death of the host organism—that makes the diet logically consistent with the theological framework of cosmocentric transfiguration.[31]

29. David Clough, *On Animals* (New York: Bloomsbury, 2014), xxiii.
30. Of course, this principle cannot apply to the microscopic level.

Interestingly enough, it is actually this diet that is prescribed in Genesis 1:29 for humans: "See, I have given you every plant *yielding seed* that is upon the face of all the earth, and every tree *with seed in its fruit*; you shall have them for food."

Holistic Systems of Life

Daniel Cowdin maintains that an "exclusive moral concern for individual animals becomes incoherent at the level of land management."[32] Concern for individual animals is inconsistent if it is not qualified by some concern for the system at large. On par with this claim, Sideris notes that animal advocates like "Singer and (especially) Regan are adamantly *un*concerned with the moral status of *larger* aggregates of beings such as species or ecosystems."[33] Those who wish to emphasize the well-being of individual creatures tend to downplay the moral significance of the system that continues to give rise to such creatures.

I have emphasized that the greatest forms of eschatological witness entail refusing the comfort that causing suffering and taking life brings when such actions are not required for some equal or greater good. Refusing to hunt, to buy cosmetic products that are tested on animals, to eat meat, to eat living (non-microscopic) organisms, to wear fur, etc. are all forms of eschatological witness. Such refusals are good—that is, appropriate vis-à-vis teleology. But these practices focus on the individual human, animal, or life forms. What of the

---

31. I must acknowledge that I am not a fruitarian. However, intellectual honesty mandates the recognition of the logic of my own position.

32. Daniel Cowdin, "The Moral Status of Otherkind in Christian Ethics," in *Christianity and Ecology: Seeking the Well-Being of Earth and Humans*, ed. Dieter T. Hessel and Rosemary Radford Ruether (Cambridge, MA: Harvard University Press, 2000), 271.

33. Lisa Sideris, *Environmental Ethics, Ecological Theology, and Natural Selection* (New York: Columbia University Press, 2003), 133.

cosmos as a whole? What about the species of which the individual is a part? What of ecosystems that require suffering and death to function? What of the general movement of life that likewise requires destruction in order to facilitate life? What does cosmocentric transfiguration have to say about these macroscopic concerns?

Sideris criticizes eschatologically-oriented ethics, much like the one I am here advocating, because they seek to "put an end to the very system that creates and maintains value, beauty, sentience, and even, perhaps, intelligibility in the world we inhabit."[34] Is this critique valid? Are eschatological ethics seeking to "put an end" to the system of nature?

I do not believe so. It is my view that cosmocentric transfiguration must at once *preserve* and *protest* nature. Herein lay the paradigm's fundamental tension. On the one hand, it is good to promote the life and well-being of individual life forms. On the other hand, it is necessary to sustain the systems that require the suffering and death of those individual life forms for life to be possible at all.

Based on this tension, I believe cosmocentric transfiguration is bound to both a preservationist and conservationist dimension. Its advocates must seek to preserve species (including predators) and ecosystems. They must advocate the well-being of the land. They must protect the lives of predators and permit those predators to take the lives of other creatures.[35] They must allow herbivores to live and to eat other non-sentient organisms. However, this preservation is not tantamount to a moral or theological approval. It is the

34. See Lisa Sideris, "Writing Straight with Crooked Lines: Holmes Rolston's Ecological Theology and Theodicy," in *Nature, Value, Duty: Life on Earth with Holmes Rolston III*, ed. Christopher J. Preston and Wayne Ouderkirk (Dordrecht, NL: Springer, 2007), 81–90.

35. In response to Daniel Deffenbaugh, cosmocentric transfiguration need not consider predators "immoral." But neither does it consider predation good. See Daniel G. Deffenbaugh, "Toward Thinking Like a Mountain: The Evolution of an Ecological Conscience," *Soundings* 78/2 (Summer 1995): 248–49. See Webb, "Ecology vs. The Peaceable Kingdom," 245–46. Though, Webb's claim that "animals do not need to exercise their predatory skills in order to live a full life" concerns me. Ibid., 249.

---

preservation of that which they protest—the letting-be and conservation of the good creation that groans for eschatological communion by maintaining the very mechanisms that reflect its isolation.

To *preserve* will mean that advocates of cosmocentric transfiguration will protect even that which they find abhorrent. They will engage in a gracious "letting-be" of and a difficult "living-with" the natural world, both wild and domesticated. These actions will include respecting the integrity of ecosystems and the natural inclinations of individual animals. Cosmocentric transfiguration cannot entail an attempt to create Eden on earth by genetically engineering vegetarian lions or killing all predators in order to protect their prey.[36] It is bound to the sigh that Wennberg conveys in his consideration of Isaiah 11: "It would truly be better if there were no predation but sadly that cannot be."[37]

To *protest* will mean that these advocates will, when possible, witness to eschatological communion through their personal actions. Jeremy Law sums up Moltmann in a manner that echoes this point: "Christian anticipation concerns the construction of representations of what is to come, resistance and protest against that which contradicts the future and solidarity with those who presently suffer."[38] Whereas preservation tends to happen on the holistic level, protest tends to happen at the level of individual life forms. In Webb's words, "We should not encourage or enhance the violence in nature."[39] Advocates of cosmocentric transfiguration will avoid hunting a deer, devouring a cow, or injecting shampoo into the eyes

36. On this point, see Wennberg, *God, Humans, and Animals*, 50–51.
37. Ibid., 49.
38. Jeremy Law, "Jürgen Moltmann's Ecological Hermeneutics," in *Ecological Hermeneutics: Biblical, Historical and Theological Perspectives*, ed. David G. Horrell Cheryl Hunt, Christopher Southgate, and Francesca Stavrakopoulou (New York: T&T Clark, 2010), 236.
39. Webb, "Ecology vs. The Peaceable Kingdom," 249.

of a rabbit while at the same time protecting ecosystems in which deer are hunted and devoured and rabbits suffer.

Cosmocentric transfigurationists preserve the system without embracing its mechanisms. For such an embrace would amount to, in the words of Webb, "a kind of Nietzschean celebration of the will to power, the recognition that the weak must be sacrificed to the strong (which is precisely the opposite of the message of Christianity, as Nietzsche well knew)."[40] Instead, advocates of cosmocentric transfiguration protest death in personal witness (and, to some extent, public policy) to individuals without trying to overthrow its hold on nature as a whole. Sideris would certainly decry my position as anthropocentric wishful thinking: "The inability to resolve conflict sometimes creates a longing, especially for religiously minded individuals, for a world in which all values *can* be brought into harmony, and benefits can be realized by all beings at once."[41] I can here only acknowledge my guilt.

To summarize the tension of cosmocentric transfiguration in a pithy alliteration: advocates of eco-eschatological ethics preserve that which they protest by protecting its integrity while they protest that which they preserve by refusing to participate in predation to whatever extent possible, thus proleptically witnessing against it.

Conclusion

I have proposed practical applications of the paradigm, including concrete principles for humanity's engagement with individual sentient creatures, individual non-sentient life forms, animal species, entire ecosystems, and the cosmos at large. I contended that, at the level of the individual, it is always a violation of the good to cause

40. Ibid., 242.
41. Sideris, *Environmental Ethics*, 224.

harm or death to a life form but that such a violation, while never justifiable in the sense of being right or good, is acceptable provided that it is necessary for the attainment of an equal or greater good. At a wider level, including that of entire animal species and ecosystems, I suggested that cosmocentric transfiguration must simultaneously preserve and protect the very mechanisms of the system that they protest. The preservation occurs on the level of a "letting-be" of the natural world while the protest occurs on the level of a proleptic witness of eschatological hope via personal actions toward individual nonhuman life forms (e.g., refusing to eat meat or to hunt).

This vision of cosmocentric transfiguration respects the integrity of the natural world without embracing the mechanisms of evolution as a divinely-ordained law. It opens up a space for a gracious letting-be while acknowledging that resurrection is the in-breaking hope for nature and all the life forms therein. It promotes practices of eschatological peace from humans without calling for the construction of the kingdom within history. It thus my contention that cosmocentric transfiguration represents the best of both worlds—that is, the natural world of history and the eschatological new creation.

Conclusion

Cosmocentric Transfiguration as the "Best of Both Worlds"

This work had two major aims. First, it set out to propose a taxonomy consisting of four paradigms of eco-theological ethics in an effort to better classify the field. Second, it sought to develop constructively the paradigm of cosmocentric transfiguration in order to better represent it among the other paradigms. Having delineated the taxonomy, its paradigms, and the contours of cosmocentric transfiguration, it is now necessary to restate and evaluate my findings, offer conclusions, and suggest possible directions for further development.

Restating the Paradigms

Part I explored three paradigms of eco-theological ethics. In anthropocentric conservation, a paradigm I expounded through the work of Saint Thomas Aquinas, all human beings are essentially unique creatures of God with individual eternal teloi. The nonhuman creation constitutes a good and ordered system of resources to aid, by way of bodily sustenance and spiritual revelation, humans in history on their journey toward communion with God. Humans must learn to embrace their role, utilizing creation in a manner commensurable with their unique telos. This manner includes distributing the resources of the cosmos justly, which also intimates preserving them for future humans.

For cosmocentric conservation, the paradigm examined through the work of Thomas Berry, the uniqueness of humans is extremely qualified. For all of creation constitutes a community. This community, including the evolutionary mechanisms that facilitate its development and ongoing existence, is fully good and in no need of redemption from the natural order that demands both suffering and death. Humans must learn to embrace their identity as part of the community of creation. This embrace entails both a gracious sharing of the world with all creatures and letting the earth be itself, respecting the integrity of the natural order.

For anthropocentric transfiguration, a paradigm established by engaging certain Eastern Orthodox theologians, humans are essentially unique in dignity. They constitute the focus of divine concern. The nonhuman creation is a gift from God to all humans meant to facilitate sacramentally the relationship among humans and between humans and the divine. This cosmic function is an eternal one, rendering the whole creation necessary even in eternity as the enduring sacrament. Humans must learn to reverence the cosmos as priests, offering it back to God and thereby realizing its sacramental telos. Such a reverence mandates that utilization of the cosmos is a sacred affair and must never be subsumed into economic or political gain.

Part II explored the work of two theologians, Jürgen Moltmann and Andrew Linzey, both of whom, in different manners, highlight an often neglected fourth paradigm of eco-theological ethics: cosmocentric transfiguration. Unlike the conservationist paradigms, this view maintains that the current order of creation, while good in many ways, does not represent God's ultimate desire for the cosmos. In particular, the shadowy dimensions of evolution (e.g., suffering, predation, and death) constitute the ultimate telos of neither the earth nor any of its inhabitants. Thus those who fit in this paradigm maintain that God embraces the entire cosmos, which includes every individual creature that is yearning for God's redemptive intervention in the midst of evolutionary emergence, in the purview of God's eschatological vision. This vision entails the consummation of the cosmic community in which God invites all creatures to participate, for their own sake, in the peace and harmony of God's triune life.

Moltmann provides theological foundations for this ethics by advocating hope for an eschatological panentheism in which the Trinity and the world, including every individual creature, will interpenetrate one another in eternity. Thus every instantiation of life will experience God's eternal peace. Furthermore, this future is, on the one hand, realized concretely in the incarnation, in which Christ becomes the redeemer of evolution, and, on the other hand, cosmically inaugurated through the presence of the Spirit. Hope for this future motivates humans to witness proleptically to it in the present.

Linzey likewise provides theological foundations for cosmocentric transfiguration by appealing to the dominant view in Christian history that the cosmos is in disarray. For Linzey, all sentient creatures endure the consequences of sin, in particular suffering, and therefore long for redemption. In Christ, God reveals a willingness to suffer with and for all creatures by taking on flesh, suffering, and death. In doing so God dies the death of all sentient beings. Yet his resurrection adumbrates their eschatological resurrection and thus their freedom from the effects of sin. For Linzey, Christians who live peacefully toward individual animals, especially by engaging in vegetarianism, approximate the eschaton by way of a proleptic witness.

Having explored representatives of all of the paradigms, I was able to present their general distinctiveness. They differed fundamentally with regard to anthropology, cosmology, and eschatology. These differences elicited different understandings about what constitutes the primary unit of moral concern. Collectively, the variations yielded a very different ethics for each paradigm. Table C.1 summarizes these findings:

	Table C.1	
	The Four Paradigms in Summation	
	Anthropocentric Conservation	**Cosmocentric Conservation**
Anthropology: Central Status/ Role of Human Beings	Essentially unique moral dignity;Subject of ultimate divine concern	Enhanced dignity;Member of creation community
Cosmology: Central Status/ Role of the Nonhuman Creation	Network of good and ordered resources/gifts for human well-being	Good and ordered interconnected community of intrinsic value
Scope of the Eschatological Community	God and humanity;Angels and elements/matter	Eschatology de-emphasized in favor of current order of world and its goodness
The Primary Unit of Moral Consideration (General or Particular)	Particular humans;General nonhumans	General
Ethical Human Engagement of the Nonhuman Creation	Proper use *in via* toward uniquely human telos	Balance of a "letting be" and a reverential "living-with"
	Anthropocentric Transfiguration	**Cosmocentric Transfiguration**
Anthropology: Central Status/ Role of Human Beings	Essentially unique moral dignity;Microcosm, co-creator, and priest	Enhanced dignity;Co-creator with God and co-traveler with nonhuman creation
Cosmology: Central Status/ Role of the Nonhuman Creation	Necessary and ultimate sacrament for divine-human drama	Community *in via* toward shared eschatological telos
Scope of the Eschatological Community	The entire cosmos	The cosmos;Individual instantiations of nonhuman life
The Primary Unit of Moral Consideration (General or Particular)	Particular humans;General nonhumans	Particular

407

Ethical Human Engagement of the Nonhuman Creation	Reverential use as sacramental gift that facilitates communion with others and God	Proleptic witness of the future peace God desires

The theological tensions of the paradigms also included whether or not the nonhuman creation is, in its natural state, unambiguously good or in need of either eschatological completion or redemption. When this tension was set beside the question of the intrinsic value of the nonhuman components of the cosmos, the paradigms naturally took shape. This shape is evident in Table C.2:

Table C.2 Theological Tensions of the Paradigms			
		Why should humans take responsibility for the created order?	
		For the sake of human beings	For the sake of the cosmos and its creatures
What is the responsibility of human beings toward creation?	Preserve the goodness and order of the unfallen cosmos.	Anthropocentric conservation	Cosmocentric conservation
What is the responsibility of human beings toward creation?	Guide the fallen and/or incomplete cosmos toward its eschatological telos.	Anthropocentric transfiguration	Cosmocentric transfiguration

As these tables reveal, at the intersection of cosmology, anthropology, and eschatology, I was able to establish a new taxonomy of eco-theological that accounts for both the question of value and the question of eschatology/soteriological destiny.

Restating the Systematic Construction
of Cosmocentric Transfiguration

In dialogue with both Moltmann and Linzey and in contradistinction with advocates and defenders of the other paradigms (or central principles of those paradigms), I have suggested the form a developed and systematic eco-theological ethics of cosmocentric transfiguration might take. This paradigm refuses to accept suffering, predation, and death as good. It thus seeks to affirm the life of every individual animal and plant. It also seeks the well-being of inanimate nature. It traces the etiology of the darker mechanisms of evolution—along with the cosmic laws that render these mechanisms necessary—to the unique space, time, and integrity allotted to creation by God. The fall is a symbol for the creation's straying in isolation at the other end of the consecratory distance that was necessary for the possibility of communion in otherness.

Thus, God has not directly willed mechanisms of evolutionary emergence such as suffering, predation, and death. Nor are these mechanisms the result of an angelic or human fall. God has willed the creation's consecratory distance for the sake of communion, not its isolation. Thus God's ultimate will, most evident in the Christ-event, is that these dimensions of transient existence entailed by the distance of isolation should ultimately be healed in transfiguration, the path to which is opened anew in Christ and maintained by the Spirit. Every single individual life and speck of matter will at the resurrection be brought into communion with God's own triune life and there experience eternity in a manner consistent with its transfigured reality.

This eschatological hope is proleptically present in history through the power of the Spirit when humans witness to it in their engagements with the nonhuman creation. This presence remains only a witness of eschatological hope. Hence, humans should not expect to construct through their Spirit-empowered efforts Isaiah's vision of the peaceable kingdom. Such a vision requires the transfiguration of the entire cosmos, including its laws. However, the proleptic witness of humans is nonetheless a symbol or sacrament of eschatological hope within history. Thus, while humans should not seek to overturn nature with any sort of finality, neither should they celebrate and embrace the darker mechanisms of evolutionary emergence.

The proper disposition of humanity toward suffering, death, and predation is one of simultaneous preservation and protest. Preservation entails the conservation of the systems that make life possible, which means protecting the balance of life and death in the world. Protest entails the refusal to participate in the darker mechanisms of evolution except when such participation is necessary to procure some equal or greater good. But even in these instances, protest mandates an oxymoronic virtuous violation of the good in which one participates in suffering, predation, and death only and always with penitence and sorrow.

Conclusions Based on Findings

Having restated the findings of this project, I will here offer my conclusions. First, I will evaluate my proposed taxonomy. Second, I will evaluate my systematic construction of cosmocentric transfiguration.

Evaluation of the New Taxonomy

As noted in the introduction, other taxonomies of eco-theological ethics tend to use a singular focus (e.g., value, salvation, geographical locale, etc.) to classify various voices in the field. These approaches, in their singularity, often overlook central tensions in eco-theological thought. An emphasis on value alone does not account for the variety of eschatological and soteriological views. An emphasis on salvation alone does not account for the value creatures have within the cosmos. Has my taxonomy addressed these issues?

No taxonomy can be without remainder. For this reason, no taxonomy should claim to be exhaustive or exact. These acknowledgements notwithstanding, it is my judgment that my multi-leveled focus on the theological loci of cosmology, anthropology, and eschatology and the dual emphasis on value and eschatological hope that these theological loci elicit provide a better taxonomy to classify eco-theological ethics than other approaches. It combines the strengths of other taxonomies and therefore creates larger and more nuanced categories for the field. It furthermore gathers eco-theology and animal theology under a larger umbrella of nonhuman ethics—thus revealing the divide between these schools of thought to be an "in house" dispute. For these reasons, I consider the proposed taxonomy successful and believe it is a viable method for clarifying dialogue within the diverse field of nonhuman theology and ethics.

Evaluation of Cosmocentric Transfiguration

The systematic proposal eveloped in chapter 4, though heavily dependent on both Moltmann and Linzey, is my own thought experiment. As such, I make no claim that either thinker would wholly—or mostly—identify with my constructive and admittedly speculative work. Even so, I believe my proposal alleviates some of the inconsistencies evident in both Moltmann and Linzey's work. It draws heavily on Moltmann's theology but is far more consistent in following that theology to its logical conclusion with regard to ethics. This ethics is similar to that of Linzey, but built upon a more thoroughly explored theological foundation followed by a more detailed and consistent consideration of the non-sentient creation, including species, ecosystems, and the general system of evolutionary emergence.

How does my construction of cosmocentric transfiguration fare vis-à-vis the other paradigms? In my judgment, none of the paradigms—including my constructive work—is without issue. However, I believe cosmocentric transfiguration, as I have delineated it, provides a consistent vision of ecological ethics that is commensurable with both science and theology.

It is consistent with science because it does not deny or downplay the troubling mechanisms inherent in evolutionary emergence. Nor does it claim these mechanisms can be ultimately overthrown within history by human effort—even when that effort is aided by grace. Furthermore, it reflects the challenges to anthropocentrism entailed in scientific thought.

It is commensurable with theology because it refuses to ignore the eschatological slant of Christian thought within history. It does not sanctify what is simply because it is. It does not deny the hope of transfiguration because it challenges present biological realities. It does not limit God's desire of the cosmos to the laws of nature. These laws will be overturned and their victims resurrected to eternal life. Thus, cosmocentric transfiguration provides stronger responses to the problem of evil than its conservationist counterparts.

Ultimately, I maintain that cosmocentric transfiguration represents the "best of both worlds" by providing grounds both to preserve the scientifically revealed realities of nature and to protest those realities (i.e., suffering, predation, and death) by way of proleptic witness. It is inclusive of all creation, extending even to non-sentient life and inanimate matter. It is inclusive of all time, ignoring neither the present realities of nature nor the eschatological possibilities of its future.

Where to Go from Here?

Certainly, further work needs to be done in order to assess more accurately the validity of this paradigm as I have delineated it. It is my hope that such work will constitute the subject of future writings. My recommendation for further research along these lines is five-fold.

First, it is pertinent to explore the congruency of cosmocentric transfiguration with the history of Christian thought. This exploration entails two key endeavors. On the one hand, work should be done with regard to the paradigm's viability vis-à-vis Christian Scripture. Such a task might take the form of exegeting passages that challenge anthropocentrism in favor of cosmocentrism and evince an eschatological hope for transfiguration. It might also take the form of seeking to identify something along the lines of Rosemary Radford Ruether's "prophetic principle," which could provide a hermeneutical key for seeing the propriety of cosmocentric transfiguration in salvation history.

On the other hand, more work needs to be done in relation to the great theologians of church history. There should be engagements with voices like Augustine and Aquinas that explore the extent to which they can, through critical retrieval, support an eco-theological ethics of cosmocentric transfiguration. Likewise, scholars should examine the great voices of Eastern thought like Irenaeus and the Cappadocian Fathers who already evince cosmic visions of transfiguration. Less prominent voices should also be explored for their potential support of this ethics—for instance voices from mysticism such as Julian of Norwich. Lastly, a great deal of work is yet to be done on the lives of saints and the theological and ethical significance of their relationships to nature, which often included transfigurative dimensions.

Second, it will be obvious that I have emphasized theology more so than science in this project. More detailed examinations are needed with regard to the viability of practices of proleptic witness (e.g., vegetarianism, refusing to hunt, and the cessation of animal experimentation) in the face of the realities of biological existence. If cosmocentric transfiguration is indeed a balance of preservation and protest, it cannot be blind to these realities, especially in situations where the very protest against death could lead to death on a larger scale by unduly disrupting natural systems. At the same time, however, protest does entail that humans ought not to use the necessity of preservation as a license to revel in the ways of nature. Scientific research should be done by scientists who remain agnostic about the goodness of the realities of biological existence with a specific eye to the extent to which human violence against the nonhuman world, both domesticated and non-domesticated, is truly necessary for the well-being of the cosmos.

Third, and in line with my second recommendation, further consideration needs to be given to the distinction between domesticated and non-domesticated (i.e., wild or free) nature.[1] How might the balance between preservation and protest apply in these

---

1. For a good start, see David Clough, *On Animals* (New York: Bloomsbury, 2014), 163–66.

different situations? These considerations ought to take the form of general inquiries and specific case studies.

With regard to non-domesticated nature, are practices such as hunting, fishing, and trapping truly necessary in most cases to procure some good that is equal to or greater than the violation of the nonhuman creature's eschatological telos? If so, how ought humans to violate this good virtuously? What reforms might be made in cases of a necessary violation of the good in order to protect the dignity of the creatures involved? It is also important to explore what cosmocentric transfiguration might have to say about human intervention in nature. Should stewards of wildlife preserves let animals suffer and die if the causes are natural? Or, is it possible to witness to eschatological hope in these cases without disrupting natural cycles?

With regard to domesticated animals, what forms might proleptic witness take? What would it look like with regard to farming? Surely factory farming would be problematic. But what about other methods of farming? Is there ever a situation in which it is necessary—in the sense described in chapter 4—to eat veal? If not, do protest and proleptic witness suggest that Christians ought to refuse to buy food from farms that participate in the selling of such meats? In addition to practices of farming, work could be done on pet-keeping from the perspective of cosmocentric transfiguration. Also, case studies about what significance the underlying principles of the paradigm might hold for zoos would be beneficial.

Fourth, further work needs to be done with regard to the viability of proportionalism and virtue vis-à-vis cosmocentric transfiguration. In chapter 4, my work scratched the surface of what ultimately remains a much larger issue that ought to constitute a separate work. In addition, this exploration must consider the appropriateness of the claim that there are inevitable and necessary evils and that one can commit these evils virtuously.

Finally, the paradigm of cosmocentric transfiguration itself requires more careful theological scrutiny. While I believe it is internally consistent, parts of it certainly require further development. In particular, more work could be done with regard to the claim that the big bang is the beginning of creation's wandering in isolation. Is such a claim convincing? How might such a claim affect theology proper? Issues such as this should be the subject of critical engagement with the paradigm.

The Final Analysis (In *this* Book)

There are real and stark differences among eco-theologians in the areas of cosmology, anthropology, and eschatology. It is my hope that identifying and classifying these differences will open spaces for better defined (and perhaps new) conversations within the field. Even if scholars do not agree on my classifications of particular thinkers, at the very least the act of classifying can facilitate a dialogue. In addition, other thinkers can consider their own thought with reference to this new taxonomy—or at least with reference to the issues it draws to the surface.

While there is still plenty of work to be done, I hope that my constructive proposal of cosmocentric transfiguration will further solidify its place at the table of discussion in eco-theological ethics. It is my view that this line of thinking has been under-represented and under-engaged in the field. Should such actually be the case, I hope this work, in conjunction with that of thinkers like Moltmann and Linzey, contributes to changing this dearth.

Finally, I hope this work is able to facilitate conversations among those who are comfortable with the classification of cosmocentric transfiguration regarding possible tensions within the paradigm itself. Such conversations will aid the development of the paradigm, particularly with regard to theological issues like the doctrine of God, the fall, and eschatology. It will furthermore highlight issues of the moral framework of this ethics, including whether proportionalism is an appropriate system for the paradigm.

Here I wish to end this project with a quote that captures in its simplicity the heart of cosmocentric transfiguration. It is offered by the great Albert Schweitzer. His work, though largely absent in this project, has nonetheless been influential on my thinking for many years.

"If I save an insect from a puddle, life has devoted itself to life, and the division of life against itself is ended."[2]

---

2. Albert Schweitzer, *Civilization and Ethics*, trans. Charles Thomas Campion, third edition (London: A & C Black, 1946), 246.

Bibliography

Aquinas, Thomas. *Summa Theologica*. Trans. Fathers of the English Domincan Province. Benzinger Brother, 1947.

_____. *Summa Contra Gentiles*. Ed. Joseph Kenny. New York: Hanover House, 1955–57.

Armstrong Susan J. and Richard G. Botzler. *Environmental Ethics: Divergence and Convergence*. Third Edition. New York: McGraw Hill, 2003.

Augustine. *The City of God*. The Fathers of the Church. Volumes 8, 14, and 24. Trans. Demetrius B. Zema, Gerald G. Walsh, Grace Monahan, and Daniel Honan. New York: The Fathers of the Church Inc, 1950–1954.

_____. *Eighty-Three Different Questions*. Trans. David L. Mosher. Washington, DC: The Catholic University of America Press, 1982.

Barad, Judith. *Aquinas on the Nature and Treatment of Animals*. San Francisco: International Scholars Publication, 1995.

Barth, Karl. *Church Dogmatics*. III/1. Ed. G. W. Bromiley and T. F. Torrance. Edinburgh: T&T Clark, 1958.

_____. *Church Dogmatics*. IV/3/2. Trans. G. W. Bromiley. Edinburgh: T&T Clark, 1962.

Bauckham, Richard. *Bible and Ecology: Rediscovering the Community of Creation*. Waco, TX: Baylor University Press, 2010.

_____. "Eschatology in *The Coming of God.*" In *God Will Be All in All: The Eschatology of Jürgen Moltmann.* Ed. Richard Bauckham. Minneapolis, MN: Fortress Press, 2001: 1–34.

_____. Editor. *God Will Be All in All: The Eschatology of Jürgen Moltmann.* Minneapolis, MN: Fortress Press, 2001.

_____. "Jesus and Animals I: What did he Teach?" *Animals on the Agenda: Questions about Animal Ethics for Theology and Ethics.* Ed. Andrew Linzey and Dorothy Yamamoto. Chicago: University of Illinois Press, 1998: 33–48.

_____. "Jesus and Animals II: What did he Practice?" *Animals on the Agenda: Questions about Animal Ethics for Theology and Ethics.* Ed. Andrew Linzey and Dorothy Yamamoto. Chicago: University of Illinois Press, 1998: 49–60.

_____. *Moltmann: Messianic Theology in the Making.* Basingstoke, UK: Marshall Pickering, 1987.

_____. *The Theology of Jürgen Moltmann.* New York: T & T Clark, 1995.

Beck, T. David. *The Holy Spirit and the Renewal of All Things: Pneumatology in Paul and Jürgen Moltmann.* Eugene, OR: Pickwick Publications, 2007.

Bekoff, Marc and Carron A. Meaney. Editors. *Encyclopedia of Animal Rights and Animal Welfare.* Westport, CT: Greenwood Press, 1998.

Benzoni, Francisco J. *Ecological Ethics and the Human Soul: Aquinas, Whitehead, and the Metaphysics of Value.* Notre Dame, IN: University of Notre Dame Press, 2007.

Berkman, John. "Towards a Thomistic Theology of Animality." *Creaturely Theology, Creaturely Theology: On God, Humans and Other Animals.* Ed. Celia Deane-Drummond and David Clough. London: SCM Press, 2009: 21–40.

Berry, R. J. Editor. *The Care of Creation: Focusing Concern and Action.* Downers Grove, IL: Intervarsity Press, 2000.

Berry, Thomas. *Befriending the Earth: A Theology of Reconciliation between Humans and the Earth*. Mystic, CT: Twenty-Third Publications, 1991.

_____. *The Christian Future and the Fate of the Earth*. Ed. Mary Evelyn Tucker and John Grim. Maryknoll, NY: Orbis Books, 2011.

_____. "Every Being Has Rights." Available online at http://www.gaiafoundation.org/ sites/default/files/documents/ Berry%20-%20Every%20Being%20has%20Rights.pdf; Internet, accessed January 2012.

_____. *The Great Work: Our Way into the Future*. New York: Bell Tower, 1999.

_____. *The Dream of the Earth*. San Francisco: Sierra Club Books, 1990.

_____. *The Sacred Universe: Faith, Spirituality, and Religion in the Twenty-First Century*. Ed. Mary Evelyn Tucker. New York: Columbia University Press, 2009.

Berry, Wendell. *The Gift of Good Land: Further Essays Cultural and Agricultural*. San Francisco: North Point Press, 1981.

Birch, Charles. "Christian Obligation for the Liberation of Nature." In *Liberating Life; Contemporary Approaches to Ecological Theology*. Ed. Charles Birch, William Eakin, and Jay McDaniel. Maryknoll, NY: Orbis Books, 1991.

Boff, Leonardo. *Cry of the Earth, Cry of the Poor*. Trans. Phillip Berryman. Maryknoll, NY: Orbis Books, 1997.

_____. *Ecology and Liberation: A New Paradigm*. Trans. John Cumming. Maryknoll, NY: Orbis Books, 1995 (original Portuguese 1993).

Bordeianu, Radu. "Maximus and Ecology: The Relevance of Maximus the Confessor's Theology of Creation for the Present Ecological Crisis." *Downside Review* 127, no. 447 (2009): 103–126.

_____. "Priesthood Natural, Universal, and Ordained: Dumitru Staniloae's Communion Ecclesiology." *Pro Ecclesia* 19, no. 4 (2010): 405–433.

Borowitz, Eugene B. *Contemporary Christologies: A Jewish Response*. New York: Paulist Press, 1980.

Bouma-Prediger, Steven. *The Greening of Theology: The ecological Models of Rosemary Radford Ruether, Joseph Sittler, and Jürgen Moltmann*. Atlanta: Scholars Press, 1995.

Brueggemann, Walter. *Genesis*. Atlanta: John Knox, 1982.

Brunner, Emil. *Dogmatics II: The Christian Doctrine of Creation and Redemption*. Trans. Olive Wyon. Philadelphia, PA: Westminster Press, 1952.

Castelo, Daniel. "Moltmann's Dismissal of Divine Impassibility: Warranted?" *The Scottish Journal of Theology* 61/4 (2008): 396–407.

The Catechism of the Catholic Church: With Modifications from the Editio Typica. New York: Doubleday, 1995.

Chester, Tim. *Mission and the Coming of God: Eschatology, the Trinity and Mission in the Theology of Jürgen Moltmann and Contemporary Evangelicalism*. Eugene, OR: Wipf & Stock Publishers, 2006.

Chryssavgis, John. "The Earth as Sacrament: Insights from Orthodox Christian Theology and Spirituality." In *The Orthodox Handbook of Religion and Ecology*. Roger S. Gottlieb, Ed. New York: Oxford University Press, 2006: 92–114.

Clark, Gillian. "The Fathers and the Animals: The Rule of Reason?" *Animals on the Agenda: Questions about Animal Ethics for Theology and Ethics*. Ed. Andrew Linzey and Dorothy Yamamoto. Chicago: University of Illinois Press, 1998), 67–79.

Clifford, Anne M. "Creation." In *Systematic Theology: Roman Catholic Perspectives*. Ed. Francis Schüssler Fiorenza and John P. Galvin. Minneapolis, MN: Fortress Press, 2011, 201–254.

_____. "Foundations for A Catholic Ecological Theology of God." *"And God Saw That It Was Good": Catholic Theology and the Environment*. Ed.

Drew Christiansen and Walter Grazer. Washington, DC: United States Catholic Conference, 1996, 19–46.

Cobb Jr., John B. and David Ray Griffin. *Process Theology: An Introductory Exposition.* Philadelphia: The Westminster Press, 1976.

Cowdin, Daniel. "The Moral Status of Otherkind in Christian Ethics." In *Christianity and Ecology: Seeking the Well-Being of Earth and Humans.* Ed. Dieter T. Hessel and Rosemary Radford Ruether. Cambridge, MA: Harvard University Press, 2000, 261–316.

Creegan, Hoggard. "Being an Animal and Being Made in the Image of God." *Colloqium* 39/2 (November 2007): 185–203.

Cullman, Oscar. *The Resurrection of the Dead or the Immortality of the Soul?: The Witness of the New Testament.* Eugene, OR: Wipf & Stock Publishers, 2010.

Cunningham, Mary Kathleen, ed. *God and Evolution: A Reader.* New York: Routledge, 2007.

Deane-Drummond, Celia. "Are Animals Moral? Taking Soundings through Vice, Virtue, Conscience and *Imago Dei.*" *Creaturely Theology, Creaturely Theology: On God, Humans and Other Animals.* Ed. Celia Deane-Drummond and David Clough. London: SCM Press, 2009: 190–210.

———. *Christ and Evolution: Wonder and Wisdom.* Minneapolis, MN: Fortress Press, 2009.

———. *Eco-Theology.* Winona, MN: Anselm Academic, 2008.

DeCrane, Susanne M. *Aquinas, Feminism, and the Common Good.* Washington, DC: Georgetown University Press, 2004.

Deffenbaugh, Daniel G. "Toward Thinking Like a Mountain: The Evolution of an Ecological Conscience." *Soundings* 78/2 (Summer 1995): 229–61.

Derrida, Jacques. "The Animal That Therefore I Am." Printed in *The Animal That Therefore I Am.* Trans. David Wills. Ed. Marie-Louise Mallet. New York: Fordham University Press, 2008.

DeWeese, Garrett J. *God and the Nature of Time*. Burlington, VT: Ashgate, 2004.

DeWitt, Calvin. *Earthwise: A Guide to Hopeful Creation Care*. Third Edition. Grand Rapids, MI: Faith Alive Christian Resources, 2011.

Edwards, Denis. "Every Sparrow that Falls to the Ground: The Cost of Evolution and the Christ-Event." *Ecotheology* 11/1 (2006): 103–23.

Ellard, Peter. "Thomas Berry as the Groundwork for a Dark Green Catholic Theology." *Confronting the Climate Crisis: Catholic Theological Perspectives*. Ed. Jame Schaefer. Milwaukee, WI: Marquette University Press, 2011, 301–20.

Ephrem the Syrian. *Commentary on Genesis*. The Fathers of the Church. Volume 91. Trans. Edward G. Mathews and Joseph P. Amar. Ed. Kathleen McVey. Washington, DC: Catholic University of America Press, 1994.

_____. *Hymns on Paradise*. Trans. Sebastian Brock. Crestwood, NY: St Vladimir's Press, 1990.

Erickson, Millard. *Christian Theology*. Second Edition. Grand Rapids, MI: Baker Books, 1998.

Fergusson, David. "Creation." In *The Oxford Handbook of Systematic Theology*. Ed. John Webster, Kathryn Tanner, and Iain Torrance. New York: Oxford University Press, 2007, 72–90.

Fellenz, Marc R. *The Moral Menagerie: Philosophy and Animal Rights*. Chicago: University of Illinois Press, 2007.

Fox, Matthew. *Creation Spirituality: Liberating Gifts for the Peoples of the Earth*. San Francisco: HarperCollins, 1991.

French, William. "Beast Machines and the Technocratic Reduction of Life." In *Good News for Animals? Christian Approaches to Animal Well-Being*. Ed. Charles Pinches and Jay B. McDaniel. New York: Orbis Books, 1993: 24–43.

_____. "Catholicism and the Common Good." In *An Ecology of the Spirit*. Ed. Michael Barnes. Lanham, MD: University Press of America Press, 1993: 177–194.

_____. "Returning to Creation: Moltmann's Eschatology Naturalized." *The Journal of Religion* 68/1 (1988): 178–81.

_____. "Subject-centered and Creation-centered Paradigms in Recent Catholic Thought." *The Journal of Religion* 70/1 (January 1990): 48–72.

Fretheim, Terrance. *God and World in the Old Testament: A Relational Theology of Creation*. Nashville, TN: Abingdon Press, 2005.

Grenz, Stanley J. and Roger E. Olson. *20th Century Theology: God & the World in a Transitional Age*. Downers Grove, IL: Intervarsity Press, 1992.

Grenz, Stanely. *The Social God and the Relational Self: A Trinitarian Theology of the Imago Dei*. Louisville, KY: Westminster John Knox Press, 2001.

Griffin, David Ray. *God, Power, and Evil*. Louisville: Westminster John Knox Press, 2004.

Gunton, Colin E. "Between Allegory and Myth: The Legacy of the Spiritualising of Genesis." In *The Doctrine of Creation: Essays in Dogmatics, History and Philosophy*. Ed. Colin E. Gunton. New York: T&T Clark International, 2004, 47–62.

Gustafson, James M. *A Sense of the Divine: The Natural Environment from a Theocentric Perspective*. Cleveland, OH: The Pilgrim Press, 1996.

_____. *Ethics from a Theocentric Perspective*. 2 volumes. Chicago: University of Chicago Press, 1981.

Guthrie, Shirley C. *Christian Doctrine*. Revised Edition. Louisville, KY: John Knox Press, 1994.

Hall, Douglas John. *Imaging God: Dominion as Stewardship*. Eugene, OR: Wipf and Stock Publishers, 1986 (Second Printing, 2004).

Hanson, Bradley C. *Introduction to Christian Theology*. Minneapolis, MN: Fortress Press, 1997.

Hart, Trevor. "Imagination for the Kingdom of God? Hope, Promise, and the Transformative Power of an Imagined Future." In *God Will Be All in All: The Eschatology of Jürgen Moltmann*. Ed. Richard Bauckham. Minneapolis, MN: Fortress Press, 2001: 61–76.

Harvie, Timothy. *Jürgen Moltmann's Ethics of Hope: Eschatological Possibilities for Moral Action*. Burlington, VT: Ashgate, 2009.

Hauerwas, Stanley and John Berkman. "A Trinitarian Theology of the 'Chief End' of 'All Flesh.'" In *Good News for Animals? Christian Approaches to Animal Well-Being*, Ed. Charles Pinches and Jay B. McDaniel. New York: Orbis Books, 1993: 62–74.

Haught, John F. *God after Darwin: A Theology of Evolution*. Second Edition. Washington, DC: Georgetown University Press, 2008.

_____. *The Promise of Nature*. Mahwah, NJ: Paulist Press, 1993.

Hauskeller, Michael. *Biotechnology and the Integrity of Life: Taking Public Fears Seriously*. Burlington, VT: Ashgate, 2007.

Healy, Nicholas J. *The Eschatology of Hans Urs von Balthasar: Being as Communion*. New York: Oxford University Press, 2005.

Hick, John. "An Irenaean Theodicy." In *Encountering Evil: Live Options in Theodicy*. Ed. Stephen T. Davis. Westminster John Knox, 2001: 29–52.

Hollenbach, David. *The Common Good and Christian Ethics* (New York: Cambridge University Press, 2002

Holt, Sally Smith. "A Review of Andrew Linzey's *Animal Theology* from a Theological Perspective." *Review and Expositor*, 102 (Winter 2005): 101–9.

Horrell, David G. Cherryl Hunt, Christopher Southgate and Francesca Stavrakopoulou, eds. *Ecological Hermeneutics: Biblical, Historical and Theological Perspectives*. New York: T & T Clark, 2010.

Hull, David L. "God of the Galapagos." *Nature* 352 (August 1992): 485–486.

Irenaeus of Lyons. *Irenaeus: Against Heresies.* Ante-Nicene Fathers. Volume 1. Ed. Alexander Roberts and James Donaldson. Grand Rapids, MI: Eerdmans, 1996.

Jenkins, Willis. *Ecologies of Grace: Environmental Ethics and Christian Theology.* New York: Oxford University Press, 2008.

Johnson, Elizabeth A. "Losing and Finding Creation in the Christian Tradition." In *Christianity and Ecology: Seeking the Well-Being of Earth and Humans.* Ed. Dieter T. Hessel and Rosemary Radford Ruether. Cambridge, MA: Harvard University Press, 2000: 3–22.

Karkkainen, Veli-Matti. *An Introduction to Ecclesiology: Ecumenical, Historical and Global Perspectives.* Downers Grove, IL: Intervarsity Press, 2002.

Kelly, David F. *Contemporary Catholic Health Care Ethics.* Washington, DC: Georgetown University Press, 2004.

Kemmerer, Lisa. *In Search of Consistency: Ethics and Animals.* Boston: Brill, 2006.

Kent, Bonnie. "Habits and Virtues (Ia IIae, qq. 49–70)." In *The Ethics of Aquinas.* Ed. Stephen J. Pope. Washington, DC: Georgetown University Press, 2002): 116–30.

Khalil, Issa J. "The Orthodox Fast and the Philosophy of Vegetarianism." *Greek Orthodox Theological Review* 35, 3 (1990): 237–259.

Kinsley, David. *Ecology and Religion: Ecological Spirituality in Cross-Cultural Perspective.* Upper Saddle River, NJ: Prentice Hall, 1995.

Law, Jerry. "Jürgen Moltmann's Ecological Hermeneutics." *Ecological Hermeneutics: Biblical, Historical and Theological Perspectives.* Ed. David G. Horrell, Cherryl Hunt, Christopher Southgate and Francesca Stavrakopoulou. New York: T & T Clark, 2010: 223–239.

Leopold, Aldo. *A Sand County Almanac—and Sketches Here and There.* New York: Oxford University Press, 1987.

Lewis, C. S. *The Problem of Pain.* New York: Macmillan Publishing Company, 1962.

Linzey, Andrew. *After Noah: Animals and the Liberation of Theology.* Herndon, VA: Mowbray, 1997.

———. *Animal Gospel.* Louisville, KY: Westminster John Knox Press, 2000.

———. *Animal Rights: A Christian Assessment.* London: SCM Press, 1976.

———. *Animal Theology.* Chicago: University of Illinois Press, 1994.

———. "C. S. Lewis's Theology of Animals." *Anglican Theological Review* 80/1 (Winter 1998): 60–81.

———. *Creatures of the Same God: Explorations in Animal Theology.* New York: Lantern Books, 2009.

———. *Christianity and the Rights of Animals.* New York: Crossroad, 1987.

———. "The Divine Worth of Other Creatures: A Response to Reviews of *Animal Theology.*" *Review and Expositor*, 102 (Winter 2005): 111–124.

———. *Why Animal Suffering Matters: Philosophy, Theology, and Practical Ethics.* New York: Oxford University Press, 2009.

Linzey, Andrew and Dorothy Yamamoto, eds. *Animals on the Agenda: Questions about Animal Ethics for Theology and Ethics.* Chicago: University of Illinois Press, 1998.

Linzey, Andrew and Tom Regan, eds. *Animals and Christianity: A Book of Readings.* Eugene, OR: Wipf and Stock, 1990.

Lossky, Vladimir. *The Mystical Theology of the Eastern Church.* Crestwood, NY: St. Vladimir's Press, 1976 (original published 1944).

Louth, Andrew. "Between Creation and Transfiguration: The Environment in the Eastern Orthodox Tradition." *Ecological Hermeneutics: Biblical, Historical and Theological Perspectives.* Ed. David G. Horrell, Cherryl Hunt, Christopher Southgate and Francesca Stavrakopoulou. New York: T & T Clark, 2010: 211–222.

———. *Maximus the Confessor.* New York: Routledge, 1996.

_____. "Eastern Orthodox Eschatology." In *The Orthodox Handbook of Eschatology*. Ed. Jerry L. Walls. New York: Oxford University Press, 2008: 233–247.

Ludlow, Morwenna. "Power and Dominion: Patristic Interpretations of Genesis 1." *Ecological Hermeneutics: Biblical, Historical and Theological Perspectives*. Ed. David G. Horrell, Cherryl Hunt, Christopher Southgate and Francesca Stavrakopoulou. New York: T & T Clark, 2010: 140–153.

MacIntyre, Alasdair. *After Virtue: A Study in Moral Theory*. Third Edition. University of Notre Dame Press, 2007.

Maximus the Confessor. *On the Cosmic Mystery of Jesus Christ*. Trans. Paul M. Blowers and Robert L. Welken. Crestwood, NY: St. Vladimir's Seminary Press, 2003.

_____. *Selected Writings*. The Classics of Western Spirituality. Mahwah, NJ: Paulist Press, 1988.

May, David M. "A Review of Andrew Linzey's *Animal Theology* from a New Testament Perspective." *Review and Expositor*, 102 (Winter 2005): 87–93.

McDougal, Dorothy. *The Cosmos as the Primary Sacrament: The Horizon for an Ecological Sacramental Theology*. New York: Peter Lang, 2003.

McDougall, Joy Ann. *Pilgrim of Love: Moltmann on the Trinity and Christian Life*. New York: Oxford University Press, 2005.

McEntire, Mark. "A Review of Andrew Linzey's *Animal Theology* from an Old Testament Perspective." *Review and Expositor*, 102 (Winter 2005): 95–99.

McFague, Sally. *The Body of God: An Ecological Theology*. Minneapolis, MN: Fortress Press, 1993.

McLaughlin, Ryan Patrick. *Christianity and the Status of Animals*. New York: Palgrave Macmillan, 2014.

Messer, Neil. "Humans, Animals, Evolution and Ends." In *Creaturely Theology: On God, Humans and Other Animals*. Ed. Celia Deane-Drummond and David Clough. London: SCM Press, 2009: 211–27.

Meyendorff, John. "Creation in the History of Orthodox Theology." *St. Vladimir's Theology Quarterly*, 27/1 (1983): 27–37.

_____. "Reply to Jürgen Moltmann's 'The Unity of the Triune God." *St. Vladimir's Theological Quarterly* 28/3 (1984): 183–188.

Meyendorff, John. *Byzantine Theology: Historical Trends*. New York: Fordham University Press, 1974.

_____. *Christ in Eastern Christian Thought*. Washington, DC: Corpus Books, 1969.

Mickey, Sam. "Contributions to Anthropocosmic Environmental Ethics." *Worldviews* 11 (2007): 226–47.

Middleton, J. Richard. "Created in the Image of Violent God? The Ethical Problem of the Conquest of Chaos in Biblical Creation Narratives." *Interpretation* 58/4 (October 2004): 341–55.

_____. *The Liberating Image: The* Imago Dei *in Genesis 1*. Grand Rapids, MI: Brazos Press, 2005.

Moltmann, Jürgen. *The Church in the Power in the Spirit: A Contribution to Messianic Ecclesiology*. Trans. Margaret Kohl. Minneapolis, MN: Fortress Press, 1993.

_____. *The Coming of God: Christian Eschatology*. Trans. Margaret Kohl. Minneapolis, MN: Fortress Press, 1996.

_____. *The Crucified God: The Cross of Christ as the Foundation and Criticism of Christian Theology*. Trans. R. A. Wilson. Minneapolis, MN: Fortress Press, 1993.

_____. *God for a Secular Society: The Public Relevance of Theology*. Trans. Margaret Kohl. Minneapolis, MN: Fortress Press, 1999.

_____. *God in Creation: A New Theology of Creation and the Spirit of God*. Trans. Margaret Kohl. Minneapolis, MN: Fortress Press, 1993.

_____. "God's Covenant and Our Responsibility." In *The Care of Creation: Focusing Concern and Action*. Ed. R. J. Berry. Downers Grove, IL: Intervarsity Press, 2000: 107–13.

_____. "God's Kenosis in the Creation and Consummation of the World," In *God and Evolution: A Reader*. Ed. Mary Kathleen Cunningham. New York: Routledge, 2007.

_____. "Horizons of Hope." *The Christian Century*. May 20 (2009): 31–33.

_____. *In the End, the Beginning: A Life of Hope*. Trans. Margaret Kohl. Minneapolism MN: Fortress Press, 2004.

_____. *Sun of Righteousness, Arise! God's Future for Humanity and the Earth*. Trans. Margaret Kohl. Minneapolis, MN: Fortress Press, 2010.

_____. "The Bible, the Exegete and the Theologian." In *God Will Be All in All: The Eschatology of Jürgen Moltmann*. Ed. Richard Bauckham. Minneapolis, MN: Fortress Press, 2001: 227–32.

_____. "The Liberation of the Future and Its Anticipations in History." In *God Will Be All in All: The Eschatology of Jürgen Moltmann*. Ed. Richard Bauckham. Minneapolis, MN: Fortress Press, 2001: 265–89.

_____. "The Logic of Hell." In *God Will Be All in All: The Eschatology of Jürgen Moltmann*. Ed. Richard Bauckham. Minneapolis, MN: Fortress Press, 2001: 43–47.

_____. *The Spirit of Life: A Universal Affirmation*. Trans. Margaret Kohl. Minneapolis, MN: Fortress Press, 1992.

_____. *Theology of Hope: On the Ground and Implications of Christian Eschatology*. Trans. James W. Leitch. London: SCM Press, 1967.

_____. *The Trinity and the Kingdom: The Doctrine of God*. Trans. Margaret Kohl. Minneapolis, MN: Fortress Press, 1993.

_____. *The Way of Jesus Christ: Christology in Messianic Dimensions*. Trans. Margaret Kohl. Minneapolis, MN: Fortress Press, 1990 (original German 1989).

_____. "The World in God or God in the Wolrd?" In *God Will Be All in All: The Eschatology of Jürgen Moltmann*. Ed. Richard Bauckham. Minneapolis, MN: Fortress Press, 2001: 35–41.

Müller-Fahrenholz, Geiko. *The Kingdom and the Power: The Theology of Jürgen Moltmann*. Trans. John Bowden. Minneapolis, MN: Fortress Press, 2001.

Munteanu, Daniel. "Cosmic Liturgy: The Theological Dignity of Creation as a Basis of an Orthodox Ecotheology." *International Journal of Public Theology* 4 (2010): 332–344.

Neal, Ryan A. *Theology as Hope: On the Ground and the Implications of Jürgen Moltmann's Doctrine of Hope*. Eugene, OR: Pickwick Publications, 2009.

Niebuhr, H. Richard. *Radical Monotheism and Western Culture—with Supplementary Essays*. Louisville, KY: Westminster/John Knox Press, 1970.

Northcott, Michael. *The Environment and Christian Ethics*. New York: Cambridge University Press, 1996.

Ormerod, Neil. *Creation, Grace, and Redemption*. Maryknoll, NY: Orbis Books, 2007.

Pannenberg, Wolfhart. *Systematic Theology*. Three Volumes. Trans. Geoffrey W. Bromiley. Grand Rapids, MI: William B. Eerdmans Publishing Company, 1991.

Peacocke, Arthur. *Theology for a Scientific Age: Being and Becoming—Natural, Divine and Human*. Minneapolis, MN: Fortress Press, 1993.

Pedersen, Kusumita. "Inclusion and Exclusion: Reflections on Moral Community and Salvation." In *Earth Habitat: Eco-Injustice and the Church's Response*. Ed. Dieter Hessel and Larry Rasmussen. Minneapolis, MN: Fortress Press, 2001: 33–52.

Phelps, Norm. *The Dominion of Love: Animal Rights According to the Bible*. New York: Lantern Books, 2002.

Pinckaers, Servais-Théodore. "The Sources of the Ethics of St. Thomas Aquinas." *The Ethics of Aquinas*. Ed. Stephen J. Pope. Washington, DC: Georgetown University Press, 2002: 17–29.

Polkinghorne, John. *Questions of Truth: Fifty One Responses to Questions.* Louisville, KY: Westminster John Knox, 2009.

———. "Jürgen Moltmann's Engagement with the Natural Sciences." In *God's Life in Trinity.* Ed. Miroslav Volf and Michael Welker. Minneapolis, MN: Fortress Press, 2006: 61–70.

———. *Science and Providence: God's Interaction with the World.* West Conshohocken, PA: Templeton University Press, 2005.

———. *Science and the Trinity: The Christian Encounter with Reality.* New Haven, CT: Yale University Press, 2004.

———. *Scientists as Theologians: A Comparison of the Writings of Ian Barbour, Arthur Peacocke, and John Polkinghorne.* London: SPCK, 1996.

———. "The Demise of Democritus." In *The Trinity and an Entangled World: Relationality in Physical Science and Theology.* Ed. John Polkinghorne. Grand Rapids, MI: William B. Eerdmans Publishing Company, 2010, 15–31.

———. *The God of Hope and the End of the World.* New Haven: Yale University Press, 2002.

Pope, Stephen J. "Overview of the Ethics of Thomas Aquinas." *The Ethics of Aquinas.* Ed. Stephen J. Pope. Washington, DC: Georgetown University Press, 2002: 30–53.

Rachel, James. *Created from Animals: The Moral Implications of Darwinism.* New York: Oxford University Press, 1990.

Rahner, Karl. *Foundations of Christian Faith: An Introduction to the Idea of Christianity.* Trans. William V. Dych. New York: The Crossroad Publishing Company, 1998.

———. *The Trinity.* Trans. Joseph Donceel. New York: The Crossroad Publishing Company, 2005.

Ratzinger, Joseph. *Eschatology: Death and Eternal Life.* Second Edition. Trans. Michael Waldstein. Washington, DC: The Catholic University of America Press, 1988.

Reed, Esther D. "Animals in Orthodox Iconography." *Creaturely Theology, Creaturely Theology: On God, Humans and Other Animals*. Ed. Celia Deane-Drummond and David Clough. London: SCM Press, 2009: 61–77.

Regan, Tom. *The Case for Animals Rights*. Second Edition. Berkley, CA: University of California Press, 2004.

Rolston III, Holmes. "Disvalues in Nature." *The Monist* 75 (April 1992): 250–78.

————. "Does Nature Need to be Redeemed?" *Zygon* 29 (1994): 205–229.

————. *Environmental Ethics: Duties to and Values in the Natural World*. Philadelphia, PA: Temple University Press, 1988.

————. "Naturalizing and Systematizing Evil." In *Is Nature Ever Evil? Religion, Science, and Value*. Ed. Willem B. Drees. London: Routledge, 2003: 67–86.

Ruether, Rosemary Radford. *Gaia and God: An Ecofeminist Theology of Earth Healing*. New York: HarperCollins Publishers, 1992.

————. *Sexism and God-Talk: Toward A Feminist Theology*. Boston: Beacon Press, 1983.

Ryder, Richard D. *Animal Revolution: Changing Attitudes towards Speciesism*. Cambridge, MA: Basil Blackwell, 1989.

Sanders, John. *The God Who Risks: A Theology of Providence*. Downers Grove: Intervarsity Press, 1998.

Santmire, Paul. *The Travail of Nature: The Ambiguous Ecological Promise of Christian Theology*. Minneapolis, MN: Fortress Press, 1985.

Schaefer, Jame. *Theological Foundations for Environmental Ethics: Reconstructing Patristic & Medieval Concepts*. Washington, DC: Georgetown University Press, 2009.

————. "Valuing Earth Intrinsically and Instrumentally: A Theological Framework for Environmental Ethics." *Theological Studies* 66 (2005): 783–814.

Schmemann, Alexander. *For the Life of the World: Sacraments and Orthodoxy.* Crestwood, NY: St Vladimir's Seminary Press, 1973.

Schwarz, Hans. *Eschatology.* Grand Rapids, MI: William B. Eerdmans Publishing Company, 2000.

Schweitzer, Albert. *Civilization and Ethics.* Third Edition. Trans. Charles Thomas Campion. London: A & C Black, 1946.

Sideris, Lisa H. *Environmental Ethics, Ecological Theology, and Natural Selection.* New York: Columbia University Press, 2003.

_____. "Writing Straight with Crooked Lines: Holmes Rolston's Ecological Theology and Theodicy." In *Nature, Value, Duty: Life on Earth with Holmes Rolston III.* Ed. Christopher J. Preston and Wayne Ouderkirk. Dordrecht, NL: Springer, 2007: 77–101.

Singer, Peter. *Animal Liberation: A New Ethics for Our Treatment of Animals.* New York: Avon Books, 1975.

Southgate, Christopher. *The Groaning of Creation: God, Evolution, and the Problem of Evil.* Louisville, KY: Westminster John Knox Press, 2008.

Staniloae, Dumitru. *The Experience of God: Orthodox Dogmatic Theology.* Volume 2 (The World: Creation and Deification). Ed. and Trans. Ioan Ionita and Robert Barringer. Brookline, MA: Hold Cross Orthodox Press, 2000.

Steenberg, Matthew Craig. *Irenaeus on Creation: The Cosmic Christ and the Saga of Redepmtion.* Boston: Brill, 2008.

Steiner, Gary. *Anthropocentrism and Its Discontents: The Moral Status of Animals in the History of Western Philosophy.* Pittsburgh, PA: University of Pittsburgh Press, 2005.

Swimme, Brian and Thomas Berry. *The Universe Story: From the Primordial Flashing Forth to the Ecozoic Era—A Celebration of the Unfolding of the Cosmos.* New York: HarperCollins, 1994.

Taylor, Angus. *Animals and Ethics: An Overview of the Philosophical Debate.* Third Edition. Buffalo, NY: Broadview Press, 2009.

Taylor, Paul W. *Respect for Nature: A Theory of Environmental Ethics.* Princeton, NJ: Princeton University Press, 1986.

The Worldwatch Institute. *Vital Signs 2012: The Trends That Are Shaping Our Future.* Washington, DC: Worldwatch Institute, 2012.

Theokritoff, Elizabeth. "Creator and Creation." In *The Cambridge Companion to Orthodox Christian Theology.* Ed. Mary B. Cunningham and Elizabeth Theokritoff. New York: Cambridge University Press, 2008: 63–77.

_____. *Living in God's Creation: Orthodox Perspectives on Ecology.* Crestwood, NY: St Vladimir's Seminary Press, 2009.

Theophilus of Antioch. *To Autolycus.* Ante-Nicene Christian Library. Volume 3. Trans. Marcus Dods. Ed. Alexander Roberts and James Donaldson. Edinburgh: T & T Clark, 1847.

Toolan, David. *At Home in the Cosmos.* Maryknoll, NY: Orbis Books, 2003.

Torrance, Alan J. "*Creatio Ex Nihilo* and the Spatio-Temporal Dimensions, with Special Reference to Jürgen Moltmann and D. C. Williams." In *The Doctrine of Creation: Essays in Dogmatics, History and Philosophy.* Ed. Colin E. Gunton. New York: T&T Clark, 1997: 83–103.

Towner, W. Sibley. "Clones of God: Genesis 1:26–28 and the Image of God in the Hebrew Bible." *Interpretation* 59/4 (October 2005): 341–356.

Tsirpanlis, Constantine N. *Introduction to Eastern Patristic Thought and Orthodox Theology.* Collegeville, MN: The Liturgical Press, 1991.

Tucker, Mary Evelyn. "A Communion of Subjects and a Multiplicity of Intelligences." In *A Communion of Subjects: Animals in Religion, Science, and Ethics.* Ed. Paul Waldau and Kimberly Patton. New York: Columbia University Press, 2006: 645–650.

_____. "Thomas Berry: A Brief Biography." *Religion and Intellectual Life* 5/4 (Summer 1988): 107–114.

Vivian, Tim. "The Peaceable Kingdom: Animals as Parables in the *Virtues of Saint Macarius.*" *Anglican Theological Review* 85/3 (Summer 2003): 477–491.

Viviano, Benedict T. "Eschatology and the Quest for the Historical Jesus." In *The Orthodox Handbook of Eschatology*. Ed. Jerry L. Walls. New York: Oxford University Press, 2008, 73–90.

Volf, Miroslav, Carmen Krieg, and Thomas Kucharz, eds. *The Future of Theology: Essays in Honor of Jürgen Moltmann*. Grand Rapids, MI: William B. Eerdmans Publishing Company, 1996.

Volf, Miroslav and Michael Welker, eds. *God's Life in Trinity*. Minneapolis, MN: Fortress Press, 2006.

von Balthasar, Hans Urs. *The Cosmic Liturgy: The Universe According to Maximus the Confessor*. San Francisco: Ignatius Press, 2004.

———. *The Last Act. Theo-Drama*, Volume 5. Trans. Graham Harrison. San Francisco: Ignatius Press, 1988.

Waldau, Paul. *The Specter of Speciesism: Buddhist and Christian Views of Animals*. New York: Oxford University Press, 2002.

Ware, Kallistos. *The Orthodox Way*. Revised Edition. Crestwood, NY: St. Vladimir's Seminary Press, 1995 (original 1979).

Webb, Stephen. "Ecology vs. The Peaceable Kingdom: Toward a Better Theology of Nature." *Soundings* 79/1–2 (Spring/Summer 1996): 239–52.

———. *Good Eating*. Grand Rapids, MI: Brazos Press, 2001.

Wennberg, Robert N. *God, Humans, and Animals: An Invitation to Enlarge Our Moral Universe*. Grand Rapids, MI: William B. Eerdmans Publishing Company, 2003.

Williams, Patricia. *Doing Without Adam and Eve: Sociobiology and Original Sin*. Minneapolis, MN: Fortress Press, 2001.

Wilkinson, Loren. "The Making of the *Declaration*." In *The Care of Creation: Focusing Concern and Action*, Ed. R. J. Berry. Downers Grove, IL: Intervarsity Press, 2000: 50–59.

White, Lynn. "The Historical Roots of Our Ecological Crisis." Reprinted in *The Care of Creation: Focusing Concern and Action*. Ed. R. J. Berry. Downers Grove, IL: Intervarsity Press, 2000: 31–42.

Wolde, Ellen van. *Stories of the Beginning: Genesis 1–11 and Other Creation Stories*. Ridgefield: Morehouse Publishing, 1995.

Wynn, Mark. "Thomas Aquinas: Reading the Idea of Dominion in the Light of the Doctrine of Creation." *Ecological Hermeneutics: Biblical, Historical and Theological Perspectives*. Ed. David G. Horrell, Cherryl Hunt, Christopher Southgate and Francesca Stavrakopoulou. New York: T & T Clark, 2010: 154–167.

Yamamoto, Dorothy. "Aquinas and Animals: Patrolling the Boundary?" *Animals on the Agenda: Questions about Animal Ethics for Theology and Ethics*. Ed. Andrew Linzey and Dorothy Yamamoto. Chicago: University of Illinois Press, 1998: 80–89.

Zizioulas, John. *Being as Communion: Studies in Personhood and the Church*. New York: Crestwood, 1985.

_____. "Ecological Asceticism: A Cultural Revolution." *Sourozh* 67 (Fall 1997): 22–25.

_____. "Preserving God's Creation: Parts I and II." *King's Theological Review* 12 (Spring 1989): 1–5.

_____. "Preserving God's Creation: Part III." *King's Theological Review* 13 (Spring 1990): 1–5.

Index

326–327, 339–343, 364, 377,
380, 407, 411
Towner, W. Sibley, 344
Transfiguration, 2, 3, 4, 5, 47, 54,
58, 60, 67, 68, 76, 125–126,
128–129, 130–137, 138, 143,
153, 166, 175, 185, 187,
194–195, 203, 207, 210, 213,
219, 221, 222, 227, 229, 255,
281, 299, 311, 337, 338, 339,
349, 352, 353, 356, 358, 361,
363, 364, 365, 367, 369,
371–375, 377, 378, 380,
407–408, 410, 411, 412
Trinity, 59, 131; and Creation,
169, 185, 195, 200–201, 222,
302, 319, 333, 390, 403;
Economic, 271; and History,
27, 171, 194; and the Image of
God, 43, 166–167, 172–173;
Immanent, 172; as the Model
for Community in Creation,
166–167, 183, 232, 236–239,
271; and the Monarchy of the
Father, 166; and Monotheism,
164, 166, 171, 187, 214; as
Open to Creation, *see* God and
Perichoresis; Social Doctrine
of, 163, 164–167, 186–187,
192, 214, 233, 306, 318–319,
320

Tucker, Mary Evelyn, 105n9, 106,
119

Utilitarianism, 21, 22, 30, 284, 285

Vatican II, 16
Veganism, 8, 147, 289, 395
Vegetarianism, 1, 8, 73, 122, 148,
224, 231–232, 268, 294–299,
301, 350, 369, 371, 373, 375,
376, 395, 398, 404, 412
Virtue, 21, 22, 79, 89, 90, 92, 98,
100, 102, 388–390, 413
Vivian, Tim, 354

Ward, Keith, 338
Ware, Kallistos, 20, 131–132, 135,
145, 332, 334n57, 357n43
Webb, Stephen, 375, 397n35, 398,
399
Weiss, Johannes, 46
Wennberg, Robert, 7n4, 20–21,
72, 75, 81, 274n38, 322, 361,
370n92, 374, 388–389, 398
Wesley, John, 252
White, Lynn, 17, 81, 103, 107,
136
Wolde, Ellen van, 34, 44
Wynn, Mark, 85–86, 87

Yamamoto, Dorothy, 83

CPSIA information can be obtained at www.ICGtesting.com
Printed in the USA
LVOW07s0239160914

404125LV00003B/5/P